# PARADIGMS OF PERSONALITY

# PARADIGMS OF PERSONALITY

## JANE LOEVINGER
Washington University in St. Louis

W. H. FREEMAN AND COMPANY
NEW YORK

Library of Congress Cataloging-in-Publication Data

Loevinger, Jane. Paradigms of personality. Includes indexes.
1. Personality—Philosophy.  I. Title.  [DNLM: 1. Personality.  BF 698 L826p]
BF698.L645  1987      155.2′01      86-25779
ISBN 0-7167-1839-1      ISBN 0-7167-1840-5 (pbk.)

The Appendix to Chapter 2 is abridged from "Solitaire: The story of Laura," in
*The fifty-minute hour* by Robert Lindner.
Copyright 1954 by Robert Lindner. All rights reserved.
Reprinted by permission of Holt, Rinehart & Winston, Publishers.

Printed in the United States of America
1 2 3 4 5 6 7 8 9 0  MP  5 4 3 2 1 0 8 9 8 7

# CONTENTS

Criticizing an introductory textbook is easy; any college freshman can do that. Writing a better one is not easy.

Three things about the available introductions to personality psychology dissatisfied me. I thought their expositions of psychoanalysis were often bowdlerized. They slighted a new field with which I am at least peripherally identified, here called cognitive developmentalism. They loaded too much information on the reader. Furthermore, much of the information struck me as being dangerously abstract; summaries of empirical work were often presented in terms of conclusions, with too little of the actual research given for the reader to have any sense of either the method or the outcome.

An introduction to the field of personality should be accessible to the beginner, who may be any educated adult; yet it should be accurate enough to be valuable for a graduate student studying for examinations. Perhaps those aims are not altogether compatible, but they are my target.

Five major theories or systems of personality occupy the bulk of this book: psychoanalysis, behaviorism, the psychometric-trait approach, social learning theory, and cognitive developmentalism. In each case, I have sought to present not the authentic beliefs of any individual psychologist but the underlying logic of the system. As a common framework, I have used T. S. Kuhn's paradigm of scientific revolutions. Although it is not always a good fit, it brings out a number of features of each system, and it does so in a different way from the usual presentations. This theme is elaborated in Chapter 1 and most clearly exemplified in Chapter 2.

The second theme is to show something of the relativistic nature of our knowledge of each system and each aspect of personality. The home base of each system is a different aspect of personality: the dynamic unconscious for psychoanalysis, behavior for behaviorism, traits for the psychometric approach, social cognition and social situations for social learning theory, and character for cognitive developmentalism. The development of relativistic thinking itself is part of cognitive developmentalism, as Chapter 6 shows, but that discussion is presaged in the discussion of Mill in Chapter 3, which invites a contrast of behaviorism and cognitive developmentalism.

A third theme may be partly antithetical to the first one: That is to set each system at least minimally into its social and historical context. No theory emerges independently of previous work in the field; every theory is in some way influenced by the intellectual climate of its time and place. Here I am doubly handicapped, by my own amateur status as well as by the difficulty of the task and the impossibility of fulfilling this aim along with the others. Nonetheless, something about the milieu must be included, lest the entire subject matter become abstract, disembodied, and artificial. An introductory book must simplify; the art is to simplify without distorting. That the average college sophomore knows less than the writer is not an acceptable excuse to distort personality theories; so it should not be an excuse to distort history.

There is a subtle but widespread misapprehension among many students and much of the general literate public. It is that all psychologists doing laboratory experiments or using complex statistics are, ipso facto, reasoning rigorously, whereas all those concerned with personality as a whole are incapable of reasoning rigorously because their thinking is vague or sentimental. Others must judge whether I offer evidence against that view.

I would like the reader to finish the book with some sense of personality psychology as a coherent structure, despite the fact that the loudest voices now speak for an opposite view of personality, and not without some reason. With that structure as framework, the many theories and experiments not mentioned in this book will fit into place.

I am not as wedded to Kuhn's model of science as the book may seem. As Kuhn recognizes, his view is also something like a paradigm and, like every paradigm, is destined to be overthrown or at least have its limitations recognized. His view of paradigms and revolutions, however, serves the purposes of this book.

My experience in using these materials as a text for an introductory personality course may be of value for readers and teachers. Although I aim at a wide audience, I cannot recommend the book to college freshmen. The discussion of Perry's system in Chapters 6 and 7 knits together the previous chapters, and with rare exceptions, only persons who have had some college experience or a good deal of life experience can fully assimilate his approach.

Because only a partial view of the field is presented here—partial both in the sense of being incomplete and in the sense of being one person's viewpoint —some supplementary reading is recommended to accompany each chapter.

For Chapter 1, Kuhn's *Structure of scientific revolutions* is the obvious choice. References to his critics are also found in Chapter 1.

In teaching psychoanalysis as a system in Chapter 2, a chief obstacle is that the students all arrive knowing the code words: ego, superego, id, oral, anal, phallic. Some students express resentment that the version of the system represented by those words is not credited in my way of teaching. "We already know about psychoanalysis," they say. "Why should we have to learn another version?" The whole system of psychoanalysis is theoretical and academic in the worst possible meanings of the words until they encounter a case history. Robert Lindner's story of Laura, appended to Chapter 2, has been one of the most popular features of my course; many of the students know someone who has suffered from at least a mild bulimia. I believe that reading Freud's Clark lectures, widely available as *Five lectures on psychoanalysis,* is also necessary for full appreciation of psychoanalysis as a system. In that small book, Freud reviews the history and develops the main ideas without using the code words that stop rational thought. I have sought supplementary readings for other chapters equivalent to the Clark lectures and the story of Laura, but I have not succeeded.

For fuller appreciation of how B. F. Skinner's ideas apply to personality, first choice would be his *Science and human behavior.* That book has a major drawback, however, in that the ideas are not directly related to his experimental work or anyone else's research. That fact conflicts directly with Kuhn's model of a scientific paradigm as the interrelation of theory, method, and data. G. H. Bower and E. R. Hilgard's *Theories of learning* has been of great help to me with respect to Chapter 3 and elsewhere.

Some of Gordon Allport's writings defending the concept of traits would be appropriate as reading with Chapter 4, but they do not relate closely to the text. With respect to Chapter 4, which is both indispensable in an introduction such as this and an uncomfortable fit with my main thesis, I recommend Stephen Jay

Gould's *Mismeasure of man* as supplementary reading. His view is not exactly mine, but it is a view unfairly neglected in standard psychology texts. Gould exemplifies a subtle point that I would like to convey, that the representatives of the humanistic view may be more knowledgeable and more rigorous than the nose-to-the-ground empiricists.

As a thoughtful, fair-minded, and accurate account of many disputed questions, I recommend Lawrence Pervin's *Current controversies and issues in personality*. The social learning point of view is well represented there in relation to a number of issues. His discussion of schools of psychotherapy in his Chapter 8 is outstanding.

For Chapter 6, my class has used the first two thirds of Perry's *Forms of intellectual and ethical development in the college years* rather than my own synopsis, given in this book. Before I assign Perry's book, I often ask the students to write an anonymous (but compulsory) evaluation of the pros and cons of the course. (It does not work to have them evaluate a different course, because they will just describe its course requirements.) A typist types all the comments together and reproduces them for handing back to the class. After they have read Perry, they are asked to read all the course comments and, ignoring their own, decide where on Perry's scale the class in general falls. They always decide that the class is somewhere between Multiplicity and Relativism. Thus, by their own decision, their immediate developmental problem is growing into relativistic thinking. I hope and believe that for some students this book helps in that process.

The choice of language is a problem in all the expositions. One should use the various authors' words enough to represent their own thinking, but, in order to convey the content in ways that are convincing to oneself and the reader, one should use chiefly one's own words. Students, too, must be persuaded that rephrasing a theory in their own language is a more convincing demonstration of comprehension than exact reproduction of text.

The order of the exposition is another problem where contradictory requirements make it impossible to succeed wholly. Some readers and teachers will find best a quite different order from the one in this text, particularly for the first presentation. For example, Chapter 1 could be postponed until after a paradigm has been illustrated. The introduction to Chapter 2, even though it may seem to wander, is in fact closely calculated to build up the original psychoanalytic paradigm. The introductory part of Chapter 3, however, inviting a contrast of behaviorism and cognitive developmentalism, only becomes fully intelligible after getting well into Chapter 6. I have elected to maintain the present order because it seems the closest one possible to an order at once chronological and logical, despite its pedagogical difficulties. A second reading of the text should verify that choice. Where the book is used in a second course in personality theory, the present order will be more satisfactory.

An advantage of beginning with psychoanalysis is that the historical threads all come together in the hands of one man, Sigmund Freud. Other schools of thought, where there are several sources and several advocates, do not arrange themselves as neatly. They are, however, more typical of the general case in science.

Most of the sources I have drawn on are evident in the text. An indispensable volume has been my superannuated copy of E. G. Boring's *History of experimental psychology*, as well as some of Boring's other essays, as cited in text. For readers who wish a more extended treatment of the schools of thought presented here or discussion of other theories, Calvin Hall and Gardner Lindzey's *Theories of personality* is authoritative.

It is fair to ask how the five fields of personality presented in Chapters 2 through 6 were selected and how the emphasis within each field was determined. Why not organic psychiatry? Why not existentialism? Why not Jung and Adler as representatives of dynamic psychiatry?

The topics covered have obviously been chosen with diversity in mind, so as to cover as many different aspects of personality as possible. A related consideration was to cover the usual bases, so that students would be about as well informed as those who study more conventional personality texts.

One substantive consideration was to follow Kuhn's model, which specifies that a scientific paradigm must begin with a great empirical discovery. I have found at least one formative discovery for each of the five major schools, but I am at a loss as to what might be the corresponding discoveries that ushered in the schools of Adler or Jung, for example. Nor is it easy to specify the great discovery that brought about the resurgence of organic psychiatry, unless it be psychotropic drugs. Existentialism surely does not claim to have sprung from any empirical scientific discoveries; it is a reinterpretation, not an empirical advance.

Three chapters — those on psychoanalysis, psychometrics, and cognitive developmentalism — cover topics in which I have a long-standing interest and a claim to a marginal status as a contributor, although I am an outsider and nonconformist in all of them. Nonetheless, familiarity with three of the five fields emboldened me to write this ambitious book.

The other two expository chapters, on behaviorism and social learning theory, are so close to the mainstream of psychology today that they could not be omitted. Because I had never found the expositions of their advocates convincing, I set myself the task of building a more logical and convincing argument for those points of view than had been done by their champions. All schools of thought represented here (and most of those not presented) are built on some solid foundation. I would rather my readers and my students master those foundations than that they become expert in the peccadilloes of each theorist.

**Jane Loevinger**
St. Louis

## ACKNOWLEDGMENTS

Augusto Blasi and Polly Young-Eisendrath have made helpful suggestions at many points in the years this manuscript has been in preparation. A discussion of chapters 2 and 6 with an interdisciplinary psychoanalytic discussion group has also been helpful.

Table 6.1 has been reprinted from Lawrence Kohlberg, *Essays on moral development.* Volume 2. *The psychology of moral development,* 1984, Harper & Row Publishers, San Francisco. I thank Larry Kohlberg for permission to reprint this table, and for many fruitful discussions over the past twenty years.

Tables 6.2 and 6.3 are reprinted from "Hierarchies of comprehension and preference in a developmental stage model of moral thinking," unpublished doctoral dissertation, University of Chicago, 1969, by James R. Rest. I thank Jim Rest for permission to reprint the tables.

Figures 1.1 and 2.1 have been adapted from similar figures in my monograph, *Scientific ways in the study of ego development,* 1979, Clark University Press, Worcester, MA. Permission to reprint has been granted by Clark University Press.

Chapter 6 contains several passages from *Forms of intellectual and ethical development in the college years: A scheme,* by William G. Perry, Jr. Copyright 1968, 1970, by Holt, Rinehart & Winston, Inc. Reprinted by permission of CBS College Publishing.

Figures 3.1 and 3.2 are adapted from figures 3.8 and 7.3 of *Theories of learning* by Gordon H. Bower and Ernest R. Hilgard, 1981, Prentice-Hall, Englewood Cliffs, NJ. Reprinted by permission of Prentice-Hall.

The Appendix to Chapter 2 is abridged from "Solitaire: The story of Laura" in *The fifty-minute hour* by Robert Lindner, 1954, Holt, Rinehart and Winston, New York. Permission to use this abridged version was granted by Holt, Rinehart & Winston Publishers.

**J. L.**

PARADIGMS OF PERSONALITY

# CHAPTER 1

# Study of Personality as Science

Several models of science have been popular in psychology texts. These models involve not only different views of the nature of science as an enterprise but also different philosophies and theories of knowledge. Some of these views will be characterized briefly, followed by a description of the view that will be followed in this book.

## SOME MODELS OF SCIENCE

A pyramid-of-science view shows physics at the base of a pyramid, overlaid by chemistry, then biology, then psychology, and topped by sociology. Each science is presumed to rest on the ones beneath it in the pyramid. According to this view, to understand psychology in principle, one needs to learn how to translate its problems into biological ones, and to understand biology one needs to translate its problems into physical-chemical terms. This view of science is a *reductionist* one; each discipline is understood in terms of the elements to which it is presumed it can be reduced. Opponents of this view have emphasized that combinations of elements have emergent properties; for example, one could not easily deduce the properties of water from the properties of hydrogen and oxygen, which make it up. Similarly, being ever so wise about biology would not be helpful in understanding the problems of psychology.

To a remarkable extent physiology, genetics, and other biological fields have today become dominated by biochemistry as the core of the discipline. Texts in biology have been written without a single picture or mention of a whole multicellular organism. These recent trends in biology, of course, lend force and credence to the reductionistic view in psychology. But surely some part of biology is lost when the science goes over entirely to biochemistry.

The belief that psychological phenomena are at bottom purely physical-physiological events is an old one. Perhaps the only older theory of personality is the belief displayed in the *Iliad* that the gods are responsible for human behavior. Belief in the organic source of all psychological ailments has never died out; it has, however, become more sophisticated. It flourishes today and can be expected to continue to do so. It is not one of the views of personality presented in the present book, but that is not meant to be a judgment on its relative importance.

The reductionistic view is often presented, at least informally, with the comment, "What else could it be?" Those who earnestly believe in this point of view cannot imagine that anyone who takes himself or herself seriously as a scientist can possibly think in any other terms. For them, the only explanations that count are the physiological, ultimately physical ones.

A second model of science is the *hypothetical-deductive* model. According to this view, science proceeds by setting up hypotheses, deducing their consequences, verifying or falsifying those consequences by research, and then accepting or rejecting the corresponding hypotheses. The best scientific research only rarely proceeds according to that plan. The requirements of two of the most common occasions for research, however, virtually force it into that format. Much research in psychology is done either as a dissertation for a doctoral degree or under grant or contract to a governmental or other funding agency. In the former situation, the graduate committee usually requires a formal hypothesis. When application is made to an agency for research funds, again the research is almost inevitably forced into the hypothetical-deductive model, as the reviewing committee judges the merits of the proposal partly on the basis of how well it fits that model. This model has the defect that it hardly allows for discovery of anything truly new in the process of doing research. Most working scientists are more freewheeling and informal in their actual procedure, despite the ocasional necessity to conform to this model.

A third model for science, and, although rarely articulated, probably the prevailing attitude of many psychologists, is the *inductive* model based on the ideas (or what are popularly supposed to be the ideas) of the sixteenth- and seventeenth-century English philosopher Francis Bacon. He proposed that the function of science is to gather together facts. When enough facts have been gathered, the ideas that summarize them will be evident by induction. Opponents of this model believe that not only what facts the scientist gathers, but how he gathers them, encodes them, and stores and retrieves them, are guided by some ideas; hence, pure fact gathering, unbiased by any ideas, is a fiction. It is neither possible nor desirable.

What unites all three conceptions of science is a belief that modern science is essentially cumulative, that each generation of scientists is ahead of all previous generations by virtue of its inheritance of all the results of previous science.

The characteristic of being cumulative clearly does not fit many nonscientific fields, such as the history of art or music. In those fields fashions change, but it is not clear that nineteenth-century music is any better than eighteenth-century music, nor do many hold that any recent poetry is superior to that of Shakespeare or the King James Bible. Modern painting and architecture are not clear improvements on those of Michelangelo in the sixteenth century or even of Giotto in the fourteenth century.

## KUHN'S MODEL OF SCIENTIFIC REVOLUTIONS

In contrast to the previous views of science is the thesis of T. S. Kuhn (1970). According to Kuhn, science works in two different modes, normal science and scientific revolutions. The great discoveries, which are rare, create *scientific revolutions*. Each such revolution creates its own school, whose followers engage in what Kuhn calls *normal science*. Normal science does not seek and is not capable of assimilating major new discoveries. When a new discovery comes, it creates another revolution; then the cycle is repeated. This process may sound like the kind of revolution that occurred with the imagists in twentieth-century poetry or the impressionists in nineteenth-century painting, in other words, the fads and fashions of the world of art and belles lettres. Looked at in more detail, Kuhn's picture of science is different.

Kuhn sees most scientific revolutions as beginning with a great *discovery*, such as the discoveries that formed the basis for thermodynamics or quantum mechanics. Often the discovery is announced in a book, such as Isaac Newton's *Principia* (1687). That great discovery becomes a kind of model experiment, or *paradigm*. The paradigm rapidly becomes a method of investigation for exploring a whole area of knowledge. Around the paradigm grow up a body of facts and a branch of theory. Kuhn at times has used the term *paradigm* for the exemplary experiment and at times for the interconnected set of investigations, findings, and theories to which the original discovery gives rise, which he now prefers to call the *disciplinary matrix*. Because scholarly usage in applying his ideas to the field of personality is not so precise as his, this book will follow the looser usage of the word *paradigm*. Each such disciplinary matrix has its own characteristic set of assumptions and kinds of problems it is equipped to solve.

The main business of normal science, Kuhn states, is not major discoveries but puzzle solving. The puzzles that most scientists are engaged in solving are meaningful only to those working within the same paradigm, or disciplinary matrix, just as contract bridge puzzles are meaningful only to those who know the rules of the game of bridge, and chess puzzles are meaningful only to those who know how to play chess. Kuhn states, however, that what marks a science as mature is that all qualified people agree on the paradigm to follow at any one time.

One of the tasks of a scientific paradigm is to account for most of the facts uncovered by its predecessor paradigms. A new paradigm, however, characteristically defines new kinds of observations as appropriate data for science. In the seventeenth century the concept of a pendulum was a new one with Galileo, for example; in ancient times the oscillation of a stone attached to a rope or chain would have been described as constrained fall because there was no concept of a pendulum.

More striking than the new kinds of data may be the entirely revised view of the world that a paradigm can lead to; there are new insights into what kinds of things there are in the universe. Think of the discovery of the microscope as a scientific instrument. The whole of the microscopic world was opened up, leading immediately to new conceptions of biology and physiology and finally to altered views of the nature of matter. Our conceptions of everyday life also ultimately changed. For example, understanding of reproduction depends in part on the idea made possible by the new techniques of observation, of the union of sperm and ovum in various species. Later, the germ theory of disease and use of asepsis in childbirth and surgery resulted. Indeed, the ramifications of the discovery of the microscopic world are so great one cannot hope to catalog them.

The discovery of X-rays and radium similarly opened up a new world previously unseen and unimaginable, another invisible universe, not detectable even with the most powerful microscope. This world too, like that of microorganisms, requires new kinds of data and has potent effects on many aspects of life. Kuhn emphasizes the revolution in physics that X-rays led to. Eventually nonphysicists, even children, have been led to a new conception of the nature of things. Medical diagnosis and treatment, warfare, energy production, the conception of indoor air pollution, foreign policy, and private fantasies have all been changed.

One way a paradigm is expanded is by being applied to new areas; that leads to new problems. Eventually more and more puzzles turn up that either cannot be solved or lead to some kind of anomaly. These unsolved problems, anomalies, and contradictions make scientists in the field uncomfortable; ultimately their uneasiness leads to the proposal of one or more new paradigms. Eventually, in a mature science, one paradigm will win over as adherents virtually all qualified persons in the field, and there will again be a single reigning paradigm. That, at any rate, is Kuhn's model (Figure 1.1).

## APPLICATION TO PSYCHOLOGY OF PERSONALITY

Many elements of Kuhn's model have use in describing interesting aspects of the psychology of personality, but one element of the model has no counterpart in the field of personality: the unanimity of qualified persons in agreeing on a paradigm. Although many psychological theorists present their own point of view as the wave of the future and alternative views as merely part of the history leading to their triumphant entry into the field—that, Kuhn points out, is characteristic of workers within any paradigm— history reveals that major alternative views of human nature and personality have existed since ancient times.

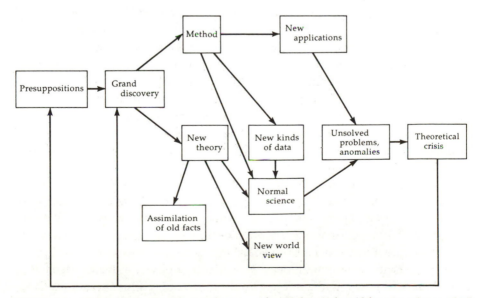

FIGURE 1.1.   Scheme of scientific revolutions, after Kuhn *(Adapted from Loevinger, 1979)*

Because so many other elements of Kuhn's model do fit and do illuminate aspects of personality theory, this model will be used, so far as possible, as the outline for presenting the several major personality theories in this book. Not all of Kuhn's colleagues in the history and philosophy of science, moreover, believe as strongly as he does either that scientists are always unanimous in accepting the prevailing paradigm or that it matters as much as Kuhn believes (Lakatos & Musgrave, 1970). Curiously, although Kuhn admits that in writing about scientific revolutions, he is describing the social psychology and sociology of scientists, he seems to resent the idea of social scientists taking over his model and applying it to their sciences, as this book will do. I therefore do not ask for nor claim his approval for my endeavor.

The excuse for the multiplicity of paradigms in psychology is sometimes given that psychology is a young science; Kuhn's use of the term *mature science* to describe one where there is a predominant paradigm would encourage this usage. I regard this argument as a form of question begging. As far back as there is any record of human inquiry, some of the best minds have been occupied with questions of the nature of human personality. How could any field of inquiry be older? Biochemistry and statistics are truly young sciences, but biochemists and statisticians do not give that as an excuse for the problems or inadequacies of their science.

There are reasons why there will always be a multiplicity of paradigms in the study of personality. One way of seeing the difference between personality theory and other disciplines is to note that one's theory of personality is itself at least partly a manifestation of one's own personality. That statement should become more meaningful by the end of this book; however, it is not the guiding principle of the book.

In psychological theory one cannot escape the problem or dilemma of *reflexivity*. As many philosophers have pointed out (see, for example, J. Bronowski, 1966), the problem of the human mind trying to understand itself is not the same as the problem of the mind trying to understand things outside itself. To put the matter in the least philosophical way possible, human beings have evolved over millennia to cope with the environment. Their sense organs and their conceptual abilities are geared to the environment, not to introspection. There is probably little or no survival value in primitive societies in being able to understand oneself. From an evolutionary point of view, self-understanding, like pickles, is an acquired taste, not a nutritional staple.

Although the use of the term *paradigm* in this book is looser than Kuhn sanctions, it is not trivial. The book will look at each of five approaches to or systems or schools of personality as a paradigm. Each will be shown to start with one or a few discoveries, which are often outside the field of personality. Those discoveries are then turned into standard methods of investigation, leading to a body of facts and a system of ideas. New kinds of observations are defined as data under the new paradigm. New applications of the fundamental methods and theories lead to small discoveries. Eventually there will turn up anomalies and problems that cannot be solved by accepted methods. That situation leads to a crisis and often to a reexamination of fundamental presuppositions. The crisis will be solved by new discoveries, if not yet, then presumably in future. That format will guide the discussion of each of five approaches to personality, as far as possible.

The presentation of the five approaches or schools will differ from more usual introductions to personality. There will be greater emphasis on empirical discoveries as leading to the founding of each school and less emphasis on the personality and personal history of the founders. Although I cannot wholly avoid giving personal data, I shall lean as far as possible in the other direction. The governing question for this book is not, What made Person A believe Theory Y? Rather, it is, What is the logical structure of Theory Y? Never mind whether that logic leads directly to the text as originally developed by Person A. (I shall make a partial exception for the two authentic geniuses, Sigmund Freud and Jean Piaget.)

The vexing question of which ideas are properly assigned to each school of thought is solved in a different way than is usual. For example, an idea is not a legitimate part of psychoanalysis just because Freud uttered it, not even if one could prove that he really and truly, deep down, believed it. An idea is a part of psychoanalysis as a system of psychology if it fits the paradigm. Similarly, behaviorism is not irrevocably tied to the political views of B. F. Skinner or anyone else; psychological testing is not tied to a belief in the importance of the genetic factor in intelligence; and the cognitive-developmental school is not tied to Lawrence Kohlberg's brand of liberalism. In place of biography, I aspire to use logic to find connections.

The approach of this book contrasts with or complements many introductions to personality in another respect, namely, in emphasizing the revolutionary discoveries and the anomalies and crises that pave the way for new revolutionary discoveries. There will be only enough of the intervening normal science to give a feel for the paradigmlike quality of the usual work in the field. Other introductions generally give a more thorough survey of current normal scientific work.

An advantage to stressing revolutions rather than normal science is that the latter quickly becomes so technical that the nonspecialist finds it hard to grasp even the bare essentials of a study or line of work, much less to master enough of the methodological complexities to evaluate contradictory findings. Revolutionary periods are just the times when the field goes back to its fundamental assumptions and first principles, Kuhn points out. The scientific work of those periods often is more intelligible to laymen, including scientists or even psychologists with other areas of specialization.

Philosophers and historians of science are by no means unanimous in praising Kuhn's model as the last word on the topic. There are many additional models of the scientific enterprise that are being discussed today. R. J. Richards (1981) discusses several such models in a way that many will find useful. The model that I am trying to avoid, describing the errors of scientists and sometimes also their discoveries in terms of their psychological makeup or social circumstances, has its advocates, for example, among proponents of Freudian and Marxian models. More generally, that is the model implied by his-father-was-a-Presbyterian-minister comments about personality theorists, although the comments may have been included to supply a personal touch rather than as a serious commitment to such a model.

An increasingly popular view is the natural-selection model of science put forth by D. T. Campbell (1960). According to this model, scientific ideas are produced in more or less the same random fashion as nature produces variants in each plant and animal species. The fittest ideas are perpetuated and survive. This model is also unlikely to achieve universal acceptance. The twentieth-century Gestalt psychologist, Wolfgang Köhler went to some trouble to establish that chimpanzees do not solve problems by random trial and success but rather by thinking about the relations of parts of the situation to one another (see Chapter 5). Not many psychologists like to think that their theories are less purposeful than the chimpanzee's problem-solving efforts. There are other models of science as well, but the merits of the various views of science are beyond the scope of a book devoted to the study of personality.

Kuhn's model was chosen partly because it is well known and partly because it provides a framework to bring out some comparative features of the different theories in ways to encourage fresh insights. Also, it embodies a way of displaying the intimate interplay of theory and data that most scientists — with the possible exception of psychologists! — recognize as the heart of the scientific enterprise. Finally, it can be seen as showing the relativity of theory to the data on which the theory is grounded. Relativistic thinking is itself a major focus of the final chapters of the book.

To put the topic into perspective, note that one aspect of Kuhn's model has minimal application in this account. A great discovery, Kuhn notes, opens up a new view of the universe. That is only minimally true of any of the paradigms in this book. One could make that assertion about psychoanalysis, but it is hard to construe any of the other paradigms in that fashion. In the grand scheme of things, the concern of this book is with a series of miniparadigms.

---

## REFERENCES

Bronowski, J. (1966). The logic of the mind. *American Scientist, 54,* 1–4.

Campbell, D. T. (1960). Blind variation and selective retention in creative thought as in other knowledge processes. *Psychological Review, 67,* 380–400.

Köhler, W. (1965). On the insight of apes. In R. J. Herrnstein & E. G. Boring (Eds.), *A source book in the history of psychology* (pp. 569–578). Cambridge, MA: Harvard University Press. (Original work published 1917.)

Kuhn, T. S. (1970). *The structure of scientific revolutions* (2nd ed.). Chicago: University of Chicago Press.

Lakatos, I., & Musgrave, A. (Eds.). (1970). *Criticism and the growth of knowledge.* Cambridge, Eng.: Cambridge University Press.

Richards, R. J. (1981). Natural selection and other models in the historiography of science. In M. B. Brewer & B. E. Collins (Eds.), *Scientific inquiry and the social sciences* (pp. 37–76). San Francisco: Jossey-Bass.

# Psychoanalysis

In the nineteenth century, psychology hardly existed as a separate discipline. What there was came under the heading of either philosophy or physiology. Corresponding to these two faces of psychology were two predominant views of human behavior. On the one hand, following Jeremy Bentham and others in the British school of associationists (see Chapter 3), behavior was seen as responsive to a "calculus of pleasure and pain." That was the philosophical face, and it yielded a psychology of consciousness.

On the other hand, behavior was seen as built up out of a complex concatenation of reflexes, which are simple responses to stimuli, similar to the presumed behavior of the lower animals. This was the biological face. It gained support from Charles Darwin's theory of evolution to the effect that if humans have evolved from lower animals, their behavior ought to be fundamentally the same. Reflex action in this context means something like stimulus-response, that is, every action is supposed to be a more or less automatic response to some prior stimulus. No stimulus, no response. This reflex arc view anticipated I. P. Pavlov's experiments on conditioned reflexes in the early twentieth century (see Chapter 3); John Dewey argued against the reflex arc point of view in a widely read article before the turn of the century (Dewey, 1896).

The British associationists analyzed consciousness in terms of ideas and the associations between them. German psychologists also assumed that the mind was a structure composed of mental elements, though they did not all agree as to what the elements were like. E. B. Titchener, one of the greatest of German-trained psychologists, though British by birth, spent much of his productive life at Cornell University and trained many of the first generation of American psychologists. His school of psychology was called *structuralism*; however, that term has different, almost opposite connotations today (see Chapter 6), and I therefore prefer to call his psychology *experimental introspectionism*. Titchener and his assistants were highly trained to analyze every stimulus, even a pinprick, in terms of the mental elements it excited.

Major modern schools of psychology have arisen as rebellions against both of those views, but particularly against the search for mental elements. William James, founder of American *functionalism*, one of the mainstreams of American psychology, said that when he introspected, he never found any mental elements, only an ever-changing stream of consciousness (James, 1890). Thus his primary emphasis was on process rather than static elements. The behaviorists disclaimed an interest in consciousness altogether, giving their attention instead to behavior; they remained, however, elementaristic, as will be seen. The psychoanalysts, rebelling in a different direction, said that consciousness was like the tip of an iceberg, with the more important nine tenths of the mind below the surface of consciousness. The Gestalt psychologists (see Chapter 5) believed that the mind operated primarily in terms of patterns rather than static elements.

The first paradigm to be treated will be that of psychoanalysis. Although many people acknowledge that psychoanalysis can hardly be understood except in the terms of its history, and although the term *paradigm* is often used in connection with psychoanalysis, there have not been many attempts to construe that history in anything like Kuhn's terms. That will be attempted here.

## BACKGROUND AND ORIGINS OF PSYCHOANALYSIS

### The Cultural Milieu

First, a brief digression to look at the cultural milieu within which psychology arose. The eighteenth century was called the Enlightenment or the Age of Reason; it was the period of the French and American revolutions, of the great Encyclopedists and Voltaire, and of interest in the classical past and confidence in reason. The Declaration of Independence and the Constitution of the United States and the discussions that led up to those documents are testimony to the unusually high caliber of rational public discourse in late eighteenth century. As always, however, there were contradictory trends. Proclamation that all men are created equal did not prevent acceptance of what John Quincy Adams later called the "peculiar institution" of slavery.

In this period the insane were often confined in prisons along with criminals and people who were merely poor or in debt or unemployed. Indeed, it was the criminals who complained of the indignity of being confined with the insane, not the other way around. Not till the end of the eighteenth century was there progress toward removing the chains that shackled the insane.

In the late eighteenth century the Age of Reason gave way to the Romantic period, which continued into the early nineteenth century. The Romantics believed that the exercise of intellect should be tempered by emotion. The greatest German poet was J. W. von Goethe, whose long life spanned the Enlightenment and the Romantic era and whose work also bridged the two. In addition to being a great poet, he was a respected scientist, who developed a phenomenological theory of color vision. Freud knew Goethe's work intimately and quoted it often. Indeed, more than once he declared that hearing a public reading of Goethe's essay on nature determined his choice of medicine as a career. (The essay is translated and its relevance for Freud's development is discussed in W. Kaufmann, 1980.)

Influenced by the Romantic movement, the early nineteenth century saw a change in the attitude of some physicians towards the mentally ill. *Moral treatment* was the name given to a movement for more humane treatment of mental patients. Physicians had discovered that in most ways the mentally ill were like other people; they had similar wishes, needs, and tastes. Good therapeutic results were built on recognition of the fundamental humanity of the patients.

By the middle of the nineteenth century, science and technology had taken off on their way to spectacular ascendancy. With the immensely successful growth of new scientific paradigms, such as thermodynamics, together with growth in knowledge of biology and physiology, there came a new faith in the power of scientific solutions to human problems, including medical and mental problems. The leading psychiatric text of the day, that of William Griesinger, described all mental diseases as diseases of the brain (Izenberg, 1976).

A paradoxical outgrowth of this belief in science was a somewhat less humane attitude toward mental illness on the part of many physicians. If mental illness is conceived of as purely physical in origin and nature, the doctor need not worry about the wishes and feelings of the patient; he need merely treat the affected organ or symptom. In Vienna, one of the leading centers of scientific medicine, the prevailing attitude toward women suffering from hysterical illnesses, illnesses that mimic physical illnesses but for which no organic basis can be found, was that the women were malingering. That attitude is not unknown today: "It's all in your head. Go home and forget about it."

Freud had a firm grasp of all three strands that made up the cultural fabric of his day— the classical and romantic, on the one hand, and the scientific, on the other. He had a fine classical education; he spoke German, French, and English and read Italian, Greek, Latin, Hebrew, Czech, and perhaps other languages. His quotations from Shakespeare and the *Iliad*, for example, are wonderfully appropriate, testifying to the depth of his knowledge of English and Greek literature. All the sources of Freud's thought, the classical and romantic sources and the scientific source, shine through his work (Holt, 1972; Izenberg, 1976).

With regard to their importance in the origin of psychoanalysis, Freud's chief biographer, Ernest Jones, put primary emphasis on Freud's natural science training (Jones, 1953). Henri Ellenberger, however, who has written a definitive history of the discovery of the unconscious, sees faith healing and its descendant psychotherapies as the primary factor in the background of psychoanalysis (Ellenberger, 1970). Ellenberger by no means intends the kinship between psychoanalysis and faith healing to be derogatory. Faith healing is a real phenomenon.

## Freud's Early Life

Sigmund Freud was born in Moravia in 1856. Following his graduation from *gymnasium* (high school, roughly corresponding to the U. S. college preparatory school plus the first two years of college), he enrolled in medical school in Vienna, the city where he then lived with his parents. Medical school was the pathway to either a medical career or one in the biological sciences, and Vienna was one of the greatest centers of medical science of that time.

Freud became a student of the great physiologist Ernst Brücke and would gladly have remained as his assistant, continuing to publish papers in evolutionary anatomy of the nervous system. At the age of 26 while still a medical student, Freud became engaged. Because both he and his fiancée came from poor families, marriage was considered out of the question until he was earning a substantial living, which was not possible as a junior assistant. Brücke's other assistants were only a little older than Freud, so the path of academic advancement appeared unlikely. Hence Freud reluctantly went into private practice of medicine as a neurologist.

As an example of Freud's neurological research, he examined and described the nerve cells of a small fish, petromyzin, supplying a missing link in the development of nerve cells from their forms in primitive species to their form in more evolved species. This and other studies of his helped to establish vital facts about the evolution and the development of the nervous system. These were observational rather than experimental studies. Characteristically, he rarely did experiments; his research consisted of observation rather than experimentation or manipulation. In his own mind, Freud seemed to remain more a scientist than a healer, more an observer than an experimenter. These predilections may have had something to do with the kind of therapy psychoanalysis has become, though they have nothing to do with the logic of the paradigm.

Because Brücke left a major impression on Freud and hence perhaps on psychoanalysis, more should be said about him. Brücke was one of a group of brilliant young scientists who were students of the great physiologist Johannes Müller in the mid-nineteenth century. Müller was the last major scientific figure who was noted as a *vitalist*; that is, he believed that in living creatures there was some "vital principle" not present in inorganic matter, a principle important to biological explanation. Müller stated that the speed of the nerve impulse could never be measured. Because the soul is unitary, it must act at once, not through any process slow enough to be measurable. A few years later, however, his student Hermann von Helmholtz succeeded in measuring the speed of the nerve impulse.

Müller's students, including Helmholtz and Brücke, banded together in a kind of brotherhood, pledging themselves to look for no other explanations of living organisms than forces that prevail in physical-chemical systems, or forces "equal in dignity." Most adherents of this school interpreted the pledge to be a commitment to a scientific reductionistic philosophy. (Freud, as will be seen, came, probably reluctantly, to a different interpretation.) Müller's vitalism can be seen as a kind of Romantic biology, whereas the reaction of his students marked them as sons of the new age of science.

### Hysteria and Hypnotism

In Freud's day most of the patients who came to a young physician setting up practice as a neuropathologist, corresponding to what today would be called a neurologist and psychiatrist, were women suffering from hysterical illnesses. They made up a large part of Freud's practice.

*Early Views of Hysteria.* Hysteria is one of the oldest known illnesses (Veith, 1977). Instances of it appear in written records dating back to the ancient Egyptians and Greeks. Characteristically a patient with hysteria has physical symptoms resembling those of any of several physical diseases but without the usual physical causes. There is no demonstrable organic basis for the symptoms, typically paralyses and anesthesias. There is, moreover, a characteristic personality picture, including a *belle indifference*, which is a bland obliviousness to serious or sad concerns and a polyannish attitude toward problems and toward the future (see M. J. Horowitz, 1977a.).

The word *hysteria* is derived from the Greek word for womb. According to the ancient Greeks and Egyptians, the disease resulted from a misplaced womb, and they prescribed treatment to force the uterus to migrate back to its proper place. For example, a persistent lump in the throat was ascribed to a misplaced womb. In defiance of what is now known of anatomy and physiology, the uterus was treated as if it were a living being that could be repelled by foul-smelling fumigants applied via nose and mouth and attracted by pleasing ones in the vulva. What is prophetic about those beliefs, naive as they may sound, is that the disease was understood to be largely — some believed exclusively — a female affliction, and that the ancients understood in their own concrete way that its origin was somehow related to sexual life.

*Mesmer and Magnetism.* Intertwined with the history of hysteria is that of another topic, also fateful for the origin of psychoanalysis; that is what is now called hypnotism. Faith healing, particularly exorcism, was commonly accepted in the eighteenth century. In the last quarter of the century, the Austrian physician Franz Mesmer and others proposed the use of magnetism as a scientific alternative to faith healing and exorcism.

To put Mesmer's ideas into context, one must note that electricity and magnetism were not well understood at this time, soon after Benjamin Franklin flew his famous kite. Mesmer believed that there was a magnetic fluid throughout the universe, as evidenced by the tides. The idea bore some resemblance to Newton's law of universal gravitation, which was by then widely accepted. The maldistribution of the magnetic fluid in the human body accounted for hysterical symptoms. In Mesmer's treatment, the patient would swallow a fluid containing some iron filings, and the physician, using magnets, altered the distribution of the magnetic fluid in the body. He was credited with many cures, as, of course, were the exorcists before him. Mesmer became convinced at some point that the iron filings and the magnets were not necessary to effect the cures. He understood that it was a matter of the personality of the magnetist and his relation to the patient. Therefore he called the technique *animal magnetism.*

For various reasons, perhaps partly because of the hostility of orthodox physicians to the new treatment (and partly because of antagonism of patients' families, who were not always pleased with cures! See G. J. Bloch, 1980, and E. R. Hilgard, 1980), Mesmer left Vienna and set up practice in Paris, where his work was also controversial. Eventually a Royal Commission was established to look into the validity of his claims concerning the universal magnetic fluid. Benjamin Franklin, the representative of the United States in France, was appointed chairman of the commission.

The commission issued two reports, one public, one never publicized. The public report dealt with the topic for which they had been appointed; it concluded that there was no such universal magnetic fluid that could be redistributed by Mesmer's magnets. The secret report did not dispute that he sometimes cured patients; however, it evaluated the hazards of the method as so great that it recommended that the successes not be publicly admitted (Perry & Laurence, 1983). Mesmer's critics noted a hazard to the patient in magnetic treatment, particularly in the case of a young woman patient and a male magnetist, namely, a fixation of the girl's affection on the magnetist that might last long beyond the treatment. Thus they had observed what Freud later called transference. Discredited again, Mesmer left for Switzerland, where he continued to live and perhaps also to practice quietly for many years. Others in France continued to practice *mesmerism*, as it was now called.

One of Mesmer's followers was Amand-Marie-Jacques de Chastenet, marquis de Puységur, a nobleman who did experiments with hypnotism. His best and most informative subject was Victor Race, whose family had for some generations been servants on the Puységur estate. In a mesmeric trance Victor proved to be more intelligent and knowledgeable than he seemed to be in everyday life (Ellenberger, 1970). This phenomenon later came to be called *hypnotic lucidity*.

*Later Experiments with Hypnotism.* A British physician, John Elliotson, took up mesmerism in 1837. His temperament can be judged from the fact that he was the first physician in England to adopt the use of the stethoscope. He also was the first to suggest that medical schools needed teaching hospitals attached to them. Nonetheless, he quit his position in both his medical school and its teaching hospital when they forbade any use of or experimentation with mesmerism (Boring, 1929). At first he used mesmerism as a method of treatment, as Mesmer had, but soon he began to use it as a mode of anesthetizing patients for surgery, as there were no other anesthetics. Apparently hundreds of operations, including leg amputations, were done this way, painlessly, by a few surgeons in England and India, though official medicine never gave it any recognition except to denounce it as fakery. James Esdaile, another British surgeon, practicing in India, reported 345 surgical operations performed with mesmeric anesthesia (Ellenberger, 1970).

What might have happened if the situation had continued is hard to guess, but in any event, use of ether, chloroform, and nitrous oxide as chemical anesthesias was discovered about this time. They became the accepted anesthetic techniques despite possible adverse effects and even some deaths, which did not occur with mesmerism.

Another nineteenth-century British physican, James Braid, whose interest was aroused by a public demonstration of mesmerism, set out to discredit it and animal magnetism as unscientific. He was, however, an open-minded experimenter. In the course of his research he became convinced that many of the claimed phenomena were real. Instead of magnets he used sensory fixation as a means of inducing trance; for example, the patient would be asked to look fixedly at a certain light. He coined the word *hypnotism* to get away from the connotations of the name Mesmer. Hypnosis refers literally to a sleeplike state;

the term *artifical somnambulism* had been used previously. The net effect of Braid's efforts was to help establish hypnotism on a more scientific basis and to bring it closer to respectability within the medical profession.

Thus the mind was shown to have a storehouse of treasures to which the person does not have ready access. This idea was known to the ancients, who had a special status of oracle for people with the gift of access to this hidden store of wisdom (Jaynes, 1977). Mainly, however, trance states had been thought of previously as states of diminished capacity.

Hypnotism as a medical technique had its ups and downs, going into and out of fashion several times. Orthodox physicians tended to be disdainful of it, despite some proven successes in curing some cases of hysterical illness and in permitting painless operations. Mesmer asserted that his methods were scientific, in contrast to the methods of the faith healers and exorcists who preceded him, but he was denounced as a charlatan. Each successive discovery of the phenomena of hypnosis was acclaimed as truly scientific, with its predecessor denounced as charlatanism, a practice that continues today, and not only with respect to hypnotism. Part of the message of Kuhn's model of scientific revolutions is that, when seen within the context of the state of knowledge of their own times, earlier workers were generally just as scientific as their successors. Only in the context of later discoveries do they appear erroneously to be unscientific or even charlatans.

*Charcot's Theory of Hysteria.* At about the time Freud was setting up practice, interest in hypnosis as a treatment for mental illness was again reviving. The leading neurologist of France, Jean-Martin Charcot, was put in charge of the hospital and clinic of Salpêtrière in Paris, where he studied hysteria and experimented with hypnosis. Charcot was interested in the symptoms of hysteria and showed that they were similar to the symptoms that were considered evidences of possession by the devil in the Middle Ages, thus providing a link with exorcism.

Railroads were coming into wide use at this time, and there were often accidents. After these accidents, many victims with only minor injuries fell ill with traumatic paralyses for which there seemed to be no organic basis. Charcot showed that the symptoms of such paralyses resembled hysterical ones. Further, by means of hypnosis, he could suggest symptoms to his patients, which were of the same kind. Hypnotic suggestion also worked to remove symptoms. Bringing these facts together, Charcot worked out the following theory: After an accident or physical trauma, a "hypnoid state" develops that makes persons who are predisposed to hysteria susceptible to the induction of hysterical symptoms, analogous to their induction by suggestion from a hypnotist. This theory was his model for all hysterical illness. Thus he had a *traumatic theory* of hysteria.

Charcot believed, as did most French psychiatrists, that the basis for hysteria was some mental degeneration or mental weakness. The ability to be hypnotized, he believed, was an abnormal phenomenon indicative of an hysterical constitution.

## The First Great Discovery

Freud obtained a traveling fellowship that enabled him to study with Charcot for a few months in 1886 and 1887. During that time he became acquainted with the work on hysteria and hypnosis that had been going on at the Salpêtrière. At Charcot's suggestion, Freud wrote a paper analyzing the differences between hysterical and organic paralyses, a paper that became the definitive one on the topic. Of the differences he found, the most important was that the distribution of organic paralyses and anesthesias follows the tracts of the nervous system, whereas hysterical symptoms are delimited according to popular ideas of organs, which do not coincide with distribution of the nerve tracts. Thus *ideas can create and shape physical symptoms.*

*Bernheim's Use of Hypnosis.* After returning to Vienna from Paris, Freud used hypnosis and suggestion on his patients, along with other traditional therapies. He found that the results of hypnotic suggestion were not adequate, partly because he was not a gifted hypnotist. Therefore, in 1889, he returned to France, this time to Nancy to study with Hippolyte Bernheim. Bernheim was a well-known physician and university professor who had become interested in the results obtained by a country doctor, Auguste Liébeault, who had been treating his patients with hypnotic suggestion during a long period when it was out of favor with medical authorities. Liébeault seems to have treated all patients by hypnotizing them and suggesting that their symptoms did not exist, regardless of the nature of their complaints. Bernheim, however, was more discriminating in his application of the method and more sophisticated in his theorizing.

Unlike Charcot, who believed that the ability to be hypnotized was an abnormality, Bernheim believed it to be a normal phenomenon; therapeutic results from the use of hypnotism, he believed, were not essentially different from those obtained from using suggestion with patients in a waking, nonhypnotized state. (This view is shared by many but not all psychologists today.) He found that hypnotism and suggestion worked best when the patient was of lower social status than the hypnotist or from a class used to unquestioning obedience, such as peasants and old soldiers.

Bernheim also performed experiments of posthypnotic suggestion. In those experiments, persons under hypnosis were told that on awakening they would perform certain actions, such as, for example, scratching their left ear. They carried out these suggestions with no memory of the suggestion having been made, inventing irrelevant excuses for the actions whose source they seemed to be ignorant of. Further, Freud learned from Bernheim that although subjects seemed, on awakening from a hypnotic trance, to be amnesic regarding what had happened to them while they were hypnotized, they could be induced by pressure and suggestion to remember what had gone on during hypnosis. Thus from Bernheim, Freud learned that ideas of which the person was not conscious had the power to affect behavior and also that they could be recovered to consciousness.

The work of Charcot and Bernheim, both because of its intrinsic merits and because of the substantial disagreement between them, brought hypnotism into focus once again as a respectable topic for physicians and medical researchers to study.

*Breuer's Use of Hypnosis.* One more train of thought must be introduced in order to have the major elements that are combined in Freud's first psychoanalytic paradigm, and that is the cathartic treatment that Josef Breuer worked out in treating — indeed, in collaboration with — Anna O. Although logically this treatment belongs last, it appears to have terminated about 1882; so it antedates other elements. Freud heard about the case from Breuer, a distinguished scientist and physician and close friend at that time, shortly after treatment was terminated, but he seems to have put it out of his mind until later when it fit his own train of thought.

Breuer's major scientific discovery was the part played by the semicircular canals in maintaining balance, which he demonstrated in humans and other animals. Like Charcot and Bernheim, he did not scoff at the symptoms of hysterical patients but listened to what they had to say. In the case of Anna O., a gifted young woman with many incapacitating hysterical symptoms, Breuer used hypnotism a new way, not to suggest away the symptoms, as Charcot, Liébeault, Bernheim, and some other psychiatrists were doing, but to recall the traumatic events that had given rise to the symptoms. When those events had been recalled and the patient had experienced in full force the emotion that had been stifled at the time the events had originally occurred, whether from politeness, embarrassment, shame, discretion, immaturity, being overwhelmed by the magnitude of the emotion, or whatever, the corresponding symptom disappeared. Here again an idea, in this case the (suppressed) memory of a traumatic event, was shown to have given rise to a symptom.

The emphasis on the importance of trauma echoes the emphasis on trauma in Charcot's theory. But for Charcot trauma meant a physical one, whereas Breuer and later Freud were talking about a *psychic trauma.* The difference is crucial, and it shows how influences that contribute to a theory do not by any means account for the theory. They can be as much hindrance as help. The influential sources must be transformed and surmounted as much as incorporated in any truly new theory.

*Freud's Work as a Neurologist.* During the period under discussion, the period that culminates in the Breuer-Freud collaborative volume, *Studies in hysteria* (1895/1955), Freud, in addition to the above studies and to earning a living in the active practice of neuropathology, published a number of scientific monographs on topics ranging from cocaine to aphasia. He was considered the leading authority on paralyses of children, the topic of another monograph.

Freud was one of the earliest to appreciate the importance of the work of the British neurologist John Hughlings-Jackson. Hughlings-Jackson showed that there are parallel nerve pathways, with those that evolved and that develop later tending to predominate over the earlier, more primitive ones. In case of injury, however, the later ones tend to be incapacitated first, leaving the earlier ones to function. This research, too, although not contributing to the discovery of the unconscious in the same way that the work with hypnotism did, finds an echo in Freud's model of the mind later on, particularly in the idea of primary and secondary process thinking (see below).

Thus Freud had a full and respectable scientific career as a neurologist by 1895. He had studied with many of the leading medical authorities in the fields of physiology, neurology, and psychiatry, both in his own country and in France and, more briefly, in Germany. The defects and illogical elements in some of his speculative writings should not obscure the fact that he was a first-rate scientist, throroughly schooled in, and an active contributor to, the best science of his day. During Freud's apprenticeship for psychoanalysis, he was a mature, productive neurologist and psychiatrist. Moreover, the cornerstone of psychoanalysis, that ideas can create and can remove physical symptoms, was not an armchair discovery but was a hard-won, even reluctant, achievement, carefully documented by numerous lines of evidence, accumulated over a period of more than a decade. It was and remains a great discovery in the best scientific tradition. That is what entitles psychoanalysis to be called a scientific revolution in Kuhn's model.

---

## THE TRAUMA PARADIGM

*Studies in hysteria* records the evolution of theory and method from Breuer's cathartic treatment to the eve of Freud's consolidation of his first paradigm, the trauma paradigm. Freud at that point was giving up the use of hypnosis to suggest away symptoms, because both he and the patients found it repugnant simply to deny the patients' suffering, which they knew was real.

### Hypnotism and Freud's Trauma Theory

Freud's use of hypnotism in treatment differed from its usual use in psychiatry, for example, by Bernheim, Charcot, and the French psychiatrist Pierre Janet (some of whose ideas are discussed briefly below). Rather than using hypnosis as a medium for transmitting the suggestion that a symptom did not exist, Freud and Breuer used hypnosis as a means to discover the meaning and historical source of the symptom. This illustrates again the transformation of elements that contributed to the paradigm. Even this use of hypnosis, essential as it was to the development of Freud's thinking, was to be given up later.

Although hypnosis is not part of psychoanalysis, indeed, a method of treatment can be called psychoanalytic only if hypnosis is not used, the study of hypnotism was the scaffolding around which psychoanalysis was erected. Freud learned the following things from the studies using hypnotism:

**1.** Through use of hypnosis, physical symptoms can be suggested to patients, and they can be suggested away; those symptoms are indistinguishable from those of hysterics. This idea was based on clinical demonstrations by Charcot and Bernheim.

**2.** A hypnotized person can be virtually compelled, through posthypnotic suggestion, to perform a series of actions for reasons he or she is unaware of and to give a seemingly rational but demonstrably irrelevant explanation, as shown by Bernheim's experiments.

**3.** Posthypnotic amnesia is not absolute; memory of the events that happened during the hypnotic trance that the person is apparently not conscious of can be recovered to consciousness, again, shown by Bernheim's experiments.

**4.** Symptoms may be caused by unconscious "memories" of traumatic events, as shown in Breuer's case of Anna O., several cases of Janet, and also of Alfred Binet (Breuer & Freud, 1895/1955).

**5.** The recovery to consciousness of the unconscious traumatic events, accompanied by fully experiencing the appropriate emotion, can eliminate the corresponding symptom, shown by Breuer.

**6.** The mind has a storehouse of information not available to consciousness but accessible under hypnosis (hypnotic lucidity), as shown by Puységur but also implied in some clinical uses of hypnosis.

The elements now begin to add up to a theory. The person has experienced some traumatic event and was unable to experience or to express fully the appropriate emotion, often because of a conflict between the feelings and the person's own moral standards. The painful memory of the experience was then repressed; it became unconscious, lost to conscious memory. Some psychic force is responsible for this *repression* of the traumatic memory. But the memory is not completely lost, and it continues to have effects. It obtrudes into consciousness only in disguised form as a symptom. When the experience can be consciously remembered, along with the repressed emotion, the symptom is relieved because indirect expression is no longer necessary.

The immediate aim of therapy is to recover to consciousness the unconscious traumatic memories, together with reexperiencing fully the emotions that occurred in the original experience. The problem that caused the trauma is often no longer a current one. Many times it became a problem only because the small child was incapable of understanding or coping with things going on or was dependent on persons whom, as an adult, he no longer needed the same way. In any case, once the patient is conscious of the real problem, it can be dealt with as any other problem is, directly rather than by the formation of symptoms. (See Figure 2.1.)

The theory that trauma plays an essential role in the origin of hysteria should be contrasted with the two theories most prevalent in Freud's time. The first theory, favored particularly by Viennese physicians, held that women who suffered from hysterical symptoms were merely malingering, because there was no physical basis for their symptoms. The second theory, favored by many French psychiatrists, was that hysteria revealed and was based on a mental weakness or mental degeneration. There had never been a demonstration of such pathology in an autopsy, but that objection was met by saying that it was a functional degeneration. Both of those theories imply a subtly derogatory attitude toward women, no surprise in that era. What is surprising is that Freud has so often been criticized for neglecting environmental factors in the origin of neurosis, for it was Freud more than any psychiatrist of his time who first brought into consideration the impact of traumatic environmental events. And whatever else may be said about Freud's attitude toward women, he took his women patients more seriously and treated them with more respect than the majority of his contemporaries did.

In *Studies in hysteria* Freud recorded in various cases using the traditional therapies of the day, including baths, massage, exercise, rest, mild electric shock, and so on. Gradually he gave up all of those treatments. He found them ineffective, and he could find no reason in his theory why they should be effective. The big discovery, the conception that ideas can cause symptoms, is first stated as "Hysterics suffer mainly from reminiscences" (Breuer & Freud, 1895/1955, p. 7).

In this connection Freud remarked that although his training led him to examine and treat a paralysis or anesthesia locally, that is, by looking at the apparently diseased organ, what he found himself doing was more like the work of a novelist, recreating with the patient her entire life history. The psychic meaning of the patient's symptoms and the associated memories were a new form of data, not previously considered grist for the scientific or psychiatric mill.

### Janet's Trauma Theory

Pierre Janet, who also studied with Charcot, had a similar but not identical theory. The similarities and differences are helpful in seeing why Freud's ideas have become important throughout Western society, why they are, indeed, household words, whereas Janet is unknown to most of the public today. Janet, using hypnosis, also found traumatic memories to be the basis of his patients' symptoms, in fact, he published case histories showing such effects in the 1880s,

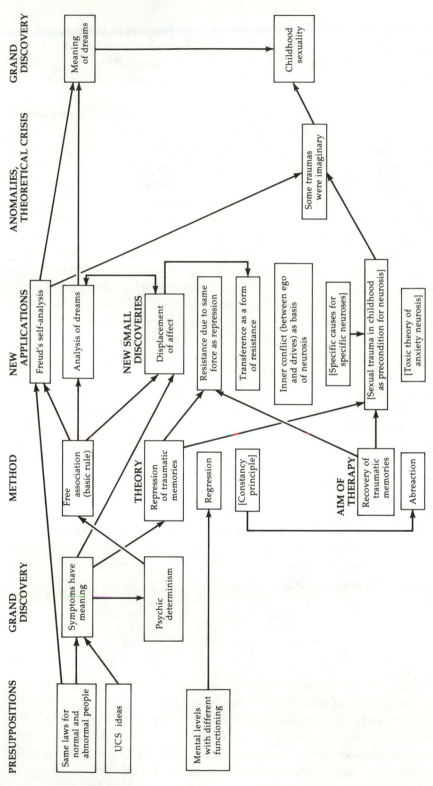

FIGURE 2.1 The trauma (proto) paradigm (*Adapted from Loevinger, 1979*). (Some of the interconnections are indicated.)

PRESUPPOSITIONS

GRAND DISCOVERY

METHOD

NEW APPLICATIONS

ANOMALIES, THEORETICAL CRISIS

GRAND DISCOVERY

Same laws for normal and abnormal people

UCS ideas

Mental levels with different functioning

Symptoms have meaning

Psychic determinism

Free association (basic rule)

Repression of traumatic memories

Regression

[Constancy principle]

Recovery of traumatic memories

Abreaction

AIM OF THERAPY

THEORY

Freud's self-analysis

Analysis of dreams

Displacement of affect

Resistance due to same force as repression

Transference as a form of resistance

Inner conflict (between ego and drives) as basis of neurosis

[Specific causes for specific neuroses]

[Sexual trauma in childhood as precondition for neurosis]

[Toxic theory of anxiety neurosis]

NEW SMALL DISCOVERIES

Some traumas were imaginary

Meaning of dreams

Childhood sexuality

before Freud did. The traumatic memories, said Janet, were like unpaid debts. Remembering the trauma and connecting it with the other parts of life were like balancing the books in Janet's metaphor, corresponding to Breuer's metaphor of catharsis.

Where Janet's practice differed from Freud's was in how Janet proceeded once the trauma was discovered. For Freud it sufficed to air the trauma by having the patient discuss it with the analyst, whereas apparently Janet hypnotized the patient again and gave the suggestion that the event had never happened (Ellenberger, 1970, pp. 361–364). That proceeding was contrary to the spirit of Freud's treatment, which was to face the truth at all costs. Anyone for whom the truth is not an appropriate treatment (for example, someone facing a terminal illness) is not an appropriate subject for psychoanalysis. Another difference between Freud's therapy and Janet's is that Janet's was almost entirely cognitive, whereas Freud from the beginning gave equal emphasis to the emotional factor (Perry & Laurence, 1984). For Janet the important thing was removing the pathogenic fixed idea, whereas for Freud the important thing was not only recalling the traumatic memory but reliving its original emotion. That, he felt, was the only way that therapy could be effective.

Freud emphasized that a difference between Janet's theory and his own was that Janet attributed the repression of traumatic memories to a degenerative change in the nervous system, manifested in a weakness in the function of psychic synthesis, whereas Freud attributed it to a dynamic conflict between opposing forces (Freud, 1910/1957). Freud and Breuer emphasized that many of their patients were gifted people, in no way mentally or morally degenerate. (There were many other facets to Janet's work that unfortunately receive too little attention today. A full and appreciative account is given by Ellenberger, 1970.)

### Resistance

Once Freud's rudimentary theory was worked out, it had a life of its own, following its own course of development, slowly, of course, for it involved breaking new ground at every step. First, Freud observed that patients become uncomfortable or go blank or change the topic when they come near painful memories or embarrassing thoughts, often the ones he was trying to help them recover. The patients themselves are not conscious of this avoidance. Freud conceived of what was happening as the operation of a force he called *resistance* or *defense*; it was as if they resisted or defended themselves against the traumatic or embarrassing memories. Then, by a leap that seems small now but was immense, he connected repression and resistance as basically the same thing. However obvious that connection may seem, it was not obvious to Janet. Janet denied that his patients experienced resistance, on the grounds, irrelevant of course, that the patients were not conscious of any such thing.

A particularly stubborn form of resistance appeared in the patient's relation to the psychoanalyst. Whatever the patient's problem might be, some version of it came out in a new edition in his relation to the analyst. This Freud called *transference*. And with this pregnant observation, *Studies in hysteria* concludes.

## Free Association

Meanwhile Freud's method of conducting treatment had undergone a sea-change to a new method that set it farther apart from standard medical practice and from previous treatments of neurosis and hysteria. Freud was not a gifted hypnotist, and the cures he obtained by means of hypnosis seemed tenuous. Besides, he reasoned, it is the patient's normal, waking personality that needs to accept the repressed memories. Hypnosis only bypasses the patient's resistance; it does not deal with it. But how is the repression to be lifted if not by hypnotism?

Here Freud drew on another element of his training, the belief in the scientific determination of biological phenomena. The way most biologists and physicians interpreted the pledge of Brücke and the group of natural scientists was as an injunction to reductionism: There is nothing in living things except physical-chemical forces. They favored physiological and physical causes for mental symptoms. But the way Freud construed their pledge was ultimately quite different. For him the crucial phrase became the last one of the pledge, "or forces equal in dignity." Psychic (*seelische* in German; see Kaufmann, 1980; Bettelheim, 1982) forces were raised to equal dignity, and Freud's basic assumption became the principle that psychic (*seelische*) events are lawful, a principle generally abbreviated as *psychic determinism*. Psychic determinism is a generalization of the discovery that hysterical symptoms have meaning, which is in turn derived from the principle whose source has been traced here, that ideas can create and can remove physical symptoms.

The hallmark of psychoanalysis became the new method of *free association*. If in mental life nothing happens by chance but everything is determined, then one need only let the patient say whatever comes to mind, and sooner or later he or she will let fall some clue to what the trouble is. The only constraint was the *basic rule* that nothing be withheld as too trivial, too embarrassing, or irrelevant. The so-called free associations are somehow determined, even though not under conscious control, indeed, especially when under the least possible conscious control. Those determinants must be unconscious, and in particular, they must be the unconscious ideas that are associated with the sought-for traumatic memories.

The method of free association thus is intimately bound with the structure of the theory. At first it was a supplement to traditional methods, but gradually it replaced all other therapeutic techniques that Freud had been trained in by his mentors, including hypnosis and finally suggestion and urging. Free association remains today the core technique of psychoanalysis. Modern psychoanalysts are much more meticulous in avoiding suggestion than Freud was at first, even after he ostensibly gave it up in favor of free association. Patients assisted Freud in that evolution, because they sometimes objected to his interruptions as disturbing to their train of thought.

Giving up all traditional, accepted therapies took unusual intellectual courage. Patients had certain expectations regarding appropriate medical treatment, and Freud, with a large family to support and many other relatives partly dependent on him, and no independent means, could not afford to spurn patients. How could he have dared to entrust the fate of the treatment to free association? How could he be confident that a source of the illness that neither he nor the patient knew at the outset would ultimately come to light by this means? He had to have faith in his theory and its fundamental discovery, psychic determinism.

### Sexual Seduction in Childhood

Another element now enters the theory, one that Freud at first thought was the key to all the rest, namely, that sexual experiences invariably seemed to appear as the original predisposing trauma. Whatever the patient's recent troubles, the memories always seemed to lead back to a childhood sexual experience, a seduction of some kind. Since Freud accepted the then-prevailing view that children lack the capacity for sexual experience, he devised an ingenious theory to account for the traumatic effect. The childhood experience, he hypothesized, caused no trouble at the time, but the memories were reawakened at puberty and at that point became traumatic. This was the weak point in the trauma theory, and it was later revised.

The use of free association as a technique probably had something to do with the emphasis on sex. Anyone can try free associating in the privacy of a solitary study room. It cannot be done for any length of time without thinking about sex in some way. To appreciate what this emphasis did to Freud's career and livelihood, one must remember that he began talking about sexual factors in the etiology of neurosis while Queen Victoria was still on the throne of England, with some years yet ahead of her. The culture of the European continent seems not to have been so prudish or so prurient as that of England, but the difference was only one of degree.

Freud was not prurient, which safeguarded him and his treatment, but in his personal life he seems to have been extremely conventional. For example, he forbade his fiancée to associate with a friend of hers who, in their delicate phrase, "got married before she got married." One of his sons revealed, years after Freud's death, that his relations with his father were permanently cooled by the fact that during adolescence, when he tried to talk to his father about masturbation, Freud expressed stern disapproval. From Freud's published remarks later in his career about the baleful effects of sexual constraints, one would never guess such facts.

The Victorian attitude toward sex as a dark and dangerous force did, however, affect Freud's theories, paradoxically, because those same theories were one important and perhaps the most crucial influence in freeing contemporary society from the most stringent of those attitudes (Breger, 1981).

## Unity of Neurotic and Normal Psychology

Related to the principle of psychic determinism is Freud's assumption that the same laws that apply to neurotic people apply to normal people. This statement has to be more in the nature of a presupposition than a discovery, though it is usually presented as a discovery of the next period, associated with his work on dreams, slips of the tongue, jokes, and so on.

Kurt Lewin in an essay on the Aristotelian and Galileian modes of thought in modern psychology, pointed out that with respect to this assumption, Freud was more in tune with modern scientific thinking than many of his critics (Lewin, 1931). In the Aristotelian mode of thought, characteristic of the scientific thinking of the ancients, the objects of study were classed into categories, and any law held only for that particular category of object. Thus Charcot and Janet believed that hysterical people were different kinds of people from normal people, characterized by some obscure mental degeneration or mental weakness. In seeking a single set of explanations for patients and normal people, including himself, Freud was taking a step comparable to Galileo when he sought common laws for the movement of the stars, falling stones, and the flight of birds, Lewin asserted. This feature of Freud's thinking, the search for universal laws of mind, is the reason that what started as a purely clinical theory of hysteria has grown to influence deeply modern thinking on personality and indeed much of life.

## Metapsychology

Freud's theory of how therapy works was at this time modeled after physical theories. The traumatic memories had a charge of emotion. That charge led to, but was never adequately discharged in, symptoms. With the recovery of the traumatic memories and abreaction (release) of the accompanying emotions, an appropriate discharge took place, and the corresponding symptom was relieved. This version of the theory is a restatement in quasi-physical terms of what has already been stated in psychological or clinical terms. That kind of restatement has come to be called Freud's *metapsychology*. Freud undoubtedly put great store by that aspect of his theorizing.

One of the problems in translating Freud's writings into English is that neologisms that have a distinctly unliterary ring in English are acceptable in literary writing in German. *Abreaction* was Breuer and Freud's word for catharsis. A central concept in the metapsychology is rendered in English as *cathexis*, a word with no other connotations, whereas the original German word, *Besetzung*, has many connotations. "Psychic energy" and "charge of emotion" are other attempts to render that idea in English.

Under the influence of his medical training, Freud in the 1890s was still looking for a physical explanation of neurosis. If there was any doubt of this, it was removed by the publication after his death (and against his express wishes) of his *Project for a scientific psychology* (1954). He had written the *Project* in 1895, lavishing much time and thought on its intricate attempt to find a totally physical explanation for the psychological phenomena he was grappling with, along with other phenomena of everyday life. He sent his friend Wilhelm Fliess several drafts of the *Project*. The fact that he never asked for the return of the last version is testimony enough that he was through with it. (There were, of course, no copying machines, and all his correspondence and writing were done longhand.) His search for a physical model foundered on the fact that its chief aim, to discover a physical explanation of repression, he could not achieve. He needed to postulate an observer in the system directing it; so there was no gain (Sulloway, 1979). He gave up the quest and turned increasingly to psychological explanations, which proved more satisfactory.

Freud's transition from seeking explanation of hysterical symptoms in terms of local, organic causes to psychological, life-history causes was not quick or easy. He did not suddenly become converted to psychic causation. In fact, he probably never completely gave up the idea that the true explanation was a physical one, and that when it was discovered, it would replace his makeshift psychological ones. To appreciate how fundamental and how painful this shift in his thinking was, one must see that what was at stake was the basic assumptions on which his medical training and thinking and that of virtually all his contemporaries rested. Gradually his theory shifted from seeing neurosis as originating in almost mechanical causes to seeing neurosis in terms of acts that have meaning (Izenberg, 1976).

As many psychologists and historians have discovered, the abandoned physical explanations left a mark on the metapsychology, which continued to occupy much of Freud's writing (Amacher, 1965; Holt, 1965). The concept of physical energy was replaced by that of *psychic energy*, whose meaning is ambiguously perched between the psychological and physical realms, incapable of a universally agreed-on definition (Holt, 1962).

Only late in his life, writing about anxiety, did Freud explicitly state that the discovery of the meaning of anxiety rendered uninteresting the source of its energy (Freud, 1926, p. 140). That statement is equivalent to saying that the psychological explanation is more interesting and important than the physiological one.

Whatever may have been the merits of the metapsychology as an aid to Freud's theorizing, many psychologists and psychoanalysts now believe the metapsychology can be entirely dispensed with (Gedo, 1979; Gill & Holzman,

1976; Schafer, 1976). The prominence Freud and many of his able followers have given to it probably reflects the cachet of natural science, particularly thermodynamics, from which it borrowed the word *energy* (though not the precise idea), rather than any contribution the metapsychology made to psychoanalysis as paradigm. I find no place for energy concepts in the paradigm (see also G. Klein, 1976.).

As to a deep explanation of how repression occurs, Freud did not at this time or probably ever achieve it. What he had done was to establish beyond doubt that it does occur. If one postulates that repression has occurred, all sorts of mental phenomena that previously seemed senseless or baffling begin to make sense, beginning with Charcot's and Bernheim's studies of hypnotism. In a similar way, Newton's theory was criticized because he did not succeed in explaining why gravity occurs; again, he merely showed its many manifestations, and that came to be what is called Newton's theory (Kuhn, 1970, p. 105).

## THE DRIVE PARADIGM

The method of free association led to a new application, dream analysis, because many patients when associating would recall their dreams. Because Freud believed in the unity of nature, that the same laws apply to the sick and the well, the psychiatrist and his patient, he applied the method of analysis to himself, over a period of years analyzing his own dreams, assisted by the technique of free association.

### Crisis and Revolution

Partly as a result of accumulated experience with patients, partly as a result of what he found in his own self-analysis, Freud came to doubt that the reports by his patients of childhood seduction could all be true. Many were not actual occurrences, he came to believe, but rather the child's fantasies. Because he had been working toward a rather tightly integrated theory that would yield a rational basis for treating neurosis, the discovery of this anomaly appeared to destroy what he had laboriously achieved over a period of about fifteen years.

He soon discovered, however, that the theory of an actual seduction was a dispensable element. In fact, psychic determinism was strengthened. Breuer and Freud had amended Charcot's theory of a physical trauma as the predisposing cause of neurosis to read psychic trauma as the cause; Freud was now going further and saying that the psychic trauma was sometimes simply a fantasy, completely or partly imaginary.

That is how this discovery is usually put, though it would be more accurate to say that many events were traumatic or not depending on the child's fantasies about the meaning of the event and his or her understanding of what the other participants were doing. If the child had been simply a victim of sexual abuse, as a recent critic (Masson, 1984) has suggested, then the fact that the child seemed to have guilt feelings, which led to inner conflict, hence ultimately to neurosis, is difficult to account for. According to Freud's new hypothesis, that the child's own fantasy is implicated, the sequence becomes more plausible.

But wait—if children have sexual fantasies, they must have sexual wishes. So childhood innocence is a myth, a retrospective cover-up of the unbridled wishes characteristic of children, who are slow to acquire the constraints of civilized, adult society. That was the next major discovery that initiated the new psychoanalytic paradigm.

Finally, and intimately related to the other discoveries, was Freud's theory of the meaning of dreams. The formula for deciphering dreams that Freud announced in *The interpretation of dreams (1900/1953)*, his greatest book, was that *Dreams are the disguised fulfillment of unconscious wishes.*

The manifest content of dreams cannot be interpreted. Only by means of the dreamer's free associations to the dream elements can one decipher the latent content of the dream, wherein the wish can be discerned. "The interpretation of dreams is the royal road to a knowledge of the unconscious activities of the mind" (Freud, 1900/1953, p. 608). The dream provides a window to the unconscious mind, in which we can see the laws by which it is governed. Freud called the processes of association thus revealed *primary process* thinking, in contrast to *secondary process* thinking characteristic of conscious, adult reasoning at its best.

Dream interpretation is recorded at least as far back as the biblical account of Joseph in Egypt predicting the seven fat years and the seven lean years. What makes dream analysis psychoanalytic is not just the mode of symbolic interpretation but the free associations of the dreamer. Thus most of the "Freudian" interpretations of literature, myth, dreams, and so on are not, strictly speaking, psychoanalysis, even when the ideas are authentically psychoanalytic. Freud did his share of such writing (Freud 1910b/1957; 1911/1958; 1914b/1953).

Freud found a place in his theory for many previous theories of dreams. The events of the dream day always play some part in bringing about the dream, but, contrary to what one might suppose, it is the unnoticed and not the striking events that are incorporated in the dream. Physical stimuli, whether bodily ones or ones in the dreamer's external environment, may also be incorporated in the dream content.

Wishes of current life may be represented in a dream and may instigate the dream, but at the heart of every dream is a childhood wish that has been aroused by events of the day. Usually it is a sexual one, according to Freud. That is one connection between the theory of dreams and the discovery of childhood sexuality. (In the kind of free translation that the interpretation of dreams permits, it is not clear to me that there is any way to distinguish a wish from a fear or a memory.)

Primary process, as seen in dreams, is characterized by condensation of elements and displacement of affect (emotion). *Condensation* refers to one dream element representing several different ideas, objects, or persons; conversely, however, a single idea, object, or person may be represented in several elements of a dream. *Displacement of affect* is an essential element of the theory. It describes the fact that an emotion appropriate to one idea may become associated with another idea to which it has no logical connection. This association may be based on a similar sounding word, contiguity in time or place, similar superficial appearance, or the like. (For example, one person named John may stand for another, or a person named John or a prostitute's "john" may be represented in a dream by a toilet, or vice versa.) Displacement of affect not only accounts for dreams, it accounts in part for formation and content of symptoms and many other manifestations of psychic life.

### Transference and the Aim of Therapy

Where resistance and transference had seemed to be obstacles to the discovery of the unconscious traumatic memories in the trauma paradigm, in the drive paradigm they became the vehicle of the therapy. Transference became the stage or arena on which old traumas, not necessarily single events but often long-lasting situations, can be reenacted safely with a new object, the analyst, who is there in a neutral, uninvolved capacity so as to insure a more favorable outcome to the drama.

Something about transference had been known at least since the time of Mesmer, whose critics worried that the patient might have a lasting emotional fixation on the hypnotist. Many therapies before and since have stressed the value of a warm, supportive relation between therapist and patient. But it is a giant step from either of those positions to Freud's account.

Transference is a complex idea, but it first became salient in a fairly simple form (Loewald, 1960/1980). The patient, Freud found, relives her most traumatic or problematic experiences in the therapy, with the psychoanalyst serving as stand-in for some important person in the past, usually the father or mother. Ordinarily this revival appears first as a passionate love, though all sorts of emotions are relived in this way, including hate, fear, jealousy, resentment, and so on. The great difference between Freud and Breuer, who had probably noticed the phenomenon in the case of Anna O., was that Freud was able to take a detached attitude, to understand that this was a form of resistance, and not to take personally the patient's emotional dependence or passionate avowals or angry denunciations.

At first Freud saw transference only as an obstacle to therapy, a form of resistance that had to be analyzed like any other resistance. Later he came to understand that reproducing earlier experiences in the physician-patient relation was a major form of remembering repressed events and emotions. Thus in the drive paradigm, transference became the core of psychoanalysis as therapy. All therapies, even physical therapies, potentially make use of transference; what distinguishes psychoanalysis from all other therapies is the analysis of transference to lay open its childhood roots.

Making the unconscious conscious is still an aim of therapy. This does not take place by sudden, startling revelations, however, as hypnotic therapy assumed, but rather by a gradual, prolonged process of overcoming resistances, bit by bit, sometimes over a period of years. The aim of therapy is broadened to encompass the successful analysis of resistance and transference.

The psychoanalyst performs mainly three things: pointing out gaps and inconsistencies in the patient's narrative that the patient is not aware of; serving as an object for the transference; and finally, interpreting the patient's behavior, symptoms, dreams, and associations. Many of the gaps and inconsistencies would be apparent to any impartial observer even without special training. The analyst's experience, however, does alert him or her to ones that others might not notice. The fact that the analyst is not a part of the patient's life outside the analytic hour enables the analyst to remain a neutral figure of transference. Giving interpretations, particularly the symbolic ones often called Freudian, is a far less prominent part of the therapeutic process than is popularly believed. The rule, in fact, is that interpretations are not offered until the patient is just about ready to discover them by herself. The vast majority of interpretations relate not to deeply unconscious traumatic memories but rather to resistances that are very close to the fabric of the patient's everyday life. Freud's term *preconscious* denotes ideas that are not in focal conscious attention but that are accessible with some effort. Although the proponents of other kinds of psychotherapy often magnify their differences with psychoanalysis, both psychoanalysis and the other psychotherapies are concerned most of the time with clarifying preconscious ideas.

Contrary to what Freud originally believed, the achievement of an important insight into an early traumatic episode does not, by itself, remove all symptomatic traces of the experience. Rather, there must be a prolonged period of following out all the ways that early experience has affected the patient's current life, behavior, and thinking in order to eradicate the traces. That process is given the technical name of *working through*. Both in the analysis of resistances and in the period of working through, most of what is going on in psychoanalytic therapy is much like what is going on in other forms of psychotherapy, that is, it is concerned with contemporary life.

Proponents of other therapies often criticize psychoanalysis for its preoccupation with the past rather than the present. In one respect, however, psychoanalysis is unique among therapies in its concentration on the immediate present. The relationship between the patient and the doctor is as close to right here, right now as one can get, and it is the topic of psychoanalysis far more than of any other therapeutic technique. Childhood memories are probably rarely provoked by the analyst; most often they are the result of following the rule of free association.

## Application to Everyday Life

In the years immediately following publication of the *Interpretation of dreams*, Freud wrote a series of books that carried further the application of psychoanalytic ideas to the everyday life of normal people. One of his best-known books is *The psychopathology of everyday life* (1901/1960), which concerns the mistakes and forgetting that characterize all of us more or less all of the time. This book is about "Freudian slips," a term frequently heard in ordinary conversation nowadays. Psychoanalysts do not use that term, for they assume that all slips are Freudian. One of the most charming books is *Jokes and their relation to the unconscious* (1905a/1960), which concerns all forms of wit and humor. These books are based on a formula that is an extension of the formula for dreams. There is a repressed or a consciously suppressed sexual or aggressive wish that is given disguised expression in mistakes or forgetting or in wit and humor. (Particularly in the case of wit and jokes, Freud makes use of the formula of discharge of energy, a theory that I cannot understand well enough to render intelligible.)

*Childhood Sexuality.* Before Freud there were only occasional glimpses of childhood sexuality. When it was acknowledged at all, it was usually considered pathological. Freud's close friend Wilhelm Fliess believed in a universal bisexual disposition and was interested in the sexuality of children; he must have influenced Freud on this point. Their friendship had been over for some time when *Three essays on theory of sexuality* (1905b/1953) appeared. Despite Freud's acknowledging Fliess's influence and priority, Fliess felt resentful at the greater credit accruing to Freud for ideas for which Fliess felt responsible. But with the ideas he took from Fliess, as with the ideas from Charcot, Bernheim, Brücke, and Breuer, it was Freud's transmutation and integration of the ideas with his other ideas that made them memorable.

The idea of childhood sexuality was elaborated on, among other topics, in *Three essays.* In order to understand the conception of *childhood sexuality* (or infantile sexuality, as the British say, but they extend the period of infancy beyond that customary in American usage), one must understand the broadened meaning Freud gave to sexuality, extending far beyond the limits of adult coitus. In this book Freud pointed out that ordinary usage with respect to sexual inversions, perversions, fetishism, and so on recognizes that broader meaning.

A couple of pages concerning stages of psychosexual development have been given extraordinary and disproportionate prominence in most elementary expositions of psychoanalysis, probably because they are concrete and pictorial, referring to the oral, anal, phallic, and genital stages. In later work Freud and others have elaborated on character types that presumably correspond to fixation at the several stages. To support these clinical hypotheses, it would be necessary to show that certain character traits go together as a syndrome—for example, stinginess, orderliness, and obstinacy, the hypothetical constitutents of the anal character type—and also that persons who have that syndrome prominently are also especially preoccupied with the corresponding bodily function of defecation. There is no impressive hard evidence to support these clinical hypotheses. Those hypotheses have not, however, been shown to be essential to the psychoanalytic paradigm and therefore do not play a role in this account.

Although the importance of psychosexual stages to psychoanalytic theory is frequently exaggerated, the theory of the Oedipus complex retains its central importance for most psychoanalysts. In its starkest form, the one that corresponds most closely to the Greek legend, the theory states that every little boy at a certain stage in his development wishes to take exclusive possession of his mother sexually and to get rid of his father. Popular opinion to the contrary notwithstanding, there never was any doubt in Freud's mind that boys also have strong affection for their fathers, and even have times when they wish they could get rid of their mother so as to have their father to themselves. How much explicit sexual imagery accompanies these thoughts in most children is not altogether clear, nor is there necessarily the same answer for all boys even within Western European and American society. The boy's affection for and identification with his father is particularly important as part of the child's defense against regression to an infantile symbiotic dependence on his mother (Loewald, 1951/1980). A modified but similar story holds for little girls.

Castration anxiety (or castration complex) and penis envy are other well-known conceptions deriving from this period of psychoanalysis. *Castration anxiety* refers to a little boy's fear that his penis will be cut off by his father or other person because of some transgression he has committed or thought of committing. For example, the father might wish to retaliate for the boy's desire to possess the mother, or he may wish to punish the boy for masturbating. Threats of castration for masturbation are not rare, but everyday observation suggests that fears of losing the penis are far more nearly universal than are the actual threats. According to Freud, the boy's discovery that there are indeed creatures, to wit, girls, who have no penis precipitates these fears.

Girls, too, are astonished when they discover the anatomical difference between the sexes. *Penis envy* is the name given to their reaction, a feeling that they have been mutilated and deprived of something of inestimable value. Penis envy and castration anxiety, like the Oedipus complex, refer to what are presumably normal aspects of child development, aspects that had been ignored by psychiatry and academic psychology prior to Freud.

*The Problem of Universality.* To what extent these phenomena are universal in Western culture, or in all cultures, remains a matter of dispute. It would be plausible that the Oedipus complex would take a somewhat different form in societies where kinship structure is entirely different. That, however, would not diminish the importance of Freud's formulation for Western culture.

Almost paradoxically, psychoanalysis in the drive paradigm places these sexual ideas and motives at the center both of normal development and of neurosis. The difference presumably is that the normal child in some sense resolves the Oedipus complex and in some way comes to terms with castration fear or penis envy. But this is an obscure part of the theory. The fact that adults are not aware of such ideas or motives is not relevant, for repression is assumed to be the fate of such ideas. Freud believed that the amnesia that most adults have for the events of their early childhood, a period when they were clearly alert, impressionable, and learning rapidly all sorts of facts that they do not forget, is accounted for precisely by the universal need to repress their childhood sexuality.

That small children are fascinated by their own and other people's sexual organs is no longer a secret known only to psychoanalysts. Still, it is hard to find other theories that ascribe much importance to the fact. Some present-day analysts assign less importance to these sexual preoccupations in their psychoanalytic treatment than was true during the heyday of the drive paradigm (Gedo, 1979; Kohut, 1977).

## Summary of Drive Paradigm

Major elements of the trauma paradigm are retained in the drive paradigm, particularly the presupposition of universal laws covering the mental life of normal and neurotic people; psychic determinism; and a set of concepts including the unconscious, repression, resistance, transference, and primary and secondary process thinking. Many of these concepts have somewhat altered meanings, however. The method of psychoanalytic treatment and investigation was expanded to include analysis of resistance and transference as the chief touchstones. New kinds of data, not previously conceived of as appropriate to scientific analysis, include dreams, mistakes, forgetting, and jokes, as well as the content of symptoms, recognized in the earlier period. In each case, Freud found sense in what had previously been considered nonsense. Instinctual drives (or, at times, wishes) were the connecting thread in the theoretical explanations.

## Public and Professional Reaction to Freud

Freud began to attract followers shortly after publication of the *Interpretation of dreams*. Public reception of psychoanalysis in its early years is hard to gauge accurately at this distance. E. Jones mentions a great deal of opprobrium, whereas Hanna Decker says that the professional public gave favorable reviews of Freud's books in Germany (Jones, 1933; Decker, 1977). Austria being a German-speaking and largely German country, that presumably is some indication of its reception there too. Havelock Ellis, writing on the psychology of sex, was in trouble with the law in England and had to have books published on the Continent. Jones, himself an early follower of Freud, was dismissed from a hospital in England for asking his patients about their sex lives, and he spent many years in Canada before returning to England. On his only trip to the United States, Freud gave a series of five lectures (1910a/1957) at the celebration in 1909 of the twentieth anniversary of the founding of Clark University, in Worcester, Massachusetts, at that time a major graduate school. Freud had been invited by G. Stanley Hall, the president of the university, who was a maverick psychologist. At most universities in the United States, however, psychoanalysis was a forbidden subject; any mention, even criticism, of psychoanalysis was said to be sufficient cause for removal of a professor in some places.

The Swiss psychiatrist, Carl Jung, at that time one of Freud's chief followers, was also invited to address the Clark convocation. He stayed on in the United States after Freud returned home. Jung wrote back to Freud that on his lecture tour he deemphasized sex and was well received. Freud grumbled that if he left out even more sex he would be even better received. A few years later there was a decisive split between Freud and Jung, who went on to develop his own complex paradigm of personality, a paradigm that still attracts many supporters.

Freud's group was at best rather beleagured. Many of the people who were attracted to it were themselves outsiders and rebels. Most were Jews. Jones, one of the few non-Jews, was a Welshman, hence a member of another oppressed minority. On the one hand, the fact that some of Freud's most prominent and trusted followers, such as Jung and the Austrian psychiatrist Alfred Adler, turned against him and against one or another aspect of his theories after a few years is often taken as a sign of Freud's intolerance and the narrowness of his theories. W. Kaufmann, on the other hand, takes their rejection as a sign of the oppositional bias that led them to psychoanalysis in the first place (Kaufmann, 1980). The paradigmatic approach in this book bypasses such arguments. Whatever the merits of political democracy, the people's will is not a safe guide to evaluation of theories.

Anti-Semitism must be ranked, along with Victorian prudery and prurience (Breger, 1981), as one of the major facts of life in Vienna at the time Freud was creating psychoanalysis (Schorske,1980). Vienna had an anti-Semitic mayor in the late 1890s. He was elected three times; each time his election was set aside by the emperor of Austria, but eventually he assumed office. Freud coveted a professorial appointment, which was bestowed only by the government, not only for the honor but also because patients chose their physicians according to such signs of merit, and he often had need of more patients to support his family. Politics and prejudice played a part in such appointments, and he obtained a professor's rank only relatively late in life, owing partly to the efforts of a former patient. There is no reason to assume, however, that such facts played much part in determining the substance of psychoanalytic theory.

---

## THE EGO PARADIGM

### From Drive to Ego

From the time the drive paradigm was well established, the problem that faced psychoanalysis was accounting for what held drives in check. In the period of the trauma paradigm, neurotic breakdown was accounted for by inner conflict between the person's drives or sexual wishes on the one hand and the controlling ego or moral standards on the other. The idea that inner conflict was the precipitating cause of neurosis continued, but parties to the conflict were at times described somewhat differently. Basically, in one form or another, the idea was always that the ego opposed and controlled the drives. What then accounted for the growth and strength of the ego? That was the problem now facing psychoanalysis.

Sandor Ferenczi, who was at the time one of Freud's closest collaborators, proposed that the ego develops by renunciation of instinctual gratification, to which the infant and child are compelled by external circumstances (Ferenczi, 1913/1916). He contrasted this idea with that of a spontaneous striving for development, an idea sponsored by Alfred Adler, whose differences with Freud concerning the importance of ego psychology had led to Adler's secession from the psychoanalytic group in 1911. More than half of Freud's Vienna group left with Adler, so it was not a trivial defection. Ferenczi was explaining ego development in terms of drives as the fundamental concept; Adler stood for independent ego motives, with drives as subordinate concepts. (Some years later the mainstream of psychoanalysis moved slowly toward something like Adler's position, but in terms of Freud's unique version of ego mastery.)

*Paradoxes of the Drive Paradigm.* In the essay "On narcissism" (1914a/1957), Freud added another element to the theory of ego development. The infant begins life in a state of complete narcissism, Freud asserted; that is the earliest form of the sexual drive. Taking the boy as prototype, he continued: The small child, who believes himself possessed of all perfections, must surrender this self-love as he accommodates himself to the increasing demands made on him by his family and society. As his perception of his own smallness and limitations becomes more realistic, he is in danger of surrendering his self-love completely, but that would be unbearably painful. To save his narcissism, he transfers his self-love to his *ego ideal*, saying, in effect, "I may not be perfect, but I can aspire to perfection." This major step in ego development, the evolution of the ego ideal in the child, is at the same time a regression to narcissism. Thus *progression is based on regression.*

This principle was new in psychoanalytic theory. It was a tour de force, because whereas previously the ego (or sometimes, ego instincts) had been conceived of as the opponent of the sexual drive, and hence a party to the neurotic conflict, now it was seen as derived from a transformation of the sexual drive. But this insight was both the high point of the drive paradigm and the beginning of its downfall. For it is, after all, a paradox that the ego would both be derived from the instinctual drives and the controller of instinctual drives.

There were other problems and paradoxes, perhaps the most insistent being the problem of resistance and the unconscious. If it is resistance that prevents repressed ideas from becoming conscious, why are we not conscious of resistance? Indeed, it was such reasoning that enabled many psychiatrists to deny that their patients experienced any such thing as resistance.

Throughout his life Freud continued to amend and expand the drive paradigm to encompass several additional findings concerning ego psychology and ego development. One cannot say that Freud ever gave up the drive paradigm in favor of a new one. Among his theoretical contributions, however, beginning with the essay on narcissism, are the major principles that have since become systematized by writers such as Erik Erikson (1950), H. Loewald (1960/1980), P. Ricoeur (1970), and others as a new or, as I shall call it, ego paradigm.

*The Principle of Mastery.* The basic principle of ego functioning is announced in *Beyond the pleasure principle* (Freud, 1920/1955). Many psychoanalysts prefer to ignore the book, because it contains Freud's postulation of the life and death instincts. Those ideas have never gained general acceptance among analysts; most consider them an embarrassment. Psychologists who wish to belittle psychoanalysis find the death instinct handy. I believe that life and death instincts cannot be considered part of any paradigm; the fact that most analysts reject the ideas is consistent with that position.

The basic principle, and the major *discovery* that lays the groundwork for the new paradigm, fitting the Kuhn model, is that *experience is mastered by actively repeating what one has passively undergone.* There were four lines of evidence for this proposition. The first and seminal one was the play of children; children play over and over again not their most gratifying experiences but the problematic, painful, or frustrating ones. Yet according to the *pleasure principle*, which Freud had previously adhered to and probably never disavowed, the most pleasurable experiences were the ones that should have been repeated. Freud's explanation is that the child masters frustration by repeating the experience under his own impetus.

Similarly, taking his own theory of dreams as given, Freud inquired why it is that persons suffering from traumatic neuroses return again in their dreams to the moments of greatest trauma. Surely it cannot be a wish to repeat those traumatic happenings. Again, by repeating the experience on its own initiative, the psyche or ego (or, more properly, the person) attempts to master the trauma. In this case, however, the effort is unsuccessful because the instigating episode remains inaccessible to consciousness. A third line of evidence is that some people seem to bring the same unhappy fate down on themselves repeatedly.

Finally, and most germane to this discussion, there is the question of how the psychoanalyst can be assured that every patient, even though she does not know the source of the current difficulties, can be counted on to present those difficulties and their sources in her transference to the analyst. Again, the most frustrating experiences are the ones most certain to be repeated, in an unconscious effort to master those experiences.

These four kinds of data serve as evidence for what Freud calls the *repetition compulsion.* On the one hand, in the case of a repeated dream referring to a repressed trauma or in the case of transference, the idea of compulsion is appropriate. Because the source is unconscious, repetition does not result in mastery. Without the help of therapy, symptoms and transference can go on with little change for many years. On the other hand, the play of children is not a part of pathology but of normal development, and under usual circumstances it does result in mastery and progressive development; thus the idea of repetition compulsion seems less appropriate.

*Ego Development as Mastery.* In the *Ego and the id* (1923/1961) and *Civilization and its discontents* (1930/1961), Freud carried further his theory of ego development. The observation on which the later works were based remains the fundamental discovery that experience is mastered by actively repeating what one has passively undergone. In the *Ego and the id,* Freud develops the theme that the ego serves three masters—the id, or instinctual life; the superego, or conscience; and the real world of the environment. The task of the ego is to master them all. In both volumes, Freud reexamines the period and events of childhood that he had previously characterized in terms of the Oedipus complex, this time from the point of view of the aggressive drive (which was more or less a representative of the death instinct, though they are conceptions of different levels of abstraction).

The child, Freud said, experiences aggressive impulses. Let us say a boy wants to hit his younger brother. Father steps in to prevent that. Having been frustrated in expressing his aggression, the boy wants now to take out that frustration by hitting his father. But that is not allowed. Father is too big; besides, the little child still needs his father's love. To solve this dilemma, the child identifies himself with his father, doing to himself what his father would have done, that is to say, controlling himself as his father would have controlled him. In so doing, the child has become divided; he now plays the part of the impulsive child and that of the controlling father. This division between impulse and control is a major step in ego development. Moreover, the process provides a general model of ego development, namely, that interpersonal relations provide both the impetus and the pattern for intrapersonal differentiation. In my words, not Freud's, *interpersonal schemas shape intrapersonal schemas* (Loevinger, 1966, 1976).

The three fundamental tenets of ego development derived from Freud's writings remain: (1) Experience is mastered by actively repeating what one has passively undergone. (2) Interpersonal relations shape and drive intrapersonal differentiation. (3) Progression is, or may be, based on regression. All of these principles appear to have been original with Freud. This is an aspect of psychoanalytic theory that does not always receive its proper due.

## Structural Theory

The paradox that we are not aware of resistance, of either the fact of repression or of the forces responsible for repression, was one anomaly that led to ego psychology. Freud met this problem (and some others too technical to detail here) by postulating, in place of the conscious and unconscious *systems* in mental life, the new *structures* of the ego, the superego, and the id. Like the psychosexual stages, this theory has been overemphasized because of its apparent concreteness. It is almost all that many people know about psychoanalysis; yet it is hard to say how this shift affected the method of therapy and investigation. According to the new theory, usually called the *structural theory*, consciousness is an attribute of some mental processes, not a system of the mind. Resistance in therapy and indeed all of a person's characterological defenses are thought of as unconscious parts of the ego, whereas what is repressed is part of the id. Thus the repressing force is now in a different mental system from the repressed content, but we need not on that account be conscious of repression.

For anyone satisfied to solve theoretical difficulties by postulating new mental entities, one problem is solved. There have always been respected psychoanalysts, however, who objected to this solution, and from the point of view of paradigm construction, it is not completely satisfactory.

## Application to Therapy

In Freud's later writings the formula for therapy became, "Where id is, there ego should be," as it is usually translated (Freud, 1933/1964, p. 80). Several authors have objected that much is lost in that translation (Bettelheim, 1982; Kaufmann, 1980). A more faithful translation is: "Where it is, I ought to become" (Brandt, 1966, p. 374). Freud himself did not use the Latinate terms *id* and *ego*, preferring terms from ordinary vocabulary, *das Es* (literally, the it) and *das Ich* (the I) (Freud, 1926b/1959). Thus the fact that his theories are often summarized solely in terms of id and ego is doubly ironic.

This formulation, even in the bowdlerized form "Where id is, there ego should be," describes the direction of movement in psychoanalytic therapy: reclaiming for conscious choice behaviors that had previously been governed by irresistible compulsions. At the same time, it is a further description of ego development and provides the theoretical basis for the claim of psychoanalysis that it leads to restructuring of character rather than merely removal of symptoms.

Anna Freud, in describing the mechanisms of defense, did much more, broadening the purview of psychoanalysis as therapy and as theory into ego psychology generally (A. Freud, 1936/1946). Similarly, Heinz Hartmann, a leading analyst, in an essay hailed at the time as revolutionary within psycho-analysis, extended the purview of psychoanalysis from psychopathology to normal adaptation (Hartmann, 1939/1958).

In the practice of psychoanalysis during the 1920s, a new obstacle was discovered in the form of certain character traits, such as, for example, insincer-ity, or cynicism, or lack of seriousness, which prevented psychotherapy from being effective (Reich, 1933/1949). Reich called such traits *character armor* and proposed treating them like symptoms. Thus they became more grist for the mill, adding a new type of data and at the same time somewhat extending the method.

A more radical extension of the method was the development of play therapy for the treatment of children. Children are too close to free association all the time for traditional psychoanalysis to be appropriate for them. Their play is more or less equivalent to dreams and daydreams of adults; it serves as the major medium of communication in therapy. Anna Freud and Erik Erikson were leaders in this development (Erikson, 1950; A. Freud, 1926/1946).

## CONTEMPORARY CROSS-CURRENTS

In the years since Freud's death in 1939, psychoanalysis, far from being a static or dead discipline, has continued to evolve.

### The "New Psychoanalytic Ego Psychology"

Under the leadership of Hartmann, Ernst Kris, and Rudolf Loewenstein, there was an ever-increasing emphasis on psychoanalytic ego psychology (Hart-mann, Kris, & Loewenstein, 1945–1962/1964). The psychologist David Rapa-port has carefully systematized the theory as expounded by this school of thought, often called the "new psychoanalytic ego psychologists" (Rapaport, 1960). As his summary reveals, the concept of psychic energy, or cathexis, remains central to the theory, whereas the new principles of ego psychology that Freud was working on in his late years, given above as the core of the new ego paradigm, are not included or at least are difficult to include. Rapaport undoubt-edly was familiar with and indeed wrote essays on the principles of ego psychol-ogy discussed above, even though he found them hard to include in his system-atic version.

Probably the major problem in integrating the ego paradigm with the drive paradigm, at least in the version that stresses the concept of cathexis, or psychic energy, is that there is a logical contradiction built into the combination. The version of the drive paradigm favored by Rapaport and the Hartmann-Kris-Loewenstein group emphasizes the concept of cathexis and with it, the *constancy hypothesis*. That is the idea that the pleasure that every human seeks consists in reducing tension to some low, constant level. Pleasure fundamentally consists of a discharge of energy; also, symptoms and symptomatic behavior are reduced when a portion of energy is discharged, according to this version of psychoanalytic theory.

This tension-reduction model is incompatible with the new formula for therapy, that progress is made by turning passive experiences into active reenactments, by the I reclaiming a portion of the territory of the it. Not only are the terms different, the direction is opposite. There is no way that going from passive to active can be construed as tension reduction.

### Schools Emphasizing the Pre-Oedipal Period

Whereas classical psychoanalysis, that is, the psychoanalysis of Freud's lifetime and of the drive paradigm, put great emphasis on the Oedipus complex as the central experience both in normal psychic development and in the development of most psychopathologies, much recent work has placed greater emphasis on the pre-Oedipal period (Eagle, 1984).

One group of recent theorists has become known as the *object relations* school; many of their most prominent members are British psychonalysts. Originally they were led or influenced by the child analyst, Melanie Klein. Their emphasis is on the longterm consequences of the child's earliest attachments, which are likely to be to the mother for both boys and girls. (In a perverse turn of phrase, *object* in psychoanalysis almost always means love object, though any person who thought of his beloved as an object would be considered sick.)

Another school of thought, whose leader has been Heinz Kohut, is called *self psychology* (Kohut, 1971, 1977). The emphasis in the therapeutic work of the self psychologists is on the formation of the self. To oversimplify their thesis, they believe that most patients do not have sufficiently strong and independent ego structure, indicating a problem in the very earliest stages of ego formation. Correspondingly, they emphasize the narcissistic stage of psychosexual development. Both the object-relations school and the self psychologists originally tended to formulate theory in terms of psychic energy, or cathexis, but that may have been more of an historical accident than a logical necessity for either school. Kohut's later work explicitly omitted cathexis as a theoretical concept but did use other hypothetical entities of the metapsychology (Kohut, 1977).

## More Radical Approaches

There are several new approaches to psychoanalytic theory that are more radical than the foregoing; they disavow cathexis theory and start out with new fundamental assumptions. All are concerned with aspects of ego psychology, but they make minimal use of the hypothetical entities of psychoanalytic metapsychology. Major insights of classical psychoanalysis with respect to drives and the importance of sexuality are not forgotten, but equal importance is given to ego motives. Many of these recent contributions to psychoanalytic theory also incorporate insights derived from other schools of psychology, both behavioristic and cognitive developmental, to be discussed in subsequent chapters.

John Gedo presents several case histories together with his revised, cognitive-dynamic approach to psychoanalysis (1979). With respect to each case, he presents first interpretations that would be given in classical psychoanalysis. In contrast, he then presents the interpretations he has found most useful both to give to his patients and to summarize their histories. His preferred versions are formulated in language much closer to the language the patients use to speak to themselves about their problems. These interpretations include values, ideals, and the patient's ways of thinking about his or her life and its problems, that is, cognitive elements. Gedo stresses, however, that his method remains that of classical psychoanalysis, free association by the patient and its complement, evenly hovering attention by the analyst.

Another cognitive-dynamic approach is that of M. J. Horowitz and a similar but less elaborate one, apparently worked out independently, by H. Wishnie (Horowitz, 1977b; Horowitz et al., 1984; Wishnie, 1977). Much of Horowitz's current work is devoted to brief psychotherapy, limited to a total of twelve sessions per patient, for reactions to acutely stressful situations. The hallmark of Horowitz's approach is a series of charts depicting the different mental states to which the patient is prone, how he or she conceives of self and other in each state, and how these states are manifested in the patient's important relationships, including the relationship with the analyst, and so on (Horowitz, 1979). By bringing into focus the circumstances or ideas that precipitate the transition from a satisfactory state to a pathological one, the patient may be helped to deal with current problems. Treatment limited to twelve sessions cannot be called psychoanalysis. Horowitz's therapy, however, like that of Gedo, uses the insights of classical psychoanalysis as well as those of more recent ego psychology. In particular, the importance of sexuality and of using the relation to the therapist as a model of other relationships bear the stamp of psychoanalysis.

One of the most interesting approaches is that of R. Schafer (1976, 1978). He wishes to forbid psychoanalysts to postulate any mental entities at all. All there are, he says, are reactions and modes of action, including "consciously" and "unconsciously" as modes of action. It remains to be seen how close Schafer's "action language" brings psychoanalysis to behaviorism. It is not clear that Schafer's approach requires any change in psychoanalysis as a method of treatment, but it mandates an enormous shift in case histories and in psychoanalytic theory, perhaps also in personality theory.

John Bowlby has drawn major insights from psychoanalysis as well as from many other fields, including ethology and experimental psychology, in formulating his theory of attachment as the central motive of infancy (Bowlby, 1969). This theory is meant to replace a now-outmoded theory, which can be found in Freud but also in behavioristic theories, that the baby's primary attachment to its mother is derived entirely from the fact that the mother has provided the baby's supply of food. Attachment, Bowlby shows, is a need separate from the need for food.

Many other theorists are working to combine insights derived from psychoanalysis with those from other branches of psychology. Most of them have not been mentioned in this chapter, and much of the work is too recent to attain the perspective necessary to decide which are the most significant approaches. Although psychoanalysts have the reputation for extreme dogmatism and for expelling members for minor heresies, some of the most radical innovations, those of Schafer, Gedo, and Horowitz, for example, are the work of psychoanalysts who are themselves entrusted with the training of the next generation of psychoanalysts.

### New Critics of Psychoanalysis

Psychoanalysis dominated the training of psychiatrists in many medical schools for a few years after World War II. That is far from being true today. However, those who a few years ago proclaimed the death of psychoanalysis spoke prematurely, in the light of recent activity. Indeed, even the exposé, denunciation, and debunking of Freud continue to be a vigorous industry, as witness the popularity of recent volumes by F. J. Sulloway (1979) and J. M. Masson (1984).

Sulloway's major thesis is that Freud's early biological theories of neurosis were false, and that falseness lives on in psychoanalysis because the biological theories are only thinly disguised in the pseudopsychological façade that the psychoanalytic metapsychology of later years provides (Sulloway, 1979). As has been shown, however, a growing number of psychoanalytic theorists have discarded most of the metapsychology (that is, cathexis theory) while retaining the essentials of the psychoanalytic paradigm. Thus Sulloway's critique is less novel than it seems and does not apply to much recent work in psychoanalysis.

Masson's thesis is almost diametrically opposed to that of Sulloway. According to Masson, Freud's original theory was true: Incest and sexual abuse of children, which Freud euphemistically referred to as seduction, are indeed the cause of neurosis (Masson, 1984). Freud abandoned the true theory in favor of a false theory of psychological trauma to cover his fondness for Fliess (there is a complex episode that shows the connection, one that does indeed show Freud in a bad light personally) and because he feared unpopularity if he exposed the actual extent of incest.

Masson's criticism is the more serious because it has consequences for the practice of psychoanalysis as therapy. Psychoanalysis as therapy is, he believes, basically invalid. For Masson's thesis to be true, the cause of neurosis would have to have been ignored by several thousand psychoanalysts and even more psychiatrists since Freud's time. Could all of them have been that stupid or that supinely enthralled by Freud's least word? For every admirer, Freud had at least one ferocious opponent, eager to expose his errors. Indeed, some of those opponents flourished in the ranks of official psychoanalysis and have provided numerous variant versions of psychoanalysis, which contain insights worth further study. Of Freud's many critics, however, Masson seems to be the first to suggest that incest or sexual abuse is the true cause of neurosis.

This chapter has sought to present the bare bones of psychoanalysis as paradigm. The wealth of variations, criticisms, and new developments is beyond the scope of this book. My hope is that rather than seeking straightway for the "truth," the beginner in the field will search first for the logic of the paradigm. Grasping that, one can more easily appreciate and fit together various subsidiary theories of Freud and other psychoanalysts and coordinate them with recent developments both within psychoanalysis proper and in various schools of thought bearing its imprint to a greater or lesser degree.

## ANALYSIS OF THE CASE OF LAURA

Most of the major elements of the psychoanalytic paradigms can be found in R. Lindner's story of Laura (Lindner, 1955). (See Appendix A, which follows.) The importance of psychic traumas in childhood in laying the basis for later neurosis is evident. Laura's father's departure was clearly a traumatic episode. Her mother's illness and subsequent crippling were also traumatic, though of a continuing kind rather than a single dramatic episode. The fighting and hatred between the parents were repeated and unrelieved traumatic situations. Thus the traumas in Laura's case were episodic, repeated, and continuing.

With regard to technique, there are a number of places where one can observe Lindner assisting Laura to free associate, for example, "There's no need to ask . . . You'll tell me in due time." An example of an intervention that assists the process of associating is the following: "There's a part of [the dream] you haven't considered. What comes to your mind when you think of the other woman in the dream, the woman the doctor was examining before you?" Another example of technique is the use of a slip of the tongue in the final episode, where the meaning was so obvious that no help from the analyst was needed.

While the part of the patient is to let it all hang out, the role of the analyst is to remain as neutral and as unobtrusive as possible, in order that the patient should discern that the drama being enacted is her own. Laura ridiculed Lindner's "objectivity" and accused him of being cold and heartless and of not doing anything to help her. Those are frequent distortions by patients of the way analysts play their prescribed role. The fact that the analyst does not respond in kind to hostile provocations or to extravagant expressions of gratitude or affection is a clue that he or she is fulfilling a function in a process rather than acting out personal feelings. But patients typically become caught up in their feelings of the moment and lose perspective on the total process; that, indeed, is also part of the process.

Resistance is noted several times in terms of muscle tension in some part of Laura's body when she approached an emotionally disturbing topic. When she described some nightmares, Lindner pressed her to describe further details. "'I can't. . . . Maybe they're so terrible I have to forget them — my dreams I mean.'" Lindner quickly interposed, "What else could you mean?" Laura then admitted that the nightmares were related to some terrible memories. What is happening there is that the memories are so painful that Laura resists reinstating them; to do so, she quickly changes "them" to "dreams," switching away from that close approach to the memories. The analyst, catching this movement, recalls her to the painful task.

The emphasis on the here and now of therapy is illustrated by Lindner's asking Laura, "But why are you doing it here today?" This is again a way of helping the patient overcome her resistance, to capture the bird on the wing, so to speak. The last two illustrations are examples of the kind of thing a person engaging in self-analysis can hardly duplicate.

Transference is displayed at numerous points throughout the case, particularly in the frequent reenactments of the theme of deserting or being deserted. The many instances of this theme show something that is often missed in introductions to psychoanalysis: Transference is not simply an emotion, it has a plot. Psychoanalysts are concerned about what may happen when the transference is acted out, rather than being talked out during the analytic hour. An example of the hazards of acting out is Laura's suicide attempt as a way to bring back the lost father-analyst. The irrational element in transference can hardly be shown better than by Laura's equating Lindner's weekend in New York with her father's permanent desertion of his family.

Laura's stomping out of the doctor's office with a great display of hatred has in it an element of identification with her father. That she also identified herself with her mother is shown by her fear that sexual intercourse or even receiving hypodermic needles may put her in a wheelchair, as the child Laura supposed they did to her mother.

Despite the physician's neutrality, necessary to permit the transference dramas to play themselves out, there cannot help but be a real relation between patient and therapist, particularly after many months of intimate communication. Lindner responded in terms of his real relation rather than his analytic role when he returned to Baltimore after Laura's suicide attempt and when he followed up her telephone calls by coming to her home during one of her eating orgies.

The theme of childhood sexuality is another pervasive one. The intensity of Laura's attachment to her father and of her vengeful hatred of her mother illustrate an aspect of the Oedipus complex. The influence of childish sexual theories is shown by Laura's unconscious belief that sexual intercourse was the cause of her mother's illness and crippling and even more clearly in her belief that there was some connection between eating and pregnancy.

The frequent reenactments of the themes of deserting and being deserted have an aspect not mentioned yet. In the original scene of the father's desertion, Laura was a passive observer. The reenactments were all Laura's doing. Thus they all represented a change from a passive to an active role, the principle of mastery that underlies all of the phenomena unique to the ego paradigm.

The principle of "Where it was, I should become" is also represented in Laura's story. In describing her eating orgies, she spoke about "it" coming to her out of nowhere. In the end, however, she acknowledged that "I" want a baby.

---

## APPENDIX

### SOLITAIRE: THE STORY OF LAURA
by Robert Lindner

*[Laura was a young woman who came to Dr. Lindner for psychoanalysis. She had two different appearances. Ordinarily attractive, though not exactly pretty, she dressed tastefully despite the fact that she was poor. She looked entirely different after her eating binges. The following is an abridged version of her case history.]*

Laura was subject to episodes of depression during which she would be seized by an overwhelming compulsion to gorge herself, to eat almost continuously. The torment Laura suffered during and after these fits (as she called them) she reported many times:

"It seems to come out of nowhere. One minute I'm fine, feeling gay, busy, loving life and people. The next minute I'm on an express highway to hell. It begins with a feeling of emptiness. Something starts to ache; something in the center of me feels as if it's opening up, like a hole appears in my vitals. The emptiness starts to throb, softly like a fluttering pulse. The pulsing turns into a regular beat and gets stronger. Soon I feel as if there's nothing to me but a vast, yawning space surrounded by skin that grabs convulsively at nothingness."

I asked her where the hunger started and the compulsion to eat entered.

"The moment I become aware of the hole opening inside I'm terrified. I have to fill it. So I start to eat — everything, anything I can find to put in my mouth, so long as it can be swallowed. As the emptiness grows, so does my hunger. But it's not really hunger, it's a frenzy, automatic and uncontrollable. If I try to stop, the hole gets bigger, I become idiot with terror, I feel as if I'm going to become the emptiness — get swallowed up by it. So I've got to eat."

I tried to find out if there was any pattern to her eating.

"No," Laura told me. "Nothing will satisfy me — because it's the emptiness that has to be filled. So I stuff anything I can find into my mouth, loathing myself while I do it, and swallowing without tasting. I eat until my jaws get numb with chewing. I eat until I swell like an animal—a pig. I get sick with eating and still I eat—swallowing, retching, vomiting. And if my supply of food runs out, I send for more. Before it comes I go mad with the growing emptiness, I shiver with fear. And when it arrives, I fall on it like someone who's been starved for weeks."

I would ask her how the frenzy ended.

"Most of the time I eat myself into unconsciousness, a state of drunkenness, or something like it. Anyhow, I pass out. Once or twice I've been stopped by exhaustion. I couldn't open my mouth any more, couldn't lift my arms. And there've been times when my body just revolted, refused to take in any more.

"But no matter how it ends, it's followed by a long sleep, sometimes for two days and nights. A sleep of sick dreams, terrible dreams I can hardly recall on awakening—thank goodness. And when I awaken I have to face the mess I've made of Laura. I can hardly believe the loathsome thing I see in the mirror is human, let alone me. I'm all swollen, I have no features. I've become a creature from hell with rottenness oozing from every pore. And I want to destroy this disgusting thing I've become."

Three months of intensive analytic work had passed before Laura first confronted me with her tragically distorted body and insisted I look at it. They had been stormy months, each analytic hour tearful and dramatic as Laura recited the story of her life. In the recounting she could find no relief, as many patients do, since it was a tale in which one dismal incident was piled upon another. Used as I am to hearing stories of abuse, neglect and unhappiness that people bring to an analyst, I was nevertheless moved by Laura's narrative, and in small ways of which I was largely unaware I communicated my compassion. This turned out to be a mistake. Misreading my attitude for one of pity, she set out to exploit it and to demand more of it. Paradoxically, just because I somehow betrayed sympathy for her, she charged me increasingly with a total lack of warmth, and upbraided me almost daily for my "coldness," my "stonelike impassivity," my "heartless indifference" to her suffering. Our meetings, therefore, followed a curious pattern after the first few weeks. They would begin with one of her moving chronicles; then she would wait for some response from me. When this was not forthcoming in the manner she desired, she would attack me viciously.

She began one hour with her usual complaint of fantastic nightmares populated by grotesque forms whose exact description and activities eluded her. These dreams occurred every night, she said, and interfered with her rest. She would awaken in terror from one, often aroused by her own frightened screams, only to have another of the same kind as soon as she fell asleep. They were weird dreams and left her with only vague memories of surrealistic scenes, faceless figures, and nameless obscenities. Water—endless, slow-moving stretches of it, or torrential cascades that beat upon her with the fury of whips; footsteps—the haunting, inexorable beat of a disembodied pair of shoes mercilessly following her through empty corridors, or the mad staccato of an angry mob of pursuers; and laughter—the echoing hysteria of a lone madwoman's howl of mockery, or the shrieking, derisive chorus of countless lunatics: These three elements were never absent from her nighttime gallery of horrors.

"But you can't remember anything more?" I asked.

"Nothing definite—only water again, and being chased, and the sound of laughter."

"Yet you speak of odd shapes, rooms, landscapes, action of some sort, scenes . . . Describe them."

"I can't," she said, covering her eyes with her hands. "Please don't keep after me so. I'm telling you everything I remember. Maybe they're so terrible I have to forget them—my dreams, I mean."

"What else could you mean?" I entered quickly.

She shrugged. "I don't know. My memories, I guess."

"Any particular memory?"

"They're all terrible . . . "

I waited for her to continue.

"I'm thinking," she began, "about the night my father left . . . "

It was raining outside. The supper dishes had been cleared away; Laura and her brother were sitting at the dining-room table doing their homework. In the kitchen Freda, the oldest child, was washing up. Their mother had moved her wheelchair into the front bedroom, where she was listening to the radio. The apartment, a railroad flat on the edge of the factory district, was cold and damp. Wind from the river whistled through newspapers that had been stuffed into cracks around the window frames. Laura's hands were stiff with cold.

When the door opened, Little Mike glanced up at her. Their eyes met in a secret communication of recognition and fear as heavy footsteps came down the hall. Bending again to their lessons, they pretended to work.

They heard their father's grunting hello and a mumbled reply from their mother. There was a creak of the springs as he sat heavily on the bed, followed by the sharp noise of his big shoes falling to the floor.

"Peasant," they heard their mother say, "if you're not going to bed, wear your shoes. It's cold in here."

"Let me alone," he replied. "I'm not cold."

"'I'm not cold,'" their mother mimicked. "Of course you're not cold. Why should you be? If I had a bellyful of whisky, I wouldn't be cold either."

"Don't start that again, Anna," he said "I'm tired."

"Tired," she mocked. "And from what are you tired? — Not from working, that's for sure."

"Oh, shut up, Anna," he said wearily as he walked through the doorway. The rasping sound of their mother's wheelchair followed him into the dining-room.

Laura looked up at her father and smiled. He bent to brush his lips against her cheek. The stiff hairs of his thick mustache scraped her skin and the smell of whisky made her slightly dizzy. Straightening, he ruffled Little Mike's hair with one huge hand, while with the other he pulled a chair away from the table.

"Freda!" he called as he sat down.

The older girl came to the door. "Yes, Papa," she answered.

"Get the old man something to eat, huh?" he asked.

Anna wheeled herself into the space between the table and the open kitchen door. "There's nothing here for you," she said. "You want to eat, come home when supper's ready. This ain't a restaurant."

He spoke over her head to Freda. "Do like I said, get me some supper."

As Freda turned to obey, Anna shouted at her. "Wait! Don't listen to him!" She glared balefully at her husband, her thin face twisted with hate. When she spoke, the veins in her long neck stood out and her shrunken body trembled. "Bum! You come home to eat when you've spent all the money on those tramps. You think I don't know. Where've you been since yesterday? Don't you know you've got a family?"

"Anna," he said, "I told you to shut up."

"I'm not shutting up. You don't care if we're cold or starving or what. All you think about is the lousy whores you give your money to. Your wife and children can rot for all it matters to you."

"Anna, the kids . . . "

"The kids," she screamed. "You think they don't know what kind of a rotten father they've got? You think they don't know where you go when you don't come home?"

He slammed his palm down on the table and stood up. "Enough!" he yelled. "I don't have to listen to that. Keep quiet!"

He started for the kitchen, but Anna whirled her chair across the entrance. "Where're you going?" she asked.

"If you won't get me something to eat I'll get it myself."

"No you won't. There's nothing in there for you."

"Get out of my way, Anna," he said menacingly, "I want to go in the kitchen."

"When you bring home money for food you can go in the kitchen," she said.

His face darkened and his hands clenched into fists. "Cripple!" he spat. "Move away or I'll —"

Her laugh was short and bitter. "You'll what? Hit me? Go ahead — hit the cripple! What're you waiting for?"

They faced each other, frozen in a tableau of mutual hatred. Laura and Little Mike sat stiffly, eyes wide and bodies rigid. In the silence they heard the rain against the windows.

Their father's hands relaxed slowly. "If you don't move out of the way," he said evenly, "I'm getting out of this house and I'm never coming back."

"So go," Anna said, leering up at him. "Who wants you here anyway?"

He stood still for a long minute; then he turned and walked swiftly towards the bedroom. When Anna became aware of what he was doing, the look of triumph gave place to alarm. Hastily, she propelled her wheel chair around the table.

"Mike," she said, "what're you doing?"

There was only the sound of the bedsprings, and the firm stamp of his shoes against the naked floorboards.

"Mike" — her voice was louder and tremulous with fright — "Where're you going? — Wait!"

The wheelchair raced into the bedroom. "Please don't go. I didn't mean it. Please. Come back. Come into the kitchen. I was only fooling, Mike. Don't go."

He pulled away from her, lifting her body from the chair. Her hands broke the fall as useless legs collapsed. The outer door slammed. Then there was the slapping sound of rain again between her heavy sobs . . .

"— He meant it," Laura said. "I guess she went too far that time. He never did come back. Once in a while he'd send a few dollars in a plain envelope. On my next birthday I got a box of salt-water taffy from Atlantic City. But we never saw him again." She dabbed at her eyes, then blew her nose.

"Well," she said, "why don't you say something?"

"What should I say?"

"You might at least express some sympathy."

"For whom?"

"For me, of course!"

"Why only you?" I asked. "What about Freda, or Little Mike, or your mother? Or even your father?"

"But I'm the one who's been most hurt by it," she said petulantly. "You know that. You should feel sorry for me."

"Is that why you told me this story, so that I'd feel sorry for you?"

She turned on the couch and looked at me, her face drawn in a grimace of absolute malice.

"You don't give an inch, do you?" she said.

"You don't want an inch, Laura," I responded quietly. "You want it all . . . from me, from everybody."

"What d'you mean?" she asked.

"Well, for example, the story you just told. Of course it's a dreadful one, and anyone hearing it would be moved, but—"

"— But you're not," she almost spat. "Not you. Because you're not human. You're a stone—a cold stone. You give nothing. You just sit there like a goddam block of wood while I tear my guts out!" Her voice, loaded with odium, rose to a trembling scream. "You and your lousy objectivity! Objectivity, my eye! Are you a man or a machine? Don't you ever feel anything? Do you have blood or ice water in your veins? Answer me! Goddam you, answer me!"

I remained silent.

"You see?" she shouted. "You say nothing. Must I die to get a word out of you? What d'you want from me?"

She stood up. "All right," she said. "Don't say anything. Don't give anything. I'm going. I can see you don't want me here. I'm going—and I'm not coming back." With a swirl of her skirt she rushed from the room.

Laura came back, of course — four times each week for the next two years. For a year Laura seemed to be standing still or losing ground. Chiefly, as in the episode just related, she reviewed her past and, in her sessions with me, either immediately or soon after, acted out their crucial aspects. My consulting room became a stage on which she dramatized her life; my person became the target against which she directed the sad effects of her experience.

The idea behind my permissiveness in therapy was to hold up a mirror of her behavior and to let her see not only the extravagance of the methods she used, but also the futility and infantilism of the desires she had been pursuing. Also, the procedure was designed to illustrate the impossibility of securing long-lasting and solid satisfactions from her accustomed behavior.

In the eleventh month of her analysis it had been a month or more since her last attack, her job at the Gallery was going well, and she had recently formed a promising relationship with an eligible young man. On the theme of this affair the first of two crucial hours began.

"I don't want to foul this one up," she said, "but I'm afraid I'm going to. I need your help desperately."

"In what way d'you think you might foul it up?" I asked.

"Oh," she replied airily, "by being my usual bitchy self. You know how possessive and demanding I become. But I'd like to have a love affair work out well for me."

"You mean you're thinking of matrimony?"

"Well," she laughed, "I've had a few daydreams about marrying Ben. But what I want now is love — I want to give it and I want to get it."

"If that attitude is genuine," I said, "you don't need my help in your affair."

"You're horrible," she complained. "Here I tell you something that I think shows real progress, and right away you throw cold water on it."

"What d'you think shows progress?"

"Why my recognition of giving, of course. I hope you noticed that I put it first. Doesn't that mean something to you? Doesn't that show how far I've come?"

"It does, if it's genuine."

"Goddammit!" she flared. "You call me insatiable; you're the one who's never satisfied. But I'll show you yet. Anyhow, that's not what I wanted to talk about today. I had a dream. Shall I tell you about it?"

When a patient presents a dream this way, announcing it first, then withholding until the analyst asks for it, the analyst must be wary. To grasp at it would be to rob his patient of the painful but necessary first steps toward responsible selfhood, and to commit himself to bargains and promises he has no right to make. Therefore, although I was most eager to hear it, I responded with the evasive but handy reminder of the "basic rule": "Your instructions are to say what comes to you during your hours here. If you're thinking of a dream, tell it."

"Well, I was in what appeared to be a ballroom or a dance hall, but I knew it was really a hospital. A man came up to me and told me to take all my clothes off. He was going to give me a gynecological examination. I did as I was told but I was very frightened. While I was undressing, I noticed that he was doing something to a woman at the other end of the room. She was sitting or lying in a funny kind of contraption with all kinds of levers and gears and pulleys attached to it. I knew that I was supposed to be next, that I would have to sit in that thing while he examined me. Suddenly he called my name and I found myself running to him. The chair or table — whatever it was — was now empty, and he told me to get on it. I refused and began to cry. It started to rain — great big drops of rain. He pushed me to the floor and spread my legs for the examination. I turned over on my stomach and began to scream. I woke myself up screaming."

"Well," she said, "what does it mean?"

"Laura, you know better than that. Associate, and we'll find out."

"The first thing I think of is Ben. He's an interne at the University. I guess that's the doctor in the dream — or maybe it was you. Whoever it was, I wouldn't let him examine me."

"Why not?"

"I've always been afraid of doctors, afraid they might hurt me."

"How will they hurt you?"

"I don't know. By jabbing me with a needle, I guess. That's funny. I never thought of it before. When I go to the dentist I don't mind getting a needle; but with a doctor it's different. I shudder when I think of having my veins punctured. I'm always afraid that's what a doctor will do to me."

"Has it ever been done?"

"Once, in college, for a blood test. I passed out cold."

"What about gynecological examinations?"

"I've never had one. I can't bear to think of someone poking around inside me." Again silence; then, "Oh," she said, "I see it now. It's sex I'm afraid of. The doctor in the dream is Ben. He wants me to have intercourse, but it scares me and I turn away from him. The other night after the concert he came to my apartment. I made coffee for us and we sat there talking. It was wonderful. Then he started to make love to me. I loved it — until it came to having intercourse. I stopped him there. I had to, I became terrified. He probably thinks I'm a virgin — or that I don't care for him enough. But it isn't that. I do — and I want him to make love to me. Oh, Dr. Lindner, that's why I need your help so much now."

"But other men have made love to you."

"Yes," she sobbed, "but I only let them as a last resort, as a way of holding on to them a little longer. And I've only had the real thing a few times. Mostly I've made love to the man — satisfied him somehow. I'd do anything to keep them from getting inside me — poking into me . . . like the needle, I guess."

"But why, Laura?"

"I don't know," she cried, "Tell me."

"I think the dream tells you. There's a part of it you haven't considered. What comes to your mind when you think of the other woman in the dream, the woman the doctor was examining before you?"

"The contraption she was sitting in," Laura exclaimed. "It was like a — like a wheelchair — my mother's wheelchair! Is that right?"

"Very likely," I said.

"But why would he be examining her? What would that mean?"

"Well, think of what that kind of examination signifies for you."

"Sex. Intercourse — that's what it means. So that's what it means! Intercourse put my mother in the wheelchair. It paralyzed her. And I'm afraid that's what it will do to me. Where did I ever get such a crazy idea?"

Like so many such "ideas" all of us have, this one was born in Laura long before the age when she could think for herself. It arose out of sensations of terror when she would awaken during the night, shocked from sleep by the mysterious noises her parents made in their passion, and incapable yet of assembling these sounds into a design purporting the tender uses of love. The heavy climate of hate between her parents made this impossible; so the sounds in the night — the "Mike, you're hurting me," the moans and cries, the protestations, even the laughter — impressed upon her the darker side of sex, the brutish animality of it and the pain. And when the disease struck her mother, an association was formed between the secret drama that played itself out while Laura slept — or awakened in fright — and the final horror of the body imprisoned on the chair.

I explained this to Laura, documenting my explanation with material the analysis had already brought out. The interpretation worked a wonder of insight. Obvious as it may seem, to Laura, from whom it had been withheld by many resistances and defenses, it came as a complete surprise. Almost immediately she felt a vast relief. The idea that sexual love was impossible for her, that she was so constructed physically that the joys of love would forever be denied her, feelings of self-dissatisfaction, and numerous other thoughts and emotions collected around the central theme of sex — these vanished.

"I feel free," Laura said as she rose from the couch when time was called. "I think this has been the most important hour of my analysis." At the door she paused and turned to me with moist, shining eyes. "I knew I could count on you," she said. "And I'm very grateful — believe me."

That was on a Saturday. On Monday, the moment I saw her I knew something had gone wrong. She sat dejectedly, chin cupped in her hands. When I greeted her, she raised her eyes listlessly.

"Ready for me?" she asked in a toneless voice.

I nodded and motioned her into the next room. She stood up wearily, dropping her coat on the chair, flopped on the couch sideways, raised one arm to her head and covered her brow with the back of her hand.

"I don't know why we bother," she said in the same flat voice. "Aren't you going to ask me what's wrong?"

"There's no need to ask. You'll tell me in due time."

"I guess I will," she said, sighing again. "I don't have to tell you I went to bed with Ben, do I?"

"If that's what you're thinking of."

"I think you must be a voyeur," she commented acidly. "That's probably the way you get your kicks. Probably why you're an analyst, too, playing Peeping Tom with your ears."

"Laura, why are you being so aggressive?"

"Because I hate your guts."

"Go on."

"That's all. I only came here today to tell you how much I despise you. I've said it and I'm finished. Can I go now?" She sat up and reached for her purse.

"If that's what you want to do," I said.

"You don't care?" she asked.

"Of course I'll be sorry to see you leave. But if that's what you want to do . . . "

"More double talk," she sighed. "All right. The hell with it. I'm here and I may as well finish out the hour — after all, I'm paying for it." She fell back on the couch and lapsed into silence again.

"Laura," I said, "you seem anxious to get me to reject you today. Why?"

"I told you — because I hate you."

"I understand that. But why are you trying to make me reject you?"

"Do we have to go through that again?" she asked. "Because that's my pattern — according to you. I try to push people to the point where they reject me, then I feel worthless and sorry for myself, and find a good excuse to punish myself. Isn't that it?"

"Approximately. But why are you doing it here today?"

"Because of what you made me do over the week end."

"With Ben?"

"Of course not. What's that got to do with it? All that happened was that I went to bed with him. We slept together. It was good, wonderful. For the first time in my life I felt like a woman."

"Then what . . . ?" I started to say.

"—Keep quiet! You wanted to know why I hate you and I'm telling you. It's got nothing to do with Ben or what happened Saturday night. It's about my mother. What we talked about last time. She's haunted me all weekend. I keep thinking about her — the awful life she had, and the way I treated her. Because you forced me to, I remembered terrible things I did to her . . . That's why I hate you." She turned on her side and looked at me over her shoulder. "And, you bastard, you purposely fixed it so I'd remember how rotten I was to her. I've spent half my life trying to forget her and that goddam wheelchair. But you brought her back from the grave to haunt me.

"It's funny how I've clung to everything I could find to keep on hating her. I always blamed her for what happened. I always thought it was her fault my father left us, that she drove him away with her nagging and complaining. I've tried to hide from myself the fact that he was just no good — a lazy, chicken-chasing, selfish son-of-a-bitch. I excused him for his drinking and his neglect of us all those years. I thought, 'Why not? Why shouldn't he run around, stay out all night, have other women? What good was she to him with those useless legs and dried-up body?' I pushed out of my head the way he was before she got sick. The truth is he was never any different, always a bum. Even when I was small he was no good, no good to her and no good to us. But I loved him — God! how I loved that man. I could hardly wait for him to come home. Drunk, sober — it didn't matter to me. He made a fuss over me and that's why I loved him. I guess I was his favorite. At least he made over me more than the others.

"When I'd hear them fighting, I always blamed her. 'What's she picking on him for?'

I'd think. 'Why doesn't she let him alone?' And when he went away, I thought it was her fault. And I made her suffer for it. I did mean things to her, things I tried to forget — did forget — until this weekend. I did them to punish her for kicking him out, for depriving me of his love. His love!

"Would you like to hear one of the things I did? I've thought this one over for two days. Maybe if I tell you I can get rid of it."

Every day on the way home from school she played the same game. That was the reason she preferred to walk home alone. Because as far as the other kids were concerned, she didn't have a father. On the high-school admission blank, where it said: "Father — living or dead," she had marked a big 'X' over "dead". So what would she say if he stepped out of a doorway, or came around a corner and grabbed her and kissed her like he used to? Could she say, "Girls, this is my father?" Of course not! So she walked home alone, pretending he was in that alley, or standing behind the coal truck, or that those footsteps behind her — the ones she kept hearing but there was no one there when she turned around — were his footsteps.

The game ended in the hallway of the tenement house. If he wasn't here, in the smelly vestibule, on the sagging stairs, or standing expectantly on the first-floor landing in front of their door, the game had to end. And he never was . . .

On the way to the rear of the apartment she glanced at her mother. In the wheelchair Anna slumped like a rag doll. Her peroxide hair, gray and brown at the roots, fell over her forehead. Her chin was on her breast, and from one corner of her mouth a trickle of spittle trailed to the collar of the shabby brown dress. The green sweater hung about her thin shoulders in rumpled folds, and from its sleeves her skinny wrists and the fingers tipped with bright red nails protruded like claws of a chicken, clutching the worn arms of the chair. Laura repressed an exclamation of contempt. In the kitchen she poured herself a glass of milk and rinsed the glass. It fell from her hand and shattered.

"Is that you, Laura?" Anna called. "Come here. I want you to do something for me. Over there, on the dresser, the check from the relief came. I wrote out the store order. You can stop on your way back and give the janitor the rent."

"All right," Laura said wearily. She took her coat from the closet. At the door to the hall she paused and turned to face Anna, who was already fumbling with the radio dial. "Anything else?" she asked, playing out their bimonthly game.

Anna smiled. "Yes," she said. "I didn't put it on the store list, but if they have some of those chocolate-covered caramels I like . . . "

Laura nodded and closed the door. When she returned, she disposed of the groceries.

"Did you get everything, Laura?" Anna called.

"Yeah."

"Pay the rent?"

"Uh-huh."

"Did they have any of those caramels?"

Laura didn't answer. Somewhere, deep inside, the low-burning flame of hate flickered to a new height.

"Laura!"

"What d'you want?"

"I asked if you got my candy."

Laura's gaze fell to the remaining package on the kitchen table. It seemed to hypnotize her, holding her eyes fast and drawing her hand toward its curled neck. Slowly her fingers untwisted the bag, plunged inside, and carried two squares of candy to her mouth. Without tasting, she chewed and swallowed rapidly.

Behind her Laura heard the shuffle of wheels. She turned to find Anna crossing the threshold of the bedroom. Snatching up the bag, she hurried into the dining room and faced her mother across the oval table.

"D'you have the candy?" Anna asked.

Laura nodded and held up the sack.

"Give it here," Anna said, extending her hand.

Laura shook her head and put the hand with the paper bag behind her back.

Puzzled, Anna sent her chair around the table toward the girl, who waited until her mother came near, then moved quickly to the opposite side.

"What kind of nonsense is this?" Anna asked. Laura put another piece of candy in her mouth.

"Laura!" Anna demanded. "Give me my candy!" She spun her chair forward, racing around the table after the girl, who skipped lightly before it. Three times Anna circled the table. Exhausted, finally, she stopped. Across from her, Laura stuffed more candy into her mouth and chewed violently.

"Laura," Anna panted, "what's got into you? Why are you doing this?"

Laura took the bag from behind her back and held it over the table. "If you want it so bad, come and get it." She shook the bag triumphantly. "See, it's almost gone. You'd better hurry."

A warm glow of exultation swept through her, filling her body with a sense of power and setting her nerves on fire. She felt like laughing, like screaming, like dancing madly. In her mouth the taste of chocolate was intoxicating.

Her mother whimpered. "Give me the candy. Please, Laura."

Laura held the bag high. "Come and get it!" she screamed, and backed away. She waited until her mother's chair came close, then she whirled and ran through the door, pulling it behind her with a loud crash.

Leaning against the banister, Laura listened to the thud of Anna's fists against the wood and her sobs of angry frustration. Her wild exhilaration mounted. Hardly conscious of her actions, she crammed the remaining candies into her mouth. Then, from deep in her body, a wave of laughter surged upward and broke through in a crazy tide of hilarity. The sound of this joyless mirth echoed from the stair well and ceiling of the narrow hallway — as it was to echo, along with the sound of footsteps and falling rain, in her dreams . . .

The weeks following were difficult for Laura. As she worked through the guilt-laden memories released from repression, her self-regard fell lower and lower. Bitterly, she recited her faults of behavior — toward her family, her friends, her teachers, her associates — throughout the years.

The time came when I found it necessary to call a halt to Laura's marathon of confession. Three factors influenced my decision. The most important was my perception of the danger in this program of self-denunciation. As she searched her memory for fresh evidence of guilt, she was becoming overwhelmed by the enormity of her past behavior. I knew she could never salve her conscience by penitential acts and renunciations, and I feared a prolonged contest between contrition and atonement could lead to a progressive lowering of self-esteem which might wind up at a point I dared not think about.

The second reason was its unproductiveness for therapy. The martyrdom she now suffered by her own hand was equivalent to the self-pity formerly induced by the rejection she had unconsciously arranged to obtain from others. She no longer exercised hate, hostility and aggressive contempt outwardly, but it was only the direction that had been altered; they remained.

Finally, my decision was also influenced by sheer boredom with what I knew to be only an act, adopted to squeeze neurotic gratification from me and the entire world which, by psychic extension from love-withholding parents, she viewed as rejective and denying.

The session that precipitated a near catastrophe took place on a Thursday afternoon. Laura was the last patient that day, since I was taking the Congressional Limited to New York, where I was scheduled to conduct a seminar that night and give a lecture on Friday. I was looking forward to the trip as a holiday from work and the first break in routine in many months. Something of this mood of impatience to get going and pleasurable anticipation must have been communicated to Laura, for she began her hour with a hardly disguised criticism of my manner and appearance.

"Somehow you seem different today. Maybe it's because of the way you're dressed. That's a new suit, isn't it?"

"No, I've worn it before."

"I don't ever remember seeing it. Anyway, you look nice."

"Thank you."

"I like to see people look nice," she continued. "When a person gets all dressed up, it makes them feel better. I think it's because they think other people will judge them on the basis of their outer appearance—and if the outer appearance is pleasing and nice, people will think what's behind is pleasing and nice, too—and being thought of that way makes you feel better. Don't you think so?"

"What exactly are you getting at?" I asked.

She shrugged. "It's not important," she said. "Just a thought. Oh! I know why you're all dressed up. Today's the day you go to New York, isn't it?"

"That's right," I said.

"That means I won't see you on Saturday, doesn't it?"

"Yes. I won't be back until Monday."

"Is the lecture on Saturday?"

"No, the lecture's tomorrow, Friday."

"—But you're going to stay over until Monday. Well, I think the rest will do you good. I think everyone needs to kick up his heels once in a while, just get away, have some fun and forget everything—if he can."

The dig at my irresponsibility toward my patients, particularly Laura, and the implication that I was going to New York to participate in some kind of orgy, were not lost on me.

"I hate to miss an hour," Laura continued in the same melancholy tone she had been using since this meeting began. "Especially now. I feel I really need to come here now. There's so much to talk about."

"In that case," I said, "you should take more advantage of the time you're here. For example, you're not using this hour very well, are you?"

"Perhaps not. It's just that I feel this is the wrong time for you to be going away."

"Now look here, Laura. You've known about missing the Saturday hour for more than a week. Please don't pretend it's a surprise to you. And, besides, it's only one hour."

"I know," she sighed. "But it feels like you're going away forever. What if I should need you?"

"I don't think you will. But if you should, you can call my home or the office here and they'll put you in touch with me."

I lit a cigarette and waited for her to go on. With the first inhalation, however, I began to cough.

"That cough of yours worries me," Laura said. "You should give up smoking. I did. It's been two months since I had a cigarette. And my cough's all gone. I feel fine. You should really try it. The first two weeks were agony, but I was determined not to give in. After all, I had a reason."

"To stop coughing?" I suggested, permitting myself to retaliate for her deliberate provocation of the past half hour.

"Of course not!" she exclaimed. "You know very well I had good reasons for giving up smoking—and other things too."

"What were they?" I asked.

"Well—it's just that I want to be a better person. You know how I used to behave. Now I want to make amends for it, to be different, better."

"And you think giving up smoking and so on will make you a better person?"

She fell silent. Glancing over at her, I noticed the rigidity of her body. Her hands, until now held loosely on her lap, were clenched into fists. I looked at my watch and cursed myself for a fool. Only ten minutes left and a train to catch! Why had I let myself rise to the bait? Why had I permitted this to come up now, when it couldn't be handled?

"Well?" I asked.

"Nothing I do is right," she said hollowly. "There's no use trying. I just make it worse."

"What are you talking about?"

"Myself," she said. "Myself and the mess I make of everything. I try to do what's right—but I never can. I think I'm working it all out—but I'm not. I'm just getting in deeper. It's too much for me."

When the hour ended, I rose and held the door open for her.

"I'll see you Monday," I said.

Her eyes were glistening. "Have a good time," she sighed.

That evening I had dinner with friends and conducted the scheduled seminar. When I returned to my hotel, the desk clerk gave me a message to call a certain long-distance operator in Baltimore. Laura answered.

"Dr. Lindner?"

"Yes, Laura. What is it?"

"I've been trying to get you for hours."

"I'm sorry. Is something wrong?"

"I don't know. I just wanted to talk with you."

"What about?"

"About the way I feel. . . . "

"How do you feel?"

"Scared."

"Scared of what?"

"I don't know. Just scared, I guess. Of nothing in particular—just everything. I don't like being alone."

"But you're alone most other nights, aren't you?"

"Yes, but somehow it's different tonight."

"Why?"

"Well, for one thing, you're not in Baltimore." The line was silent as I waited for her to continue. "And then, I think you're angry with me."

"Why do you think that?"

"The way I acted this afternoon. It was mean of me, I know. But I couldn't help it. Something was egging me on."

"What was it?"

"I don't know. I haven't figured it out. Something. . . . "

"We'll talk about it Monday," I said.

After a pause, she sobbed, "Do you forgive me?"

"We'll review the whole hour on Monday," I said, seeking a way out of this awkward situation. "Right now you'd better get to bed."

"All right," she said meekly. "I'm sorry I bothered you."

"No bother at all," I said. "Good night, Laura"—and hung up with relief.

I gave the lecture on Friday afternoon and had returned to my room for a nap when the phone rang. It was my wife, calling from Baltimore. Laura had slashed her wrists: I had better come home quick . . .

The doctor and I sat in the corner of the room, talking in whispers. On the bed, heavily sedated, Laura breathed noisily. Even in the dim light the white bandages at her wrists and the pallor of her face were discernible.

"I doubt that it was a serious attempt," the physician was saying. "You've got to saw away hard to get down where it counts. The cut on the left wrist is fairly deep, but not deep enough, and the ones on the right wrist are superficial.

"Right after she slashed herself she began screaming. A neighbor ran in and called me. My office is in the same building, and I happened to be there. I rushed upstairs, took a look at the cuts and saw they weren't too bad, so I slapped a couple of tourniquets on, phoned the hospital that I was sending her in, then called the ambulance. I followed it here to Sinai. In the Accident Room they cleaned her up and had her wrists sutured by the time I arrived. She was still quite excited, so I decided to put her in for a day or two. I gave her a shot of morphine and sent her upstairs."

"Who called my home?" I asked.

"Her neighbor called Laura's sister and told her what happened. I think the sister tried to get hold of you."

"She knows Laura's in treatment with me," I said.

"She's a lulu. I don't think you've got anything to worry about as far as her physical condition goes, though. She'll be fine in the morning. Maybe a little groggy, that's all."

Laura had her hour on Saturday — in the hospital. During many sessions we worked out the reasons for her self-destructive gesture. As the physician had observed, her act was a dramatic demonstration without serious intent, although it could have miscarried to a less fortunate conclusion. Its immediate purpose was to recall me from my holiday and to reawaken the sympathetic attention she believe herself to have prejudiced by her hostile provocativeness on Thursday. But the whole affair had much deeper roots.

The motivation was twofold. Unconsciously, it represented an effort to re-enact, with a more satisfying outcome, the desertion of her father; and, at the same time, it served as extreme penance for "sins" of behavior and thought-crimes between the ages of twelve and twenty-four. So far as the first is concerned, Laura interpreted my brief interruption of therapy as an abandonment similar to that abrupt and permanent departure of her father. This time, however, as indicated by the phone call to my hotel, she believed herself to have been at least in part responsible, to have driven him (in the person of the analyst) away. To call him back, her distraught mind conceived the suicidal act, which was a frenzied effort — planned, so it appeared, but not executed, more than a decade before — to repeat the original drama but insure a different and more cordial ending.

The mad act was also powered dynamically by the fantastic arithmetic of confession and penance that Laura had invented to discharge her guilty memories. As I had feared, the mental balance sheet with her testament of culpability and the increasing asceticism of her life could never be stabilized and had to lead to martyrdom of some kind. My effort to prevent this miscarried because it was sloppily executed.

Laura made a rapid recovery and returned to the analysis much sobered by her encounter with death. The episode provided her with many useful insights and led her to abandon her false asceticism and to stop playing the role of the "well-analyzed," "adjusted" paragon among her friends. But no progress had been made against the complaint which brought her into treatment, the seizures of uncontrollable hunger and furious eating.

Laura was seldom late for appointments, nor had she ever missed one without canceling for a good cause well in advance. On the day, therefore, when she failed to appear at the appointed time, I grew anxious. After a half hour when there was still no sign of Laura, I asked my secretary to call her apartment. There was no answer.

During the afternoon, caught up in work with other patients, I gave only passing thought to Laura's absence. At the close of the day, I tried to recall her previous session for some clue to this unusual delinquency. Since none came, I pushed the matter from my mind and prepared to leave the office. We were in the corridor awaiting the elevator when we heard the telephone. Jeanne returned to answer. A few moments later she reappeared, shrugging her shoulders.

"Must have been a wrong number," she said. "All I heard was a funny noise and then the line went dead."

I arrived home after six o'clock and dressed to receive guests who were coming for dinner. While in the shower, I heard the telephone. On emerging from the bathroom, I asked my wife who had called.

"That was the queerest thing," she said. "The party on the other end sounded like a drunk and I couldn't make out a word."

During dinner, near the edges of consciousness something nagged uncomfortably. When the telephone again rang while we were having coffee, I rushed to answer it.

"Hello?" In response, came a gurgling, throaty noise. Unmistakably produced by the human voice, it had a gasping, breathless quality, yet somehow seemed animal in nature. It produced a series of meaningless syllables, urgent in tone but unidentifiable.

"Who is this?" I demanded.

There was a pause, then, laboriously, I heard the first longdrawn syllable of her name.

"Laura! Where are you?"

Again the pause, followed by an effortful intake of breath. "Home . . . "

"Is something wrong?"

"Eat-ing."

"Since when?"

"Don't—know."

"How d'you feel?" I asked, aware of the absurdity of the question but desparately at a loss to know what else to say.

"Aw-ful . . . No—more—food . . . Hungry . . . "

My mind raced. What was there to do?

"Help—me," she said—and I heard the click of the instrument as it fell into its cradle.

"Laura," I said. "Wait!"—But the connection had been broken. I called her. There was no answer.

Excusing myself from our guests, I got my car and drove to where Laura lived. On the way there, I thought about what some of my colleagues would say of such a breach of orthodoxy. To me, psychoanalysis is a vital art, and there are occasions when genuine human feelings take precedence over the rituals and dogmas of the craft.

I searched the mailboxes in the vestibule for Laura's name, then ran up the stairs to the second floor. I pushed the button forcefully time after time, but no one came to the door. Finally, I turned the knob with one hand and pounded the panel with the flat of the other. I heard something heavy crashing to the floor, then the shuffling of feet.

"Laura!" I called. "Open the door!"

I heard what sounded like sobs and faint moaning, then a voice that slowly pronounced the words, "Go—away."

I shook the knob violently. "Open up!" I commanded. "Let me in!"

The knob turned in my hand and the door opened. I pushed against it, but a chain on the jamb caught and held. In the dim light of the hallway, against the darkness inside, something white shone. It was Laura's face, but she withdrew it quickly.

"Go—away" she said in a thick voice..

She leaned against the door, trying to close it again. I put my foot in the opening.

"Take the chain off," I said with all the authority I could muster. "At once!"

The chain slid away and I walked into the room. It was dark, and before I found the light switch, Laura ran past me into the room beyond. I turned on the light. Everywhere was a litter of stained papers, torn boxes, empty bottles, open cans, broken crockery and dirty dishes. On the floor and on the tables large puddles gleamed wetly. Bits of food—crumbs, gnawed bones, fishheads, sodden chunks of unknown stuffs—were strewn all about. The place looked as if the contents of a garbage can had been emptied in it, and the stench was sickening.

I swallowed hard against a wave of nausea and hurried into the room where Laura had disappeared. In the shaft of light that came through the archway, I saw a rumpled bed, similarly piled with rubbish, in a corner, the crouching figure of Laura.

As the light went on, Laura covered her face and shrank against the wall. I went over to her, extending my hands.

"Come," I said "stand up."

She shook her head violently. I bent down and lifted her to her feet. When she stood up, her fingers still hid her face. Gently, I pulled them away. Then I stepped back and looked at Laura. Her face was like a ceremonial mask on which some maniac had depicted every corruption of the flesh. Depravity and abomination seemed to ooze from great pores that the puffed tautness of skin revealed.

I closed my eyes momentarily against this apparition of degradation. When I opened them, I saw the tears welling from holes where her eyes should have been, course in thin streams down the bloated cheeks, and fall on her nightgown. And then I saw it!

Laura was wearing a night robe of some sheer stuff that fell loosely from straps at her shoulders. Originally white, it was now soiled and stained. It bulged below her middle in a sweeping arc, ballooning outward from her body as if she were pregnant.

I gasped with disbelief, and my hand went out automatically to touch the place where her nightgown swelled. My fingers encountered a softness that yielded to their pressure. Questioning, I raised my eyes. Her face twisted into what I took for a smile. The mouth opened and closed to form a word that it labored to pronounce.

"Ba-by," Laura said.

"Ba-by?" I repeated. "Whose baby?"

"Lau-ra's ba-by . . . Lo-ok."

She bent forward drunkenly and grasped her gown by the hem. Slowly she raised the garment, until her hands were high above her head. There, where my fingers had probed, a pillow was strapped to her skin with long bands of adhesive. Laura let the nightgown fall.

"See?" she said."Looks — real — this way."

Her hands went up to cover her face again. Great sobs shook her, and tears poured through her fingers. I led her to the bed and sat on its edge, trying to order the turmoil of my thoughts while she wept. Once more the lost mouth worked to make words.

"I — want — a baby," she said, and fell over on the bed asleep.

I covered Laura with a blanket and called a practical nurse who I knew would be available. I briefed her quickly: The apartment was to be cleaned and aired. When Laura awakened, the doctor downstairs was to examine her and advise on treatment and diet. She was to report to me regularly, and in two days she was to bring Laura to my office.

Two days later, while her nurse sat in the outer room, Laura and I began to put together the final pieces in the puzzle of her neurosis. As always, she had only a vague, confused memory of events during her seizure, recollecting them hazily through a fog of total intoxication. Until I recounted the episode, she had no clear remembrance of my visit and thought she had dreamed it. Of her pitiful imitation of pregnancy, not the slightest memorial trace remained.

It was clear that Laura's compelling desire was to have a child, that her feelings of emptiness arose from this desire, and that her convulsions of ravenous appetite were unconsciously designed to produce its illusory satisfaction. What was not apparent was why this natural feminine wish underwent such extravagant distortion, why it had become so intense, and why it had to express itself in so monstrous and self-destructive a manner.

About a week after the incident, Laura and I were reviewing it again. I was intrigued by the contrivance she wore that night to simulate the appearance of a pregnant woman, and asked for details about its construction. Laura could supply none. Apparently, she said, she had fashioned it in an advanced stage of her intoxication from food.

"Was this the first time you made anything like that?" I asked.

"I don't know," she said, somewhat hesitantly. "I can't be sure. Maybe I did and destroyed the thing before I came out of the fog. It seems to me I remember finding something like you described a couple years ago after an attack, but I didn't know — or didn't want to know — what it was, so I just took it apart and forgot about it."

"You'd better look around the apartment carefully," I said, half joking. "Perhaps there's a spare hidden away some place."

"I doubt it," she replied in the same mood. "I guess I have to mike a new baby every . . . " Her hand went over her mouth.

"My God!" she exclaimed. "Did you hear what I just said?"

Mike was her father's name; and of course it was his baby she wanted. It was for this impossible fulfillment that Laura hungered — and now was starved no more.

## REFERENCES

Amacher, P. (1965). Freud's neurological education and its influence on psychoanalytic theory. *Psychological Issues*, 4 (4, Whole no. 16).

Bettelheim, B. (1982). *Freud and man's soul.* New York: Knopf.

Bloch, G. J. (Ed.). (1980). *Mesmerism: A translation of the original medical and scientific writings of F. A. Mesmer, M. D.* Los Altos, CA: William Kaufmann.

Bowlby, J. (1969). *Attachment and loss.* Vol. 1. *Attachment.* New York: Basic Books.

Boring, E. G. (1929). *A history of experimental psychology.* New York: Century.

Brandt, L. W. (1966). Process or structure? *Psychoanalytic Review, 53,* 374–378.

Breger, L. (1981). *Freud's unfinished journey: Conventional and critical perspectives in psychoanalytic theory.* London: Routledge & Kegan Paul.

Breuer, J., & Freud, S. (1955). Studies on hysteria. *Standard edition* (Vol. 2). London: Hogarth Press. (Original work published 1895.)

Decker, H. S. (1977). Freud in Germany: Revolution and reaction in science, 1893–1907. *Psychological Issues, 11* (1, Whole no. 41).

Dewey, J. (1896). The reflex arc concept in psychology. *Psychological Review, 3,* 357–370.

Eagle, M. (1984). *Recent developments in psychoanalysis.* New York: McGraw-Hill.

Ellenberger, H. F. (1970). *The discovery of the unconscious.* New York: Basic Books.

Erikson, E. H. (1950). *Childhood and society.* New York: Norton.

Ferenczi, S. (1916). Stages in the development of the sense of reality. In *Sex in psychoanalysis* (pp. 181–203). Boston: Gorham Press. (Original work published 1913.)

Freud, A. (1946). *The ego and the mechanisms of defence.* New York: International Universities Press. (Original work published 1936.)

Freud, A. (1946). *The psycho-analytic treatment of children.* New York: International Universities Press. (Original work published 1926.)

Freud, S. (1953). The interpretation of dreams. *Standard edition* (Vols. 4 & 5). London: Hogarth Press. (Original work published 1900.)

Freud, S. (1960). The psychopathology of everyday life. *Standard edition* (Vol. 6). London: Hogarth Press. (Original work published 1901.)

Freud, S. (1960). Jokes and their relation to the unconscious. *Standard edition* (Vol. 8). London: Hogarth Press. (Original work published 1905a.)

Freud, S. (1953). Three essays on the theory of sexuality. *Standard edition* (Vol. 7, pp. 125–243). London: Hogarth Press. (Original work published 1905b.)

Freud, S. (1957). Five lectures on psychoanalysis. *Standard edition* (Vol. 11, pp. 3–55). London: Hogarth Press. (Original work published 1910a.)

Freud, S. (1957). Leonardo da Vinci and a memory of his childhood. *Standard edition* (Vol. 11, pp. 59–137). London: Hogarth Press. (Original work published 1910b.)

Freud, S. (1958). Psychoanalytic notes upon an autobiographical account of a case of paranoia (dementia paranoides). *Standard edition* (Vol. 12, pp. 3–82). London: Hogarth Press. (Original work published 1911.)

Freud, S. (1957). On narcissism: An introduction. *Standard edition* (Vol. 14, pp. 67–102). London: Hogarth Press. (Original work published 1914a.)

Freud, S. (1953). The Moses of Michelangelo. *Standard edition* (Vol. 13, pp. 211–238). London: Hogarth Press. (Original work published 1914b.)

Freud, S. (1955). Beyond the pleasure principle. *Standard edition* (Vol. 18, pp. 3–64). London: Hogarth Press. (Original work published 1920.)

Freud, S. (1961). The ego and the id. *Standard edition* (Vol. 19, pp. 3–66). London: Hogarth Press. (Original work published 1923.)

Freud, S. (1959). Inhibitions, symptoms, and anxiety. *Standard edition* (Vol. 20, pp. 77–174). London: Hogarth Press. (Original work published 1926a.)

Freud, S. (1959). The question of lay analysis. *Standard edition* (Vol. 20, pp. 179–258). London: Hogarth Press. (Original work published 1926b.)

Freud, S. (1961). Civilization and its discontents. *Standard edition* (Vol. 21, pp. 59–145). London: Hogarth Press. (Original work published 1930.)

Freud, S. (1964). New introductory lectures on psychoanalysis. *Standard edition* (Vol. 22, pp. 3–182). London: Hogarth Press. (Original work published 1933.)

Freud, S. (1954). Project for a scientific psychology. In M. Bonaparte, A. Freud, & E. Kris (Eds.), *The origins of psycho-analysis: Letters to Wilhelm Fliess, Drafts and Notes: 1887–1902* (pp. 347–445). New York: Basic Books.

Gedo, J. E. (1979). *Beyond interpretation: Toward a revised theory for psychoanalysis.* New York: International Universities Press.

Gill, M. M., & Holzman, P. S. (Eds.). (1976). Psychology versus metapsychology. *Psychological Issues, 9* (4, Whole No. 36).

Hartmann, H. (1958). *Ego psychology and the problem of adaptation.* New York: International Universities Press. (Original work published 1939.)

Hartmann, H., Kris, E., & Loewenstein, R. M. (1964). Papers on psychoanalytic psychology. *Psychological Issues, 4* (2, Whole no. 14). (Original work published 1945–1962.)

Hilgard, E. R. (1980). Introduction. In G. J. Bloch (Ed.), *Mesmerism: A translation of the original medical and scientific writings of F. A. Mesmer, M. D.* (pp. xi–xxiii). Los Altos, CA: William Kaufmann.

Holt, R. R. (1962). A critical examination of Freud's concept of bound vs. free cathexis. *Journal of the American Psychoanalytic Association, 10,* 474–525.

Holt, R. R. (1965). A review of some of Freud's biological assumptions and their influence on his theories. In N. S. Greenfield & W. C. Lewis (Eds.), *Psychoanalysis and current biological thought* (pp. 93–124). Madison, WI: University of Wisconsin Press.

Holt, R. R. (1972). Freud's mechanistic and humanistic images of man. In R. R. Holt & E. Peterfreund (Eds.), *Psychoanalysis and Contemporary Science, 1,* 3–24.

Horowitz, M. J. (1977). The core characteristics of the hysterical personality. In M. J. Horowitz (Ed.), *The hysterical personality* (pp. 3–6). New York: Jason Aronson. (a)

Horowitz, M. J. (1977). Structure and the processes of change. In M. J. Horowitz (Ed.), *The hysterical personality* (pp. 329–399). New York: Jason Aronson. (b)

Horowitz, M. J. (1979). *States of mind: Analysis of change in psychotherapy.* New York: Plenum.

Horowitz, M. J., Marmar, C., Krupnick, J., Wilner, N., Kaltreider, N., & Wallerstein, R. (1984). *Personality styles and brief psychotherapy.* New York: Basic Books.

Izenberg, G. (1976). *The existentialist critique of Freud: The crisis of autonomy.* Princeton, NJ: Princeton University Press.

James, W. (1890). *The principles of psychology.* New York: Holt, Rinehart & Winston.

Jaynes, J. (1977). *The origin of consciousness in the breakdown of the bicameral mind.* Boston: Houghton Mifflin.

Jones, E. (1953). *The life and work of Sigmund Freud.* Vol. 1. *The formative years and the great discoveries.* New York: Basic Books.

Kaufmann, W. (1980). *Discovering the mind.* Vol. 3. *Freud versus Adler and Jung.* New York: McGraw-Hill.

Klein, G. (1976). Freud's two theories of sexuality. In M. M. Gill & P. S. Holzman (Eds.), *Psychology versus metapsychology* (pp. 14–70). *Psychological Issues, 9* (4, Whole no. 36).

Kohut, H. (1971). *The analysis of the self. Monographs, Psychoanalytic Study of the Child,* No. 4. New York: International Universities Press.

Kohut, H. (1977). *The restoration of the self.* New York: International Universities Press.

Kuhn, T. S. (1970). *The structure of scientific revolutions* (2nd ed.). Chicago: University of Chicago Press.

Lewin, K. (1931). The conflict between Aristotelian and Galileian modes of thought in contemporary psychology. *Journal of General Psychology, 5,* 141–177.

Lindner, R. (1955). Solitaire: The story of Laura. In *The fifty-minute hour* (pp. 79–118). New York: Holt, Rinehart & Winston.

Loevinger, J. (1966). Three principles for a psychoanalytic psychology. *Journal of Abnormal Psychology, 71,* 432–443.

Loevinger, J. (1976). *Ego development: Conceptions and theories.* San Francisco: Jossey-Bass.

Loewald, H. (1980). Ego and reality. In *Papers on psychoanalysis* (pp. 3–32). New Haven, CT: Yale University Press. (Original work published 1951.)

Loewald, H. (1980). On the therapeutic action of psychoanalysis. In *Papers on psychoanalysis* (pp. 221–256). New Haven, CT: Yale University Press. (Original work published 1960.)

Masson, J. M. (1984). *The assault on truth.* New York: Farrar Straus & Giroux.

Perry, C., & Laurence, J. -R. (1983). Hypnosis, surgery, and mind-body interaction: An historical evaluation. *Canadian Journal of Behavioral Science, 15,* 351–372.

Perry, C., & Laurence, J. -R. (1984). Mental processing outside of awareness: The contributions of Freud and Janet. In K. S. Bowers & D. Meichenbaum (Eds.), *The unconscious reconsidered.* New York: Wiley.

Rapaport, D. (1960). The structure of psychoanalytic theory. *Psychological Issues, 2* (2, Whole no. 6).

Reich, W. (1949). *Character analysis.* New York: Farrar, Straus & Giroux. (Original work published 1933.)

Ricoeur, P. (1970). *Freud and philosophy: An essay on interpretation.* New Haven, CT: Yale University Press.

Schafer, R. (1976). *A new language for psychoanalysis.* New Haven, CT: Yale University Press.

Schafer, R. (1978). *Language and insight.* New Haven, CT: Yale University Press.

Schorske, C. (1980). *Fin-de-siècle Vienna.* New York: Knopf.

Sulloway, F. J. (1979). *Freud: Biologist of the mind.* New York: Basic Books.

Veith, I. (1977). Four thousand years of hysteria. In M. J. Horowitz (Ed.), *The hysterical personality* (pp. 7–93). New York: Jason Aronson.

Wishnie, H. (1977). *The impulsive personality.* New York: Plenum.

# CHAPTER 3

# Behaviorism

Two opposing views of human nature have been advocated throughout history. On the one hand, our actions are seen as resulting from things done to us; on the other, they are seen as originating within ourselves and resulting at least partly from each individual's unique character and personality. As an example of the first view, in Homer's *Iliad*, people's actions are depicted as being dictated by their gods, that is, by forces outside themselves. What motivated the gods was evidently not a question to ask, though their faults were depicted as all too

human. In contrast, exemplifying the second view, is Aristotle's idea of developing oneself to realize one's full potential.

Gordon Allport, an American psychologist who maintained an interest in
personality during a long period when it was scarcely a respectable occupation
for psychologists to do so, has written of the former as a *reactive* view, the latter
as a *proactive* view (Allport, 1960). Those are convenient summary terms,
though there have been many versions of the reactive and proactive views, each
with a unique stamp.

The proactive view is more likely than the reactive one to be associated with
an interest in the development of personality and character, particularly in their
development to their fullest potential. One might interpret the mandate of a
book about personality as being largely concerned with the proactive view, but
in fact the field at present is, if anything, dominated by psychologists more or
less partial to the reactive view. These psychologists, both behaviorists and
social learning theorists (see Chapter 5), tend to belittle the effect of one's unique
personality on one's behavior.

## BACKGROUND IN NINETEENTH CENTURY THOUGHT

### Bentham and Mill as Precursors of Modern Personality Theories

Two nineteenth-century philosophers, Jeremy Bentham and John Stuart Mill,
provide background for modern versions of the reactive and proactive views,
particularly B. F. Skinner's behaviorism and the cognitive developmental
theories (see Chapter 6). In addition to the intrinsic interest of the theories of Mill
and Bentham, their lives were fatefully intertwined in ways relevant to their
theories of human nature.

Jeremy Bentham's main contribution was in the area of jurisprudence and
legal philosophy. Like many or perhaps all political philosophers, he built his
philosophy on an underlying theory of human nature; unlike some political
philosophers, Bentham made his psychology explicit. He would not reason
about anything until he had resolved it into its parts (Mill, 1838/1962); hence,
unlike those behaviorists who label the parts of every action as stimulus and
response, he had lists everywhere in his writings. One of his lists is of the
"Springs of Action," or, as we would say, of human motives.

The "sovereign masters" of human conduct, Bentham stated, are pain and
pleasure (Bentham, 1789/1962), motives that today are usually labeled in terms
of their external counterpart, reward and punishment, or, under the influence of
B. F. Skinner, simply reinforcement. Pleasures differ only quantitatively, not
qualitatively; the same holds for pains. Pleasures and pains differ in intensity,
duration, frequency, probability of occurrence, and purity, which is the absence
of the mixture of the opposite. Pleasure unmixed with pain is preferable to the
same intensity, duration, etc. of pleasure mixed with pain. (These quantitative

aspects turn out to anticipate approximately what Skinner calls schedules of reinforcement.) Bentham's disregard of the quality of pleasure he memorialized in a phrase that, translated into modern idiom, becomes: "Pinball is as good as poetry so long as it gives equal pleasure."

Among Bentham's followers was a younger, well-known British philosopher, James Mill. The two men became acquainted at about the time that Mill's oldest child, John Stuart Mill, was two years old. The two men took the raising of this child as an opportunity to see what could be accomplished by shaping a creature entirely to their theories, with the aim of making him their prime disciple. (Probably they never wrote an explicit description for shaping children. I do not know that Skinner has done so either, and certainly he would not endorse the details of their method. Nonetheless, shaping behavior has become the trademark of applied Skinnerian behaviorism.)

John Stuart Mill was a brilliant and precocious child. He learned Greek at three or four years, arithmetic and Latin at eight, logic at twelve, and economics at thirteen. At fourteen he began studying law. He was not permitted to play as other children were but instead associated with his father's friends, the British utilitarian philosophers. Any spare time he spent instructing his eight younger brothers and sisters. What can one expect to be the outcome of such a program of shaping behavior? Bentham and James Mill must have believed that John Stuart would accept and further their philosophy. I do not endorse the dubious idea that a given program of child-rearing has one and only one possible outcome, but nonetheless one can examine what happened to John Stuart Mill.

A striking result of his training, less bewildering today than it must have been to his father and Bentham, was that at about the age of twenty, John Stuart went into a profound depression lasting more than a year (Warnock, 1962). Another result was a brilliant essay giving an analysis, appreciation, and evaluation of Bentham's philosophy and impact on the law and a devastating criticism of Bentham's psychology (Mill, 1838/1962).

Mill thought it valuable that Bentham introduced the method of detail into philosophy and that he declined to reason about wholes until they were resolved into parts or about abstractions until they were reduced to things. But in dismissing all philosophy done by other methods as "vague generalities," Mill pointed out, Bentham forgot that those vague generalities contain the "whole unanalyzed experience of the human race" (Mill, 1838/1962).

In reducing human motives to pleasures and pains, Bentham showed too simple a view of human nature, said Mill. What about the pursuit of spiritual perfection as an end in itself? he asked. What about "desiring, for its own sake, the conformity of his own character to his standard of excellence, without hope of good or fear of evil from other source than his own inward consciousness"? Then there is a sense of honor and personal dignity, which may act in independence of others' opinions, or even in defiance of them. There are also the love of beauty; the love of order; "the love of power, not in the limited form of power over other human beings, but abstract power, the power of making our volitions effectual; the love of action, the thirst for movement and activity, a principle scarcely of less influence in human life than its opposite, the love of ease" (Mill, 1838/1962, pp. 100–101). None of these motives appear among the "Springs of Action," Bentham's catalog of motives.

For Mill, individuality is itself a good thing, and the pressure to conform to the ways of the majority is a form of despotism comparable to that of an absolute monarch. Most people, he said, even in private matters and in things done for pleasure, do not ask themselves what they prefer but only what is proper to their station and circumstance; on this point he would agree with the social learning theorists (see Chapter 5). "Peculiarity of taste, eccentricity of conduct, are shunned equally with crimes: until by dint of not following their own nature they have no nature to follow: their human capacities are withered and starved" (Mill, 1859/1962, p. 190), a somewhat different conclusion from that of the social learning theorists.

Despite their differences, Mill and Bentham both classed themselves as utilitarians. For Bentham the doctrine of utility was that the ethical thing to do was that which produced the greatest good for the greatest number. Mill, although not disagreeing with the formula, emphasized the ethical importance of looking at the consequences of actions rather than of calculating the gains and losses for affected parties. Mill added, as Bentham certainly did not, that among the consequences to be considered were the effects of an action upon the inward consciousness of the actor. That brings up the topic of character and its development. That topic, usually neglected by the behaviorists, is within the purview of the cognitive developmental approach (see Chapter 6).

In the chapter on individuality in *On liberty* Mill wrote:

> Among the works of man, which human life is rightly employed in perfecting and beautifying, the first in importance surely is man himself. Supposing it were possible to get houses built, corn grown, battles fought, causes tried, and even churches erected and prayers said, by machinery—by automatons in human form—it would be a considerable loss to exchange for these automatons even the men and women who at present inhabit the more civilised parts of the world, and who assuredly are but starved specimens of what nature can and will produce. Human nature is not a machine to be built after a model, and set to do exactly the work prescribed for it, but a tree, which requires to grow and develop itself on all sides, according to the tendency of the inward forces which make it a living thing. (Mill, 1859/1962, p. 188)

This passage was written long before anyone imagined that robots programmed by computers based on microchips would be commonplace in scientific laboratories and close to realization as household items.

An essential tenet of the cognitive developmental school (see Chapter 6) is that those at higher stages of development can understand those at lower stages, whereas those at lower stages cannot understand those at higher stages. Mill anticipated the point in the following passage:

> Those who are equally acquainted with, and equally ca-pable of appreciating and enjoying, both, do give a most marked preference to the manner of existence which employs their higher faculties. Few human creatures would consent to be changed into any of the lower animals, for a promise of the fullest allowance of a beast's pleasures; no intelligent human being would consent to be a fool, no instructed person would be an ignoramus, no person of feeling and conscience would be selfish and base, even though they should be persuaded that the fool, the dunce, or the rascal is better satisfied with his lot then they are with theirs. . . . A being of higher faculties requires more to make him happy, is capable probably of more acute suffering, and certainly accessible to it at more points, than one of an inferior type; but in spite of these liabilities, he can never really wish to sink into what he feels to be a lower grade of existence. . . . [The most appropriate explanation] is a sense of dignity. . . . It is better to be a human being dissatisfied than a pig satisfied; better to be Socrates dissatisfied than a fool satisfied. And if the fool, or the pig, are of a different opinion, it is because they only know their own side of the question. The other party to the compari-son knows both sides. (Mill, 1863/1962, pp. 259–260)

Skinner may not acknowledge Bentham as his predecessor, but he under-stands that Mill is an adversary, for he has called one of his books *Beyond freedom and dignity* (Skinner, 1971).

This then is part of the philosophical heritage of the generation to which Freud introduced psychoanalysis. Freud, though writing in a different spirit, was familiar with and admired many of the writings of Mill. In terms of basic ideas, modern behaviorists and cognitive developmentalists in some ways are reminiscent of Bentham and Mill. But modern psychology contributes a wealth of factual material based on experimental and research paradigms that permit many more specific assertions about the matters at issue.

Some supporters of each of the three points of view — the behaviorists, the developmentalists, and the psychoanalysts — wrap the mantle of science about themselves and declare themselves and their movement to be leading the way to the psychology of the future. History belies those claims. Only psychoanalysis is truly new; the other theories have survived for millennia; and there is good reason to suppose that all three views will survive in some revised form long beyond the present generation.

For that one can be grateful, as Mill has instructed. If all mankind but one were of a given opinion, Mill said, it is as important that the majority not silence the one as that the one not silence the majority (Mill, 1859/1962). There are three reasons. One is that the one might be right and the majority wrong. The second and more likely is that neither opinion contains all of the truth, but that each has some element of truth. The third reason is the most interesting: that when the opponents of any opinion are silenced, the heart and meaning of that opinion are lost, and it becomes only dead clichés. "He who knows only his own side of the case, knows little of that" (Mill, 1859/1962, p. 163). Large controversy stirs up even average people to achieve dignity and intellectual stature.

That is why even in the unlikely case that one theory of personality were surely "right" or "true," it would still be appropriate to present sympathetic versions of several theories in an introduction to the psychology of personality.

### The Problems of Knowledge and Language

In the nineteenth century the central problem of psychology was considered to be epistemology. How do people, including infants, know or learn anything? Do the facts of the environment filter through our senses and impress themselves on our minds? Or does the mind impose its own rational order on the material presented to it? The former position is called *empiricism*, the latter, *rationalism*. Empiricism is the forerunner of modern behaviorism, rationalism the forerunner of the cognitive developmental approach. In terms of that issue, Mill and Bentham are both considered empiricists (Robinson, 1982).

Most but not all modern psychologists, especially in the United States, are empiricists in the sense that they consider empirical data essential to psychology. The present book is written entirely in that vein: Theory and data are equally important, but theory must always be informed by data. Empiricism in the present discussion has a different meaning. At its extreme, the empiricist doctrine states that there is nothing in the mind but what comes through the senses or is generated by combinations of ideas that come through the senses.

The empiricist view has four implications (Bower & Hilgard, 1981, Ch. 1): sensationalism, reductionism, associationism, and mechanism. *Sensationalism* means that the original source of all we know is our senses. *Reductionism* means that complex ideas can be reduced to, and understood in terms of, their simple elements. *Associationism* means that complex ideas are built out of simple sensations by the sensations being associated together, mostly by contiguity in time or space. *Mechanism* means that the mind is a passive agent, observing the inexorable laws of the association of ideas. Clearly, Mill was not an extreme empiricist.

The *rationalist* view sees the mind as endowed originally with certain innate ideas. Raw experience, the rationalists assert, is nothing but a formless chaos of impressions until the mind imposes on it its shape, given by the innate ideas. In the eighteenth century Immanuel Kant stated that space and time are not ideas that could possibly arise in experience. Rather, they are innate ideas imposed on experience virtually from the outset.

Interesting arguments and even some data were brought to bear on such questions. For example, it can be shown that the image projected on the retina is not that of the object as we see it and as we know it to be. Our ideas do not correspond to our visual sensations; that discrepancy is evidence against the sensationalist view. There are equal difficulties in consistently maintaining a rationalist point of view. Although such arguments may sound dated, the issues are not dead. They reappear in connection with modern psycholinguistics, to be discussed later.

Darwin's theory of evolution raised the emotional issue of whether humans are descended from some earlier kind of primate, or, as his opponents phrased it, whether man came from a monkey. For the majority of psychologists who accepted, at least in principle, the theory of evolution, Darwin's theory encouraged a belief in the fundamental continuity of psychological processes between animals and people. But precisely the problem of language posed a special problem for the theory. The anti-Darwinians stated that however strong the evidence for evolution elsewhere in the animal kingdom, the existence of language is uniquely human and sets humankind off from all other living creatures. Language, they said, is a Rubicon that no "brute" could cross (Müller, 1861, p. 354). Those rare instances in which animals learn single words do not constitute a major exception, because the animals do not put the words together in the manner of a human language.

One of Darwin's strongest defenders was George John Romanes, who wrote books on mental evolution in man and animals (Romanes, 1884, 1888). His argument for continuity rested on largely anecdotal evidence of reasoning in animals, mostly people's pets. Most of the evidence was interpreted in an anthropomorphic way; the motives that a human might have had when performing a similar act were ascribed to the animal in the anecdote. For Romanes, animals demonstrated that they had minds by behavior that was adaptive and not reflex, showing that they had made some choice. The mental state of the animal, he said, can be known only by projecting human mental states into it. Having set himself this rule, he proceeded to ascribe parental affection, puzzlement, anger, jealousy, and imagination to animals such as caterpillars, spiders, fish, and crustacea (Knoll, 1986).

Needless to say, psychologists reacted against Romanes's approach. But they also could not accept the alternative favored by the Creationists, that the behavior of each species was largely accounted for by elaborately preprogrammed instincts.

William McDougall's psychology extended the concept of instinct as explanation to human behavior (McDougall, 1908/1928). (Perhaps Freud did, too, though that is a matter of dispute, complicated by the problem of translating from German to English.) Instinct in the writings of early twentieth century psychologists such as McDougall (and Freud) must not be confused, however, with the concept of *innate releasing mechanism* of current ethological theory. Instincts were conceived of as flexible; in fact, McDougall saw them as purposive behavior, with flexibility in pursuit of purpose being a defining feature (compare E. C. Tolman, Chapter 5).

## THE DISCOVERIES

The origins of the behaviorist revolution lie in I. P. Pavlov's work on conditioned reflexes and Edward Lee Thorndike's on trial-and-error learning; major discoveries of both men occurred around the turn of the century. Although it is questionable whether either discovery ranks in novelty or revolutionary force with Freud's discovery of the dynamic unconscious, their work is interpreted in this book as the basis for a new paradigm in psychology, in accord with Kuhn's model. The research of both Pavlov and Thorndike pointed to substituting a more or less mechanical learning process for either the reasoning that Romanes discerned in animal behavior or the instincts postulated by the Creationists. The importance for the study of personality lies in the implication that much or all of the behavior of people follows the same mechanical model.

### Pavlov's Conditioned Reflexes

Ivan Pavlov, a Russian physiologist, was studying the salivary secretion of dogs. For this purpose, he put each dog in an apparatus that held it still and permitted measuring the secretion after meat powder was put in the dog's mouth. He noticed that the secretion began when all preparations had been made, before the meat powder was actually introduced. Such "psychic secretions" had been noted at least a hundred years earlier. What was distinctive about Pavlov's discovery was that he saw in this setup a new experimental method that could be used to study a wide variety of problems.

In the typical, or exemplary, experiment, the animal is presented with a stimulus like food, which results in a reflex response, salivation in the case of food. This occurs naturally, prior to any training. The stimulus is called an *unconditioned stimulus* and the response an *unconditioned response.* Then on a series of occasions the unconditioned stimulus is preceded or accompanied by some arbitrary stimulus, say, a light or a bell, which after several trials becomes a *conditioned stimulus.* The response to the conditioned stimulus is called the *conditioned reflex,* or conditioned response; it typically resembles the unconditioned response and, after training, occurs even in the absence of the unconditioned stimulus (Figure 3.1).

| A | US (food) | ——————————————→ | UR | (salivation) |
| B | $S_1$ (light) | ——→ US (food) ——→ | UR | (salivation) |
| C | $S_1$ (light) | ——————————————→ | CR | (salivation) |
| D | $S_2$ (bell) | ——→ $S_1$ (light) ——→ | CR | (salivation) |
| E | $S_2$ (bell) | ——————————————→ | CR | (salivation) |

A: Unconditioned reflex or response
B & C: First-order conditioned response
D & E: Second-order conditioned response

FIGURE 3.1    First- and second-order conditioning *(Adapted from Bower & Hilgard, 1981)*

With this simple model experiment, much can be done. Repetition of the original situation results in learning, and repeating for enough trials the conditioned stimulus without the unconditioned stimulus results in disappearance of the conditioned reflex; that disappearance is called *experimental extinction.* After experimental extinction and an interval with no trials, the conditioned reflex will spontaneously recover to some extent. Much work was done on time relations that optimize conditioning; the conditioned stimulus should slightly precede or accompany the unconditioned stimulus. The animal will ordinarily generalize and thus respond to stimuli that differ somewhat from the original stimulus. The closer the new stimulus is to the original, the closer the response will come to equaling the original response. The animal can then be taught to discriminate between two somewhat similar stimuli, treating one as positive, to be followed by the unconditioned stimulus, and the other as negative, not to be so followed. This fact can be used as a method of discovering what sensory discriminations the animal is capable of making (Pavlov, 1927).

The implications for personality of the phenomena of conditioning are increased by the phenomenon of *secondary conditioning.* A conditioned stimulus can serve in the same role as an unconditioned stimulus to condition a new stimulus. If an animal learns that a light signals food, and a bell is then frequently paired with the light, eventually the bell will elicit salivation (Figure 3.1). By extension, this mechanism can account for how conditioning colors many aspects of life where it is not immediately evident.

Pavlov discovered, again by accident, that when a discrimination is established and the positive and negative stimuli are then gradually made so much alike that the animal can no longer discriminate between them, the animal behaves in a disturbed manner analogous to that of a neurotic individual (Pavlov, 1941). He considered this experiment to provide an experimental model of neurosis. Late in his life he worked on this model for its psychiatric implications. Pavlov's work was highly honored in the Soviet Union, perhaps in part because the government was hostile to an alternative psychodynamic approach to mental illness.

All in all, the work on conditioned reflexes lends itself to a mechanical picture of learning. The question then becomes how much of human learning can be accounted for by such mechanisms.

## Thorndike's Connectionism

Edward Lee Thorndike, one of the first American psychologists, has left his stamp on many fields, including learning theory, measurement of intelligence, character development, and educational psychology. He was annoyed by the unscientific approach in Romanes's work, but he did not wish to attack the theory of evolution, which Romanes was defending. Rather, he sought a more scientific approach to animal and human learning than that of the nineteenth century anecdotal accounts; so he took on the problem of accounting for as much as possible of both human and animal learning with as mechanical a model as possible.

In a typical experiment in Thorndike's early work a motivated animal is presented with a puzzle and rewarded for solving it. His original experiment involved placing a cat in a puzzle box with slatted sides. The cat was hungry and could see food outside. The door to the box was held by a latch that could be operated by the cat. Inside the box, the cat would run through its repertory of actions, such as rubbing, clawing, biting, scratching, and purring, until it accidentally tripped the latch. On succeeding trials the cat tended to solve the problem more quickly, until finally it learned to go directly to the latch and release itself (Thorndike, 1898).

A trial in this apparatus is evaluated in terms of time to solution. A curve plotting time to finish against number of trials produced a picture of the course of learning, and averaging learning curves for several animals produced a smooth curve. The fact that the average curves showed a gradual decrease in time rather than a sudden drop was taken by Thorndike as evidence that the animal does not learn to understand the problem. Rather, the correct response is gradually "stamped in," and all errors are gradually "stamped out." Thus he had an automatic, or mechanistic, explanation for learning. He called this *trial-and-error learning* or, later, *selecting and connecting*. The latter name shows Thorndike's deliberate reference to Darwin's theory of evolution by natural selection.

The chief outcome of Thorndike's many experiments in this mode was his *law of effect:* Responses that are accompanied or immediately followed by satisfaction will, other things being equal, become more firmly connected with the situation; those accompanied or followed by discomfort will have their connections with the situation weakened (Thorndike, 1911).

Thorndike, like Pavlov, had a neurological or quasi-neurological theory. He thought that corresponding to each connection there was a neural "bond," whose exact nature, however, he did not explain. Thorndike aimed to be ultraempirical and not to go beyond the data given. He apparently thought that neural bonds were not hypothetical, for what else could account for the connections between ideas? Modern neurology, however, does not sanction Thorndike's equation of neural bonds with the association of ideas. (Indeed, Freud had already argued against such an idea in his book *On aphasia,* 1891/1953.)

Whatever may be the weaknesses in Thorndike's neurological hypotheses, his practical approach to problems of learning had some good effects for school children. In his day it was customary to require children to learn many things, such as Greek and Latin grammar, for the sake of "mental discipline." Thorndike disputed this supposed value; the only carry-over from learning one thing to learning another lies in whatever identical elements the two performances share, he declared.

Thorndike carried his behavioristic philosophy into other branches of psychology, where he made a considerable impact. He said that there is no such thing as general intelligence (Thorndike, 1927). Two tests correlate to the extent that they call on identical elements, or identical "bonds." In fact, he constructed a test of general intelligence, but he refused to call it that; he called it "Intellect CAVD." CAVD stands for completions, arithmetic problems, vocabulary, and following directions, which are the subtests included in the test. Thorndike elevated his point of view to a doctrine, his *doctrine of specificity.* He belittled all talk of general traits that cut across different situations; any relation between behavior in one situation and that in another is due to common elements in the situations or the behaviors. This point of view is alive today, particularly in the work of some social learning theorists. The study of character by his protegés Hugh Hartshorne and Mark A. May will be reviewed in Chapter 5.

## BEHAVIORISM AS A SCHOOL OF THOUGHT

### Watson, Founder of Behaviorism

John B. Watson, another American psychologist, took up the methods of Thorndike and particularly Pavlov and turned them into an ideology, which he called *behaviorism* (Watson, 1919). Although his early experimentation was entirely with animals, he saw behaviorism as the program for psychology as a science, and he was explicit about its application to people. With appropriate conditioning, he said, any infant could be turned into any kind of adult. Introspection and any considerations relative to consciousness should, on principle, be excluded from psychology. Verbal reports viewed as behavior were admissable. Thinking, he hypothesized, was subvocal speech, tiny movements of the mouth and tongue or minimal movements in other parts of the body. Like Thorndike with his hypothetical neural bonds, Watson was not bothered by the fact that those tiny mouth and limb movements were just as hypothetical as the ideas or mental processes that they were meant to displace.

Watson's most famous experiment was performed on a small child called

Little Albert. Watson believed that the original human emotions to be found in infancy were fear, rage, and love, and the child is originally afraid only of loud noises and sudden loss of support. He began his experiment when Albert was about nine months old (Watson & Rayner, 1920). At no time did Albert show fear when suddenly confronted with a white rat, a rabbit, a dog, a monkey, masks with or without hair, or other stimuli. Even loss of support did not frighten him, but a sudden loud noise did. At eleven months, over a series of several trials on each of several days, Albert was suddenly presented with a white rat; at first he began to reach for it, but just as he did so, a sudden loud noise was sounded behind him. This was done on each trial. On the third day of experimental trials, the fear reaction had generalized, though in attenuated form, to a rabbit, a dog, a fur coat, some cotton, and Watson's hair — but not the hair of Watson's assistants. At this point the child was removed from the hospital, so that, unfortunately, no attempt could be made to de-condition the fears.

Although this experiment is often quoted in approximately those terms, recent research has raised some doubts (Samelson, 1980). First, the conditioned fear reaction is not easily established, and Watson's first attempts with other children were unsuccessful. Second, with Albert the experiment did not work well if he was allowed to suck his thumb; it was necessary for experimenters to remove his thumb from his mouth during the experimental trials. Finally, the experiment appears never to have been replicated. It is quite unusual and perhaps unwise for an experiment to play as large a part in the history of psychology as this one has without repetition.

Mary Cover Jones, a student of Watson's, did the reverse experiment with Little Peter (Jones, 1924, 1974). At the age of three, Peter was extremely afraid of furry animals. By application of conditioning principles, she was able to rid the child of the fear. The experiments with Albert and Peter are the forerunners of modern behavior modification therapy.

Watson's doctrines were widely publicized just before and after World War I, and they had a major influence on the child-rearing practices of many people (Jones, 1974). He recommended, for example, that babies not be cuddled; at most, the parents could kiss them on the forehead at bedtime and shake hands with them in the morning. Babies themselves probably were the strongest opponents of his theories. The logical connection between his recommendations and his experimental work is not clear.

## Kinds of Behaviorism

There have been many theories of learning, and because learning is so essential to all of psychology, they have become major schools of psychology. They have been predominantly of two types, both behavioristic. One type stresses learning by *association,* chiefly contiguity and most often governed by frequency; the other type stresses *reward.* (Latterly, reward is called reinforcement, but, as

Edward Tolman pointed out, whether reward constitutes reinforcement is the question.) The theories that stressed association generally had closer kinship to Pavlov's model of learning, whereas those that stressed reward had closer kinship to Thorndike's model. (For an example of a learning theory based on association, see chapter 4 on Edwin F. Guthrie in G. H. Bower & E. R. Hilgard, 1981.)

The most important dissenter from the emphasis on reward in early American behaviorism was Tolman, who argued for a cognitive behaviorism, or, as he called it, *purposive behaviorism,* even for the rat. In his formulation, reward conveys information to the animal, but it does not stamp in anything. (His work will be discussed further in Chapter 5.)

What remains most impressive about behaviorism is that the laws, or, to be more accurate, generalizations, about learning that Pavlov and others derived from the studies of conditioned reflexes, now often called *classical conditioning,* hold virtually unchanged when one turns to learning mazes and puzzle boxes, such as Thorndike studied, now often called *instrumental conditioning.* The common elements include the work on generalization and discrimination of stimuli and extinction and spontaneous recovery of the conditioned response. Experimental neurosis, which Pavlov studied by making a discrimination so difficult as to be impossible, is studied in instrumental learning by training an animal to approach and to avoid the same stimulus situation. For example, food or a sex object will await the animal only in a place where it will also receive a painful shock. Again, the result appears to be analogous to neurosis in people.

### Model Experiment: The Rat in the Maze

The typical experiment for animal learning involved some variant of the following format: An animal is not fed for approximately twenty-four hours. Then it is put in an elevated maze. The rat is a convenient animal to use because it is cheap and easy to maintain, it reproduces fairly rapidly, and it can walk on a narrow runway without sides. Typically, the maze consists of several Ts, with each T appended to the tip of one arm of the previous one. The rat runs down a series of short runways, and at the end of each it must choose to go right or left. At the end of the maze there is a box with the animal's ration of food.

The curve displaying the animal's rate of learning will usually have trials on the abscissa (X axis) and either time to get to the end or number of errors (blind alleys entered) on the ordinate (Y axis). Curves for individual rats are irregular, but average curves for a group show a rapid decline in time and errors at first, followed by a more gradual decrease.

Possible variations on this experiment are enormous. Changes can occur in the size and shape of the maze, the animal's deprivation schedule, appropriate or inappropriate reward, cues for the correct alley, and so on. There may, for example, be a door to pass through in each arm of the T; the correct door need not always be on the same side but may be shifted, with some sign such as a square or circle to indicate the correct one. This model experiment proved to be more flexible than Thorndike's original puzzle box.

---

## SKINNER'S RADICAL BEHAVIORISM

B. F. Skinner is one of the best known contemporary psychologists and one of the most radical and consistent behaviorists ever. His work is worth studying for both reasons, as well as for its own merits.

### Basic Concepts

Skinner, like Watson, aspires to eliminate all mentalistic terms from his psychological discourse. In this respect he is stricter than was Thorndike, whose law of effect stressed reward and punishment, or satisfiers and annoyers. Thorndike did not mind that those terms have mental connotations. Skinner substitutes the term *reinforcement* for whatever strengthens the tendency to make a response. For some reason *punishment* slips through his anti-mentalistic screening. Whereas reinforcement leads to increasing some behavior, punishment leads to decreasing a behavior. *Positive reinforcer* is Skinner's name for a stimulus that, when following a response, increases the probability that that response will recur. *Punishment* is the presentation of an unpleasant, or, as psychologists say, aversive, stimulus. Depriving a subject of a reinforcement he calls *negative punishment,* and ending a punishment he calls *negative reinforcement.*

The only truly scientific method for psychology, according to Skinner, is his own approach, analyzing all behavior in terms of the organism's history of reinforcement (Skinner, 1953). In Allport's terms, Skinner is an extreme proponent of the reactive view. He opposes all postulation of mythical inner entities or agencies, which, he says, merely duplicate inside, invisibly, the behavior that has already been observed visibly; neurological entities, such as Thorndike's neural bonds, are as taboo as mental entities. That kind of theory, he says, psychology does not need. We understand a behavior, Skinner asserts, when we know how to produce it or eliminate it by manipulating the environmental contingencies.

Although a behaviorist, Skinner is in one sense not a stimulus-response psychologist, as many earlier behaviorists were. He rejects the slogan of Watson, "No stimulus, no response." Rather, he begins by observing that there are two kinds of actions, one, a *respondent,* which is *elicited* by a definite stimulus, the other, an *operant,* which is *emitted* by the organism with no definite stimulus. Reflexes such as salivation or blinking one's eyes when something comes close to them are respondent. Most human behavior, however, is operant. (Indeed,

Tolman confined the realm of behavior to what Skinner calls the operant realm. See Chapter 5.) Pavlov's classical conditioning was concerned with respondent behavior; Thorndike's instrumental conditioning of the cat in the puzzle box was concerned with operant behavior.

Respondent behavior is generally governed by the autonomic nervous system, is involuntary, and usually involves smooth muscles and glands. Operant behavior usually involves skeletal muscles and is voluntary. Those characterizations are not absolute; the blink of the eye, which can be classically conditioned, involves skeletal muscles, and symptomatic behavior is usually operant but not altogether voluntary.

Stimuli play an important part in operant behavior, even though they do not elicit the behavior in the same sense that they elicit respondent behavior. The organism learns to discriminate between different stimuli, and the discriminated stimuli become the occasions for responding or not, in accord with available reinforcement. Thorndike's cats emitted all sorts of behavior before they got out of the puzzle box; when they learned to discriminate the latch from the rest of the box, their response became more efficient. That behavior is classed as operant, because the latch does not compel the cat to trip it in the way that meat elicits salivation.

An organism that has learned a response to one particular stimulus will ordinarily give a similar response to a category of similar stimuli; that is *generalization,* or, as Skinner sometimes calls it, induction or transfer. In a sense, all attempts to teach anybody anything useful would be futile without that effect. Every child must carry what is learned in school into other situations, else school accomplishes nothing. Much of what psychoanalysis calls transference (see Chapter 2) can be looked at in this way, though Skinner himself deals with psychoanalysis mainly in terms of obsolete concepts such as cathexis, rather than in terms of resistance and transference.

The opposite or complement of generalization is *discrimination.* All operant conditioning is based on learning to discriminate between the appropriate stimuli and responses and inappropriate ones; however, the technical term refers to learning to differentiate between two similar stimuli, only one of which is reinforced.

### Shaping Responses and Fading Stimuli

Skinner, Keller Breland, and Norman Guttman (Skinner, 1958) discovered, perhaps partly by accident, a method for producing a kind of behavior that was radically different from the animal's original repertory. They were working on a war project in a laboratory on the top floor of a flour mill. Because of bureaucratic delays, they had time to do experiments with pigeons that landed on the window sills.

> We built a magnetic food-magazine, which dispensed
> grain on the principle of an automatic peanut vendor, and
> conditioned pigeons to turn at the sound it made and eat the
> grain it discharged into a cup. . . . We built a gauge to mea-
> sure the force with which a pigeon pecked a horizontal block,
> and by differentially reinforcing harder pecks we built up
> such forceful blows that the base of the pigeon's peak quickly
> became inflamed. . . . One day we decided to teach a pigeon
> to bowl. The pigeon was to send a wooden ball down a minia-
> ture alley toward a set of toy pins by swiping the ball with a
> sharp sideward movement of the beak. To condition the re-
> sponse, we put the ball on the floor of an experimental box
> and prepared to operate the food-magazine as soon as the first
> swipe occurred. But nothing happened. . . . We decided to
> reinforce any response which had the slightest resemblance to
> a swipe — perhaps, at first, merely the behavior of looking at
> the ball — and then to select responses which more closely
> approximated the final form. The result amazed us. In a few
> minutes, the ball was caroming off the walls of the box as if
> the pigeon had been a champion squash player. The spectacle
> so impressed Keller Breland that he gave up a promising ca-
> reer in psychology and went into the commercial production
> of behavior. (Skinner, 1958, p. 94)

Skinner's explanation of the speed of the conditioning is that the pigeon
was first trained to respond to the sound of the food magazine by turning and
approaching the food tray. The sound of the magazine became a *conditioned
reinforcer*, by a mechanism analogous to Pavlov's secondary conditioning, and it
could follow the desired response instantly. Even short delays, they found, may
result in reinforcing unintended intervening behaviors. Further, because the
experimenter held the switch that operated the food magazine, they could break
up the behavior into small, arbitrary fragments or approximations.

Although he does not subscribe to the slogan "No stimulus, no response,"
Skinner does analyze behavior in terms of stimuli and responses. What Skinner
and his followers have refined to an art is analyzing observable behavior into
small, discrete fragments. A chain of such fragments makes up a relatively
simple response. Breaking the behavior into fragments aids training efforts,
since one fragment at a time can be trained.

Such a functional analysis of behavior is the key to many practical applications of Skinner's work to behavior modification in animal training, child training, psychotherapy, and elsewhere. As he noted with the pigeons, close analysis
often reveals that the last response just prior to reinforcement is not at all the one
that the trainer desires to strengthen. "Your father will punish you when he

comes home" is poor disciplinary technique, according to Skinner; to be effective, rewards and punishments must be swift.

On the stimulus side, what corresponds to shaping response is called *fading* of stimuli. The evidence seems to show that a response, at least under some circumstances, can be established more securely if the wrong one is never made (Bower & Hilgard, 1981, p. 173 ff.). For example, in some experiments, the animal has been thoroughly trained to make the correct choice with no alternative visible. The wrong choice is then gradually introduced, but at first as a very faint stimulus. When subsequently the wrong choice is clearly visible, the animal will not ever choose it. The correct habit will be more firmly established than would be possible if the task had been presented at the outset as a choice between two visible alternatives. Similarly, a difficult discrimination can be taught an animal by superimposing the new clues on a well-learned old pair, easily discriminated.

The pigeon can easily discriminate between red and green, but it has a hard time discriminating a horizontal bar from a vertical bar. Teach the pigeon to discriminate a red key from a green one; then superimpose the horizontal and vertical bars over the colored keys. When the red and green colors are gradually faded out, leaving only the horizontal and vertical bars, the difficult discrimination will have been learned.

## Schedules of Reinforcement

Some of the best-known work of Skinner and his colleagues has to do not with shaping behavior but with maintaining it at a given rate. Skinner has demonstrated that schedules of reinforcement are the crucial element in determining those rates. For his work on schedules of reinforcement Skinner found that he did not need to have the animal perform an elaborate task, such as running even a simple maze (Ferster & Skinner, 1957). He stripped the task down to its bare essentials. For rats, that consisted of simply pushing a lever to obtain a pellet of food. For pigeons, the corresponding task was pecking at a key to obtain a bit of food (Skinner, 1956).

To study behavior in a realistic way, an experiment was needed that did not reward the animal for each and every effort, for in nature not every foray for food or other goods is successful. Skinner therefore devised an apparatus that rewarded the animal only intermittently or a certain percentage of the time. What he sought to find out was the rate of responding per unit of time as a function of the rate of reward.

To understand this work one must have some idea of the nature of the apparatus, which is usually now called the Skinner box, though not by Skinner. The animal, say, the rat, is put in a box from which it cannot escape. The box has in it a little lever that the rat can press with a paw. Near it there is a food magazine that drops one pellet of food within the rat's reach, according to some prearranged schedule, after certain paw presses. The rat will ordinarily be hungry when put in the box, though that is not what Skinner would say. He would say something like, "The animal was not fed for twenty-four hours before each trial." The animal is trained to press the lever for food; that training is not the essential part of the experiment and may not even be reported. In an adjoining room is a recording device, which has a sheet of paper and a pen arranged so that the pen moves across the paper with time irrespective of what the rat does (or the paper is on a drum that rotates at a constant rate). The other dimension records each time the rat presses the lever. Thus, in Figure 3.2, the X axis in each panel records the time, the Y axis the total number of lever presses to that point in time. A similar apparatus can be used for a pigeon, except that it records when the pigeon pecks for its food.

Suppose that no matter how many times the rat pushes the lever, it will not be given a pellet more often than once every five minutes; the pellet appears for the first press after five minutes have elapsed since the last pellet. That is called a *fixed-interval* schedule. The typical rate of responding is studied after the animal has completely mastered the situation and settled down to a steady rate. In that case, the response rate will resemble that of panel A of Figure 3.2. There is typically a scalloped effect; the animal after receiving a reinforcement responds only at a very low rate, but as the end of the five-minute interval approaches, the rate increases till it is at a maximum just before the reinforcement is given. Then the process begins again.

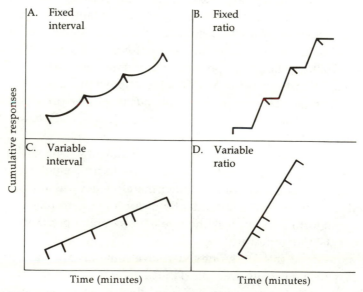

FIGURE 3.2  Scheme of cumulative response records on four schedules of reinforcement. *(From Bower & Hilgard, 1981)*

The scalloped effect disappears if the animal is reinforced not according to a fixed interval but according to a *variable interval*, which, however, may average five minutes. (Obviously, five minutes is only chosen as an example; another interval would do as well.) The point is that when the total number of reinforcements is the same as for a fixed interval, the rate of responding tends to be constant, as in panel C of Figure 3.2, rather than scalloped.

Another schedule varies the ratio of reinforced to unreinforced responses instead of the interval between reinforcements. Suppose the animal receives a food pellet every tenth bar press, no matter how much time has elapsed. That is a *fixed-ratio* schedule. The response curve for a fixed-ratio schedule is depicted in panel B of Figure 3.2. Again, there is a period of little or no responding immediately after a reinforcement is given, followed by a period of rapid responding until the next reinforcement is given.

For a *variable-ratio* schedule, the animal is reinforced after some number of responses, but the number varies from one reinforcement to the next in some random sequence. With that schedule, the likelihood of receiving a reinforcement is greater, the faster the rate of response; thus the animal is usually responding rapidly when reinforced and settles down to a uniformly high rate of response, as in panel D of Figure 3.2, even when the frequency of reinforcement is no greater than for other schedules.

One of the most remarkable features of the rates of response depicted in Figure 3.2 is that these same findings hold almost regardless of the species studied, whether it be rat, pigeon, or person (Skinner, 1956). Such findings justify a certain *hubris* on the part of the psychologist who discovers them. There are not many psychological findings at once so specific in form and so general in application.

Not only does intermittent reinforcement affect the rate of response; it also affects the persistence of a response for long periods during which it is not reinforced. In particular, a variable-interval or variable-ratio schedule will make the animal very resistant to experimental extinction of the response. With appropriate prior training, a pigeon may emit as many as 10,000 successive responses without reinforcement (Bower & Hilgard, 1981, p. 180).

One can easily understand that effect if one permits oneself to anthropomorphize, by saying that the animal still *expects* to get a reward sooner or later. Skinner would disapprove of that. He has no use for terms like "expects." For Skinner, adding expectation or any other mentalistic term merely reduplicates inside the mind what is already observed in the behavior.

There is, of course, a paradox here, one that Bentham, Thorndike, and every behaviorist who stresses pleasure or reward or reinforcement should find embarrassing. If each instance of reward stamps in or reinforces the preceding response, why is it that a response established by a variable-ratio schedule is more resistant to extinction than one reinforced every time it occurs? Skinner sidesteps the problem by declaring that he has no interest in theory, that psychology needs no such theories. In Chapter 5 Tolman's answer will be presented.

## Application to Personality

Skinner is saying that whatever may be true about personality apart from the way it is shown in observable behavior, scientific study of human nature must be restricted to observable behavior. For Skinner, science means prediction and control (Skinner, 1953). These, he states, are possible through study of behavior itself, objectively, without reference to any hypothetical traits or other personality variables or inner processes. That topic, however, continues to be debated among personality, social, and clinical psychologists. The majority of psychologists today, and not just clinicians, believe that one cannot study psychology, much less personality, without reference to cognitive aspects. Few would deny, however, that Skinner proceeds far toward explaining behavior in his terms.

*Kinds of reinforcers.* At first glance, one may think that any behavioral generalizations that apply to rewards or reinforcers apply equally, with an appropriate change of sign, to punishments. But many exceptions to that rule are found. Thorndike at first did not concern himself with the differences, but later he came to believe that under many circumstances rewards are much more effective in assisting learning than are punishments.

Skinner has made an extensive analysis of the efficacy of punishment and its alternatives. Punishment, he believes, has many unfortunate consequences. He distinguishes punishment from both *forgetting* and *extinction.* Each must be evaluated with respect to both its speed of achieving the main objective and its possible undesirable side effects. Suppose your child cries for candy when you take him to the grocery store. You could slap him; that would be punishment. You could ignore him and hope that the behavior would suffer extinction. Or you could stop taking him to the grocery store for a while and hope he would forget that conduct before he goes with you again.

On the whole, although not denying the possible efficacy of punishment, Skinner favors, as did Thorndike, judicious use of rewards to improve behavior. Obviously, this is different from the practice of many parents and teachers. But if psychologists never arrive at some counter-intuitive conclusions, they labor in vain. By Skinner's reasoning, a teacher should dismiss her class early on days, even at the moment, they are behaving especially well (Skinner, 1958, p. 98).

It is not clear, however, that all of the elements in the situation have entered into his calculations. Parents and teachers usually have a desire to punish irritating behavior; that feeling is also a fact of human nature, however unwelcome. Another neglected possibility is that learning something in school may be intrinsically rewarding, especially when the children are behaving well, in which case dismissing the class would be a punishment. The topic of intrinsic motivation will be discussed again in Chapter 5.

Suppose research were to prove that reinforcement of good behavior is more effective at extinguishing criminal behavior than punishing crime. Rearrangement of the penal system around that fact would surely create public resentment, as one can observe every time prisons are made more humane. Why reward criminals, people say, when there are more deserving poor who remain in need? Considerations of equity limit application of Skinner's conclusions, whether they are based on his laboratory results or purely on his philosophy.

*Token economies.* One effective application of operant behavioral techniques has come in the token economies put into effect in certain institutions, including homes for the retarded, mental hospitals, and prisons. In a token economy, the person is awarded a token or a point every time he or she performs a specified behavior. Once a certain number of points or tokens has been accumulated, they can be exchanged for some valuable reward, which may be a tangible item or a privilege. This system gets around certain problems involved in rewarding behaviors every time they occur; large rewards, such as a weekend pass, are not effectively given on an immediate basis, for example.

Difficult and unruly conduct can usually be mastered effectively by a token economy in a relatively short time. Of course, the behavior need not be rewarded on each occurrence. Indeed, when it is, the behavior is likely to drop off sharply as soon as the reinforcement is discontinued. Typically, the reward is not discontinued but given intermittently, on either a variable-ratio or variable-interval schedule. By tapering off rewards on an appropriate schedule, the desired behavior will continue long after all contrived rewards cease. When the targeted behaviors are ones that become either habitual or self-rewarding, such as washing one's face or eating with a fork, they will presumably ultimately continue without further reward.

Some civil liberties advocates have protested the use of token economies in prison on the grounds that prisoners do not have the option of freely giving or withholding informed consent. The alternative options frequently have been worse: a straitjacket in days gone by, stupefying drugs in more recent times. The drugs, once hailed as the solution to the problem of mental illness, have been shown to have serious long-term consequences, particularly tardive dyskinesia, a form of uncoordinated and uncontrollable movements. Whatever the legal issues may be, from a psychological view token economies can in some circumstances be valuable and, in reasonable hands, humane.

*Gambling and self-destructive habits.* Why do people continue to gamble money they cannot afford to lose, in the face of proven odds that their mathematical expectation (the algebraic sum of their possible gains and losses, each multiplied by its probability of happening) is always of loss? In the case of state-sponsored lotteries, for example, the state announces in advance that something like one half the proceeds will be taken by the state and only the remainder distributed as prizes. Yet millions of people invest; in one instance a municipality close to bankruptcy did so. Skinner's explanation is that rewards for gambling, when they come, are immediate and powerful, whereas losses are long-term, thus more attenuated in their effect. The immediacy of the rewards can be shown by laboratory studies to have a more powerful effect than the long-term punishment of financial losses.

A somewhat similar analysis probably explains at least some cases of drug addiction. The "rush" that follows imbibing or smoking or injecting drugs is far more potent as a reinforcer than the long-term negative consequences, according to this theory, partly because it comes so fast after taking the drug. The high is immediate; the hangover does not come till the next day.

*The self and self-control.* The concept of self, according to Skinner, is "simply a device for representing a functionally unified system of responses" (Skinner, 1953, p. 285). What unifies the system of responses may be a discriminated stimulus, such as behaving differently with one's family than with business associates; a reinforcer, such as food or a sexual object; some emotion; or a drug, for example. However, the concept of self encourages one to overestimate the unity of behavior.

Self-control eventually must be accounted for by variables outside the self, he states. (Note that Skinner is here assuming his conclusion.) For the most part, people control themselves the same way they control children, by changing the stimulus, by depriving themselves of reinforcement, by interposing aversive stimuli, and so on. Self-punishment is accounted for by the fact that it permits the person to escape a more aversive condition, namely, guilt feelings.

Self-control refers to responses organized around primary reinforcers. Social conscience and superego are nothing but names for behavior working to the advantage of the community, according to Skinner. Antisocial personality, correspondingly, is nothing but a name for behavior where the competition between people for the available reinforcers makes the behavior so labeled aversive to others.

Skinner does not deny the existence of what psychoanalysts call repression, but he reinterprets it in his own terms. When a certain behavior in a child is punished, he says, the child learns to engage in competing behavior instead of the punished behavior. Then the child may stop thinking about the behavior that was punished, because the memory is unpleasant. Then the child or person may go further and deny having behaved in the way that was punished, even in the face of proof to the contrary. That is *repression.* Thus repression is nothing but competing behavior that avoids aversive stimulation, according to Skinner.

Skinner has not just renamed ideas gleaned from earlier behaviorists. He has redefined them carefully in line with his own view of what constitutes rigorously scientific psychology. Further, by means of ingenious experiments, he has demonstrated a number of new and interesting phenomena. His view of scientific psychology and of human nature and his experimental discoveries have implications for the psychology of personality. Skinner not only points that out but goes further and finds political implications (Skinner, 1953). But his views on topics such as the self, culture, and social systems are a kind of folk wisdom, chatty and discursive. They are applications of his philosophy, but they contain almost no direct references to experiments, even his own, and certainly not to other contemporary experimental work.

---

## OBJECTIONS TO RADICAL BEHAVIORISM

Perhaps no other psychological theory can account for as much of actual, day-to-day behavior as the theory of operant conditioning. But every theory has its limits, and radical behaviorism is a big enough target to attract many arrows.

### Breland and Breland on Instinctive Drift

Keller Breland left Skinner's laboratory to pursue a career in shaping animal behavior, using the techniques that he, Skinner, and others had worked out. "We have controlled a wide range of animal behavior. . . . Conditioned behavior has been exhibited at various municipal zoos and museums of natural history and has been used for department store displays, for fair and trade convention exhibits, for entertainment at tourist attractions, on television shows, and in the production of television commercials. Thirty-eight species, totaling over 6,000 individual animals, have been conditioned" (Breland & Breland, 1961, p. 681), including reindeer, cockatoos, raccoons, porpoises, and whales. Reinforced by their successes, they departed from established laboratory procedures. In so doing, they began encountering a pattern of failures, of which they recount several at length.

Because raccoons condition easily, have hands about like primates, and have good appetites, the Brelands set out to teach one, a tame and eager subject, to pick up coins and deposit them in a five-inch metal box. First the subject was reinforced for picking up one coin. Then the metal box was introduced; the raccoon was supposed to drop the coin in it. "He seemed to have a great deal of trouble letting go of the coin. He would rub it up against the inside of the container, pull it back out, and clutch it firmly for several seconds. However, he would finally turn it loose and receive his food reinforcement" (ibid., p. 682). Finally, the animal was supposed to pick up and deposit both coins in order to receive food. "Not only could he not let go of the coins, but he spent seconds, even minutes, rubbing them together . . . and dipping them into the container. . . . The rubbing behavior became worse and worse as time went on, in spite of nonreinforcement" (ibid., p. 682).

In a similar experiment, pigs were taught to pick up large wooden coins and carry them several feet to deposit in a "piggy bank." Pigs have ravenous appetites, condition readily, and are able to take ratios. Therefore the Brelands set about to establish a ratio of four or five coins deposited per reinforcement. Problems developed in pig after pig. "At first the pig would eagerly pick up one dollar, carry it to the bank, run back, get another, carry it rapidly and neatly, and so on, until the ratio was complete. Thereafter, over a period of weeks, the behavior would become slower and slower. He might run over eagerly for each dollar, but on the way back, instead of carrying the dollar and depositing it simply and cleanly, he would repeatedly drop it, root it, drop it again, root it along the way, pick it up, toss it up in the air, drop it, root it some more, and so on" (ibid., p. 683). Finally the problem behavior interfered with the conditioned behavior to the extent that the pigs would not get enough to eat during the day; increasing their hunger made matters worse. Similar problems were encountered in chickens, hamsters, porpoises, whales, cows, and so on. In each instance, the animals substituted for the reinforced behavior their own instinctive pattern, at the cost of greater effort and longer time before reinforcement. Increasing drive intensified the effect.

Such failures of prediction and control could not be accounted for within the tenets of behaviorism. Breland and Breland label the effects they have observed *instinctive drift*. "It can easily be seen that these particular behaviors to which the animals drift are clear-cut examples of instinctive behaviors having to do with the natural food getting behaviors of the particular species" (ibid., p. 683). The raccoon's behavior is called "washing behavior" and may result in removing the exoskeleton of crayfish. The pigs' rooting and shaking are part of their food-getting repertoire. Breland and Breland summarize their conclusion as "wherever an animal has strong instinctive behaviors in the area of the conditioned response, after continued running the organism will drift toward the instinctive behavior to the detriment of the conditioned behavior and even to the delay or preclusion of the reinforcement" (ibid., p. 684), or, in brief, "learned behavior drifts toward instinctive behavior." Their experiments contradict what they identify as the implicit assumptions of behaviorism, that animals enter the laboratory as more or less blank slates on which the experimenter can write, that species differences are not great, and that one can condition almost any response to almost any stimulus. The concept of instinct, whose banishment was one of the original aims of behaviorism, thus comes back into psychology.

### Intrinsic Motivation

Although the criticisms that Breland and Breland make of behaviorism are effective, in principle the facts can probably be accommodated within a strictly behavioristic paradigm. Skinner, for example, never denied the role of heredity in determining the individual's behavior. Instincts simply could be acknowledged as parameters of conditioned behavior.

It is harder to see how behaviorism can absorb any proof that raising motivation may actually decrease how much is learned. But that is the thesis of a recent line of research. To recount the relevant studies and reasoning takes the discussion into the relation of behavior and cognition. That is a realm all its own, and the topic is deferred therefore to Chapter 5.

## Chomsky's Criticism

In the introduction of this chapter, language was mentioned as a particularly difficult area for behavioristic systems to explain. Skinner met the challenge forthrightly many years ago with a book on what he calls verbal behavior, his name for language and linguistics (Skinner, 1957). In a lengthy review of the book, Noam Chomsky mounted one of the severest criticisms of Skinner's entire system (Chomsky, 1959).

Consider the problem of how language is acquired. At first it appears to be obvious that children learn language by copying older children and adults whom they hear speak. Recent studies have shown that the situation is not that simple. A small child, commenting on where Daddy has disappeared to, will normally say something like "Daddy go office." That is, at first the child will use only present tense, whether the adults around him adapt their own speaking to his style or not. When the child first learns the past tense, he is likely to say something like "Daddy go-ed office." Now, although adults may use present tense in speaking to the child, they will not form the past tense of the irregular verb *to go* as if it were a regular verb.

Children learn whatever language is spoken by those about them; so no one maintains that any words are innate. What Chomsky argues is rather that they are born with the potentiality to construct certain grammatical rules that apply to all languages (Chomsky, 1959). The explanation for a sentence like "Daddy go-ed to office" (or one little boy's proud declaration, "I knewed it") is that the child does not learn language word by word but rather masters the rules needed to generate a vast number of sentences, few of which he or she has ever heard anyone speak. The rule for forming the past tense for regular verbs is mastered before the child learns even common irregular forms of verbs. This argument is part of Chomsky's case against Skinner's behaviorism.

Skinner begins from a base of experiments on bar pressing and key pecking. Terms such as *stimulus, response,* and *stimulus control* (meaning control of behavior by the immediate stimulus) are borrowed from that situation and applied to the everyday life of people as if the terms could be used with the same meanings. But, says Chomsky, the terms shift in meaning, so that there is almost no resemblance between the way the terms are used in the animal laboratory and the way they are applied to everyday human life. Those terms, which Skinner uses to give a seemingly objective description of the development and use of language, are at best metaphorical, cloaking commonsense mentalistic ideas in pseudo-objective terms.

Chomsky gives as an example of the elusiveness of Skinner's concepts that he leans heavily on self-reinforcement by people to show the ubiquity of reinforcement as potential explanation of behavior. But when Skinner says that a person is reinforced by X, he clearly means that the person wants X, or likes X, or is interested in X, or something of that sort, as Chomsky demonstrates by examples. So mentalistic references are not at all eliminated, merely disguised by a change of terms. In fact, substituting reinforcement for wanting, liking, being interested in, and so on introduces unnecessary ambiguity.

Skinner's refusal to consider what is in the black box of the mind rules out any real understanding of what is happening when children learn to talk. There is no basis in his or anyone's research nor is there any conclusive argument to support his claim that language learning can be accounted for by pure reinforcement and need not invoke any contribution from the person.

If Skinner's terms of *stimulus, response, stimulus control*, and *reinforcement* are taken literally, says Chomsky, they cover almost none of verbal behavior. If they are taken as metaphors, then they offer no improvement over traditional explanations of language learning.

---

## REFERENCES

Allport, G. W. (1960). The open system in personality theory. In *Personality and social encounter: Selected essays* (pp. 39–54). Boston; Beacon Press.

Bentham, J. (1962). Introduction to the principles of morals and legislation. In M. Warnock (Ed.), *John Stuart Mill: Utilitarianism, On liberty, essay on Bentham, together with selected writings of Jeremy Bentham and John Austin* (pp. 33–77). Cleveland: World Publishing. (Original work published 1789.)

Bower, G. H., & Hilgard, E. R. (1981). *Theories of learning.* (5th ed.). Englewood Cliffs, NJ: Prentice-Hall.

Breland, K., & Breland, M. (1961). The misbehavior of organisms. *American Psychologist, 16,* 681–684.

Chomsky, N. (1959). Review of *Verbal behavior* by B. F. Skinner. *Language, 35,* 26–58.

Ferster, C. S., & Skinner, B. F. (1957). *Schedules of reinforcement.* New York: Appleton-Century-Crofts.

Freud, S. (1953). *On aphasia.* New York: International Universities Press. (Original work published 1891.)

Jones, M. C. (1924). A laboratory study of fear: The case of Peter. *Pedagogical Seminary, 31,* 308–315.

Jones, M. C. (1974). Albert, Peter, and John B. Watson. *American Psychologist, 29,* 581–583.

Knoll, E. (1986). The science of language and the evolution of mind: Max Müller's quarrel with Darwinism. *Journal of the History of the Behavioral Sciences, 22,* 3–22.

McDougall, W. (1928). *An introduction to social psychology* (enlarged ed.). London: Methuen. (Original work published 1908.)

Mill, J. S. (1962). Bentham. In M. Warnock (Ed.), *John Stuart Mill: Utilitarianism, On liberty, essay on Bentham, together with selected writings of Jeremy Bentham and John Austin* (pp. 78–125). Cleveland: World Publishing. (Original work published 1838.)

Mill, J. S. (1962). On liberty. In M. Warnock (Ed.), *John Stuart Mill: Utilitarianism, On liberty, essay on Bentham, together with selected writings of Jeremy Bentham and John Austin* (pp. 126–250). Cleveland: World Publishing. (Original work published 1859.)

Mill, J. S. (1962). Utilitarianism. In M. Warnock (Ed.), *John Stuart Mill: Utilitarianism, On liberty, essay on Bentham, together with selected writings of Jeremy Bentham and John Austin* (pp. 251–321). Cleveland: World Publishing. (Original work published 1863.)

Müller, F. M. (1861). *Lectures on the science of language.* London: Longmans Green.

Pavlov, I. P. (1927). *Conditioned reflexes.* London: Clarendon Press.

Pavlov, I. P. (1941). *Conditioned reflexes and psychiatry.* New York: International Publishers.

Robinson, D. N. (1982). *Toward a science of human nature.* New York: Columbia University Press.

Romanes, G. J. (1884). *Mental evolution in animals.* London: Kegan Paul, Trench.

Romanes, G. J. (1888). *Mental evolution in man.* London: Kegan Paul, Trench.

Samelson, F. (1980). J. B. Watson's Little Albert, Cyril Burt's twins, and the need for a critical science. *American Psychologist, 35,* 619–625.

Skinner, B. F. (1953). *Science and human behavior.* New York: Free Press.

Skinner, B. F. (1956). A case history in scientific method. *American Psychologist, 11,* 221–233.

Skinner, B. F. (1957). *Verbal behavior.* Englewood Cliffs, NJ: Prentice-Hall.

Skinner, B. F. (1958). Reinforcement today. *American Psychologist, 15,* 94–99.

Skinner, B. F. (1971). *Beyond freedom and dignity.* New York: Knopf.

Thorndike, E. L. (1898). Animal intelligence: An experimental study of the associative processes in animals. *Psychological Review, Monograph Supplement, 2* (8).

Thorndike, E. L. (1911). *Animal intelligence.* New York; Macmillan.

Thorndike, E. L., & others. (1927). *The measurement of intelligence.* New York: Bureau of Publications, Teachers College, Columbia University.

Warnock, M. (1962). Introduction. In M. Warnock (Ed.), *John Stuart Mill: Utilitarianism, On liberty, essay on Bentham, together with selected writings of Jeremy Bentham and John Austin* (pp. 7–31). Cleveland: World Publishing.

Watson, J. B. (1919). *Psychology from the standpoint of a behaviorist.* Philadelphia: J. B. Lippincott.

Watson, J. B., & Rayner, R. (1920). Conditioned emotional reactions. *Journal of Experimental Psychology, 3,* 1–14.

# CHAPTER 4

# The Psychometric Approach: Traits

In everyday speech the term *personality* is often used as an expression for what is unique and individual about a person. Individual differences in personality are obvious; those differences are referred to in terms of traits. Characterizing persons in terms of trait differences is as old as recorded thought. In the *Iliad*, Homer referred to "long-suffering brilliant Odysseus" and "Achilleus of the swift feet."

Individual differences as part of the science of personality involves something more and quite different from those ancient observations. Doing psychological research on traits necessarily implies that one has some way of measuring or at least classifying traits; so the study of personality traits requires some introduction to the topic of measurement in psychology.

This book arbitrarily casts diverse, major approaches to personality in the format of Kuhn's model of scientific paradigms. Although the psychometric-trait approach to personality is considered by its enthusiastic practitioners to be the quintessentially scientific approach to personality, it is the hardest of the book's topics to squeeze into the mold, not so much because it is unscientific as because it is not entirely successful. Kuhn's model assumes at least an initial success, a great discovery.

If there is a great discovery, it is simply that measurement is possible in psychology. Thus the first question is how the idea of psychological measurement ever came to be accepted, in the face of longstanding belief that such measurement was impossible and philosophically absurd.

Psychological tests did not spring fullblown from the heads of modern psychologists. The possibility entered by a roundabout route, beginning with measurements only peripheral to psychology of personality and with statistical ideas in biology.

## BACKGROUND OF PSYCHOLOGICAL MEASUREMENT

### Is the Psyche Measurable?

There has always been a theme among philosophers and humanistic thinkers that psychology, the realm of the human spirit, is apart from science. Science is experimental, mathematical, and intersubjectively observable. The human soul is none of those and hence is immune to scientific observation. The problem was compounded among Continental philosophers of the nineteenth century by the fact that there was a single word for the soul and the mind in German *(Seele)* and in French *(l'âme)* (Boring, 1950), thus making the distinction between mind and soul hard even to name.

Goethe, among his many professions, was a psychologist with a respected phenomenological theory of color vision. He castigated Newton's theory of color vision, based on the wave lengths of colored light. According to Goethe, those numerical values are just what color is not.

Kant stated that space and time are the framework of all experience. Therefore, they cannot possibly be constructed from experience. Thus he opposed the belief that permeated the thinking of John Locke and subsequent British empiricists that all knowledge comes from experience. Moreover, Kant stated specifically that there cannot be a science of psychology, because science requires observations in space and time, whereas mental events occur in time but not in space (Kant, 1786/1970). Mental events, he said, cannot be measured, and measurement is necessary for science.

In the early nineteenth century, philosophers and physiologists believed that because the soul is unitary and indivisible, voluntary action must be virtually instantaneous. Therefore, the speed of psychological processes could not be measured. In 1850 von Helmholtz measured the speed of the nerve impulse in the frog's leg, showing it to be slower than the speed of sound, rather than faster than the speed of light, as some physiologists had hypothesized. That was an opening wedge for the idea of measuring in psychology (Boring, 1929, p. 42).

Boring outlined four main sources of measurement in psychology: psychophysics, reaction times, learning theory, and individual differences and statistics (Boring, 1961). The main concern of theory of personality is of course the last, but in passing landmarks of the other areas may be noted. G. T. Fechner's work on psychophysics used the just noticeable difference as the unit for quantifying sensation, which phenomenologists previously assumed was not quantifiable (Fechner, 1860).

Differences in reaction times had been noted in the eighteenth century by astronomers trying to record the exact time of the passage of certain stars, but they had called the differences errors. In the nineteenth century those differences were recognized as an instance of legitimate individual differences and studied under the heading of the *personal equation* of the observer. An elaborate algebra grew up around this field: The time for a simple reaction was subtracted from the time for a more complex reaction as a way of estimating the time taken to process the complexities. That was a neat way to quantify mental operations, but the premise proved false. People do not approach a complex problem in terms of its simpler constituents in the way that theory implied.

The study of learning evolved many more or less indirect methods of measuring. Beginning with H. Ebbinghaus's 1885 study of memory, those methods included the trials taken to master a list of nonsense syllables, the time that forgetting takes, the savings of time when relearning forgotten material, and so on (Ebbinghaus, 1885/1913). Other methods of measurement were mentioned in Chapter 3, including strength of conditioned response (e.g., amount of saliva), number of errors per trial, and rate of response per unit of time. Each of these methods defines a kind of psychological measurement.

### Origins of Statistics

The idea of a population appears first in the work of John Graunt, a seventeenth-century London tradesman. He published tables of births and deaths in London covering the years 1604 to 1661 (Graunt, 1662/1956). On the insistence of King Charles II, who recognized the value of these tables, Graunt was elected to the Royal Academy of Science despite his low social status.

Actuarial tables essentially like those used today began with the work of Edmund Halley, the seventeenth century English astronomer who discovered the famous comet. Halley recognized that actuarial tables usable for insurance purposes needed to be based on a population without much in- or out-migration. For that purpose he chose the Polish city of Breslau (modern Wroclaw) (Halley, 1693/1956). His work shows how practical problems inspired advances in statistics.

The idea of probability is even older than the idea of population, and games of chance provided part of the impetus for probability theory. The seventeenth-century Swiss mathematician Jacob Bernoulli proved the law of large numbers, which is the basis for our confidence that by increasing the size of a sample, we increase the likely accuracy of statistics derived from the sample. The French mathematician Pierre Laplace published a famous essay on the laws of probability in 1814.

Probably the greatest mathematical genius of all time was the nineteenth-century German Carl Friedrich Gauss. The normal curve of distribution, ubiquitous in psychology, is often called the Gaussian distribution. Gauss used this distribution to describe errors of scientific observers, and it is often called the normal law of error. The Belgian astronomer Adolphe Quetelet was the first to apply the normal law to physical traits and social data in humans in 1835. The implication was that nature aims at an ideal, the mean value represents that ideal, and the variations are nature's errors (Boring, 1929, p. 468). Thus the normal curve did not begin as a way of describing people but as a property of certain statistical distributions. There is nothing abnormal about a distribution that does not follow the normal curve.

Some statistical concepts that apply specifically to psychological tests are introduced briefly in Appendix B.

## INDIVIDUAL DIFFERENCES

In the late eighteenth century, Thomas Malthus, a British economist, wrote a treatise on the relation between overpopulation and food supply and coined the phrase the *struggle for existence*. Darwin, who influenced psychology in many ways, took up Malthus's idea and added the idea of variation as an essential condition for the occurrence of evolution. Overpopulation, variation among individual members, struggle for existence, and survival of the fittest became key terms in Darwin's theory of evolution (Darwin, 1859). Thus individual variation is embedded in the theory of evolution, a central tenet of most biological science since Darwin. The question for psychology was how to conceptualize and describe individual variation.

## Faculties

In the nineteenth century the prevailing view of the organization of the mind was based on its division into several *faculties*, such as will, intellect, imagination, and so on. The faculties included both what would be called abilities and personality traits. (Alfred Binet's initial list of faculties is given below.) The list varied from author to author, and there was no accepted way to decide on a final list. That was one weakness in the approach. Indeed, until 1838, when Jean E. D. Esquirol, a French psychiatrist, published a book on mental disorders, there was not even a clear distinction drawn between feeblemindedness and mental illness (Goodenough, 1949). As recently as the first two decades of the twentieth century there was confusion between mental illness, delinquency, and feeblemindedness, even among some psychologists.

Some eighteenth- and nineteenth-century physiologists, notably Franz Joseph Gall and his student Johann K. Spurzheim, believed that the relative predominance of any faculty could be assessed by the shape of the skull (Boring, 1929, p. 49). Assessment of intelligence and personality by head contour was known as *phrenology*. Phrenology, we now know, was based on a number of errors. The shape of the skull gives no clue to the shape of the brain except in rare cases of extreme pathology. And the shape of the brain similarly gives no clue to the nature of personality or intelligence. Gall and Spurzheim at least were correct, however, in locating intelligence in the brain, which was not taken for granted in their time. The problem of localization of function within the brain continues to be important, but nothing in present-day psychology or brain physiology justifies either the idea of faculties or their location in specific parts of the brain.

If not by skull shape, how can any psychological characteristics be assessed? What are the basic characteristics worth measuring? In what terms, that is, should personality be described? Those are the questions that have persisted for the psychology of personality.

## Galton and the Biometric Approach

Francis Galton, the last of the great nonprofessional English scientists, could be called the founder of the scientific study of individual differences. He came from a distinguished family; Darwin was a first cousin. Galton's explorations of Africa as a young man led to an interest in anthropology and thence to differential psychology. His interests included many problems: intellectual distinction, inheritance of psychological characteristics (1869), eugenics, imagery (1883), and association of ideas. Galton invented the standard score, that is, expressing a person's score on any measure in terms of its deviation from the mean of the group, divided by the standard deviation of the group. Because deviations from average were considered "nature's errors" in striving for an ideal or average type, Galton's approach was needed. It dignified individual differences, raising them to the status of facts worth studying (Dunnette & Kirchner, 1965).

Galton was impressed with Locke's empiricist epistemology, which asserted (to put it too simply) that everything in the mind had to come through the senses. (An opposing view is that people are born already possessing certain innate ideas.) But if everything comes through the senses, Galton reasoned, it must follow that the most capable individuals have the most acute senses. The fact that the lowest grade of idiots often have sensory defects seemed to confirm this line of thinking. Some such reasoning encouraged Galton, and later others, to try to measure intelligence by sensorimotor tests, such as tests of discrimination and reaction time, which were similar to methods then being used in experimental psychology. Galton probably was the first to use a psychological questionnaire (DuBois, 1970); he invented the association test, in which the subject is given a list of words and writes after each one the first word he thinks of (Peterson, 1925).

By appropriate measurement, Galton thought, the most capable individuals could be selected and then rewarded for marrying and having children; the least capable and most dangerous could somehow be discouraged from reproducing. Criminality and feeblemindedness were believed to be closely connected; Galton would have been astounded by the cleverness of modern computerized crime. He was one of the founders of the eugenics movement.

In the belief that superior intelligence would be accompanied by superior physical vigor and other observable physical signs, Galton gave a wide battery of physical tests to more than nine thousand visitors to the London Exhibition (world's fair) of 1884. To his disappointment, measurements of eminent scientists did not reveal any superiority to the general population in head size, strength of grip, and other such characteristics. Thus this early attempt to find rigorously measurable characteristics that are a clue to intelligence was a failure.

In the course of studying inheritance, Galton measured heights of fathers and their adult sons, and he invented the idea of correlation to express the relation between the two sets of measures. The term *regression toward the mean,* which is still used in statistics, comes from his description of the relation of the son's height to the father's height. The sons of exceptionally tall men will be taller than average but on average not as tall as their fathers; hence, they regress to the mean. The corresponding observation holds for sons of exceptionally short men, and, of course, the same is true of other inherited traits that depend on several genes. Such statements, of course, apply to group trends and are not predictive of particular cases. This result is purely a statistical artifact, though the term *regression* may mislead one to suspect a physical cause. The *product-moment coefficient,* the most often-used measure of the relation between two variables, was proposed by Galton's student Karl Pearson.

### The Genetic Approach

Students of genetics and heredity in the early years of the twentieth century divided mainly into two groups — those like Pearson who advocated statistical, or as they called them, biometric, methods of study of human characteristics, and those who were committed to studying inheritance in terms of the nine-teenth-century Austrian botanist Gregor Mendel's recently rediscovered ideas about genes. The latter group went so far at times as to advocate that mental defect was determined by a single gene. Both groups yielded for many years a large number of advocates for sterilization of humans. Several thousand persons were sterilized in the United States in an attempt to improve the quality of the racial stock (Gould, 1981).

Sterilization proved to entail many risks, and the public eventually revolted against it. One objection was that it was applied in a discriminatory way. Candidates for sterilization were all drawn from public institutions that served the lower classes and minority races; equally retarded persons in private institutions were not sterilized. A second objection was that the science on which the proposals for race improvement were based was at best flimsy. An example of such unscientific thinking is that many different conditions were lumped together in the category of the feebleminded, including prostitution, drug addiction, and so on. Such people may not have been fit parents, but others do not have to pass a test to become parents. Those miscellaneous defects were in most cases unlikely to be inherited by their offspring.

Even in the case of a defect caused by a single gene, such as Huntington's disease, sterilization can be appropriately applied only to those who display the defect, who must thus be homozygous for the recessive gene. Heterozygous individuals have no sign of the disease and usually have normal offspring. Moreover, the recessive gene may be widespread in the population, even in families that do not know they carry it. For a characteristic such as intelligence, which depends on many genes, the possibility of improvement in the racial stock in a few generations is chimerical, even with a drastic sterilization policy. The final blow to any enthusiasm for sterilization was Hitler's policy of mass sterilization, often of perfectly normal persons of persecuted groups, such as Jews and gypsies, and of persons with minor defects such as club feet.

---

## MEASUREMENT OF ABILITY

### Early Mental Tests

In the early years of experimental psychology a century ago, appropriate subjects for study were normal, white, adult men. Wilhelm Wundt, a German scientist generally considered the founder of modern scientific psychology, did not welcome the study of individual differences. Nonetheless, J. McKeen Cattell, an American who did his graduate work with Wundt, took individual differences as his dissertation topic, influenced by Galton's work in England. He probably was the first to use the terms *individual differences* and *mental tests* (Cattell, 1890). He became the first official professor of psychology in the United States, first at the University of Pennsylvania and then for many years at Columbia University.

Cattell argued that each intelligent action must begin with a sensation and include memory and response. On this basis, he proposed a series of tests, mostly sensory and motor but a few of a more psychological nature. They included rate of movement, strength of grip (dynamometer pressure), and number of letters remembered after a single hearing, for example. He reasoned that the sum of many such tests would correlate with a college student's academic standing.

Clark Wissler, a student of Cattell's, studied the data Cattell had collected on a large sample of Columbia University students, using the kind of tests the theory called for (Wissler, 1901). The tests correlated with college grades no better than chance. Similar results were obtained by other investigators. Consequently, mental tests fell into disrepute for a while. Nonetheless, based on his background in experimental methods, Cattell had introduced the idea of clear standardization of testing conditions, and he had established one important principle: No matter how carefully laboratory conditions are controlled, individual differences in performance remain.

During the same period, Ebbinghaus in Germany was critical of psychologists for failing to study complex mental processes. He studied human memory and opposed breaking down complex processes into elemental sensory and motor components, as Galton and Cattell had been doing. Most of his experiments on memory were on himself, so individual differences were not his topic. He also invented the completion test, however, which is still in use in modified form (Ebbinghaus, 1897).

### Individual Tests

One of psychology's major practical accomplishments, however flawed it may be in the eyes of social critics, has been individual tests of intelligence. Alfred Binet was the major innovator, although probably Lewis M. Terman should be given more credit than he usually is. David Wechsler extended individual testing to adults.

*Binet's test of general intelligence.* By far the most important of the psychologists working on the higher mental processes was Binet, a versatile French psychologist who did research on topics ranging from hypnotism to inkblots, from graphology to memory in chess players. He studied his young daughters extensively, recording differences between them that would now be called introversion versus extraversion (Binet, 1902). His chief interests, however, were in mental deficiency and mental measurement.

Binet and his student Victor Henri published in 1896 a paper containing a series of tests of eleven different mental faculties or processes: memory, mental imagery, imagination, attention, comprehension, suggestibility, esthetic appreciation, will as measured by muscular effort, moral sentiments, motor skill, and spatial judgment. That is a typical list of faculties. (Note the absence of the usual modern categories of verbal and mathematical abilities.) Each faculty was measured by a number of different tests, in order to cover different aspects. Thus Binet began, as was to be expected, with an approach typical of the faculty psychology of his day.

He introduced early, however, an innovation, namely, testing the tests. Each test was evaluated in terms of whether it discriminated between children of different ages and school grades and also between children the teachers considered bright and those they considered dull. By these criteria some tests proved to be better than others. Over a period of years he tried out many kinds of tasks, continuing to select those that discriminated well and dropping those that did not.

Binet did not begin with a rigorous definition of intelligence, which he then translated into a scientific instrument. That would better describe the approach of Cattell, whose tests finally proved of no value for estimating intelligence. Binet began with a commonsense conception that intelligence included reasoning, judgment, and comprehension. He correctly perceived that the simple tasks Cattell proposed did not tap this stratum of mind. He understood, too, that he was not measuring intelligence in any strict sense and that intelligence was manifest in different special ways in different persons (Peterson, 1925, p. 142).

Binet published several articles in 1901 on head measurements in relation to intelligence. Galton by then was convinced that there was no relation, but many other psychologists still believed in a close connection. Binet discovered that the head measurements a psychologist obtained for pupils identified by their teachers as bright or not bright depended partly on which hypothesis the research worker believed. (This topic, the effect of the *experimenter's bias* on the results obtained, has been a lively subject for investigation in recent years.) Binet therefore did his study, again with children chosen from the extremes of the distribution, making sure that he had no clue as to which children had been identified as more or less intelligent. In a total of about 250 children, he found those of superior intelligence had on average slightly bigger head measurements, but that the difference was not consistent enough to be of any value in estimation of intelligence. On the basis of these and later studies, Binet concluded that the physical appearance of intelligence can be deceptive and that intuitive impressions must be guarded against (Gould, 1981).

In 1904, when the French government became concerned about the problems caused by mental defectives in school classes, Binet was the person they called on for help. In response, Binet and his colleague Theodore Simon put together their first Binet-Simon scale, which is the ancestor of most tests of general intelligence now in use (Binet & Simon, 1905).

This test differed in several ways from previous attempts to measure intelligence. First and most important, each subtest was chosen to tap a higher mental process, as opposed to simple sensorimotor skills, reaction times, or bodily or cranial measures that most other psychologists were then using. These tests had been developed over a period of years by Binet, Ebbinghaus, and others.

The second innovation was that the 1905 scale was the first to be composed of a battery of tests. That reflected Binet's insight that because of the complexity of intellectual functions, no single test, however good, would suffice (Peterson, 1925).

Third, Binet and Simon gave up the idea of mental faculties as a guide to testing ability. The subtests were arranged in order of difficulty, mixing together all the different types — memory, reasoning, vocabulary, and so on — rather than having all the memory tests together, all the reasoning tests together, and all the vocabulary items together. This was a retreat from the idea of rigorous measurement of each separate faculty, in the direction of practical classification of the child's general level of development, as Binet was aware. The score was a kind of average of several quite different subtests; individuals who obtained the same overall score might have quite different patterns of abilities.

Fourth, each subtest was scored right or wrong, according to whether performance reached an arbitrary standard. That contrasted with most other tests, each of which yielded a quantitative measure, such as time to finish, strength of grip, number of errors, and so on. Most previous psychological tests registered some actual physical quantity.

Finally, each subtest in the Binet-Simon scale had to be justified by simultaneously passing a series of criteria, including improvement with age and school grade and differentiation between children whom the teachers regarded as bright or dull. Within a single school grade, Binet assumed that the oldest and largest children would generally be less bright than the others, because they presumably had been held back. Thus each test of intelligence should show improvement (positive correlation) with age when all children are considered, but, in effect, a negative correlation with age when only the children from a given class are considered. The simultaneous use of several criteria for choice of subtests anticipates what is today called construct validation. *Construct validity* refers to evidence that the test actually measures the trait or construct that the psychologist set out to measure. (See Appendix B.)

In 1908 Binet and Simon brought out a revision of their scale, this time with another major innovation, the concept of mental age (MA). For most school ages the test included five subtests, chosen so that average children of the given age could usually pass them. Each child was to be given the tests from an age where he or she passed all, or all but one, to an age where he or she failed all, with the credit for intermediate ages determined by how many subtests were right. (A refinement of that scheme is still in use.) The mental age was determined to be approximately the age for which the tested child would match the performance of the average child. Mental age obviously is a more meaningful reference score than simply the number of subtests passed.

Because Binet measured vaguer, more elusive higher mental processes, which were not resolved into their supposed component elements, because many of his tests were scored pass-fail rather than in terms of a physical quantity, and because he did not make use of elaborate scientific apparatus, Binet's methods were scorned as unscientific by many experimental psychologists. "If we can't be more scientific than that," they seemed to say, "we'd rather not measure intelligence at all." Ironically, today it is the inheritors of the Binet tradition of mental testing who seem to be saying that to the proponents of projective tests.

*Terman and the IQ.* In the United States, Lewis Terman was working on many of the same ideas at more or less the same time as Binet. He adapted Binet's methods, added some subtests of his own, and added a significant new idea, the intelligence quotient, or IQ, which had been proposed by Wilhelm Stern (1912), a German psychologist. Stern had noted that what it meant for a child to be two years ahead in mental age (MA) depended on the child's chronological age (CA). It was more significant for a four-year-old to be two years advanced than for a ten-year-old. Similarly, two years retardation is more significant at four years than at ten. The ratio MA/CA takes this fact into account. (In practice, the IQ is taken as 100 MA/CA, in order to remove decimals.) Terman's (1916) Stanford-Binet test was the first to incorporate this measure. It also was the first mental test standardized on hundreds of average children (DuBois, 1970).

The significance of the IQ lies in the assumption that the rate of growth remains constant during childhood and adolescence. Although this measure has captured the popular fancy and is often spoken of as if it were as strictly measurable as height and as stable as eye color, it has no meaning in maturity. The functions measured by tests of intelligence do not change much between late adolescence and old or at least middle age, when they begin to decline; so there is no rate of growth to measure. People go on learning, but IQ tests are not intended to reflect what has been learned but something more like capacity for learning. Some tests now express their results in terms of the child's rank in his or her age cohort; again, the importance depends on the assumption, only approximately true, that each person will retain a proportionate place in relation to the age cohort. This assumption is equivalent to the assumption of the constant IQ. Notice that the mean IQ in the population must be about 100; that follows from the definition of MA.

The Stanford-Binet test has been revised three times (Terman & Merrill, 1937, 1960, 1973) and is currently being revised again. It has set the standard for individual tests of intelligence for many years. It was exemplary in the explicitness of instructions for administering and scoring. Small deviations in method of administration, such as giving little hints to the child as to correct answers or permitting the child's mother to remain in the testing room and give hints, can make a big difference in the score and hence are not permitted. The 1937 revision was standardized on the most comprehensive sampling of normal children that had been attempted to that time, and the 1960 version was an improvement. The 1973 version broadened the base of the standardization sample, including representatives of ethnic minorities for the first time. The standard deviation of IQ is about 16 for the 1960 version. That means that about two thirds of the children have IQs between 84 and 116. Although new insights were undoubtedly embodied in each revision, the main reason for the revisions is to bring the content of the test questions up to date.

Terman's interest in normal and superior children differed from Binet's focus on the retarded. It was soon established in many studies that the Stanford-Binet test predicted future school achievement better than previous tests had done.

Although some psychologists have interpreted the relative constancy of the IQ and its predictive power for school achievement as proving that intelligence is largely inherited, there is no necessary connection, and the problem of the relative importance of heredity and environment in determining intellectual status remains a contested question (see, e.g., L. A. Pervin, 1984).

While Binet and Simon were working out their tests, Charles Spearman, an English psychologist, was supplying a theoretical basis for the Binet type of test. Spearman's theory was that there is a general factor in intelligence, which he called $g$, which partially determines the score on any mental test whatsoever. In addition, the score on each subtest is partially determined by a factor specific to that test. By averaging many subtests, all with different content, the specific factors tend to average out, and the score is then determined almost entirely by general intelligence, which is exactly what is wanted (Spearman, 1904). The statistical proof of Spearman's proposition is powerful and depends for its application chiefly on the extent to which the specific factors really are different in each subtest. Even so small a thing as having all the subtests be paper-and-pencil tests would be a partial violation, though of course a minimal one, compared, say, to having all the subtests be arithmetic tests, or, for that matter, having all be verbal tests.

*Wechsler's test for adults.* Several intelligence tests made originally by the American psychologist David Wechsler but now revised by a corporation of psychologists are the major competition for the Stanford-Binet test. Wechsler profited from the years of experience with the Binet and Stanford-Binet tests to choose content somewhat similar, though there was some change to make the test suitable for adults (Wechsler, 1939). Because the IQ scale, being in the first instance a measure of the rate of growth, does not logically apply to adults (assuming that intellectual growth has stopped at maturity), Wechsler began his scale for adults using a point scale rather than an IQ scale. His format was in some respects like the pre-Binet one. The person is given all the subtest items of a given type in succession, say, all the vocabulary items, or all the items requiring memory for numbers. The points for each subtest are totaled, then translated into something called an IQ that is scaled so that the average person at any age has an IQ of 100 and 50 percent of the IQs fall between 90 and 110. (Note that the Wechsler tests do not use MA as an intermediate step in the computation.) The test yields a separate verbal IQ, performance IQ, and total IQ. There are now separate Wechsler scales for adults, school children, and preschool children.

One reason for his use of the format of subtests with common content running through several ages was that Wechsler hoped to extract additional information about each subject from the pattern of scores on the subtests. If, for example, a person does poorly on the verbal part of the scale but relatively well on the performance tests (arranging pictures in sequence to depict a story, copying a design made with a set of colored blocks, and the like), perhaps there is a language handicap that leads to underestimating the person's ability and potentiality. Some patterns may also, Wechsler thought, indicate an emotional rather than an intellectual handicap. Research results have failed, however, to verify the value of many such predictions, and the test is usually used as a measure of general, verbal, and performance ability.

## Group Tests

When the United States entered World War I in 1917, psychologists were look-ing for ways that their profession could aid the war effort. A group of leading psychologists, headed by Robert Yerkes, was given the task of constructing a quick method for screening incompetent recruits, and perhaps also specially competent ones as candidates for officer training. Arthur S. Otis had been working on a test for intelligence that could be given to a whole group at once, rather than administered individually, as the Stanford-Binet was. Yerkes's com-mittee, building on the work of Otis, devised the first widely used group test of intelligence, the Army Alpha test. The Army Beta was a performance test de-vised for use with illiterate or non-English-speaking recruits.

Recruits in 1917 and 1918 were generally given the Alpha or Beta test. One result was the widely publicized conclusion that the average American has the intelligence or mentality of a twelve-year-old. That conclusion, besides being not quite accurate (because the recruits tested turned out not to be a random sample of the population), is misleading. At worst, the conclusion ought to be that on the tasks included in the Alpha and Beta examinations, people on average reach their adult level by age twelve. More recent research has indicated that people reach their mature level on various subtests of the Stanford-Binet between fourteen and twenty-two years of age (Kleinmuntz, 1982, p. 321).

There have been many group tests of intelligence in recent years. Probably most school children in the United States today are subjected to at least one of them, and often more than one. Undoubtedly they are of great value for quick screening of large groups, but where a crucial decision about a child's future hangs in the balance, there is no substitute for an individual test, with an examiner observing and responding to the individual child.

## Special and Component Abilities

In the United States in the 1930s and 1940s there grew up a major school of thought regarding mental measurement that emphasized diverse abilities rather than general ability. The diverse abilities included different kinds of reasoning, verbal fluency, perceptual speed, and so on. The major figure was L. L. Thurstone, whose work depended heavily on the technique of *factor analysis,* a mathematical method of analyzing a large group of tests to find a smaller number of statistical groupings (Thurstone, 1935, 1947). Those statistical groups of tests are said to reveal the mental factors, or abilities, that must be postulated to account for the performance on the actual tests. For many years great claims were made for the power of factor analysis to reveal the structure of mind. This school of thought attracted most of the psychometrically and statistically qualified psychologists for many years. To this day, however, the results of their many large studies have led to few if any applications. Faced with the need for practical tests, such as college board examinations, psychologists usually stay with verbal and quantitative measures of general ability, or, for younger ages, verbal and performance tests. The distinction between verbal and quantitative abilities and between verbal and performance tests reflects common sense and pre-factor analytic wisdom rather than the results of recent factor analytic research.

Many problems concerning the measurement of abilities are still being studied and argued about by psychologists in that field. A relatively new branch of psychology, cognition, has led to new ways of looking at the components of intellectual performance (Sternberg, 1982, 1985). The failure of the psychologists before Binet to find an effective way to break the intelligent act into its component parts does not mean that the new analyses will fail, for they are based on sounder theory and much additional experimental evidence. However, psychologists will await evidence as to whether they result in tests of value in predicting school or other achievements.

In any event, measurement of general ability stands out as one of psychology's major tangible accomplishments. That success led to an extension of the methods into the field of personality, where they have been less successful.

## MEASUREMENT OF PERSONALITY

Measurement is the hallmark of most modern sciences, and inevitably psychologists were emboldened by their success in measuring general ability to try the more difficult task of measuring personality. Exactly how to translate methods from one field to the other has not been clear. Abilities and traits are not the same. Abilities in general increase with age, at least until maturity; not so with traits, which may have periods of increasing and of decreasing. Abilities rarely interfere with each other. Two abilities may be positively correlated or they may be uncorrelated, but they will rarely be negatively correlated. One can easily think of traits that are negatively correlated.

The term *objective* is usually applied to personality tests answered by making check marks on paper; thus the scoring is objective, no matter what the mental process of the subject taking the test. Projective tests are in free response form. They are more difficult to score but may bring out a richer picture of the subject's personality. There are other tests formats, too, but those are the major types.

### Objective Tests

The method of test construction for objective tests can vary widely, and the kind of test that results will be entirely different for different methods. Some tests have been made up by psychologists without use of any data, just using their common sense and general knowledge of their field. Other tests are constructed by rigorously empirical methods, sometimes with no consideration given to whether the resulting test makes theoretical sense.

*A priori scales.* One of the earliest personality tests was R. S. Woodworth's *Personal Data Sheet*, used during World War I as a partial substitute for a psychiatric interview to screen out maladjusted or mentally ill recruits (Woodworth, 1919). Each subject was asked a number of true-false questions. Most of the questions referred to obviously symptomatic behavior. The score was the number of symptoms admitted or claimed, as the case might be. This method of test construction, asking the subjects to report on their own symptomatic behavior and constructing a scoring key in advance of any data, was the usual method of creating personality tests for a number of years thereafter.

An early test of this type is the Bernreuter Personality Inventory, which purports to measure neuroticism, self-sufficiency, extraversion-introversion, and dominance-submission (Bernreuter, 1933). Thus, in addition to one scale measuring neuroticism, or pathology, it includes three scales measuring individual differences in ordinary personality traits. Probably more than a million copies of this test were sold, though there was little or no proof that the tests measured the traits proclaimed by the titles of the scoring keys. Many other tests of this type have been marketed over the years. Such tests probably were a large part of the reason that the American Psychological Association appointed a committee to establish minimum standards for tests sold to the public (American Psychological Association, 1954).

Certain problems surfaced repeatedly in all such tests. Many of the problems fall under the heading of *response bias,* which means a more or less automatic tendency to answer a certain way, regardless of the content of the item. Thus some people will say yes to almost anything asked them, whereas others tend to say no regardless of content. A subtler form of response bias, and a more pervasive one, is usually called, somewhat ungrammatically, *social desirability.* That is, some people habitually put up a good or socially approved front, not necessarily from a conscious desire to deceive, whereas others tend to exaggerate their peccadillos and foibles. There are circumstances, such as trying to evade being drafted into the military or trying to obtain a job, where one may consciously portray oneself specially favorably or unfavorably. Even where there is no conscious intention to deceive, people may unintentionally shade their answers in accord with their general tendency to either optimism or pessimism, self-depreciation or self-aggrandizement. Such problems are much less important in tests of ability, where most people, all but the most recalcitrant or incompetent ones, know that they are supposed to give the right answer and are more or less willing to cooperate with the tester.

An even more serious problem turned up in personality tests. With tests of ability, the tester can almost always distinguish the most capable from the least capable people, even if fine discriminations in the middle of the range are uncertain. That is not always true with tests of personality or of psychopathology. A psychopathic person may answer a test in a way that only the healthiest persons are expected to answer (Hathaway, 1939). Except in such obvious cases as where there is a foreign language problem, a sensory defect, or open defiance, a complete miss of that sort can hardly occur in ability testing. In personality tests, however, a person may appear especially healthy just because his pathology leads him to answer in a certain way.

*The MMPI: Its empirical derivation.* Of the objective personality tests descended from the Binet tradition, the most important is the Minnesota Multiphasic Personality Inventory (MMPI), whose chief authors have been Starke Hathaway, a psychologist; J. C. McKinley, a neuropsychiatrist; and later Paul E. Meehl, also a psychologist (Hathaway & McKinley, 1940; Meehl & Hathaway 1946). Many others have contributed to the thousands of studies using this test, and many subsequent tests are modified derivatives from it.

In starting out, Hathaway and McKinley had this problem: Psychiatrists interview incoming patients and then assign some diagnosis. That time-consuming process could be eliminated if an adequate test could be found that would perform the diagnostic evaluation. Many personality and diagnostic tests were in use; their questions partly overlapped. Hathaway and McKinley wanted to replace those tests with a single set of questions covering many areas. Furthermore, there was evidence that use of diagnostic labels varied greatly from one hospital or clinic to another. In some clinics, almost everyone was called schizophrenic, whereas other clinics that drew on similar populations labeled few people schizophrenics. The difference seemed to be mostly a matter of how the labels were applied. A test could help to standardize usage.

Hathaway and McKinley started by collecting all the questions they could find from every published psychiatric-intake interview and personality or social-attitude scale. Then they culled near duplicates, changed the wording on some so that yes would about as often be the healthy as the symptomatic answer, and added some questions to test whether the person was trying to put himself or herself in an improbably acceptable or unacceptable light. Their original pool of more than 1,000 questions was reduced to just over 500. All of the items were put into simple English to make the test intelligible to people with minimal education.

Each item was typed on a separate small card. To take the test, the subject sorted the cards into three boxes, marked True, False, and Cannot Say. The purpose of having the subject handle the cards was to direct attention to each item separately; however, the test is most often given now as an ordinary paper-and-pencil test with an answer sheet, and it is often scored by machine. (Computer administration of tests is the next step, now becoming common-place.)

The "multiphasic" in the test's title stands for the fact that it was intended from the beginning to be a multiple-score test. It is intended to serve for a number of diagnostic decisions, just as an interview is. The decision with respect to each of the several diagnoses is supposed to depend on a separate scale, or scoring key. Items on all the various topics are randomly intermixed. Each score on the test reflects how the subject does on a particular subset of items, which do not occur together but are scattered throughout the test. Which items should be considered together to constitute a scoring key, or scale, was determined empirically, with reference to empirical data, not according to any advance theory. In that way, the MMPI reflects a thoroughly behavioristic point of view. It is a radical departure from the previous kind of test, whose items were picked by the test constructor in accord with his own theory of the trait to be measured, on the assumption that people can be counted on to report their feelings and behavior fairly accurately. The MMPI assumes that an answer to one item is a bit of behavior whose meaning is sought in its correlates; the item is not assumed to be a veridical report of the person (Meehl, 1945).

The original diagnostic scales for the test were called Hypochondriasis, Depression, Hysteria, Psychopathic Deviate, Paranoia, Psychasthenia, Schizophrenia, and Hypomania. There is also a masculinity-femininity scale. Currently they are usually referred to by number instead of name, and thereby hangs a tale. Each of the diagnostic scales was constructed as follows. A sizable group of patients in the diagnostic category of the title was given all of the test items, and their responses were recorded. A large control group was established by giving the same test to persons who were presumably psychiatrically normal but otherwise drawn from the same population as the psychiatric cases. They included relatives who came to visit psychiatric patients, outpatients in the same clinics, and patients in nonpsychiatric wards. All the patients and relatives were clients of the University of Minnesota Hospital, a major teaching hospital, which draws on a large urban and rural area.

The schizophrenia scale, for example, consisted of whatever items best differentiated the fifty patients diagnosed as schizophrenic from the normal control sample. The method of constituting the control group assured that the differences would not be just a matter of social class or intelligence. As a further check on the diagnostic usefulness of the items, a second control group was used, which consisted of high school seniors who came for counseling about college entry plus college freshmen and sophomores who came to the University of Minnesota counseling service for some reason. A third control group was composed of a sample of residents of Minneapolis. Finally, the items were screened for their ability to distinguish the category of patient for which the scale was named from the general psychiatric population of the hospital.

The scores on all the scales of the MMPI are expressed in standardized form. A score corresponding to the average of the general population becomes a standard score of 50; 60 represents a score one standard deviation above the mean; 70 represents a score two standard deviations above the mean. Scores above 70 are considered diagnostically significant. In interpreting scores, however, special norms for specific groups are usually considered. College students, for example, normally show a different pattern of scores from the norms for the general population.

Three scales were built into the test from the start to ascertain whether the subjects were giving valid, or veridical, responses; they are called *validity scales*. What is at issue is not the validity of the MMPI but the trustworthiness of the responses of a particular person.

1. The *Lie*, or *L, scale* is intended to detect whether the person is consciously lying to make a good impression. As an example, there are questions such as whether one has as good table manners when eating at home alone as when eating in a restaurant, and whether one reads all the editorials in the newspaper every day. For those questions the apparently socially approved response is in one direction, but what most people actually do is in the other. No single answer is important, and a normal person might actually do a few of those things for some reason, but if a person answers many of the questions in the supposedly approved direction, their answers on the entire test are suspect.

2. A second validity scale consists of the number of Cannot Say answers; again, too large a number of these renders the test protocol unscorable or at least suspect.

3. The third validity scale is called the *F scale*, where *F* stands for frequency. This scale consists of a number of items, purposely chosen to be diverse, that, irrespective of content, are answered in one direction by almost everyone. An example might be "Everything tastes the same." Again, no single answer is

important, but an appreciable number of rare responses suggests that the whole test protocol is invalid. The subject may, for example, have been sorting or marking the questions at random, without bothering to read them, or may not understand the instructions. In either of those situations, by chance the person would answer about half the items in the rare direction. Alternatively, the patient may have a serious thought disorder, may understand ordinary words in an entirely different way from the accepted one, or may have delusional beliefs about himself or herself. The latter instances would be psychiatrically significant.

Although the original diagnostic scales were all derived empirically, the three original validity scales were a priori scales. (However, the F scale did take into account empirical frequencies.) The idea for the validity scales was not entirely original. In particular, the study of children's honesty by H. Hartshorne and M. A. May (see Chapter 5) had a scale like the L scale.

The durability of the MMPI reflects the fact that in its day it represented the best in the practice of test construction, nor can one readily point to an improved technique today.

Most likely the authors of the MMPI thought that by administering it to an incoming patient and scoring the eight diagnostic scales, one could sort most patients into one of those eight diagnostic categories according to which scale was highest. Being rigorously empirical, how could it fail?

*The MMPI: Problems and uses.* The MMPI, for all its virtues, did fail in its original aim to substitute a set of pathology scales for a set of diagnostic decisions. Indeed, even the authors of the test have recommended that the separate scales not be referred to by the name of the diagnostic category but rather by number. The test is now interpreted mainly with respect to the total pattern of scores rather than the scores on individual scales. The two main considerations in using the scores now concern the general level, that is, how many scores are above 70, and the pattern, in particular, which two scales are the highest. Interpretation of the pattern is a more complicated process than was originally envisaged in setting up the test and goes beyond what can be considered here.

One source of the problem is that although the authors of the test picked the items that would separate hypochondriacs, for example, from normal people, they did not have a way to pick those items that would simultaneously separate hypochondriacs from depressives and hysterics, the two groups whose answers most resemble those of the hypochondriacs.

A second source of difficulty concerns the validity of the diagnostic categories themselves; some of the diagnostic categories are no longer used. This topic leads into the revision (3rd ed.) of the *Diagnostic and statistical manual* of the American Psychiatric Association (1980) (usually abbreviated as DSM III), but that is also beyond the scope of this book.

Finally, the test did not succeed to the extent and in the way planned because of the intrinsically probabilistic nature of human behavior. Prediction failed because people are unpredictable. Having a psychiatric syndrome does not completely determine the person's answers to the MMPI or any other test. This source of difficulty is the most important, because it defines the limits not just of the MMPI but of any similar test and indeed of the entire behavioristic-psychometric approach to measurement.

Although the test does not serve as a straightforward replacement for psychiatric diagnosis, as originally intended, many psychologists and psychiatrists find it useful as an aid in diagnosis, as a way to describe personality, and as a research instrument. It is the most widely used of the hundreds of objective personality tests. Many other widely used personality tests were more or less based on the MMPI and its findings. That is odd, considering that it was originally intended as a diagnostic instrument and not as a test of personality traits at all.

There are several computerized scoring services that not only score but provide by computer a narrative interpretation of a person's test protocol. At present, however, there is not a sound basis in research for such computerized interpretations (Matarazzo, 1986).

*The MMPI: Correcting for defensiveness.* A major study of the errors of classification by the MMPI was done early on by Meehl and Hathaway (1946). For several scales they compared the answers of false positive cases with false negatives. A *false positive* case is one wrongly classed as being in a diagnostic category, say, hysteria, though the person is not in fact diagnosed as hysterical by psychiatrists. A *false negative* is a case not diagnosed by the test when, in fact, psychiatrists diagnose the case that way. Some people are diagnosed as ill when they are not because they exaggerate their symptoms; in other cases a diagnosis is missed because people minimize their symptoms or symptomatic answers. Meehl and Hathaway made a series of studies looking for a set of items that would give a clue to whether the subject was overestimating or underestimating symptoms. This set of items could then be used to apply a correction to the original scales and improve diagnostic accuracy. Contrasting the responses of the false positive cases with the false negative cases, a separate correction key was worked out for each of several diagnostic scales. If a correction score based on those telltale items is added to the corresponding diagnostic scale, fewer false positives and false negatives occur.

Groups of college students were used for additional studies. Each student in the group was given the test with the usual instructions. Then the same students were asked to answer the questions again, this time so as to make a completely normal, or good, impression. Other groups were given instructions to pretend to be mentally ill, or to make a bad impression. It would be possible to construct a scoring key from any of those small studies that could be used to detect and correct conscious faking.

The remarkable discovery was that one such correction key was much like the others, and a key derived one way served about as well for any of the purposes as for its own. Putting together the many studies of faking good and bad scores and of errors made by the diagnostic scales, Meehl and Hathaway constructed a single scale, which they called the *K scale*, to be used for all of these purposes, to correct the errors of the diagnostic scales and to detect conscious faking (Meehl & Hathaway, 1946). The K scale has been much analyzed and is often interpreted as a measure of defensiveness. A very defensive person may partly conceal pathology, whereas a person abnormally low in this trait, if it is a trait, may seem to be sicker than he or she really is.

Thus the K scale, which began as an empirical correction factor, or validity scale, to enable the original scales to work better, may turn out to be an interesting psychological trait. There is a long-standing debate among psychologists as to whether whatever is measured by the K scale merely vitiates measurement of personality or whether it provides valuable new information about the person. The K scale, like all the others, operates with probabilities, not certainties, and the conclusion that the original diagnostic scales should be referred to by numbers, not names, still holds.

## Projective Tests

Projective tests provide an entirely different approach to personality measurement. In part, they counter some of the adverse criticism of objective tests, but they present problems of their own. The fundamental principle underlying all projective techniques, the *projective hypothesis*, is that people will structure or perceive ambiguous stimuli in accord with their own strivings, dispositions, and conflicts, including or especially unconscious ones (Lindzey, 1952). Although the ancestry of projective techniques would seem to be the psychoanalytic principle of psychic determinism, in fact Binet and Henri (1896) first proposed using inkblots to study personality, long before Rorschach did, and they were certainly uninfluenced by psychoanalysis.

*Rorschach and inkblots.* Hermann Rorschach, a Swiss psychiatrist, experimented with hundreds of inkblots before arriving at the set of ten blots that constitute his famous Rorschach test, first published in 1921. The blots were made by dropping some ink on a paper and folding it in two. As a result, all the blots are bilaterally symmetrical. Some are black and white only, others colored. As a result of a printer's error, one edition appeared with shades of gray in some parts of the blot, rather than pure black and white. Rorschach recognized that shading introduced a new element that brought out interesting responses; so subsequent editions have been intentionally made that way.

The Rorschach test has a more varied theoretical background than the MMPI. Rorschach himself was familiar with Freudian psychoanalysis and with Jung's system of analytical psychology. Following his death soon after the publication of *Psychodiagnostik*, several other psychologists undertook to complete the work. The major systems for interpreting the test are the work of Bruno Klopfer, Samuel Beck, Marguerite Hertz, Zygmund Piotrowski, and David Rapaport and Roy Schafer, operating as a team (Exner, 1974). Klopfer had been trained in Germany and was oriented to a phenomenological approach to psychology; he was also interested in Jung's approach to psychotherapy. Beck was trained at Columbia University. His intellectual commitment was to empirical, even behavioristic science; however, he was also interested in Freudian psychoanalysis. Hertz was trained at Western Reserve University, where she was schooled in the psychometric approach. Piotrowski graduated from the University of Poznan in Poland with a speciality in experimental psychology. He had further training in clinical psychology after emigrating to New York and studied the Rorschach test under Klopfer. Rapaport and Schafer included the Rorschach test in their proposed test battery for diagnostic psychological evaluation (Rapaport, Gill, & Schafer, 1946). Each of the authors (including Rapaport and Schafer as one author) has worked out a somewhat individual and unique approach to administering, scoring, and interpreting the test. All have incorporated much of Rorschach's original thinking but have elaborated it in different directions. Each of the systems has stimulated extensive research and clinical applications.

John E. Exner, Jr. first studied systematically all of the scoring systems and the validational research. Then he assembled his own comprehensive scoring system, which incorporates the best features from each of the others plus some additional features. His first consideration was Rorschach's original reasoning, which he found still valid for the most part. His second consideration was to look at the research findings related to Rorschach's arguments and those of the other systematizers, in the hope of finding a way to reconcile differences. Usually that was not possible, so he selected the suggestion most in line with contemporary research evidence. Where there was little or no research evidence available, the third consideration was the reasonableness of the arguments put forth in behalf of a particular scoring rule. The fourth consideration was the opinions and current practices of two large samples of clinical psychologists who were currently using the Rorschach technique. Finally, he decided doubtful issues by trying out different possibilities on a large sample of Rorschach protocols administered and interpreted by a variety of psychologists (Exner, 1974). The exposition that follows is guided by his system.

In interpreting responses to the Rorschach test, consideration is given to location, determinant, content, popularity, and the organizational quality of the response. *Location* refers to whether the response concerns the whole blot, a large detail, a small detail, or the white space surrounding the blot. *Determinant* refers to whether the response is determined by the form of the blot, its color, its shading, or by perceived movement. (An example of the kind of question Exner had to resolve in making his composite system is whether animal movements should be counted as movement responses; the solution is that they are counted if the animals are making human movements, like reading or dancing.) *Content* refers to mention of humans, animals, mythological creatures, anatomical details, explosions, geography, landscapes, clothing, and so on. Rare or *original* responses and very common (*popular*) ones are also noted. Finally, the *quality* of the response is considered, particularly whether different elements have been combined plausibly and whether the percept is a reasonable interpretation of the particular part of the blot where the subject claims to see it. Rules of Rorschach interpretation require that each of the foregoing elements be interpreted in the light of all the others; therefore, it is not possible to give a simple example of how each is interpreted.

People are ordinarily aware of the content of their response, though they probably do not surmise how the psychologist will interpret the various contents displayed in their Rorschach responses. It probably does not even occur to most people, however, that the psychologist attaches meaning to which part of the blot they see a figure in or what the determinant is. An even subtler factor in scoring is the balance of the elements, such as the ratio of movement to color responses. The exact formulas used to compute the balance of different elements of a protocol (one person's test responses) are apparently derived solely from intuition, and their basis or validity is unknown. Because the most important factors in the scoring system are far from commonsense ones, conscious attempts to make socially acceptable responses or otherwise to alter one's score are not a major problem.

The basic logic of Rorschach interpretation is hard to capture in a few sentences (Schafer, 1954). The clinicians who use it probably depend to some extent on a vaguely psychoanalytic symbolism. The connection between the detailed, explicit rules of Rorschach interpretation and the most solidly established psychoanalytic principles, however, is tenuous. The Rorschach test may stand or fall on the validity of psychic determinism, but certainly psychoanalysis does not stand or fall on the validity of Rorschach interpretation.

With the Rorschach test, unlike most objective tests, what the tester finally arrives at is a complicated personality description, rather than a single score or set of scores. Experienced clinicians can often make remarkably insightful inferences on the basis of Rorschach protocols, but hard-boiled research with the test has not yielded many findings that are impressive to those outside the Rorschach coterie. Several problems dog the steps of researchers in this field.

A specific problem is that the number of responses ($R$) varies widely from case to case. Suppose a person gives three responses showing human movement. (An example of human movement would be "two people dancing.") Does that have the same significance in a protocol with ten percepts as it does in a protocol with fifty or sixty percepts? Simply dividing by R does not solve the problem, as it turns out.

Another problem is that the clinician can pin the interpretation to what is unique to the case at hand, whereas research must concern itself with common elements that occur in large numbers of cases (Loevinger, 1963). If I say that the subject wore shoes, that does not give much information about him, whereas if I say he stood on his head while answering the test, that is unique. Not enough people stand on their heads while being tested to enable the researcher to ascertain what it means; however, in a particular case a clinician may make a plausible guess and almost certainly learn more than from the fact that the person wore shoes. But the price of having substituted intuition for empirical research is that if another person turns up standing on his head while being tested, the examiner has no basis for assuming that what applied to the first case applies equally to the second. Research almost has to be concerned with characteristics that split the sample more nearly equally.

But perhaps the main problem is that the rules require that every scored element of the responses be interpreted in the light of the other elements. That makes every case unique and precludes any simple approach to validational research.

The Holtzman Inkblot Test has been devised to meet some of the problems of the Rorschach test. (Holtzman 1961; Holtzman, Thorpe, Swartz, & Herron, 1961). It has forty-five different inkblots, and the subject is instructed to make one response to each blot. This device solves the problem of interpreting scores with respect to number of responses, because the number of responses is constant. The test is not used as widely as the Rorschach despite its superior psychometric logic. Whether the preference for the Rorschach test is merely a matter of clinging to tradition or whether the Rorschach has some real clinical superiority is unknown, at least to me.

*Morgan and Murray and the TAT.* Another well-known projective test is the Thematic Apperception test (*TAT*), originated by Christiana Morgan and Henry Murray (1935). In this test, a set of slightly out-of-focus photographs of people is shown to the person, one at a time. The subject is asked to tell what is happening, what led up to it, and what will happen next. Different pictures are used for men, women, girls, and boys. In most pictures there should be a character with whom the person tested can identify. The number of pictures given and the mode of interpretation have not been as rigidly standardized as in other tests. Various ways of scoring have been proposed. Murray has an elaborate categorization of needs and environmental presses that he uses in classifying and interpreting stories; it is partly an elaboration of psychoanalytic theory, but as with the Rorschach, the connection is not easily made explicit or compelling. The needs most often studied by other psychologists have been the needs for achievement, aggression, affiliation, power, intimacy, and autonomy.

A major problem in interpreting the test lies in the unpredictable appearance of the Walter Mitty (or Baron Munchhausen) effect. Does the person who gives many achievement responses display his own drive toward achievement, or is he, like Walter Mitty in the story by James Thurber, dreaming of achievements as a substitute for doing anything? In fact, there is no logical necessity for the possibilities to be limited by those alternatives. There could be still other possible meanings, although those two are most obvious.

David McClelland has for many years used the TAT to study the need for achievement and other needs. Borrowing terms from Skinner, he describes the TAT as being an *operant* test, as compared to objective personality tests, which are usually more like what Skinner calls *respondent* behavior, because the test itself dictates the kind of response called for within narrow limits (McClelland,

1980). He believes operant tests are better for revealing the subject's motives, whereas respondent measures better reveal the cognitive determinants of behavior.

### Idiographic Measures

Some psychologists within the loosely grouped humanistic, phenomenological, and existentialist schools object to the idea of psychological measurement altogether. Somewhat like Goethe, they maintain that what can be specified and measured is precisely what is not psychological, or what is of least interest to psychology. At the same time, other psychologists within these schools have made major contributions to measurement of personality.

*Allport and the study of values.* Gordon Allport was the best-known trait theorist of his generation. He championed traits during an era dominated by behaviorists on the one hand and psychoanalysts on the other. One of his distinctive ideas is that of unique traits, that is, traits that characterize the central theme of one person's life rather than being a dimension along which all people can be arrayed. He maintained that every person was best characterized in terms of his or her own unique traits. Holding strictly to that dictum would undercut the possibility of measurement, because measurement requires common dimensions for all people. But Allport was also the originator of one of the first and most important tests used to measure people's sense of values, the Allport-Vernon Study of Values (Allport & Vernon, 1931).

The Study of Values, currently revised (Allport, Vernon & Lindzey 1951), is based on a set of six values derived from E. Spränger (1928) that are more or less characteristic of different styles of life. A person whose primary interest is *theoretical* emphasizes empirical, critical, and rational search for truth. One whose primary interest is *economic* emphasizes what is useful, practical, and applicable. One whose outlook is basically *esthetic* emphasizes form, harmony, grace, symmetry, and fitness. A person whose chief concern is *social* emphasizes altruistic and philanthropic love of people. Someone whose chief concern is *political* emphasizes personal power, influence, and renown. A person whose fundamental outlook is *religious* emphasizes the mystical and the unity of the cosmos. Obviously the meanings of these different values are not totally contained in a single word.

The current version has forty-five items, and the test is self-administering. The following is a sample item:

> In your opinion, can a man who works in business all the week best spend Sunday in
> a. trying to educate himself by reading serious books
> b. trying to win at golf, or racing
> c. going to an orchestral concert
> d. hearing a really good sermon

The subject's instructions are to rank those alternatives in order of his or her preference. Each alternative represents a separate value, and points are credited to that value in accord with the person's priority for it.

Items of that sort represent comparisons of the person with himself or herself. The test is constructed so that there is no meaning to the idea of a general level, such as in the Stanford-Binet test of intelligence or in the MMPI. In the case of the Stanford-Binet test, the general level of the scores is the most important and the only well-validated bit of information that one can obtain from the test. In the case of the MMPI, the most important thing to note is the general level of the person's scores. If there are several scores above 65 or 70, the tester should be alert to the possibility of some pathology. The pattern of scores is the second thing to take into account. With the Study of Values, however, the general level is the same for everyone and is therefore not meaningful. The pattern of the scores is all that matters.

*Rogers and the Q sort.* Carl Rogers is another psychologist who has reservations about measurement in psychology but has also contributed to it. Rogers, best known as the originator of client-centered counseling, believes that the condition under which positive change, that is, therapy, can occur is that the counselor should have unconditional positive regard for the client. That attitude is incompatible with evaluating the person, as a clinician does in administering tests and writing a diagnostic report, he asserts. Hence Rogers opposes diagnostic study as a prelude to counseling or other therapy. But Rogers has also done some of the best-known research in clinical psychology, using his own kind of measurement (Rogers & Dymond, 1954).

One measure of adjustment in Rogers's theory is the congruence between the person's perceived self and ideal self. With ingenuity, this congruence can be measured. The instrument used in this and a good deal of other research is the *Q sort*. A series of statements is generated that can be applied widely. These statements can be of various sorts, depending on the topic of research. An example might be a series of adjectives, such as conscientious, beautiful, stubborn, impulsive, tall, intelligent, and so on. There may be as many as 50 or 100 such adjectives or phrases. Each subject is then given an arbitrary quasi-normal distribution, anchored by phrases such as "Not at all like me" at one extreme and "Just like me" at the other. The distribution for a total of 68 adjectives could be 1, 2, 6, 15, 20, 15, 6, 2, 1. The subject's task is to sort the designated number of adjectives into each position on the distribution. A good exposition of the Q-sort technique is given by J. Block (1961), although his version is not exactly the one used by Rogers.

In filling out the Q sort, the person is comparing one of his or her traits to another. There is no direct reference to a comparison with other people. Having described himself, the person can then use the same format to describe his ideal self. As a result of the two sets of ratings, each adjective will have two numbers. The correlation between those two ratings is a measure of the congruence of the person's own conception of real self and ideal self. The congruence of his self-conception with other people's conception of him can also be measured by an extension of this method. That would constitute another element of Rogers's idea of adjustment. The ratings of individual adjectives all must add up to the same total for everyone, because the distribution was given in advance. The correlation between real and ideal self (or between self-ratings and ratings by others) does, however, have a meaningful level.

Research using this technique has shown that college students seeking counseling have a lower correlation between real and ideal self than a matched group of students not seeking counseling. After completing counseling, their correlation goes up. These results, however, are less favorable to the use of the technique than they sound at first, because those who gained the most from counseling are not the same ones whose correlation between real and ideal self gained the most (Kleinmuntz, 1982).

This chapter has introduced the idea of psychological measurement, a fragment of its history, and some of the best-known attempts to measure personality. The tests mentioned have been the subject of thousands of research studies, as well as being widely used in clinical practice. Despite controversy concerning their merits and weaknesses, they have endured. That alone gives them some value in terms of the cumulated wisdom and expertise built into them by clinical experience, intuition, and research.

Overall, measurement of general intelligence is one of psychology's successes; measurement of personality is still open to some question.

---

## OPPOSITION TO PSYCHOLOGICAL MEASUREMENT

Despite the triumphs of measurement in psychology, from Helmholtz to Binet, opposition to the idea of measurement has not ceased.

Many psychoanalysts belittle every approach to personality other than their own kind of intensive case study. Everything else, such critics believe, is necessarily superficial. Thus they discount the possibility of indirect use of other kinds of evidence to make inferences about aspects of personality that they are privileged to approach more directly. Their position is not altogether logical, for if the psychological depths did not have effects accessible to more superficial approaches, the depths could be ignored. All the symptoms and malaise that lead a person to become a patient are examples, as well as dreams, slips of the tongue, and jokes. In fairness, there are also psychoanalysts and psychoanalytically trained psychologists who use in their research either standard measures of personality or original ones.

Another group of opponents has been mentioned: some of the psychologists and philosophers in the humanistic movement, including some phenomenologists and existentialists.

Perhaps more significant is the opposition coming from within the ranks of other scientists. Stephen Jay Gould, an acclaimed biologist, has devoted a book to the "mismeasure of man" (Gould, 1981). He does not object to mathematization for itself. His objections to measurement in psychology are mainly political and moral, and in that he is not alone. He chronicles a disgraceful history of racial and sexual prejudice on the part of psychologists and other proponents of genetics in the nineteenth and early twentieth century. His arguments against the nativist, or hereditarian, view of intelligence and against all attempts to assign a percentage of causation to heredity and environment in relation to intelligence are strong ones, based on his firm understanding of biology.

In the end, however, he declares that the real error consists in construing intelligence as a thing that can be measured. He appears to believe that the very attempt to measure intelligence implies that it is somehow a concrete entity. That argument appears to be weak. There may be psychologists who reify whatever they are studying, but Gould's argument, if credited, undercuts any kind of abstract entity in psychology. Intelligence is no more real than any other abstract concept, but no less.

Many psychologists have shared Gould's anticonceptual bias, from Thorndike (1927), with his CAVD test, which he refused to call a test of intelligence, to Robert C. Tryon (1935) and Godfrey Thomson (1946), who worked out approximate methods of factor analysis, while belittling the reality of factors.

For psychologists engaged in measuring personality, the criticism that hits closest to home is that of Walter Mischel, which will be discussed in the next chapter.

---

**APPENDIX**

## PSYCHOMETRIC THEORY

We are accustomed to think of psychological tests as a way of measuring and comparing people. The topic of this section requires a change of focus. Granted that tests are used to select persons, how do we select the tests? Imagine two professors independently constructing an examination for the same college course. Now suppose the class takes both tests. Scores on one test will be somewhat similar to scores on the other, but it is unlikely that all the students will get exactly the same grades on the two tests or achieve exactly the same class rank. How should the psychologist construct or evaluate the test, prior to using it to select or evaluate students, job applicants, patients, defendants, and so on?

When psychologists first began making tests, they naively believed that by naming a test as a measure of what they wanted to measure, ipso facto they had a test of that ability or trait. Thus originally psychologists did not see the problem. Charles Spearman, the same psychologist who originated the idea of general intelligence (g) as the general factor in all intellectual tasks (Spearman, 1904), originated classical psychometric theory with two simple ideas, reliability and validity (Spearman, 1910). Those were the psychometric properties in terms of which tests were to be evaluated. (Other properties, such as ease of administration and scoring and the time it takes to give the test are not germane to the psychometric issues.)

*Reliability* was defined as the self-correlation of the test, *validity* as the correlation of a test with a criterion. Both of those ideas proved to be flawed under critical examination. Nonetheless, the realization that the worth of a psychological test must be critically examined and evaluated was an immense step forward.

## Reliability

Criticism began soon after Spearman proposed the idea of reliability, but it reached its peak in the 1950s, when the American Psychological Association appointed a committee to review standards for psychological tests (American Psychological Association, 1954). The idea of the committee on tests was that the public and the users of the tests, who were often educators without extensive training in psychometrics, should be protected from the sale of worthless but well-advertised tests. Prior to that time there were only vague standards of what the ethical limitations were in advertising tests.

The definition of reliability as the self-correlation of a test is of course paradoxical, because every test correlates perfectly with itself. But there is a commonsense meaning to reliability that encompasses what this kind of coefficient was meant to ascertain. To what extent is the test a dependable measure of whatever it measures, versus being an accidental result of more or less chance events, such as the particular items chosen or the particular occasion?

The two traditional ways of estimating reliability actually correspond to different sources of unreliability. The psychologist can give a test, then a few days or a few weeks later give it again to the same sample of people. The correlation between their scores on the two administrations of the test is the *retest reliability* coefficient, now often called a *coefficient of stability*. The other type of reliability coefficient correlates the score on half the items with the score on the other half the items, usually odd items versus even items, after a single administration of the test to a sample of people. That procedure yields the *split-half reliability* coefficient, which is a measure of the test's *homogeneity*. In Spearman's original work and in much statistical theory for many years afterwards those two kinds of coefficient were both referred to as reliability and treated as if they were interchangeable (Loevinger, 1947).

Reliability today is generally studied in terms of several independent elements. Some of these elements apply to objectively scored tests, often called objective tests for short; others apply only to projective tests.

The first element of unreliability lies in the subject taking the test. The person may exhibit a given trait or ability to a different degree on different occasions, for reasons of health, interest, fatigue, distractions, or whatever. The extent of such effects is measured in terms of a coefficient of stability. There is a problem, however, for the second test is, by being second, not exactly the same test as the first one. In some tests, which depend on figuring out a problem or responding to unusual stimuli such as inkblots, one clearly cannot give exactly the same test and expect to obtain comparable results, because some subjects may remember, some may purposely vary their responses, and so on. In these cases an equivalent form of test is given. But then it is not exactly the same test. Retesting a person with a psychological test cannot be made to be the same as measuring height on two occasions. People have memory.

The second element of unreliability in an objective test is concerned with internal consistency, or homogeneity. Do all the items in a test measure the same thing? Again, there are problems. Apparent internal consistency can be increased by introducing irrelevant variables, such as speed. Another way is to use only one kind of test item. For example, contrary to Binet's practice of measuring general intelligence by the sum of a variety of subtests, one could measure intelligence by a test made up only of long-division items or by a test made up only of vocabulary items. Such tests would be much more homogeneous than a Binet-type test, hence more reliable in that sense. Obviously they would be less good as measures of general intelligence. Homogeneity becomes an important property of a test just to the extent that it is manifest in items that are apparently diverse with respect to content and item format. In that situation it represents a real finding, real evidence that some common trait or ability underlies the apparently diverse performances.

The issue of whether a test is too homogeneous becomes more important in relation to personality and attitude measurement than in relation to tests of ability. Surprisingly, the format in which questions are asked is in many instances as important as the content of the questions, and sometimes it is more important (Campbell & Fiske, 1959). The simple device of having all questions be in the same format may insure that the consistency of the test will be quite high, almost regardless of content. To clarify this point, some people tend to say yes, others to say no, almost no matter what one asks them. If an adjustment questionnaire is presented for which all the sypmtomatic answers are yes, the yea-sayers will appear to be sicker than they are, whereas the nay-sayers will appear healthier than they are. The authors of the MMPI took these tendencies into account in wording their items, so that symptomatic answers do not all require the same answer.

In relation to projective tests and to individually administered tests of intelligence (such as the various revisions of the Binet scales and the Wechsler scales), another kind of reliability refers to how much two psychologists scoring the same performance arrive at the same score. This is called *inter-rater reliability*. Not only must it be asked how much Rater A agrees with Rater B, there may even be a question (rarely investigated, however) whether Rater A on one day would agree with himself a week later.

In some tests there is also a problem of whether two persons would administer the test exactly the same way, though in general people should not be considered qualified as testers until they are virtually letter-perfect in this respect. That is a standard more easily achieved with ability than with some projective tests, which allow for an inquiry to explore the meaning of the subject's responses. Also, in testing very young children, special skills may be important, ones that not every tester can be assumed to have, in order to keep their interest and cooperation. Some clinicians are said to feel justified in modifying tests for their patients. In such cases, the results are not comparable to tests given under standardized conditions. In general, certified psychologists can be assumed to be rigorously trained in this respect.

## Validity

The topic of validity at first seemed more obvious and unproblematic than reliability: Simply find a good criterion of whatever the test purports to measure and correlate the test with the criterion. The problem was that there never was a good criterion, though this seemed to come to psychologists as a fresh surprise on each occasion. In fact, if there had been a good criterion, usually no one would have bothered to construct a new test of that trait. While many psychologists were more or less independently groping with the problem of the criterion, a subcommittee of the American Psychological Association Committee on Tests, consisting of Paul E. Meehl and Lee J. Cronbach, set about to clarify a new idea that the committee was proposing, namely, *construct validity* (Cronbach & Meehl, 1955). Although the term was new, it embodied the best practice of previous test constructors, particularly Alfred Binet.

Three kinds of test validity are today officially recognized: content, criterion, and construct validity, or, as they are now officially labeled, content-related, criterion-related, and construct-related validity (American Psychological Association, 1985).

*Content validity* refers to the validation of a test by the test constructor's judgment that the content of the test items covers the material for which the test is intended. It is the usual kind of validation for many educational achievement tests; an instructor ordinarily has no other option in constructing course tests than to include whatever material she believes the course should have covered. In relation to tests of personality and attitude measurement, other options are possible but difficult and expensive. But hope springs eternal in each new generation of researchers that a valid and useful test can be constructed a priori.

What seems to happen is that the researchers (especially young ones or professionals in a neighboring discipline such as psychiatry or social work), looking over the tests available in relation to the chosen topic, find that none quite measures what they are looking for. Therefore, they conclude, they should define exactly what is needed and construct a test for that putative trait. But where reliance in test construction is placed solely on content validation, psychometrics is back right where Spearman found it, with each test constructor naively believing in the infallibility of his or her own intuition, or at best, the infallibility of the consensus of the test constructor and a few colleagues.

*Criterion validity* includes two slightly different types of validity, predictive and concurrent. *Predictive validity* refers to how well a test predicts a specific criterion performance; it can ordinarily be measured by a single correlation coefficient. That used to be thought of as the obvious, ultimate form of validation. The difficulty in finding a suitable criterion and the likelihood that conditions will change, and therefore the correlations will change, have shaken the faith in that kind of test validation if used alone.

*Concurrent validity* also refers to correlation with an external criterion, but a contemporary rather than a future one. Thus it refers to the present discriminating ability of the test with respect to whatever it is supposed to measure. A test used to evaluate whether a patient is currently schizophrenic might conceivably be quite different from one used to predict whether he or she will in future become schizophrenic, though in practice examples of the difference between predictive and concurrent validity are hard to find. Hence both are currently subsumed as criterion validity.

*Construct validity* refers to how well a test measures the trait or ability (construct) that it is supposed to. Evidence for any of the other kinds of validity is germane, and in general all of those kinds of evidence are necessary to establish construct validity (Loevinger, 1957). Current usage of criterion-related, content-related, and construct-related validity reflects the fact that no kind of evidence can be legitimately excluded in evaluating a test's validity (American Psychological Association, 1985).

Although the term *construct validity* dates from approximately 1954, one of the best examples is that of Binet's work. Binet began by looking at the content of the subtests and excluded those that did not seem to tap such higher mental processes as judgment and reasoning. He did not try for a strict, logical definition of intelligence, but he knew the domain that he wanted to test. Next, he looked for several external criteria to pick the best subtests. No single criterion by itself was very good. The failure of all available criteria for differentiating bright and dull students was the reason he had been called on to devise a test. Though each single criterion had its flaws, he understood that by using several criteria jointly, he could select a group of tests that would do better than any previous method had done. (For some people, that insight is obvious; others, who find it difficult to understand, may appreciate the magnitude of Binet's discovery.)

The errors teachers made when asked to pick the brightest and dullest students in the class were the reason Binet was called on to construct a test. Their errors most likely were of the sort that some average children were selected to be among the bright nominees, possibly because of pleasing appearance or personality, and other average children were called dull, perhaps because of a dull look or mischievous behavior. But despite these errors, one can safely assume, as Binet did, that on the average those called the brightest were in fact somewhat brighter than those called the dullest. Therefore, a valid test of intelligence should show higher average scores for the students that the teacher nominated as bright than for those in the same classroom nominated as dull.

Obviously, within any age cohort there is a wide range of intellectual ability. On average, however, one can assume that older children have greater ability than younger children. Here, then, Binet found a second criterion for his tests, and one completely independent of teacher nomination. Each subtest chosen for his battery of tests had to show an increase in the performance of average children with age. In principle, that topic is best studied by following a given group of children *longitudinally*, that is, with periodic retesting. In fact, Binet followed the more practical course of getting independent samples of children of successive ages. Age has one big advantage over other criteria for intellectual ability, namely, that it can be ascertained virtually without error. It is thus completely reliable in the psychometric sense.

Thus the subtests Binet and Simon chose to make up the first Binet-Simon scale had these characteristics: Each subtest had some content that could be interpreted as a higher mental process; it differentiated children that teachers called bright from those they called dull; it gave higher scores to older children than to younger ones when the children were drawn from a wide age range; and within a school grade it tended to give higher scores to younger ones. It may seem paradoxical, but no subtest should have too high a correlation with age, because we know that age itself is not a perfect measure of ability. The same holds for teacher nomination.

## REFERENCES

Allport, G. W. (1961). *Pattern and growth in personality.* New York: Holt, Rinehart & Winston.

Allport, G. W., & Vernon, P. E. (1931). *Study of values: A scale for measuring the dominant interests in personality.* Boston: Houghton Mifflin.

Allport, G. W., Vernon, P. E., & Lindzey, G. (1951). *Study of values* (rev. ed.). Boston: Houghton Mifflin.

American Psychiatric Association.(1980). *Diagnostic and statistical manual of mental disorders* (3rd ed.). Washington, DC: Author.

American Psychological Association. (1954). *Technical recommendations for psychological tests and diagnostic techniques.* Washington, DC.: Author.

American Psychological Association. (1985). *Standards for educational and psychological testing.* Washington, DC: Author.

Bernreuter, R. G. (1933). The theory and construction of the personality inventory. *Journal of Social Psychology, 4,* 387–405.

Binet, A. (1902). *L'Etude expérimentale de l'intelligence* [Experimental study of intelligence]. Paris: Ancienne Librairie Schleicher.

Binet, A., & Henri, V. (1896). La psychologie individuelle [Individual psychology]. *L'Année Psychologique, 2,* 411–465.

Binet, A., & Simon, T. (1905). Methodes nouvelles pour le diagnostic du niveau intellectuel des anormaux [New methods for diagnosis of the intellectual level of abnormals]. *L'Année Psychologique, 11,* 191–244.

Binet, A., & Simon, T. (1908). Le développement de l'intelligence chez les enfants [Development of intelligence in children]. *L'Année Psychologique, 14,* 1–94.

Block, J. (1961). *The Q-sort method in personality assessment and psychiatric research.* Springfield, IL: C. C. Thomas.

Boring, E. G. (1929). *A history of experimental psychology.* New York: Appleton-Century-Crofts.

Boring, E. G. (1950). The influence of evolutionary theory upon American psychological thought. In S. Persons (Ed.), *Evolutionary thought in America* (pp. 267–298). New Haven: Yale University Press.

Boring, E. G. (1961). The beginning and growth of measurement in psychology. *Isis, 52,* 238–257.

Campbell, D. T., & Fiske, D. W. (1959). Convergent and discriminant validation by the multitrait-multimethod matrix. *Psychological Bulletin, 56,* 81–105.

Cattell, J. McK. (1890). Mental tests and measurements. *Mind, 15,* 373–380.

Cronbach, L. J.,, & Meehl, P. E. (1955). Construct validity in psychological tests. *Psychological Bulletin, 52*, 281–302.

Darwin, C. F. (1859). *On the origin of species by means of natural selection, or the preservation of favored races in the struggle for life.* London:

DuBois, P. H. (1970). *A history of psychological testing.* Boston: Allyn & Bacon.

Dunnette, M. D., & Kirchner, W. K. (1965). *Psychology applied to industry.* New York: Appleton-Century-Crofts.

Ebbinghaus, H. (1913). *Memory* (H. Ruger & C. Bussenius, Trans.). New York: Bureau of Publications, Teachers College, Columbia University. (Original work published 1885.)

Ebbinghaus, H. (1897). Über eine neue Methode zur Prüfung geistiger Fähigkeiten und ihre Anwendung bei Schulkindern [A new method for testing mental capacities and its use with school children]. *Zeitschrift für Psychologie und Physiologie der Sinnesorgane, 13*, 401–459.

Exner, J. E., Jr. (1974). *The Rorschach: A comprehensive system.* New York: Wiley.

Fechner, G. T. (1860). *Elemente der Psychophysik* [Elements of psychophysics]. Leipzig: Breitkopf & Härtel.

Galton, F. (1869). *Hereditary genius.* London: Macmillan.

Galton, F. (1883). *Inquiries into human faculty and its development.* London: Macmillan.

Goodenough, F. (1949). *Mental testing.* New York: Holt, Rinehart & Winston.

Gould, S. J. (1981). *The mismeasure of man.* New York: Norton.

Graunt, J. (1956). Natural and political observations made upon the bills of mortality. In J. R. Newman (Ed.), *The world of mathematics* (pp. 1421–1435). New York: Simon & Schuster. (Original work published 1662.)

Halley, E. (1956). An estimate of the degrees of the mortality of mankind, drawn from curious tables of the births and funerals at the city of Breslaw; with an attempt to ascertain the price of annuities upon lives. In J. R. Newman (Ed.), *The world of mathematics* (pp. 1437–1447). New York: Simon & Schuster. (Original work published 1693.)

Hathaway, S. R. (1939). The personality inventory as an aid in diagnosing psychopathic inferiors. *Journal of Consulting Psychology, 3*, 112–117.

Hathaway, S. R., & McKinley, J. C. (1940). A multiphasic personality schedule (Minnesota). I. Construction of the schedule. *Journal of Psychology, 10*, 249–254.

Holtzman, W. H. (1961). *Holtzman Inkblot Technique.* New York: Psychological Corporation.

Holtzman, W. H., Thorpe, J. S., Swartz, J. D., & Herron, E. W. (1961). *Inkblot perception and personality.* Austin, TX: University of Texas Press.

Kant, I. (1970). Preface. *Metaphysical foundations of natural science* (J. Ellington, Trans.). In R. I. Watson, Sr. (Ed.), *Basic writings in the history of psychology* (pp. 87–88). New York: Oxford University Press. (Original work published 1786.)

Kleinmuntz, B. (1982). *Personality and psychological assessment.* New York: St. Martin's Press.

Lindzey, G. (1952). Thematic Apperception Test: Interpretive assumptions and related empirical evidence. *Psychological Bulletin, 49*, 1–25.

Loevinger, J. (1947). A systematic approach to the construction and evaluation of tests of ability. *Psychological Monographs, 61* (Whole no. 285).

Loevinger, J. (1957). Objective tests as instruments of psychological theory. *Psychological Reports, 3,* 635–694.

Loevinger, J. (1963). Conflict of commitment in clinical research. *American Psychologist, 18,* 241–251.

Matarazzo, J. D. (1986). Computerized clinical psychological test interpretations: Unvalidated plus all mean and no sigma. *American Psychologist, 41,* 14–24.

McClelland, D. C. (1980). Motive dispositions: The merits of operant and respondent measures. *Review of Personality and Social Psychology, 1,* 10–41.

Meehl, P. E. (1945). The dynamics of "structured" personality tests. *Journal of Clinical Psychology, 1,* 296–303.

Meehl, P. E., & Hathaway, S. R. (1946). The K factor as a suppressor variable in the MMPI. *Journal of Applied Psychology, 30,* 525–564.

Mischel, W. (1968). *Personality assessment.* New York: Wiley.

Morgan, C. D., & Murray, H. A. (1935). A method for investigating fantasies. *Archives of Neurology and Psychiatry, 34,* 289–306.

Pervin, L. A. (1984). *Current controversies and issues in personality* (2nd ed). New York: Wiley.

Peterson, J. (1925). *Early conceptions and tests of intelligence.* Yonkers-on-Hudson, NY: World Book.

Quetelet, L. A. J. (1835). *Sur l'homme et le developpement de ses facultés, ou essai de physique sociale* [Man and the development of his faculties]. Paris: Bachelier.

Rapaport, D., Gill, M., & Schafer, R. (1946). *Diagnostic psychological testing.* Vols. 1 & 2. Chicago: Yearbook Publishers.

Rogers, C. R., & Dymond, R. F. (Eds.). (1954). *Psychotherapy and personality change.* Chicago: University of Chicago Press.

Rorschach, H. (1921). *Psychodiagnostics.* Berne: Bircher.

Schafer, R. (1954). *Psychoanalytic interpretations in Rorschach testing.* NY: Grune & Stratton.

Spearman, C. (1904). "General intelligence" objectively determined and measured. *American Journal of Psychology, 15,* 201–292.

Spearman, C. (1910). Correlation calculated from faulty data. *British Journal of Psychology, 3,* 271–295.

Spränger, E. (1928). *Lebensformen* [Types of men]. New York: G. E. Stechert.

Stern, W. (1912). *Psychologischen Methoden der Intelligenz Prüfung* [Psychological methods of intelligence testing]. Leipzig: Barth.

Sternberg, R. J. (Ed.). (1982). *Handbook of human intelligence.* New York: Cambridge University Press.

Sternberg, R. J. (1985). *Beyond IQ: A triarchic theory of intelligence.* New York: Cambridge University Press.

Terman, L. M. (1916). *The measurement of intelligence.* Boston: Houghton, Mifflin.

Terman, L. M., & Merrill, M. A. (1937). *Measuring intelligence.* Boston: Houghton Mifflin.

Terman, L. M., & Merrill, M. A. (1960). *Stanford-Binet Intelligence Scale: Manual for the third revision, form L-M.* Boston: Houghton Mifflin.

Terman, L. M. & Merrill, M. A. (1973). *Stanford-Binet Intelligence Scale: 1972 norms edition.* Boston: Houghton Mifflin.

Thomson, G. H. (1946). *The factorial analysis of human ability*. Boston: Houghton Mifflin.

Thorndike, E. L. (1927). *The measurement of intelligence.* New York: Bureau of Publications, Teachers College, Columbia University.

Thurstone, L. L. (1935). *The vectors of the mind.* Chicago: University of Chicago Press.

Thurstone, L. L. (1947). *Multiple factor analysis.* Chicago: University of Chicago Press.

Tryon, R. C. (1935). A theory of psychological components — an alternative to "mathematical factors." *Psychological Review, 42,* 425 – 454.

Wechsler, D. (1939). *The measurement of adult intelligence.* Baltimore: Williams & Wilkins.

Wissler, C. (1901). The correlation of mental and physical traits. *Psychological Review, Monograph Supplements, 3* (no. 6).

Woodworth, R. S. (1919). Examination of emotional fitness for warfare. *Psychological Bulletin, 16,* 59 – 60.

# Cognitive Behaviorism and Social Learning Theory

Trait theory was the predominant view of personality among psychologists concerned with individual differences. Most psychologists, however, have been concerned not with individual differences but with general laws that apply to all people, especially the laws of learning. In this field, the behaviorist view (see Chapter 3) quickly rose to predominance in the 1920s. In its purest form, as enunciated, for example, by John B. Watson, it asserts that psychology as a science need by concerned with nothing but behavior, overt and, in principle, observable. At times Watson seemed to be saying that all behavior is reducible to muscle twitches and glandular secretions, but at other times behavior definitely concerned action sequences as well.

As happens in most fields, once any view becomes widely accepted, many people have a stake in contradicting it, one way or another, and others are deeply invested in defending it. Behaviorism was opposed by the psychoanalysts and also by existential and humanistic psychologists.

Another group of psychologists, the cognitive behaviorists, opposes an extreme philosophical behaviorism but nonetheless agrees with the behaviorists that the data of psychology are primarily behavior. They need terms like purpose, plan, map, model, expectation, goal, and motivation to explain the behavior they see. The data, however, are not introspective accounts of those variables; they find objective indicators of them. Cognitive behaviorism is a general description but not a specific school of personality theory. The corresponding school of personality psychology is social learning theory.

---

## ORIGINS OF SOCIAL LEARNING THEORY

### Gestalt Psychology

The predominant school of thought in nineteenth century psychology I will call *experimental introspectionism* (though it is more often called structuralism, a term now recycled for the Piagetians, as will be seen in the next chapter). For the experimental introspectionists, the central problem of psychology was to determine with exactitude the mental elements. Like the British associationists and other philosophical introspectionists before them, they took it for granted that the contents of the mind are reducible to a set of elements, which together make up the stream of thought and account for all the products of the mind. Rather than simply introspect to find those elements, however, they performed experiments to determine the exact properties of the mind.

E. B. Titchener at one time made a tally of sensation qualities, as follows: eye, 32,820; ear (audition), 11,600; nose, ?; tongue, 4; skin, 4; muscle, 2; tendon, 1; joint, 1; alimentary canal, 3?; blood-vessels, ?; lungs, 1; sex organs, 1; ear (static sense), 1 (Titchener, 1896). Thus there are, by this count, more than 44,000 elementary sensations. Each is a conscious element of mind, but it has no meaning. To include meaning there must be at least two sensations, thus some context for the sensation. A sensation plus its context is or creates a perception. The laws of association show how ideas are thus generated.

As an example of the kind of experimentation these psychologists did, one prominent question was, How far apart must two pointed objects touching the skin be in order that they be perceived as two points rather than as one point? On the finger tips, the points can be very close together, but on the back, the points must be quite far apart to be perceived as two.

Both psychoanalysis and behaviorism were rebellions against this kind of introspective psychology, psychoanalysis by emphasizing the unconscious in contrast to consciousness, behaviorism by denying that psychology need be concerned with consciousness. Gestalt psychology, in turn, arose as a rebellion against behaviorism but also against the older experimental introspectionism. *Gestalt* is the German word for form or pattern. The Gestalt psychologists were originally centered in Germany, but the leaders — Max Wertheimer, Kurt Koffka, Wolfgang Köhler, and Kurt Lewin — all went to the United States during the Nazi era.

The chief thrust of the work of the Gestalt psychologists was that perception always involves patterns and is not reducible to the sum of separate elements. When a child learns to recognize or sing "Yankee Doodle," she does not learn one note at a time; rather, the child learns the pattern or relation between notes and recognizes the tune even if it is played in a different key than she has ever heard it in before.

*Wertheimer on perception.* Max Wertheimer, the founder of Gestalt psychology, objected to the resolution of perceptions into elements, such as Titchener was doing, on phenomenological grounds. If I stand at the window and see a house, a tree, and the sky, he wrote, that cannot be reduced to 327 brightnesses and tones of color. A melody of 17 tones with its accompaniment of 32 tones is heard as melody and accompaniment, not as 49 tones, and certainly not as something that could be divided arbitrarily into 20 plus 29 tones rather than 17 plus 32 (Wertheimer, 1923/1965).

A discovery of Wertheimer's that became one of the starting points for Gestalt psychology was the perception of apparent movement. When a person views in rapid succession two frames, first a vertical strip, then a horizontal one, which is what he would see if the strip actually rotated, the person will see it as if the strip had moved from one position to the other. The strip is not "seen" at intermediate positions; rather, one apparently sees movement, or, as the Gestalt psychologists would say, one sees *apparent movement*. Wertheimer called this the *phi phenomenon* (Wertheimer, 1912).

*Köhler's experiments with apes.* An important instance of work outside the field of perception is that of Wolfgang Köhler, who experimented with the great apes on the Spanish island of Tenerife off the coast of Africa from 1913 to 1917. He presented a different view of their learning process from the trial-and-error view of Thorndike (Köhler, 1917/1925).

Some of the more intelligent apes, he showed, could master the use of simple tools and show reasoning, not simply blind trial and error, in solving novel problems. For example, most apes when caged, seeing food outside the bars that they could not reach, learned to detour away from the food in order to pick up a stick that could then be used as a tool to reach the banana. Köhler considered the ability to detour a crucial aspect of intelligence, or reasoning. One especially intelligent ape, who liked to put sticks into holes, happened to put one stick into the hole in the end of another one. When he had done so, he realized that he had a long stick that would enable him to reach an otherwise unattainable banana.

A similar problem involved a banana suspended inside the cage but out of reach even when the ape was jumping. The ape had to learn how to move a stool over and to jump from the stool to reach the banana. Again, it was necessary to detour away from the direction of the banana in order to bring the stool under the banana. The next task required the ape to balance one stool on top of another in order to jump to reach a higher banana. One ape was able to master this feat. The animals had difficulty not so much in the conception as in the execution, particularly learning to balance one stool securely on another.

Köhler emphasized that it is possible to present problems to an ape that will disrupt his behavior and lead to apparently blind trial and error. For most problems presented to them, however, their behavior is radically different, being what in a person we would call thoughtful rather than a blind thrashing about. On the basis of these and many other experiments, Köhler defined *insight learning*. Insight rather than blind trial and error must be postulated when the animal first pauses to assay the lay of the land, then proceeds to carry out his actions smoothly without disruption and shifts from one strategy to another by abrupt breaks; once mastered, the accomplishment is secure.

### Tolman's Purposive Behaviorism

Edward C. Tolman, an American influenced by the Gestalt psychologists, called his system *purposive behaviorism* at first, later expectancy theory or *sign-Gestalt* theory (Tolman, 1932). The business of psychology is studying molar, not molecular behavior, he said, borrowing the terms from chemistry. The muscle twitches and glandular secretions studied by the extreme Watsonians he called the *molecules* of behavior, whereas actions, the large units of behavior, he called *molar* behavior. Just as perception is not a mosaic of discrete sensations, so actions are not a mosaic of discrete muscular movements. In fact, the particular muscular movements are usually not important because they can be interchanged with alternative movements to achieve the same results.

Purpose, he said, is not something peripheral or incidental to behavior but rather is part of the definition of behavior. There is no behavior without purpose. Thus the patellar reflex (knee jerk) is not behavior by his definition. Behavior is always *docile* in the pursuit of some purpose. The purpose need not be consciously entertained; indeed, most of his work was done with white rats (to whom he dedicated his first and best book). Purpose is something given in and inferred from behavior, equally in rats and people. By "docile" Tolman meant that people or other animals learn to reach their goals more efficiently in successive trials. That is Tolman's definition of behavior. If you block one of an animal's ways of approaching a goal, it will search for another way to the same goal. If it is presented with the situation again, it will tend to do it a bit better.

Thorndike's studies of cats in puzzle boxes are included, but Pavlov's studies of conditioned reflexes, for the most part, are not.

As an example of a behavioristic definition of a cognitive concept, Tolman cited O. L. Tinkelpaugh's experiment (Tinkelpaugh, 1928). A monkey watched while the experimenter put food under one of two containers. Then a screen was put between the monkey and the two containers. The animal was not allowed to reach the containers for a few seconds. When it did, it invariably chose the correct one and consumed the food, either a lettuce leaf or a banana, which it much preferred. Now here is the experiment. The monkey watches while a banana is hidden under one cup. While the screen is up and the animal cannot see what is being done, the banana is removed and a leaf of lettuce is substituted. The monkey turns over the cup but rejects the food, throws the lettuce on the floor, searches around, and generally shows disruption of a previously smooth behavior pattern. Is it farfetched to say the animal expected to find a banana and was then disappointed and frustrated? There does not seem to be a simpler way of conveying the pattern of its response.

Similarly, M. H. Elliott, one of Tolman's students, using white rats, substituted a less favored food, sunflower seed, for a favored food, bran mash, at the end of the maze, achieving a similar disruption of behavior and similar searching responses (Elliott, 1928). "Such 'searching,' i.e. disruption, is to be taken as the empirical evidence for, and definition of, an immanent expectation of the previously obtained bran mash" (Tolman, 1932, p. 74).

*Latent learning in rats.* Tolman and his students undertook a major program of research around the idea of purposive behavior and expectancies, mostly using white rats. He was careful to distinguish performance from competence or knowledge through an ingenious series of experiments. Hungry rats were put, one at a time of course, in rather complex mazes. Sometimes they were put first in the final station, where they found food, then started at the beginning. Other times they were simply started in the maze and allowed to discover for themselves that there was food at the end. Eventually they found their way through to the food box. On subsequent days they were merely put in the start box, and they ran through to the food. There are two main ways to measure learning in a maze, by the number of errors, that is, entries into blind alleys, and by the time it takes to get from start to finish. On successive days the rats gradually eliminated their errors and decreased their time to reach the food.

In the following experiment, the rat received only a small portion of its day's ration as a reward in the maze, with the remainder given to it a couple of hours later in another place. Rats run under those conditions were the control group. Then hungry rats with no previous maze experience were put in the maze with no food in it. The rats in this group, like those in the former group, were fed a couple of hours later in another place. They simply wandered around in the maze. They eventually reached the end, but on successive trials they eliminated errors very slowly and also decreased their running time slowly. The crucial test, the experiment, is as follows. On the eleventh trial, when the rats who had been fed every time were running the maze quickly and almost without errors and the others were just ambling along, the rats that had not received food in the maze suddenly found some in the food box. On the next trial, they ran as well as or better than those that had been fed all along. Similarly, if those who have been fed in the maze find no food, their performance will deteriorate somewhat. The fact that rats in the experimental group were evidently learning the maze even while showing almost no improvement Tolman called *latent learning*.

Thorndike's law of effect (see Chapter 3), that rewards stamp in the right responses, does not account for latent learning. Even if one stretches the idea of reward to say the rats were rewarded by being taken out of the maze, one cannot thereby explain the results, for the control group had that reward in addition to food. There were many variations on this impressive experiment.

*Cognitive maps in rats.* How is latent learning possible? Tolman postulated that the rat exploring the maze in a leisurely way is forming a *cognitive map* of it. As a test of this theory and a further refutation of Watson's molecular theory of learning, Tolman's student Donald Macfarlane did the following experiment (Macfarlane, 1930). He installed a maze inside a tank and flooded it to the extent that the rat had to swim to reach the food box. Under these circumstances, the rats learned the maze. Then he installed a platform a little below the level of the water, so that the rat now had to wade through rather than swimming. The actual muscular movements of wading or running are entirely different from swimming. On the first trial after the change, the rats showed disruption of behavior, as usually happens with animals who have found a situation different from the one they expected. After one trial, however, they ran through as efficiently as they had formerly swum, with an evident carryover of the previous learning process. Thus the animal has shown that it has formed a cognitive map of the maze, in the absence of previous rewards for wading through it.

Note that in Tolman's system there is a subtle shift in what the animal is viewed as learning. In the typical case of instrumental learning, such as those studied by Thorndike and many other behaviorists, the animal learns a response to a stimulus. The behaviorists are often referred to as S-R theorists, where S stands for stimulus and R for response. When learning consists of constructing a cognitive map, however, the animal is forming S-S associations, not S-R associations; it is learning the relation of the stimulus elements to each other, not to particular responses.

*Reward versus reinforcement.* Tolman disagreed with Thorndike's law of effect. Reward or the state of satisfaction following reward does not, by itself, stamp in connections, Tolman believed. The animal learns what leads to what by experiencing them together, and rewards and punishments are not necessary for learning, though they may induce performance of what has been learned. Rewards and punishments do have an effect in calling the animal's attention to elements of the situation to be specially attended to. Reward is a bit of information, not a reinforcer.

The fact that animals rewarded or punished only part of the time showed more resistance to experimental extinction than those invariably rewarded was never a major difficulty for Tolman's theory, and some of the early work on probabilistic learning (that is, learning in situations where a reward is not always obtained, what Skinner refers to by *schedules of reinforcement*) was done by psychologists in that group. The classical S-R theorists, such as Thorndike or Watson, did have difficulty with these facts. The animal rewarded every time during training ought to have the stronger association or habit and be more resistant to extinction, according to their theories, which needed ad hoc amendments to accommodate the actual facts.

Skinner (see Chapter 3) turned the situation around and made intermittent schedules of reinforcement the centerpiece of his theory. Yet it is hard to think about what Skinner has found without saying to oneself, "Of course a variable-ratio schedule of reinforcement is resistant to extinction; the animal keeps expecting that another reinforcement can still come." The word *expecting* makes that Tolman's type of account, not Skinner's. Tolman, however, objects to Skinner substituting the word *reinforcement* for *reward*. Whether reward is in fact reinforcing is the question, Tolman said. Although Tolman made a telling point there, Skinner has prevailed as to vocabulary. Most psychologists today appear automatically to use the term *reinforcement* when they mean reward or punishment, even when they do not accept Skinner's theory that reward is what determines learning.

Tolman's explanation of why intermittently rewarded behavior is more resistant to extinction than invariably rewarded behavior is a discrimination hypothesis: "Expectancies and behavior change at a faster rate the greater the discriminability of the change of conditions between training and testing series" (Bower & Hilgard, 1981, p. 341). Thus the longer extinction time for variable-interval and variable-ratio schedules results from the fact that they are harder to discriminate from no reward than are invariably rewarded or even fixed-interval and fixed-ratio rewards.

Some experiments face rats with a difficult decision. A typical one requires the rat to jump across a gap to one of two doors, which may be distinguished by position or by some different mark or color. One door opens to a food box, the other is closed, and the rat who has jumped to it consequently falls to the ground. Faced with this choice, the rat who has not completely mastered the required discrimination hesitates and looks back and forth at the two doors, Tolman noted. This behavior he called *vicarious trial and error*, or VTE. VTE is Tolman's behavioristic definition of thinking or of the decision process.

---

## APPLICATION TO PERSONALITY

Behaviorism and especially cognitive behaviorism have had an immense influence on contemporary psychiatry, clinical psychology, and personality theory, second only to the influence of psychoanalysis (and often proudly proclaimed as more important than psychoanalysis because more "scientific"). But how does one go from Tolman's rats to personality theory and psychotherapy?

The discoveries of Tolman's group justify assuming that reward and punishment cannot be given total credit for human or even animal learning. It can be left up in the air whether Tolman was right that reward and punishment function only as sources of information and motivation for performance. When one turns to human learning, it seems reasonable to assume that the cognitive element in behavior, such as purposes, plans, maps, models, and expectations, is even larger than in animals. One can hardly speak about human behavior without such terms. Nonetheless, many behaviorists, especially the Skinnerians, continue to emphasize reward and punishment, renamed reinforcement, in theories of human learning and in prescriptions for teaching, for psychotherapy, for social reform (Skinner, 1981, and elsewhere), and for other practical applications.

There is a new element in human learning. People, perhaps especially children, learn vicariously. Vicarious trial and error, the VTE that Tolman's rats showed by head waggles, takes other forms in children; an enormous amount of human learning involves vicarious learning from *social models*. James Mark Baldwin, one of the earliest and greatest developmental psychologists, made *imitation* the central motive of his psychology (Baldwin, 1897/1906). Imitation obviously is learning from social models. Freud did not talk of imitation, but some of the same phenomena are covered in his discussions of *identification*. Bandura, in fact, uses the terms *imitation, identification*, and *observational learning* interchangeably to refer to learning from social models (Bandura, 1969, p. 219).

Probably the predominant school of personality psychology today is social learning theory. It has several central tenets, each of which is championed by a different investigator. Julian B. Rotter has stressed the expectation for and value of rewards as determinants of behavior (Rotter, 1954, 1972). Albert Bandura has stressed that one can learn behaviors vicariously through social models, regardless of rewards or even practice (Bandura, 1969, 1977b). Walter Mischel has stressed the importance of the situation as opposed to traits in determining behavior (Mischel, 1968, 1973).

### Rotter on Expectation of Reward

Rotter was one of the first to promulgate social learning theory. He begins by emphasizing that behavior is determined by the situation, the expectation of rewards, and the value of the rewards expected (Rotter, 1954). Those factors are compatible with Tolman's findings. Because, however, Rotter is concerned with people instead of rats, he can use a technique Tolman could not, namely, a questionnaire.

*Generalized expectancy.* Granted that the expectation of rewards, based on past experiences in that specific situation, is a major factor, there is another factor that presumably is minimal in animal learning; that is a *generalized expectancy* with regard to a class of similar situations. There are many ways of categorizing situations, and people may have generalized expectancies with respect to any or all ways of categorizing. Behavior in any situation is a function of expectancies with respect to that situation plus all relevant general expectancies. The more often the specific situation has previously occurred, the more the person will depend on specific expectancies. The more novel the situation, the more important will generalized expectancies be. What one expects in a given situation is, obviously, specific to that situation, and minor changes in the situation can alter what one expects to happen and hence alter behavior. The generalized expectancies, however, are built up through many experiences and operate in many different circumstances.

The effect of reinforcement, Rotter states, is not an automatic stamping in of the preceding behavior. Its effect depends on whether the reward is viewed as contingent on the behavior. Where the outcome of a task is seen as entirely a matter of luck or chance (or entirely under the experimenter's control), the effect of reward is likely to be the opposite of what behavioristic learning theory predicts: The response preceding the reward is less likely rather than more likely to be chosen the next time. That paradox is the result of the *gambler's fallacy*, that is, the belief that randomly occurring events in fact follow a pattern, namely, that behavior that paid off one time is for that very reason less likely to pay off the next time. Thus the gambler's fallacy operates in the opposite direction from classical reinforcement (Rotter, 1966).

*Internal versus external locus of control.* On the basis of such considerations, Rotter and his students have devoted much attention to one particular generalized expectancy, which he has named *internal versus external control of reinforcement*. This characteristic refers to whether one believes one's rewards are largely contingent on one's own efforts and permanent characteristics or are outside one's own control. Some people are prone to believe that whether they attain what they want depends on their own efforts and characteristics, whereas others tend to believe that what they attain is in the hands of luck or fate or circumstances or other people. Rotter calls his test for this variable the I-E test (Rotter, 1966).

The format of the I-E test is paired choice, that is, each item consists of a pair of statements, one of which represents a typical belief of a person who feels controlled by luck, by fate, or by others and the other a typical belief of a person who feels in charge of his or her own destiny, whether because of inborn traits or current efforts. Both statements relate to the same topic. The pairs of statements refer to influencing political events, to the causation of war, to whether grades are due to studying or to some mysterious process of the teacher, and to many other topics. Some of the pairs are phrased in the first person; others refer to people in general. For each pair of statements, subjects are to choose the one that they prefer or that is closer to their own idea. The score is the number of times the person answers in the external direction.

> The following is a typical item from the test:
> **a.** Many of the unhappy things in people's lives are partly due to bad luck.
> **b.** People's misfortunes result from the mistakes they make.

A great deal of research has been done with the I-E test, and many of the findings associated with Rotter's version of social learning theory involve its use. Learning theory predicted that behavior reinforced 100 percent of the time would be extinguished more quickly than that reinforced 50 percent of the time (see Chapter 3). Experimental results show, however, that if the task is perceived as dependent on the person's skill, behavior reinforced 100 percent is extinguished more slowly than that reinforced 50 percent of the time. The Externals, persons who score toward the external side, have been shown to make more gambler's fallacy shifts, that is, to have higher expectations after a failure than after a success, compared with the Internals, those scoring on the internal side (Rotter, 1966).

Rotter suggested that those scoring at either extreme are likely to be maladjusted. That is understandable in view of the content of the test, which does not separate realistic beliefs in one's control over events from unrealistic beliefs. It is generally unrealistic to think that one's grades are usually the result of the teacher's peculiarities; it is quite realistic to believe that ordinary people have little effect on questions of war and peace. In view of the fact that such questions are lumped together in the test, the number of significant correlations that have been found with the test is all the more remarkable. Rotter has criticized many applications of the test for failing to take account of the factors affecting the specific situation and expecting the correlation in a specific instance to be carried entirely by this measure of generalized expectancy (Rotter, 1975).

Many studies done with the I-E test confirmed the hypotheses with which they began, though usually the confirmation was a barely significant statistical trend. Other hypotheses were not confirmed by research. The problem is that the theory does not specify which of its predictions are central to its thesis and which are peripheral. So nonconfirmation does not much weaken Rotter's theory, but then confirmation correspondingly does not much strengthen it.

Rotter acknowledges that his test accounts for relatively little of the variance of behavior, and that the link between theory and research predictions is not strong. The I-E test is not unique in these respects. Rotter is simply more candid than most psychologists. Although the central theme of the present book is that theories and research on personality can be looked at as a species of science, the weakness of the link between most personality theories and their experimental tests is a warning of the gulf between most of psychology and more exact sciences.

In principle one could study any number of traits in the way Rotter and his group have studied internal-external control, beginning by making a separate test for each generalized expectancy. One generalized expectancy for which he has created another test is that of the tendency to trust other people (Rotter, 1980).

Locus of control as a topic of study has not stopped with the I-E test but has grown to be a substantial research area, or miniparadigm (Lefcourt, 1981, 1982). Much of the research begins with the obvious complexity of the I-E test. Thus, to believe that one's outcomes are governed by powerful others is quite different from attributing outcomes to luck or chance (Levenson, 1981). Separate tests have been constructed for these attitudes and also for other ways of dividing up the construct of the locus of control. Some such tests have been based on statistical analysis of the original test, others on logical analysis. The statistical analysis is technically called *factor analysis*; it always involves empirical analysis of data from a particular sample of persons. The logical analysis is based on examination of the apparent content, that is, on the wording of the test.

Does the I-E test measure a trait? Certainly it refers to a generalized disposition; that is its essence. Rotter, however, is not sympathetic to attempts to factor analyze the test with a view to setting up a kind of permanent taxonomy of its components (Rotter, 1975). Those components, he thinks, would prove to be different with different samples of people facing different situations. He takes an intermediate position with respect to traits. He is not a fanatical opponent of the idea of traits, but at the same time he does not readily reify traits either. That position is a safe one; one can hardly prove Rotter wrong on that point. At the same time, it partly undercuts the value of the I-E test as an insight into personality.

The predilection of Rotter and other social learning theorists for the term *reinforcement* rather than the everyday-language term *reward* is ironic, given that Skinner chose the term *reinforcement* because it is noncognitive, whereas the social learning theorists are explicitly dedicated to reintroducing the cognitive element in behavior.

### Bandura on Social Models

Perhaps the most widely recognized advocate of social learning theory today is Albert Bandura. He began with the task of setting off his theory against that of operant learning theory, as expounded by Skinner and his followers (Bandura, 1977b). Operant learning theory, Bandura believes, does not adequately explain an important form of learning, namely, learning by observing other people as models. The operant version is approximately as follows: The model is a discriminated stimulus; imitation of the model is the response; a rewarding stimulus following the modeled response reinforces the behavior. Later, because imitation has often been reinforced, the child develops a tendency to imitate that does not require constant reinforcement.

Bandura replies with an alternative model. People can learn vicariously through social models without experiencing or observing any rewards or punishments, without practicing the relevant responses in the presence of the model, and without the model being present during the reproduction of the behavior. Therefore, observational learning can take place without any element of the standard operant learning procedure being present (Bandura, 1971).

*The effect of aggressive models.* A typical experiment by Bandura is as follows (Bandura, Ross, & Ross, 1961): A group of nursery school children were brought individually into a room where they were given a quiet task to do in one corner. In the opposite corner an adult was taken to a small table containing a tinker toy set, a mallet, and a Bobo doll (an inflated toy with a weighted bottom, so that if you hit it down, it springs up automatically). There were two adult models, one man and one woman; half of the boys saw the male model, half the female, and the same for the girls. In the major part of the experiment, designed to show the importance of aggressive models, the adult displayed four different and novel kinds of aggressive behavior toward the doll: The adult (1) laid the doll on its side, sat on it, and punched its nose; (2) then raised the doll up and hit it on the head with a mallet; (3) then picked the doll up and threw it; and (4) then kicked it around. This sequence was repeated three times, accompanied by aggressive exclamations, such as "Sock him in the head," "Kick him," and "Pow," and also the remarks, "He keeps coming back for more," and "He sure is a tough fella."

In the nonaggressive behavior condition, the children saw the adult quietly putting tinker toys together, ignoring the Bobo doll and the mallet. The third group of children, the control group, omitted this part of the experiment. There were twenty-four children in each of these conditions.

After ten minutes in the room with either adult model, the children were taken into another room and frustrated to make them feel a bit aggressive. The frustration consisted in putting them in a room filled with attractive toys, then, just as they were beginning to play with them, interrupting on a flimsy pretext and taking them to a different room. The control children were frustrated in the same way. Following the frustrating experience, the test of delayed imitation began. The room in which the children were tested contained a number of toys, including a Bobo doll, a mallet, and other toys appropriate to aggressive and to nonaggressive play. The children spent twenty minutes in this room, where they were watched through one-way mirrors by trained observers.

Of the twenty-four children who saw the aggressive behavior, all but two showed a good deal of physical and verbal aggression similar to that of the models. Those behaviors were virtually absent from both the other two groups of children. One third of the children who observed aggressive models also imitated the nonaggressive remarks of the model they had observed. General aggression, just punching the Bobo doll, as a child who had not seen the adult model might do spontaneously, did not differ between the group exposed to the aggressive model and the control group; however, the children who had seen the nonaggressive model showed less aggression. The reason for using the novel aggressive act was, of course, to differentiate the general aggressive from the imitative aggressive responses.

In an extension of this experiment, a corresponding procedure was followed for another forty-eight children, half of whom saw the same two models in a ten-minute film of the same aggressive actions, the other half seeing a similarly aggressive cartoon (Bandura, Ross, & Ross, 1963). The filmed model and the cartoon model were as effective in producing aggression as the model actually in the room with the children.

Thus in this series of experiments the children imitated models who received no visible rewards or punishments; the children had no practice in the presence of the model; and the model was not present when the children imitated. These experiments exemplify Bandura's objection to operant learning theory.

In another experiment, one group of children had seen a filmed model severely punished for novel aggressive actions, and a second group of children saw the filmed model rewarded with food and with approval for her aggressive behavior (Bandura, 1965). The third group of children saw a version with neither reward nor punishment. At the conclusion of the film, the three groups were given the opportunity to play with the same kind of doll. Those who had seen the model punished displayed the least aggressive behavior. There was no difference in the amount of aggression displayed by those who had seen the model rewarded and those who had observed no consequence. Under all three conditions, the boys displayed much more aggressive behavior than the girls. In order to find out what the children had learned, as distinct from what they performed spontaneously, after an interval all groups were given an incentive to reproduce as much of the behavior they had seen as they could. Under these circumstances there were no differences among the three groups, and the differences between the boys and girls were almost eliminated. All groups displayed more aggression than before. Thus rewarding or punishing the model changed the observers' spontaneous performance but not what they learned.

*Modeling in social learning theory.* This experimental format has the merit of providing a framework or paradigm within which many variations can fruitfully be explored. Other experiments in this general format have shown which characteristics of models make behavior most likely to be imitated, which characteristics of children make them most likely to imitate models, and which situations are most conducive to imitation. As an example of a characteristic of a model that is important, models of high status relative to the observer are more likely to be imitated. It is also true, however, that models are more likely to be imitated the more similar they are to the child who is the subject. Hostile and aggressive responses are particularly likely to be imitated, but so are self-rewarding and self-regulatory responses. Children who tend to be dependent on adults are more likely to be imitative than less dependent children of the same age (Bower & Hilgard, 1981, p. 463).

Granting, as surely one must, the importance of social models in shaping behavior, turning from the laboratory to real-life situations shows how complex the matter is. Everyone past infancy has observed countless models displaying countless different kinds of behaviors with all sorts of consequences, many behaviors bringing rewards or punishments that directly contradict the consequences of other instances of the same or similar behavior. Bandura, of course, is aware of that fact. How people put together those experiences to shape their own future conduct may be no more than the inevitable consequence of their own past experiences and present situation, but that has not been proved, nor is it easy to see how it could be.

The experiments of Bandura and his colleagues show that imitation occurs, but that presumably has always been known (except, perhaps, by psychologists in love with contrary theories). More weighty is the fact that people can be induced to do some things by watching others being rewarded and punished for doing or not doing them, without receiving any direct reward or punishment themselves, or even simply by observing the behavior with no visible rewards attached. What is the mechanism for that effect? What does it imply for psychological theory?

Bandura has addressed these questions. The position he outlines for social learning theory is that reinforcement is not an automatic or mechanistic response to reward. Rather, reward acts as a source of information and motivation, an idea that Tolman had proposed previously. Observing a reward being given to a model is just as informative as being rewarded oneself (Bandura, 1977b).

As is often true in psychology, the position Bandura ascribes to his opponents, the behaviorists, may not be one that they recognize as their own. The term *reinforcement* does indeed suggest an automatic or mechanistic effect, and the thrust of Skinner's thinking may appear to be compatible with some such assumption, but Skinner himself, on purpose, says nothing at all about what is taking place in the "black box," which is how he looks at the unfathomable, impenetrable person who is doing the learning.

### Situationism

One of the oldest issues debated in psychology is the extent to which people's behavior is guided by the situation versus the extent to which it is governed by the person's traits and dispositions. Nineteenth-century faculty psychology laid great emphasis on the person's faculties, an amalgam of abilities and traits (see Chapter 4). Perhaps the best evidence of continued advocacy of traits as determinants of behavior is the great interest in and talent devoted to factor analysis of psychological tests by R. B. Cattell and other investigators (Cattell, 1957). (For a summary of Cattell's personality theory, see Hall & Lindzey, 1978, ch. 14.)

The issue is entwined with another, namely, the issue of the generality versus the specificity of behavior. To the extent that behavior is governed by broad traits and dispositions, it has generality. To the extent that it is specific to the situation, rather than depending on the person's traits, it does not have generality. (That is how the argument is usually presented. One could make a case that there are very specific dispositions, even inborn ones, whereas situations can appropriately be classed in broad categories. That is not usually how the issue is argued, however.)

*Hartshorne and May's study of character.* The original advocate of the doctrine of specificity was E. L. Thorndike (see Chapters 3 and 4). He initiated and organized one of the first major studies of individual differences with respect to an aspect of personality, the Character Education Inquiry, conducted by Hugh Hartshorne, Mark May, and their several collaborators (1928, 1929, 1930).

The original aim of the study was to evaluate the effect of various character-building organizations, such as boys' clubs and Sunday school, on children's moral behavior. More than 10,000 children, mainly from the fourth through the eighth grade, from several public and private school systems, were studied with respect to a large number of tests, tasks, and games. The experiments were conducted at home, in the classroom, on the playground or in the gym, and at parties, thus tapping a wide range of typical settings and situations.

There was a variety of small experiments in which each child could cheat, lie, or steal, seemingly without being detected. The studies were planned with remarkable care and ingenuity. For example, tests were given in the classroom, then the papers taken to the office and copied, then returned to the students with answer keys, so that they could grade their own papers. The excess of the score when they graded their own papers over the original score was a measure of cheating. In a speed test, such as crossing out all the a's on a page of letters, the children had a chance when grading their papers to cross out some more a's. Care was taken that all the tests, tasks, and contests were the kind that the children were used to, that every child was given a chance to cheat, and that they had no inkling that cheating could be detected, so that the usual constraints against cheating, such as observation by other students, were missing.

For athletic contests each child was tested alone, because their mutual surveillance would have inhibited any natural tendency to cheat. They were shown attractive badges to be awarded to the winners, in order to arouse a motivation to do well. Then each task, say, a broad jump, was practiced a couple of times in front of the experimenter, who surreptitiously noticed the distance jumped. Then the experimenter left the child alone to record his own "real" trials. The differences between the values the experimenter recorded and those the child did, when improbably large, were considered signs of cheating. Other tasks set impossibly difficult puzzles to be worked on in a short time; claiming success was considered a likely indication of cheating. Among party games, where a child was able to pin the tail on the donkey perfectly, it was assumed that she had peeked beneath the blindfold, as was possible. In tests where there was a chance of improvement in the second score, the discrepancy between the two scores had to be great enough (as determined by precise reliability studies) to rule out genuine change for the score to be taken as evidence of cheating.

Another test gave the children a chance to use boxes that contained coins. The children had an opportunity to take a dime (a lot of money for a school child in those days) before returning the box. The children did not know that the boxes were marked with their seat number, so that they could be identified.

A final set of data consisted of a questionnaire concerning whether the child had been dishonest in some way on the previous tasks. Thus in addition to knowing who cheated or stole and who did not, the experimenters found some who confessed having done so and others who denied it, thus lying to cover up.

Contrary to what might be expected, Hartshorne and May found that resisting the temptation to cheat, steal, or lie in one such situation was not very predictive of resisting temptation in another. The correlation between two such tasks or tests, although in general statistically significant (that is, presumably not due to chance), was usually not high and varied according to whether the tasks, the settings, and the modes by which cheating could occur were the same or different. The correlation between two different tests at school was higher than that between the same two tests, one conducted at school and one at home. The correlation between two similar tasks was higher than that between two entirely different ones. But only where tests or experiments were of the same type and in the same setting were the average intercorrelations reasonably high, ranging from an average of .84 for intercorrelation of tests of lying to an average of .44 for intercorrelation of tests of speed. But whereas copying from a scoring key on one test correlated on average .70 with copying from a scoring key on another test, and adding on scores on a speed test on average correlated .44 with adding on scores on another test, copying from a scoring key correlated only .29 with adding on scores. Thus the conclusion from this first set of studies was that cheating, stealing, and lying do not constitute a general trait of dishonesty but are largely specific to the particular situation in which they are studied.

Hartshorne and May noted, however, as the social learning theorists who quote them do not always do, that the size of the correlation between specific tests was about the same as the size of the correlation between specific subtests of a general intelligence or achievement test. If one allows that there are real differences in ability or achievement (never mind if those differences are originally due to heredity or environment), these data are not grounds for rejecting the idea of somewhat general differences in honesty between children. The tests agree with the teacher's ratings of the children for honesty almost as well as intelligence tests agree with teacher's ratings for intelligence (Hartshorne & May, 1928, p. 139).

In their second set of studies, the experimenters dealt with measures of service and self-control in the same way with similar results, that is, only modest generality from one situation to another (Hartshorne, May, & Maller, 1929).

The final set of studies was concerned with the organization of character (Hartshorne, May, & Shuttleworth, 1930). In these studies they contrived a way of rendering the scores on a variety of tests on a comparable scale (*normalizing* is the technical term for that operation). Having done so, they were in a position to ask about each of the children, not just how honest a child was in a specific situation, but how variable with respect to honesty he or she was in going from test to test or from situation to situation. Surprisingly, in view of their previous findings, they found the degree of integration quite high. Moreover, the more honest pupils were also the more integrated. The experimenters concluded that honesty is often an integrated character trait, but dishonesty is specific to the situation.

With respect to the original aim of the research, to study character education, results indicated no consistent gain from having participated in character-building organizations, such as Sunday school or boys' clubs. The results have usually been taken as a rebuff to psychologists who expect a high degree of generalizability from one measure of honesty to another, or even as disproving the postulate of conscience or superego (Mischel, 1981, pp. 481–482). The results are even more striking as a rebuff to those who expect a straightforward influence of character-building environments on behavior. The low degree of generality does not establish a high degree of importance of environmental influences; the major factors that account for honest behavior simply are not known.

This set of studies has provided a rich lode that later psychologists, unwilling or unable to undertake again so huge an empirical study, have mined repeatedly. One way of reanalyzing goes as follows. Suppose each subtest is treated as if it were an item in a test. Then a series of subtests must be added together to make a single reasonably reliable score. That is treating the data the way ability data are treated. If this is done, the composite score on one occasion does indeed show a respectably high correlation with a similar composite score obtained on another occasion (Epstein, 1984).

The research of Hartshorne, May, and their collaborators is often cited in current psychological literature as the primary source of a situationist view, though perhaps that is an injustice to the original authors. In any event, taken in its entirety, it lends itself to alternative interpretations.

*Mischel on delay of gratification.* Walter Mischel has been investigating the capacity to delay gratification, presumably because it is a necessary ingredient of mature behavior in general and conscience in particular. His most typical experiments occur in the following format: A child is left alone in a situation where he or she has been promised one of two awards, a larger or preferred reward and a smaller or less preferred one. Which reward the child receives depends on willingness to wait. If the child must have the reward immediately, the smaller or less preferred one is given; if the child is willing to wait for the experimenter to return, the larger or more preferred one is given. The question is, Under what circumstances are children willing to wait for the larger reward rather than settling immediately for the smaller one?

Mischel's first studies of the topic were done with children between the ages of seven and nine in a rural school in Trinidad in the 1950s. The children answered a simple little questionnaire, then were promised a piece of candy, a small piece immediately or a larger piece if they would wait till the experimenter returned in a week. The children checked their preference on the questionnaire, providing the researcher with a written record of the choice. Of the seven-year-olds, about 80 percent chose the small piece now; the eight-year-olds were split about 50–50; of the nine-year-olds, 80 percent chose the larger, delayed reward (Mischel, 1958).

This experimental setup proved to be one capable of many fruitful variations and modifications. For example, Trinidadian school children who, according to their own self-reports, were relatively low on social responsibility and reliability also tended to be low on ability to delay gratification. Delinquents especially were low in ability to wait for larger rewards (Mischel, 1961). Children capable of delaying longer cheat less and are more socially responsible (Mischel & Gilligan, 1964), are more achievement oriented (Mischel, 1961), and are a little brighter (Mischel & Metzner, 1962). Perhaps most surprising, recent research indicates that social adjustment in high school is related to ability to delay gratification in the preschool years (Mischel, 1984, p. 277). Thus Mischel's own work provides remarkable evidence of a capacity—one hardly dares say trait—that generalizes across time and across situations.

Most of Mischel's studies have been devoted to showing situational influences on the ability to delay gratification. Much of the work having been done with nursery school children, it is not surprising that small changes in procedure can strongly affect the child's ability to wait for a preferred treat rather than accept the less preferred one available. The key variable in many of the experiments turned out to be distraction; the more children's attention was distracted from the desired treat, the longer they could wait. Most mothers of small children discover that. More interesting is that the children themselves discovered how to wait effectively. Below the age of four years, they seem to have no strategy. By five or six they may cover up the rewards or think about something else. Between third and sixth grade they develop sophisticated strategies to aid in distraction and delay and can give clear reasons for them (Yates & Mischel, 1979).

*Interactionism.* Despite the success of his own work in establishing ability to delay gratification as a general tendency or trait, Mischel has become an advocate of the importance of situations as opposed to traits or other personality dispositions (which latter he calls states) as determinants of behavior (Mischel, 1968). At times he has seemed to take as his mission to discredit both psychoanalysis and trait psychology, which, despite their almost total lack of communality (compare, for example, Chapters 2 and 4), he lumps together as trait-state psychology. He particularly has argued that traits are largely chimerical, that there is only minimal evidence for action tendencies that hold across diverse situations. Surely he is correct in assuming that measurement of personality makes no sense if there are no cross-situational tendencies. Although Mischel has retreated considerably from the extreme position denigrating traits that he once espoused, he is still a leading advocate of situationism (Mischel, 1973, 1984).

Aligned on the other side have been a number of other major figures in personality psychology. S. Epstein has argued that the low correlations in many studies that have tried to predict behavior from personality tests result from the fact that the baseline for the predictions is too narrow (Epstein, 1984). When the average of a number measures of a given trait, averaged either over time or over the different situations in which the trait might be manifest, is correlated with an appropriate criterion measure, perhaps also an average of some sort, correlations are appropriately high. Jack Block has made similar arguments (Block, 1977). In addition, he has cited data from long-term studies of children followed into maturity to show that data gathered originally for other purposes can yield some quite remarkable long-term predictions, a finding that he documents in more detail than Mischel does (Block, 1971).

Block has argued another point, a subtle one but one of great generality in its ramifications. Simply by doing sloppy, poorly conceived, poorly controlled, or generally inadequate research, one can almost guarantee very low correlations. That is because poor research introduces random effects, and random effects almost invariably result in erasing differences that actually exist in the population or that would be demonstrated in careful research. The actual relationship is attenuated by poor research technique (Block, 1977).

But perhaps nothing has been more characteristic of the debate over situationism than the conquest of straw men. Everyone admits that people's behavior is determined largely by the situations they find themselves in. People automatically behave differently in the classroom, the dining room, and the bathroom, for example. Were that not so, the person would have to be confined to an institution, and even there, the situation would be paramount in determining behavior. Few if any people say that everyone reacts to a situation like everyone else, that there are no enduring differences between people. If there were no carry-over of what is learned in one situation to a new one, no one would ever learn anything, Epstein has pointed out, for no situation is ever reproduced exactly (Epstein, 1984).

Virtually all psychologists who write in this area today claim to occupy middle ground of *interactionism*, if they do not actually claim to have discovered it. The interactionist position states that behavior is not determined by the situation alone, nor is it determined by the traits and dispositions of the person alone. Rather behavior is determined by the interaction of the person with the situation. That statement is just common sense, and it is difficult to find anyone who has contradicted it, even among those most committed to one side of the issue.

---

## EVIDENCE FROM SOCIAL-PSYCHOLOGICAL EXPERIMENTS

Impressive and ingenious as many of the laboratory experiments of the social learning theorists are, they do not compare in impact with some almost larger-than-life social-psychological experiments.

### Zimbardo's Prison Study

One of the most striking and persuasive evidences for the importance of the situation in determining behavior is the prison experiment done at Stanford University (Haney, Banks, & Zimbardo, 1973). Philip Zimbardo advertised for college undergraduate men who were spending the summer in the Stanford area to volunteer for a prison experiment, for which they would be paid $15 per day for two weeks. They understood that they might be assigned the role of either prisoner or guard. Of the seventy-five volunteers, twenty-four were picked on a variety of criteria to represent particularly healthy, competent, and invulnerable young men, with no evidence of previous antisocial behavior. By design, none of them knew one another beforehand.

The subjects were assembled and told whether they would play the part of a prisoner or a guard and briefed on what to expect. Because the assignment to those roles was random, there was little likelihood that a particular kind of person would tend to be found in one role more than in another. Prisoners were to be incarcerated in cells in the basement of a Stanford building for twenty-four hours a day. The guards stood eight-hour shifts; they had no restrictions on their own hours. The experiment involved a total of ten prisoners and eleven guards.

The experiment began in a somewhat unexpected way, namely, local police went out in the middle of the night to "arrest on suspicion of burglary" the students who had been assigned the role of prisoners. Then the prisoner students were put into a makeshift prison, three per small cell, in the basement of the Stanford psychology building. Doors had been removed and black, iron-barred ones substituted. The only furniture was a cot, mattress, sheet, and pillow for each prisoner.

Many features of prison life could not be reproduced for ethical and practical reasons, features such as homosexuality, beatings, and knowing that one faced a long term. In order to simulate some of the effects, the prisoners were deprived of all their clothes and other possessions and issued smocks, with no underwear permitted. They wore rubber sandals and had a chain and lock around one ankle. They each wore a cap made of a nylon stocking, to simulate the short haircut given in prisons. Each prisoner had a number, which was printed on the front and back of his smock. Instructions were to call the prisoner by number rather than name. These provisions succeeded in inducing some of the emasculation and deindividuation of the prison experience.

The guards were given plain khaki uniforms, plus a night stick and a whistle as signs of their authority, and reflecting sunglasses to keep them from making eye contact with the prisoners. They were intentionally given only minimal instructions on what to do, other than to keep order. The vagueness of this assignment permitted their own predilections to come out.

Within a few hours the students had thrown themselves into their roles to an amazing extent. The guards were being verbally brutal and overbearing; the prisoners were servile and sullen and planning escapes. Physical aggression was firmly prohibited, and there were experimenter-observers present at all times, though not necessarily visible to the participants. Most of the aggression was in the form of hostile or insulting remarks addressed to the prisoners by the guards. Over time, the guards became more harassing in their behavior, the prisoners more passive. Half of the prisoners were so upset that they had to be excused from completing the experiment. The entire experiment was terminated after six days instead of two weeks for similar reasons. All of the prisoners were de- lighted. The guards, who had grown to like their opportunity for exercising arbitrary power, were sorry to have the experiment stop.

The reactions for which some prisoners were released from the experiment were depression, crying, rage, and acute anxiety. These reactions began as early as the second day of the experiment. The guards also had negative feelings, but they always turned up for work, and some voluntarily worked extra hours without extra pay.

Although there were no constraints on what prisoners and guards could talk about, there were almost no conversations about anything except the prison experience, even when prisoners were alone in their cells. When participants spoke to one another, they almost never used names or nicknames but instead used some depersonalizing reference, such as "you."

Zimbardo and his colleagues point out that customarily the behavior of real-life guards and prisoners is attributed to dispositional factors. Prison guards are said to be selected for their sadistic potential, the prisoners for their antisocial tendencies. Because similar behaviors were displayed in this study by college students selected only for their apparent normality, the dispositional hypothesis just does not hold here. Only a situational explanation is convincing.

Note that the major effects Zimbardo and his colleagues observed are not so much examples of social imitation as of the influence of a preassigned social role, together with a stereotyped conception of what the role calls for. There were, nonetheless, individual differences in the reactions of the prisoners and guards. Half the prisoners stuck it out to the end of the experiment, for example. Of the three shifts of guards, the evening shift was by all measures the most harassing to the prisoners. Some guards were brutal, some tough but fair, and some never initiated any harassment of the prisoners. Such individual differences as were observed could not be related to any traits evident in the individual tests given before the experiment. (To preserve the independence of the observers, the tests were not scored until after the experiment.) However, the total numbers were too small and the initial choice of subjects — all college students — too homogeneous to provide a fair test of what individual differences might turn up in a broader experiment.

### Milgram's Obedience-to-Authority Study

Another well-known research program that has some bearing on the question of social learning is the series of experiments by Stanley Milgram at Yale University on the subject of obedience to authority. The question Milgram set out to study was, Why do people obey orders that authorities issue when the orders conflict with their own conscience (Milgram, 1974)? His standard setup will be considered first, then the variations he introduced to clarify the crucial elements in the situation.

*The standard experimental setup.* First, Milgram set up a situation that was presented as, and appeared to the subject to be, one kind of a study but was in fact a quite different kind. When the subject appeared in the psychology laboratory, he was told that it was a study of conditions under which learning would take place, and in particular of the effects of punishment, as, for example, when parents spank their children. Two people showed up at one time; one was to be the Teacher, and other the Learner. Although ostensibly determined by lot, the subject was always the Teacher. (In what follows, "Teacher," "Learner,"' and "Experimenter" will refer to the person's role within the experiment, not to real-life roles).

The Learner's task was to learn a long list of pairs of words. The Teacher's task was to present the first word for each pair and to punish the Learner if he did not get the paired word correct. Punishment consisted of an electric shock, administered by electrodes connected to one arm of the Learner and governed by a panel in front of the Teacher. The Learner was strapped into his chair, presumably to help administer the shock but also to give an unspoken impression that he could not escape. In fact, the Learner was an accomplice of Milgram, and no real shocks were administered.

The Learner was a forty-seven-year-old accountant who was trained to play his part as victim convincingly, shrieking in pain, protesting, and demanding that the experiment be halted, as called for by the script. The Experimenter was a thirty-one-year-old high school biology teacher, who maintained an impassive attitude throughout as he urged the subjects (i.e., the Teachers) who wished to quit that they should continue the experiment.

Rather than following an unfortunate tradition in psychological research to use psychology students as subjects, Milgram advertised to the New Haven community, offering $4 per hour plus carfare for subjects. For most of his experiments, 40 percent of the subjects were skilled or unskilled workers; 40 percent were white-collar, sales, and business people; and 20 percent were professionals. With respect to age, 40 percent were in their forties, 40 percent were in their thirties, and 20 percent were in their twenties. For most of the experiments, there were forty subjects, all men.

The thirty levels of shock were labeled from 15 to 450 volts. They were also labeled in terms of their effects, as Slight Shock, Moderate Shock, Strong Shock, Very Strong Shock, Intense Shock, Extreme Intensity Shock, Danger: Severe Shock, and XXX. The gimmick was that with each failure, the Teacher was instructed to move to the next higher level of shock. Moreover, to insure that the Teacher was aware of the level, part of his task was to announce the voltage level of the shock before administering it. The Learner asked and the Experimenter explained that the shocks can be painful but they would cause no permanent tissue damage.

Unknown to the Teacher, the Learner was given a schedule of answers to follow, of which three out of four were wrong. After the 75-volt shock, he complained of discomfort; after 120 volts, he shouted that it was painful; after 150 volts, he begged to be released; after 270 volts, he let out an agonizing scream; after 300 volts, he refused to answer any more. The Experimenter instructed the Teacher that not answering was considered the same as a wrong answer, and he should continue to shock the Learner.

Many Teachers, who of course were the only real subjects in most of the experiments, were made extremely uncomfortable by the Learner's apparent suffering, and they turned to the Experimenter for further instructions. The Experimenter replied, "Please go on." If that did not suffice, he next said, "The experiment requires that you continue." If necessary, these prods were followed by "It is absolutely essential that you continue," and "You have no other choice, you *must* go on." If the subject still refused, the experiment was terminated.

After participating, every subject was debriefed about the experiment, including the information that there were no shocks, and given a chance to have a pleasant talk with the supposed victim. Subjects who defied the Experimenter and quit were supported in their decision; those who continued to administer shock were told that their behavior was normal, as indeed it was.

Most people would like to think that in such circumstances their conscience would prevail over orders issued by an arbitrary authority. In public lectures to psychiatrists, middle-class adults, and college students, Milgram asked each member of the audience to guess how many shocks they themselves would administer in such an experiment before insisting on quitting. People in those audiences estimated that number to average around eight or nine, which is in the range of moderate to strong shocks. All predicted that they would defy the Experimenter before reaching the maximum level of shock. Some persons said they would refuse to administer any shocks. None thought they would go higher than 300 volts, in the range called Extreme Intensity Shock. However, as will appear, no groups acted the way these groups anticipated they would.

*Proximity and nature of the victim.* In Experiment 1, the Learner's voice could not be heard by the subject, but he could hear the Learner pounding on the wall after the 300-volt shock. Of the forty subjects, five refused to continue after that; twenty-six proceeded to the maximum shock level. Thus 65 percent of the subjects were obedient to the end; the mean number of shocks administered was twenty-seven out of thirty. In Experiment 2, the victim's verbal complaints could be heard. The mean number of obedient subjects fell slightly, to 62.5 percent, and the mean number of shocks was twenty-five. Experiment 3 was the same except that the Learner was in the same room as the subject. There were 40 percent obedient subjects, and the mean number of shocks was twenty-one. In Experiment 4, when the subject had to hold the Learner's hand to the shock plate, only 30 percent were obedient, and the mean number of shocks was eighteen. These four experiments show the importance of the proximity of the victim in arousing or enforcing the conscience of the person administering punishment.

The answers the subjects gave to a postexperiment interview are needed to complete the picture. Most of them reported anywhere from moderate to extreme tension and nervousness during the experiment. Most of the subjects had been protesting all along about the procedure of hurting the innocent victim and expressed their disapproval of the procedure and even their unwillingness to continue. Yet when urged to do so, they did in fact continue to shock the victim while also continuing to express disapproval.

Perhaps the specific persons posing as the Experimenter and the Learner, by the accidental quirks of their personality, account for the results. In Experiment 6, a second team was chosen, who were more or less reversed in personal qualities, the new Learner being more like the old Experimenter and the new Experimenter being more like the old Learner. There was little difference in the results.

In Experiment 9, the Teacher heard the Learner make a proviso in his agreement to take part that he can quit when he wants to; other conditions were like those of Experiment 6, that is, the Learner made the usual protestations that he wants to quit, it is painful, he demanded to be let out, etc. Only a few more subjects quit under these circumstances. Of the forty subjects, sixteen were obedient, compared to twenty in the comparison experiment.

*Proximity and prestige of the authority.* The initial experiments took place in an elegant, well-appointed laboratory at Yale, so the objection could be made that the influence of authority in this situation was in part due to the prestige of Yale University. Experiment 5 was a variation of Experiment 2, except that it was carried out in a plain basement laboratory, and the verbal protests of the Learner were altered somewhat. The most significant alteration was that the Learner mentioned that he had a heart condition. There was no change in the level of obedience; twenty six of the forty subjects remained obedient and proceeded to the highest shock level.

Is it the proximity of the Experimenter giving the orders to continue that accounts for the obedience? In Experiment 7, the Experimenter left the laboratory and the Teacher called him by telephone to ask any questions, mostly concerning continuation of the experiment, of course. Under these circumstances, the number of obedient subjects dropped to nine out of forty. Moreover, many of the subjects "cheated" and, when the Experimenter was not present, administered lower shocks than they were supposed to.

In Experiment 10, the imprimatur of Yale was completely removed from the research. It was moved to an unprepossessing location in Bridgeport, an industrial city, to a building that appeared only marginally respectable. The group responsible described themselves as the "Research Associates of Bridgeport," a made-up name. Other aspects of the research, such as the method of recruiting subjects, the socioeconomic mix, and the pay, remained the same. Of the forty subjects, nineteen remained fully obedient compared to twenty-six in the most comparable experiments at Yale, despite the fact that many subjects did express their doubts about the legitimacy of the sponsor and of the enterprise.

In Experiment 12, the Learner demanded that the shocks continue, whereas the Experimenter said the experiment should terminate. Under these circumstances, no one continued.

Experiment 13 addressed the question, What if orders to continue giving shocks come from an ordinary man, not from a person in a laboratory coat with the trappings of authority? To contrive this situation, three people arrived at the laboratory together. By a rigged drawing, the usual person became the Learner, the subject administered the shock, and the other arrival recorded times at the Experimenter's desk. The Experimenter was called away by the telephone when he had explained that shocks would be given but had said nothing about what level of shock. The second accomplice decided, in the Experimenter's absence, that they would follow the scheme of escalating the shock at each wrong answer. He was also the one that insisted that this scheme be followed. Only four of twenty subjects remained obedient, one-third as many as when the ostensible Experimenter was present and made the decision.

In the instance of the sixteen subjects who defied the "ordinary man" serving as Experimenter and refused to continue giving shocks, the ordinary man then took over the job of shocking the Learner and asked the subject to assume his role of recording times. Almost all protested the continuation of the experiment, but most continued to fulfill their part in recording times. Five, however, actually did bodily restrain the accomplice from going on with the shocks and thus terminated the experiment.

What happens if the victim is also a person in authority? In Experiment 14 before the experiment even began, the Learner objected to being shocked. The Experimenter said he must fulfill his quota of subjects and so induced the accomplice to agree to serve as Learner if he, the Experimenter, would serve as Learner first. Thus the person receiving the shocks and demanding that the experiment be ended was the person who originally appeared to be the authority. All subjects ended the experiment under these conditions.

What happens when authorities disagree? In Experiment 15 there were two Experimenters of equal status but conflicting advice; one wanted to stop when they reached 150 volts, the other to continue. All subjects stopped.

In Experiment 16, the subject arrived to find two Experimenters. One drew with the subject to see who would be Learner; the accomplice was chosen. Now there were two authorities, but one was in the subordinate position of Learner. In this condition, thirteen of the twenty subjects remained fully obedient, the same proportion as when the victim was an ordinary person rather than an authority. Of the remainder, all but one quit immediately when the Learner demanded it. But for the majority, the authority at the control desk was the only one who mattered.

*Characteristics of the subject.* What if the subjects are women instead of men? Women have a reputation for being more soft-hearted but also for being more compliant and obedient. Experiment 8, a repetition of the basic experiment with women, showed no difference; twenty-six of the forty were obedient to the end, administering the maximum shock.

Is the average person a sadist? Is that why people go on administering shocks? Experiment 11 was the same as Experiment 5 except that the subject was free to choose his own shock level. The mean level across trials that subjects chose was between the third and fourth level. To put that into perspective, the lowest level at which discomfort is expressed by the Learner is the fifth level. Thus the motive of the subjects is obedience, not the desire to hurt for the sake of hurting.

*Conformity versus obedience.* Obedience to authority and conformity to group (or peer) pressure are often not distinguished, either in everyday thinking or in psychological theory. Milgram points out several conspicuous differences. Obedience always implies a hierarchy of people, with the obedient person lower in the hierarchy, whereas conformity implies equal status of participants. Imitation governs conformity, but is usually not implied in instances of obedience. Obedience generally refers to explicit instructions, whereas conformity is usually less well defined. Obedience is voluntary in circumstances portrayed in these experiments. The subjects are proud of having been obedient and often mention the fact in their interviews. In experiments designed to illustrate conformity, subjects are usually unaware of having conformed to the opinions of others.

Two experiments were designed to bring out the contrasts. In Experiment 17, two accomplices served as fellow Teachers to the subject of the experiment, with the Teacher's duties divided between them and the subject. One of the subject's peers quit after the 150-volt shock, another after the 210-volt shock. Only four of the forty subjects remained fully obedient in the face of such examples. Thus a natural tendency to be obedient and to seek approval of authority can be largely counteracted by a clear example of defiance of authority by one's peers.

In Experiment 18, however, where the peer (an accomplice of Experimenter) actually administered the shock and the subject needed only attend to the paperwork, thirty-seven of the forty were fully obedient, an exceptionally high percent. This circumstance unfortunately resembles closely the actual position of most people with respect to crimes committed by their government, that is, they do not have direct responsibility but play only a minor, subsidiary role, perhaps no more than failing to object.

*Implications of the study.* By encircling the topic as he did, Milgram has made a definitive study of obedience to authority. Usually this is considered a topic appropriate to the field of social psychology. By inserting the study in the discussion of cognitive behaviorism, I mean to bring out its relation to the effect of the social situation on personality and conduct. To begin with, the biggest influence is being in the experimental situation, for that already sets up the experimenter as the authority and the subject as voluntarily under his direction. The effect is to induce people to do things that they would not normally do and that most people find repugnant to the point of being extremely painful.

Some changes in the experimental situation make a big difference in how people act. These changes include nearness or remoteness of the victim, nearness or remoteness of the authority, presence or absence of peers who defy authority, and having the subject actuate the shock versus playing a more subsidiary role.

Other situational manipulations have smaller effects. The academic aura of Yale compared to that of an anonymous research organization in Bridgeport had only a minor effect, despite the suspicious comments about the organization as the experiment proceeded. Thus it is the fact of authority per se, not how high or how much respected the authority is, that counts most.

With regard to the relative importance of situational versus internal, or personal, determinants of behavior, experimental procedures by their very nature tip the scales toward situational determinants. Moreover, Milgram provides only minimal information about the differences between those who were obedient and those who disobeyed. Perhaps it was only a coincidence, but two of the individual cases Milgram cited of persons who disobeyed had had personal experience of living under Hitler. A paper-and-pencil test of authoritarian or fascist tendencies, the Berkeley F-scale (Adorno, Frenkel-Brunswik, Levinson, & Sanford, 1950), did show an average difference between the two groups in the expected direction. Also, those higher on Kohlberg's scale of moral development (see Chapter 6) were more likely to disobey. But these effects were not large, and those studies seem not to have been repeated. Overall, the research illustrates a powerful influence of the environment on most people, yet there remain important individual differences in susceptibility to environmental pressures.

In order to become part of a hierarchical organization, as virtually everyone in modern society must, Milgram points out, it is necessary to surrender some autonomy. Some submission to authority is an essential ingredient of all social life. Moreover, obedience is consistently rewarded throughout life. Thus perhaps it is disobedience that is remarkable and must be accounted for.

Milgram gives many instances of persons in his research displaying a sweet, sensitive, submissive attitude toward the Experimenter's wishes and at the same time a callous, or indifferent, or authoritative and arrogant attitude toward the Learner. Many, for example, stated that it was the Learner's own fault he received so many shocks, because he learned so slowly. To those many psychologists who limit themselves to a strictly observational, behavioristic point of view, such a combination of behaviors is grossly inconsistent. Those who permit themselves to be a little more cognitive and inferential, however, can discover how consistent those behaviors are. The authoritarian personality is subservient toward those of higher status but domineering toward those of lower status.

Returning to the issue of the relative importance of traits and situations, the contrast between seeing the submissive and arrogant behavior of the authoritarian person as consistent or inconsistent should be a warning. If we do not understand the nature of the traits studied, we cannot expect to find consistency. The nature of traits is not automatically given by behavioristic observation but must be constructed with some hypotheses in mind. The next chapter will consider some bold hypotheses as to some aspects of personality.

---

## THE SELF, ITS MOTIVATION AND REGULATION

In Gestalt psychology, in Tolman's expectancy theory, in Rotter's study of generalized expectancies, in Bandura's early studies of social models, and in early situational studies there was little mention of the self as a concept. But sooner or later the reasoning on these topics, as applied to the human personality, requires mention of that pervasive yet elusive topic. How then do the social learning theorists integrate it with the rest of their theories and data? In particular, how does the self start a behavioral sequence, and how does it stop one? Or, as usually phrased, how is behavior motivated and how is it regulated?

### Agency and Efficacy

As Milgram coordinated his studies, seeking a theoretical explanation of the effects, he found that the central concept was what he called the *agentic state*. That is his name for the feeling that one is simply an authorized agent of someone else who is in charge and bears responsibility. The agentic state he contrasts with the feeling of autonomy that most adults have most of the time. Milgram's choice of terms is unfortunate, because other psychologists refer to the feeling of autonomy as a feeling of agency; so the majority are using the term *agency* in exactly the opposite sense from Milgram's. For this reason it will be avoided here.

D. Bakan, for example, contrasts the two fundamental modalities of agency and communion (Bakan, 1966). Agency is manifested by self-assertion, self-expansion, and self-protection. Communion refers to seeing oneself as part of a larger organism. Bakan sees the mitigation of autonomy by communion as a developmental task of maturity, but Milgram's results suggest the opposite, that mitigation of communion by autonomy may often be more of a problem. Other social learning theorists, when they push their own explanations and experiments to their limits, find a similar concern, though each has chosen a slightly different vocabulary to express it.

The issue of self-control and self-regulation obviously is central to Mischel's research on delay of gratification. He has also stated that the person's sense of self is one of the more enduring, transsituational aspects of personality (Mischel, 1973).

Much of Bandura's recent research concerns his concept of *self-efficacy* (Bandura, 1977a). Behavior, he asserts, is governed not only by what rewards one expects to result from a given course of conduct but also by how strongly one expects to be able to carry out that course of conduct. How confident is the person, he asks, that he can achieve what he knows is required in the situation? A particularly important application of the idea of self-efficacy lies in his work on behavioral therapy, which will be discussed presently.

Psychoanalysts and psychologists who think in psychoanalytic terms also have turned attention to similar phenomena. R. W. White documented evidence for the proposition that a feeling of *effectance*, of seeing the effects of one's own actions, is an independent ego motive, not derived from sexual or other drives (White, 1963). Such motives were neglected in the early years of psychoanalysis, when the discoveries about drives and the unconscious were of greatest interest. Other psychoanalysts have argued for a similar position, often with different vocabulary, such as instinct for mastery (Hendrick, 1942). Freud recognized the importance of mastery in *Beyond the Pleasure Principle* (1920/1955) and in *The Ego and the Id* (1923/1961); in classical psychoanalysis the principle of mastery takes a special form, that one masters experience by actively repeating what one has passively undergone (see Chapter 2).

Perhaps the clearest terms are those of R. deCharms, who talks about being a *pawn* versus being the *origin* of one's own destiny (DeCharms, 1968, 1981). What Milgram calls the agentic state is much like what deCharms calls seeing oneself as a pawn. M. R. Lepper and D. Greene discuss related phenomena in terms of intrinsic motivation (Lepper & Greene, 1978).

These authors are not all writing about exactly the same thing in different words. Each begins from a different vantage point, with a different set of observational or experimental studies as his foundation, subsuming slightly different aspects of personality. Is the opposite of effectance (or self-efficacy) learned helplessness (Seligman, 1975), or is it communion? The difference is enormous. The point is not to slur over the differences in the experimental and research traditions but to indicate that from many points of view, there is something more than stimuli and responses. There is, finally, the person's self (or, one might say, the person himself) who must be taken into account.

## Self-regulation

Social learning theorists begin with a solid respect for the behaviorist tradition in psychology. They recognize, however, that there are certain problems or anomalies that confront behaviorists in accounting for human behavior, indeed, as Tolman showed, even in accounting for animal behavior. Thus they include cognitive elements in their account, as the Skinnerian behaviorists do not. Expectations, vicarious rewards, and even observation of unrewarded models can influence behavior, they have shown.

But if one goes a step further and says that some behavior cannot be accounted for on the basis of any rewards or punishments, whether administered to the person involved or another person observed, nor even on the basis of the behavior of any model observed, what then? Is there anything left of the behaviorism with which social learning theory started? That has become one of the central issues for its critics, and some of its adherents have dealt with it. The question is whether they have remained within their own paradigm in doing so. The problem is not whether self-regulation of behavior exists. That is no new discovery, though older learning theories often ignored the fact. The problem is whether social learning theory is in principle compatible with some explanation of self-regulation that can reasonably be interpreted as part of the theory.

Bandura takes for granted that an important element in self-regulation of behavior is self-reinforcement, that is, administering rewards and punishments to oneself, even if only in the form of praise and blame. (He believes this explanation is antithetical to an explanation in terms of superego or conscience, though a case could be made that he is describing the same phenomena from another point of view.) But the critic (e.g., C. Taylor, 1977) might ask, who is instructing the self who is reinforcing the person, so that the self knows when and how to reinforce behavior? And is that instruction imparted by reinforcement?

Rather than address that question, F. H. Kanfer and A. R. Marston showed in a series of studies that people's self-reinforcement is at least initially governed largely by external reinforcement (Kanfer & Marston, 1963). An argument in favor of their point is that in the long run persons who reward themselves inappropriately for inadequate performance will incur social disapproval, which is itself a punishment.

Bandura and C. J. Kupers carried the point further. There do not have to be externally imposed rewards and punishments. The pattern of self-reinforcement can be the result of observations of the self-reinforcement practiced by available models. For their study, eighty boys and eighty girls ranging from seven to nine years old were drawn from a school playground, one at a time. The ostensible topic of study was skill at bowling. A miniature bowling game was contrived that made it difficult for the subjects to assess the number of points they had just won and therefore easy for the experimenter to manipulate the scores artificially. That was done so that the models achieved the same scores in front of each subject, and all subjects achieved the same scores. A bowl of M and M candies was available from which the subjects were free to help themselves; any subject who refused to take some at the beginning was disqualified from the experiment.

One third of the subjects were in each of the following conditions: watching an adult model play first, watching a peer (an accomplice of the experimenter) play first, and seeing no model before playing. Both the adult and peer models for half the subjects rewarded themselves only for excellent performance, 20 points or over, and for half the subjects rewarded themselves also for mediocre performance, 10 points or more. In addition to taking candies, one for just exceeding standard, two for far exceeding standard, the models made self-approving or disapproving comments on their own performances.

Children who had observed no model helped themselves to candies about equally no matter how many points they made bowling. Those who had seen the low-criterion model rarely rewarded themselves for low performance (below 10) but rewarded themselves generously for any score over 10. Those who had seen the high-criterion model rewarded themselves far more for excellent performance (20 to 30 points) than the other children and hardly at all for lower performance. These results held whether the model was an adult or a peer and regardless of the sex of the subject or model. Children who had observed models made many self-evaluative statements similar to those of the models, whereas children in the control group made no such statements (Bandura & Kupers, 1964).

Overall, these results support the hypothesis that children can acquire the capacity for self-regulation by observing appropriate models, without the standards being either initiated or maintained by direct external rewards or punishments. Bandura believes that his results contradict relevant psychoanalytic doctrines. Psychoanalysts have their own version of similar observations, however, in their hypothesis that the child's conscience is likely to be modeled after the parent's own conscience rather than be shaped by what the parent deliberately tries to instill. In psychoanalytic theory the explanation is that the child identifies himself with the parent. It is not clear what in social learning theory corresponds to the mechanism of identification; imitation is too pale in this context.

Psychoanalysis, in fact, has several dynamic explanatory factors, corresponding to the complexity of conscience (Loevinger, 1976b). Clinicians have noted that many children impose on themselves a conscience of a rigor entirely disproportionate to what their parents would wish for them. The explanation

Freud gave was that the child's aggressive impulses, when restrained or frustrated, may turn against the self (Freud, 1930/1961). The stringency of the conscience that develops under those circumstances may reflect not the stringency of the parent's constraint but the strength of the child's frustrated aggression and fantasy of parental retaliation.

## Intrinsic Motivation

One of the greatest challenges to both behaviorism and social learning theory has been the demonstration of circumstances under which rewards can actually decrease performance on some tasks. M. R. Lepper and D. Greene (1978) and E. L. Deci and J. Porac (1978) have summarized a great deal of research on the question of the adverse effects of rewards on performance and motivation.

One of the first and most typical experiments was the following. Preschool children were introduced to an attractive drawing activity during a free play period when they had a number of other activities to choose from. Children who were interested in drawing were selected for study in one of three groups. One group was offered a Good Player certificate in return for making the drawings. A second group was not offered anything but received the same reward for drawing. The third group drew but neither expected or received any award. Two weeks later the drawing materials were again introduced in the free play period. Children who had expected and received an award for drawing used the drawing materials significantly less than those who had either received an unexpected reward or who had not been rewarded. The conclusion is that when the children work for a reward, they lose some of their intrinsic interest, their interest in the activity for its own sake (Lepper, Greene, & Nisbett, 1973).

Many other studies with children of various ages have confirmed the pattern of results. Lepper and Greene are not asserting that rewards have no effect on behavior or that they always have adverse effects. The conditions under which they expect adverse effects are fairly precise: Generally, people's attention must be drawn to the reason they are doing the activity, the activity must be one that is intrinsically interesting, they must believe that engaging in the activity has netted them a reward. Under those conditions, they seem to attribute their engaging in the activity to the reward rather than to an interest in the activity. Then on future occasions when the activity is available but clearly not going to be rewarded, they will engage in it less than people who think of their previous practice of the activity as being done just for fun. Psychologists have discovered what Mark Twain knew: If you call it a privilege instead of work, people will even want to paint a fence.

This effect is only one among several relevant ones, however. There are circumstances under which some children can be induced to take part in learning activities only with the help of extrinsic rewards; having mastered the activity, they may then find it intrinsically rewarding. Such circumstances are favorable for the use of token economies, which are particularly effective with psychotic, retarded, and delinquent persons, who may otherwise be difficult to reach.

Learning to read is an example of an activity whose rewards are far more evident to the proficient than to the apprentice student. Imagine a delinquent fifth-grade boy who is a nonreader. Rewards would probably be necessary to induce him to make the effort to master the essentials, but pride in his own ability as well as interest in what he is reading would become important motives once he had learned to read.

On the other hand, offering a small child rewards for eating is probably harmful if the child comes to think of eating as something done for a reward rather than to satisfy hunger.

---

## PRACTICAL APPLICATIONS

### Problems in Child Rearing

Social learning theorists, like the psychoanalysts and many behaviorists, often feel called upon to advise the public on how to raise their children. The advice of the different schools is often contradictory and probably only tenuously related to the theory and experiments that lend the cachet of authority to the advice givers.

Take a particular problem, the problem of aggression. What makes people aggressive? Since the term *aggressive* has many meanings, from assertive to competitive to hostile to destructive, the question must be limited further. What makes people too aggressive? Is it given in biology? A result of past experiences? Or of the present situation? There are many possibilities. One must think first of whether aggression is in some sense an instinct or a biological drive, then whether biology accounts for differences between people. Then there is the question of how much to attribute to past experience, how much to the present situation.

Freud is usually said to have emphasized biology. That statement can only apply to his metapsychological theory, not at all to his therapy. Psychoanalysis as therapy, which in the approach of this book is taken as the touchstone for what is essential in the psychoanalytic paradigm, has nothing specifically biological in it, being a purely verbal transaction. To the extent that Freud's metapsychology did emphasize biological aggression, it was mainly an emphasis on everyone's biological inheritance, not on individual differences.

The social learning theorists tend to emphasize current situational influences in producing aggression, as in producing other personality characteristics. Obviously, however, people react differently to current situations. This fact is accommodated by the social learning theorist by calling on the influence of past experiences as well as on the present situation. Since past and present experiences are the sum total of what the psychoanalytic transaction is about, one might reason that there is little difference between the social learning theorists and the psychoanalysts. In their theoretical writings, however, both Bandura and Mischel aim frequent barbs at what they claim to be unproved and unprovable assertions of psychoanalytic theory. Moreover, in a practical situation there may be a real difference.

Suppose a little boy or, for that matter, a little girl is too aggressive. Say, he hits his parents. Assume that all parents wish to have their children grow up to be reasonably behaved adults. It was at one time popularly supposed that the lesson of psychoanalysis was that if children were forced to bottle up their aggressions, all sorts of harm would come to them in later life. (In another version, the aggression would have to explode in a different direction in their current life.) It is doubtful that any such lesson could be logically deduced from the tenets of psychoanalysis, but that was a popular interpretation or misinterpretation. (Today and for many years past, psychoanalysts who give lectures to parents on bringing up children are far more likely to stress the positive value of setting limits, as a way to give the child a needed sense of security, than on the harm of bottling up aggression.)

At this point, learning theory takes a radically different tack. Its proponents say that by practicing aggressive behavior the child is not getting rid of anything but rather is learning to be aggressive. Research data, to the extent that any are relevant, seem to bear out the learning theory conclusion (Bandura, 1973); of course, the learning theorists are the ones planning the research and gathering the data.

Just how far this line of reasoning can be taken is not clear. If a one-year-old continues to nurse at the breast or a bottle, is he practicing a habit that will later be hard to break? Or is he getting the need to suck out of his system? Answers to questions like that are not obvious; there are no relevant hard data.

### Behavioral Therapy

In recent years psychotherapy, at least among psychologists, has come increasingly to be dominated by a group of approaches variously termed *behavior therapy*, *behavioral therapy*, and *behavior modification*. This group of therapies draws on various aspects of learning theory but includes a variety of techniques drawn from theories not entirely compatible with one another. The therapies have in common emphasizing specific behaviors; they say nothing about underlying motives, conflicts, or drives; they do not stress insight; and they do not claim to stimulate psychic growth. Thus they are differentiated clearly from psychoanalysis and a variety of psychotherapies more or less derived from psychoanalysis. Behavioral therapy is also differentiated from the medical model of neurotic illness, often espoused by psychiatrists, particularly those who prescribe drug therapies. The basic assumption of the behavioral approaches is that neurotic behavior is learned behavior that happens to be personally, socially, or legally disapproved or deviant. People learn to be miserable, and they can learn not to be.

*Systematic desensitization and aversion therapy.* Two kinds of behavioral therapy are based on classical conditioning, systematic desensitization and aversion therapy. They owe their origin to Watson's experiment with Little Albert, anticipating aversion training, and Mary Jones's work with Little Peter, anticipating desensitization.

J. Wolpe (1958) has worked out a theory, which he calls *systematic desensitization*, that both accounts for those experiments and provides a basis for further systematic use of the method (Wolpe, 1958). Although his theory is complex, its essence appears to be counterconditioning of the anxiety response. Anxiety is conceived of as a response that has been inappropriately (classically) conditioned to some stimulus or stimulus complex. In a typical case, the client comes with a complaint of a severe phobia, say, a fear of taking examinations. With the client's help the therapist constructs a graded series of occasions on which increasing anxiety is aroused. Then the client is taught complete muscular relaxation. While completely relaxed, she is told to imagine the least anxiety-provoking image in her hierarchy of frightening situations. If the client is able to remain relaxed, the therapist then asks her to move one step up the hierarchy to the next most frightening image. The method continues until the client ceases to be relaxed; then the therapist will drop back a few steps and start again. Eventually, after a series of such sessions, during which, of course no untoward events are likely to occur, the anxiety response to examinations should suffer extinction, and the patient should be ready to take them without anxiety. A similar program would be used to handle something like snake phobias or fear of flying. Just as Jones had reasoned that, with Little Peter, eating was incompatible with fear response, so Wolpe believes that anxiety is incompatible with complete muscular relaxation.

In aversion therapy an unpleasant stimulus is introduced just before the person reaches for the desired or forbidden object. For example, giving a patient antabuse will make the next drink he takes nauseating. Similarly, a smoker may be guided to smoke one cigarette after another until she becomes nauseated. Aversion therapy depends on creating a conditioned response where none existed before, whereas systematic desensitization depends on extinction of a learned fear response.

*Behavior modification by reward.* The program of behavior modification inspired originally by Skinner's behaviorism takes instrumental (operant) conditioning rather than classical conditioning as its model. The therapist's task is to find the controlling stimuli or reinforcers that are maintaining the symptoms and replace them so as to bring about more preferred behavior. The persons involved with the client—parents, teachers, attendants in an institutional setting, and so on—must learn to cease rewarding undesirable behavior and start rewarding desirable behavior. This method has now become a major one in outpatient clinics and in institutional management, but it is not as simple as it sounds.

The art of the therapist is to discover exactly what the deviant behaviors are and exactly what the sustaining stimuli and rewards are. A parent might complain that a child is sloppy, mean, aggressive, shy, reclusive, disobedient, or whatever, but all those words are abstractions and inferences. They describe traits, not explicit behaviors. With the help of the therapist, the parent, teacher, or nurse must identify specific behaviors and exactly what the situations are where the behaviors do and do not occur. Then they must identify exactly what they are doing that reinforces the symptomatic behavior. The reward, for example, may be nothing more than paying attention to the child. In that event, one part of the solution would be to pay no attention to symptomatic behavior but to give lavish attention to the child when he is not displaying the deviant symptom.

Other frequent elements of behavior modification programs include finding a way to measure the rate or frequency of the undesirable behavior in order to be able to monitor the improvement.The goals of the therapy should be described in behavioral terms, with the help of the client and, if appropriate, the rest of the family. Before any intervention is started, an agreement should be reached with the client and his or her family specifying what the contingencies of reward will be in the clearest, most understandable terms possible. The rate or frequency of undesirable behavior should be monitored during the program. If the method is not working, it is started over, perhaps altering the contingencies of reward. Ideally, when the goals of therapy have been met, the interventions should be phased out, because good behavior should be sustained by its own rewards. There should be provision for follow-up checks, however, with booster treatments if necessary. Smoking and weight loss programs, for example, are notorious for the high percentage of relapses that follow within a year of treatment.

Rewards for desirable behavior must be tailored to the individual client. Accumulating points or gold stars to exchange for a candy bar at the end of the week might be appropriate for some school-age children; some relatively mature children would consider that condescending and demeaning; small children and very impulsive ones would be unable to wait for a reward till the end of the week. Generally speaking, any preferred activity can become a reward for a less-preferred activity, as D. Premack (1965) has shown. The client who is sufficiently cooperative will often be the best contingency manager, able to monitor and record the behavior and administer the rewards. Generally, rewards are regarded with more favor than punishments in managing behavior. With children, often a place is designated for "time-out" or isolation in place of a more active punishment.

Behavior modification using rewards has played a large part in treatment of autistic children in recent years. Autistic children often will sit and bang their heads against a wall or the back of a chair for long periods of time. A nurse or parent may be in the habit of running up and hugging the child at that time, to protect the child and to supply any longed-for affection. The therapist would probably decree that one should not notice head banging but should give much attention and affection at other times.

Other symptoms of the autistic syndrome may include not looking people in the eye and not talking. A child may be seated opposite the parent or other trainer and asked to look in the speaker's eyes. The child is rewarded, say with candy, when he does so. If the behavior never occurs spontaneously, it can be shaped via Skinner's methods. After eye contact is established, the trainer can demand some vocalization before giving food, then move up to some simple words, and ultimately require the child to name the food wanted.

*Cognitive behavioral therapies.* Bandura's current method of therapy, modeling plus guided participation, is based on his experimental research; it does not follow precisely either the Wolpe or the behavior modification model. Originally his therapy rested on the idea of modeling. Recently he has added to that rationale further theory stressing the importance of the client's feelings of self-efficacy. To treat snake phobias, for example, the method calls for the client to observe someone else approaching and handling snakes. Then gradually the client must approach the snake closer and closer, always with the presence of the participant therapist who is able to handle snakes. Finally the client should be able to handle snakes herself. Bandura believes the chief vehicle of change is the client's belief in being able to perform the previously feared behavior; practice with guided participation is the best way to encourage such belief in self-efficacy (Bandura, 1977a). Some studies have shown the superiority of his method over other therapies in some circumstances, but every therapy has its own claims and records of success in some kinds of cases (Frank, 1972).

Because of his stress on the element of belief in one's own self-efficacy, Bandura's therapy is close to a whole group of therapies that stress cognitive components of change, that is, the importance of changes in attitudes and beliefs in effecting therapeutic change. Albert Ellis, the originator of Rational-Emotive Therapy (RET), has been one of the first and most prominent of the cognitive therapists (Ellis, 1973; Ellis & Grieger, 1977). He has identified many common beliefs that people entertain that cripple them for an enjoyable life. For example, "Everything I do must be perfect, or else it is no good at all." This belief is patently irrational, and the client who holds such a belief ordinarily is not clearly aware of it. Once clearly articulated, its falsity may be self-evident. If not, the therapist may have to do some persuading, even by way of cajoling or ridiculing the belief. Many neurotic people have numerous such irrational beliefs. They are often astounded to hear themselves uttering them when the therapist helps to bring the beliefs out in the open. Group therapy is appropriate for many cases, because members of the group, although cherishing similar irrational beliefs, have no trouble pointing out other people's irrationalities.

In addition to those described above, there are dozens of other approaches to psychotherapy in general and behavior modification in particular. Many practicing therapists are more eclectic in their approach than those described.

Some have no consistent theory; others are comfortable working out their own private compromise between theories. Ideally, the best therapy in each case will be chosen specifically for that client, but in practice most therapists have their preferred methods to which they are committed by experience or by conviction, and there is no guarantee that only suitable clients will seek their help.

*Effects of therapy.* Do people actually change in therapy? That is a topic of current debate, and resolution of the issue lies beyond the scope of this book. There is evidence on both sides, and not many psychologists are sufficiently unbiased to give an evaluation of the overall evidence that their opponents will trust. I would evaluate the preponderance of evidence as saying therapy often is better than no treatment at all, particularly if one is fortunate enough to find an appropriate therapist. In some cases, I am convinced, it is life-saving. L. A. Pervin gives a balanced presentation of many forms of psychotherapy and of the issue of the effects of therapy (Pervin, 1984, ch. 8).

The problems in doing good research on the effects of therapy are enormous. How does one obtain an adequate untreated control group? How does one make sure that the therapist did not simply accept the cases that were more amenable to cure? How does one equate one therapist with another? And is it ethical to intervene in treatment decisions just to achieve an experimental group? And so on, through many additional difficulties.

Two of the most common problems for which people seek the help of psychologists and other therapists are smoking and obesity. Typically, a variety of programs to help either condition have about 80 percent effectiveness at the end of the program, but only about 10 to 20 percent of the clients remain cured at the end of a year. S. Schachter was able to interview almost all members of two small communities, an academic psychology department and a small rural community in eastern Long Island (Schachter, 1982). As the purpose of the study was to contrast the weight and smoking histories of persons who were not self-selected with the histories of those who came to psychotherapists, it is significant that eighty-three of the eighty-four eligible members of the academic group were interviewed, and seventy-eight of the seventy-nine eligible small-town residents. For the two samples combined, a total of ninety-four people had a history of smoking. Forty-six persons had a history of obesity, defined as having been at least 15 percent overweight by standard tables. Of the forty-six, forty had made active attempts to lose weight. In contrast to the difficulty of giving up cigarettes or losing weight with the help of a psychotherapist's program, Schachter found that more than 60 percent of the people in his two samples had cured themselves of smoking or obesity, mostly without the help of any therapy.

That contrast raises many interesting questions, not yet resolved. Do psychotherapists actually do harm, then, and prevent successful treatment? That is possible in an occasional case, but it is not the most plausible explanation. More likely, those who go to therapists for help are those who have not been able to stop smoking or limit their eating on their own. That would mean that the potentially most successful cases have managed without help, which accords with common sense. Thus the failure rate of psychotherapists may reflect lack of determination or other relevant characteristics of their clients rather than the weakness of their methods. In other words, the therapists get the hard cases.

Schachter adds another explanation. Although there is only about a 10 or 20 percent success rate for a single weight-loss or antismoking program, many relapsed clients then try a different one. Because of the repeated efforts, those ultimately successful are far greater than 20 percent. The latter explanation is somewhat weakened by the data of Lee Robins, which Schachter cites, concerning the self-cure of heroin addiction by returning Vietnam veterans. A large group of veterans who were identified as having been heavily addicted to heroin before discharge were followed up later by Robins; other than detoxifixation before discharge, they had received no treatment. Half of them used no narcotics at all after return to the United States, and only 14 percent became readdicted (Robins, 1974; Robins, Helzer, Hesselbock, & Wish, 1980). This figure is in startling contrast to the almost hopeless prognosis for most drug-treatment programs.

However Schachter's results are construed, they support the thesis that something about the person is the crucial factor in the therapy and outweighs external contingencies. Robins's data, on the other hand, testify to the importance of the situation. Clearly, both are important.

When psychotherapy does achieve positive results, what element is responsible? In the foregoing paragraphs, the rationale of several methods has been presented, but that is not necessarily the basis of the method's successes. Jerome Frank has a different theory of why therapies succeed. All patients, he says, are alike when they enter therapy in at least one respect: They are demoralized and cannot cope with some aspect of their life. All therapies have certain things in common: The therapist represents himself as promoting psychological well-being, has some theory to back up any improvement that takes place, conducts therapy in a setting that becomes associated with psychological improvement, and encourages a confidential emotional relationship with the patient. The essence of the healing lies in these nonspecific elements: The patient is offered hope, empathy, and a rationale for pursuing the treatment (Frank, 1972).

## THE PROBLEM OF DEVELOPMENT: WHAT IS REWARDING?

What is reinforcing? That question Skinner leaves completely open. For him, what is reinforcing is defined entirely by the fact of change in behavior. He takes no stand on what classes of things people seek or crave.

Bandura, who even more than Skinner seeks to advise people on how to raise their children, conduct therapy, etc., has addressed the question more directly (Bandura, 1977b). There is, he asserts, a developmental hierarchy of incentives. For the smallest children, material consequences are all that matter. With increasing age, symbolic consequences, such as social approval, become increasingly important. Beyond that point, social-contractual arrangements take over as producers of incentive. Finally, at the highest level, individuals take over their own reinforcement, evaluating their own behavior and using the knowledge that they have done well as a form of reward, along with other self-administered rewards. Thus self-esteem becomes a major reward.

These observations raise a problem that has already been encountered, that of secondary drive and secondary reinforcement (see Chapter 3). Why do the incentives people seek evolve in that way? Bandura appears to believe that the rewards higher in the hierarchy take over as a consequence of their association with those lower in the hierarchy. He puts it this way: "The effectiveness of social reactions as incentives derives from their predictive value rather than inhering in the reactions themselves. For this reason, the approval or disapproval of people who exercise rewarding and punishing power is more influential than similar expressions by individuals who cannot affect one's life" (Bandura, 1977b, pp. 101–102). Basically, this position reduces development to another instance of learning.

Psychologists are clever, and almost any theory can be stretched to cover almost any data produced by the proponents of opposing theories. But the stretch marks show. Development is not the home territory of the social learning theorists. It is doubtful if they would have spent much time worrying about how to account for the self or its development or the development of motives if there were not other theories that account for them more readily.

The next chapter will examine an alternative point of view on the nature of development in general and of the development of motives and incentives and of the self in particular.

---

## RESERVATIONS ABOUT SOCIAL LEARNING THEORY

Perhaps every psychological theory has built into it subtle philosophical paradoxes (Smedslund, 1978). In any event, consider some that arise in connection with current theorizing in the social learning school.

Social learning theorists apparently begin with a respectful attitude to the claims of scientific exactitude of the strict behaviorists, particularly those of Skinner's school. They almost universally adopt the antiseptic term *reinforcement* in place of the colloquial terms *reward, punishment,* and *consequences.* To be sure, "reinforcement" does have the convenience of covering both reward and punishment, but that does not seem to be their reasoning. The term *reinforcement* has built into it an entire theory, as Tolman used to point out, and it is precisely the theory that social learning theorists reject. Learning, they have shown, is not the automatic consequence of rewards received but rather is based on many social and cognitive elements, such as expectations, values, and observations of social models. Past and future rewards are only part of that complex. If one believed that past history of reinforcement in Skinner's sense determined behavior, the major research instruments of Rotter, Bandura, and Mischel would be hard to understand. Rotter's study of internal versus external control of reinforcement, Bandura's study of imitation of social models, and Mischel's study of small, immediate rewards versus later, larger ones only make sense in terms of reinforcement if the term is given a different meaning from Skinner's usage.

Furthermore, unlike Skinner, the social learning theorists are interested not only in recording but also in explaining behavior. They begin by admitting cognitive elements. Tolman and his cohorts introduced behavioristic definitions of terms such as maps and hypotheses, preferences and expectations. Such terms are not much different from the expectancies and values of the social learning theorists; however, in social models they have introduced a new element.

As J. Aronfreed pointed out, Bandura at the time he wrote was "more comfortable with invisible external agencies than with hypothetical internal agencies" (Aronfreed, 1972, p.108). As the social learning theorists pursue their explanations, however, they now regularly go beyond the cognitive elements and invoke something more: self-efficacy in Bandura, an agentic state in Milgram, and a self in Mischel. This indispensable something does not clearly fit any psychological theory. Certainly it is not derived from any theory studied so far. It intrudes despite theory and is then claimed by psychoanalysts, other psychodynamic theorists (Adlerians, Jungians, and others), and social learning theorists as their own exclusive province. The trait theorists claim a piece of it with many measures of self-concept (Wylie, 1979), most of which are only tests of self-esteem (McGuire, 1984).

Any reservations about social learning theory as theory do not diminish the value of the therapeutic methods it has led to. The doubts do bring up a question about the self-consistency of the theory and the relation of the theory to the therapies.

The next chapter will examine some research that aims directly at the intrusive domain: not so much behavior or trait but the structure of personality. How that elusive self, or ego, or personality structure, and particularly its moral or ethical component, can be rendered observable to a scientific eye will be the challenge addressed by the new field of research.

## REFERENCES

Adorno, T. W., Frenkel-Brunswik, E., Levinson, D., & Sanford, R. N. (1950). *The authoritarian personality.* New York: Harper & Row.

Aronfreed, J. (1972). A developmental memoir of "social learning theory." In R. D. Parke (Ed.), *Recent trends in social learning theory* (pp. 93–108). New York: Academic Press.

Bakan, D. (1966). *The duality of human existence.* Chicago: Rand McNally.

Baldwin, J. M. (1906). *Social and ethical interpretations in mental development.* New York: Macmillan. (Original work published 1897.)

Bandura, A. (1965). Vicarious processes: A case of no-trial learning. In L. Berkowitz (Ed.), *Advances in Experimental Social Psychology* Vol. 2, pp. 3–55. New York: Academic Press.

Bandura, A. (1969). *Principles of behavior modification.* New York: Holt, Rinehart & Winston.

Bandura, A. (1971). *Social learning theory.* Morristown, NJ: General Learning Press.

Bandura, A. (1973). *Aggression: A social-learning analysis.* Englewood Cliffs, NJ: Prentice-Hall.

Bandura, A. (1977). Self-efficacy: Toward a unifying theory of behavioral change. *Psychological Review, 84,* 191–215. (a)

Bandura, A. (1977). *Social learning theory.* Englewood Cliffs, NJ: Prentice-Hall. (b)

Bandura, A., & Kupers, C. J. (1964). The transmission of patterns of self-reinforcement through modeling. *Journal of Abnormal and Social Psychology, 69,* 1–9.

Bandura, A., Ross, D., & Ross, S. A. (1961). Transmission of aggression through imitation of aggressive models. *Journal of Abnormal and Social Psychology, 63,* 575–582.

Bandura, A., Ross, D., & Ross, S. A. (1963). Imitation of film-mediated aggressive models. *Journal of Abnormal and Social Psychology, 66,* 3–11.

Block, J. (1971). *Lives through time.* Berkeley, CA: Bancroft Books.

Block, J. (1977). Advancing the psychology of personality: Paradigmatic shift or improving the quality of research? In D. Magnusson & N. S. Endler (Eds.), *Personality at the crossroads* (pp. 37-63). New York: Erlbaum.

Bower, G. H., & Hilgard, E. R. (1981). *Theories of learning* (5th ed). Englewood Cliffs, NJ: Prentice-Hall.

Cattell, R. B. (1957). *Personality and motivation structure and measurement.* New York: Harcourt, Brace, Jovanovich.

deCharms, R. (1968). *Personal causation: The rational affective determinants of behavior.* New York: Academic Press.

deCharms, R. (1981). Personal causation and locus of control: Two different traditions and two uncorrelated measures. In H. M. Lefcourt (Ed.), *Research with the locus of control construct* (pp. 337–358). New York: Academic Press.

Deci, E. L., and Porac, J. (1978). Cognitive evaluation theory and the study of human motivation. In M. R. Lepper & D. Greene (Eds.), *The hidden costs of rewards* (pp. 149–176). New York: Erlbaum.

Elliott, M. H. (1928). The effect of change of reward on the maze performance of rats. *University of California Publications in Psychology, 4,* 19–30.

Ellis, A. (1973). *Humanistic psychotherapy: The rational-emotive approach* (Ed., E. Sagarin). New York: Julian Press.

Ellis, A., & Grieger, R. (Eds.) (1977). *Handbook of rational-emotive therapy.* New York: Springer.

Epstein, S. (1984). The stability of behavior across time and situations. In R. A. Zucker, J. Aronoff, & A. I. Rabin (Eds.), *Personality and the prediction of behavior* (pp. 209–268). Orlando, FL: Academic Press.

Frank, J. D. (1972). The bewildering world of psychotherapy. *Journal of Social Issues, 28,* 27–43.

Freud, S. (1955). Beyond the pleasure principle. *Standard edition* (Vol. 18, pp. 3–64). London: Hogarth Press. (Original work published 1920.)

Freud, S. (1961). The ego and the id. *Standard edition.* (Vol. 19, pp. 3–66). London: Hogarth Press. (Original work published 1923.)

Hall, C. S., & Lindzey, G. (1978). *Theories of personality* (3rd ed.). New York: Wiley.

Haney, C., Banks, C., & Zimbardo, P. (1973). Interpersonal dynamics in a simulated prison. *International Journal of Criminology and Penology, 1,* 69–97.

Hartshorne, H., & May, M. A. (1928). *Studies in the nature of character.* Vol. 1. *Studies in deceit.* New York: Macmillan.

Hartshorne, H., May, M. A., & Maller, J. B. (1929). *Studies in the nature of character.* Vol 2. *Studies in service and self-control.* New York: Macmillan.

Hartshorne, H., May, M. A., & Shuttleworth, F. K. (1930). *Studies in the nature of character.* Vol. 3. *Studies in the organization of character.* New York: Macmillan.

Hendrick, I. (1942). Instinct and the ego during infancy. *Psychoanalytic Quarterly, 11,* 33–58.

Kanfer, F. H., & Marston, A. R. (1963). Determinants of self-reinforcement in human learning. *Journal of Experimental Psychology,, 66,* 245–254.

Köhler, W. (1925). *The mentality of apes* (rev. ed.). New York: Harcourt, Brace. (Original work published 1917.)

Lefcourt, H. M. (1981). *Research with the locus of control construct.* Vol. 1. *Assessment methods.* New York: Academic Press.

Lefcourt, H. M. (1982). *Locus of control: Current trends in theory and research* (2nd ed.) New York: Erlbaum.

Lepper, M. R., & Greene, D. (1978). Overjustification research and beyond: Toward a means-end analysis of intrinsic and extrinsic motivation. In M. R. Lepper & D. Greene (Eds.), *The hidden costs of rewards* (pp. 109–148). New York: Erlbaum.

Lepper, M. R., Greene, D., & Nisbett, R. E. (1973). Undermining children's intrinsic interest with extrinsic rewards: A test of the "overjustification" hypothesis. *Journal of Personality and Social Psychology, 28,* 129–137.

Levenson, H. (1981). Differentiating among internality, powerful others, and chance. In H. M. Lefcourt (Ed.), *Research with the locus of control construct.* Vol. 1. *Assessment methods* (pp. 15–63). New York: Academic Press.

Macfarlane, D. (1930). The role of kinesthesis in maze learning. *University of California Publications in Psychology, 4,* 277–305.

McGuire, W. J. (1984). Search for the self: Going beyond self-esteem and the reactive self. In R. A. Zucker, J. Aronoff, & A. I. Rabin (Eds.), *Personality and the prediction of behavior* (pp. 73–120). Orlando, FL: Academic Press.

Milgram, S. (1974). *Obedience to authority: An experimental view.* New York: Harper & Row.

Mischel, W. (1958). Preference for delayed reinforcement: An experimental study of a cultural observation. *Journal of Abnormal and Social Psychology, 56,* 57–61.

Mischel, W. (1961). Delay of gratification, need for achievement, and acquiescence in another culture. *Journal of Abnormal and Social Psychology, 62,* 543–552.

Mischel, W. (1968). *Personality and assessment.* New York: Wiley.

Mischel, W. (1973). Toward a cognitive social learning reconceptualization of personality. *Psychological Review, 80,* 252–283.

Mischel, W. (1981). *Introduction to personality* (3rd ed.). New York: Holt, Rinehart, & Winston.

Mischel, W. (1984). On the predictability of behavior and the structure of personality. In R. A. Zucker, J. Aronoff, & A. I. Rabin (Eds.), *Personality and the prediction of behavior* (pp. 269–305). Orlando, FL: Academic Press.

Mischel, W., & Gilligan, C. (1964). Delay of gratification, motivation for the prohibited gratification, and responses to temptation. *Journal of Abnormal and Social Psychology, 69,* 411–417.

Mischel, W., & Metzner, R. (1962). Preference for delayed reward as a function of age, intelligence, and length of delay interval. *Journal of Abnormal and Social Psychology, 64,* 425–431.

Pervin, L. A. (1984). *Current controversies and issues in personality* (rev. ed.). New York: Wiley.

Premack, D. (1965). Reinforcement theory. In D. Levine (Ed.) *Nebraska Symposium on Motivation: 1965* (pp. 123–188). Lincoln NB: University of Nebraska Press.

Robins, L. (1974). The Vietnam drug user returns. *Special Action Office Monograph,* Series A (No. 2).

Robins, L., Helzer, J. E., Hesselbrock, M., & Wish, E. (1980). Vietnam veterans three years after Vietnam. In L. Brill & C. Winick (Eds.), *The yearbook of substance use and abuse.* Vol. 11. New York: Human Sciences Press.

Rotter, J. B. (1954). *Social learning and clinical psychology.* Englewood Cliffs, NJ: Prentice-Hall.

Rotter, J. B. (1966). Generalized expectancies for internal versus external control of reinforcement. *Psychological Monographs, 80,* (1, Whole No. 609).

Rotter, J. B. (1972). Beliefs, social attitudes, and behavior: A social learning analysis. In J. B. Rotter, J. E. Chance, & E. J. Phares (Eds.), *Applications of a social learning theory of personality* (pp. 335–350). New York: Holt, Rinehart & Winston.

Rotter, J. B. (1975). Some problems and misconceptions related to the construct of internal versus external control of reinforcement. *Journal of Consulting and Clinical Psychology, 43,* 56–67.

Rotter, J. B. (1980). Trust, trustworthiness, and gullibility. *American Psychologist, 35,* 1–7.

Schachter, S. (1982). Recidivism and self-cure of smoking and obesity. *American Psychologist, 37,* 436–444.

Seligman, M. E. (1975). *Helplessness.* San Francisco: W. H. Freeman.

Smedslund, J. (1978). Bandura's theory of self-efficacy: A set of common sense theorems. *Scandinavian Journal of Psychology, 19,* 1–14.

Skinner, B. F. (1981). Selection by consequences. *Science, 23,* 501–504.

Taylor, C. (1977). What is human agency? In T. Mischel (Ed.), *The self: Psychological and philosophical issues* (pp. 103–135). Totowa, NJ: Rowman, Littlefield.

Tinkelpaugh, O. L. (1928). An experimental study of representative factors in monkeys. *Journal of Comparative Psychology, 8,* 197–236.

Titchener, E. B. (1896). *An outline of psychology.* New York: Macmillan.

Tolman, E. C. (1932). *Purposive behavior in animals and men.* New York: Appleton-Century-Crofts.

Wertheimer, M. (1912). Experimentelle Studien über das Sehen von Bewegung [Experimental studies of seen movement]. *Zeitschrift für Psychologie, 61,* 221–227.

Wertheimer, M. (1965). On objects as immediately given to consciousness. In R. J. Herrnstein & E. G. Boring (Eds.), *A source book in the history of psychology* (pp. 201–203). Cambridge, MA: Harvard University Press. (Original work published 1923.)

White, R. W. (1963). Ego and reality in psychoanalytic theory. *Psychological Issues, 3* (3, Whole No. 11).

Wolpe, J. (1958). *Psychotherapy by reciprocal inhibition.* Stanford, CA: Stanford University Press.

Wylie, R. C. (1979). *The self concept* (rev. ed.). Vols. 1 & 2. Lincoln, NB: University of Nebraska Press.

Yates, B. T., & Mischel, W. (1979). Young children's preferred attentional strategies for delaying gratification. *Journal of Personality and Social Psychology, 37,* 286–300.

# Cognitive Developmentalism

One of Alfred Binet's greatest contributions to psychology is the concept of mental age. Rather than simply looking at children as bright or dull, he used the average increase in ability with age as a kind of ladder or scale of measurement along which children could be arranged. The points on the scale were defined by the performance of the average child of that age. This method works up through the mid-teens, at which point people reach their adult level with respect to much of what intelligence tests measure. The mental age scale can be thought of as derived from an earlier conception of children as miniature adults, whose job is just to grow "up."

The Swiss psychologist, Jean Piaget, began from a different basic assumption. What if children are viewed not as miniature adults but as creatures of a different sort? The children who make mistakes in reasoning by adult standards are also reasoning in some fashion; there are patterns to their thinking. When any scientist begins from a new set of assumptions, one should look for a scientific revolution. By Kuhn's standard, a revolution requires that some genuine discoveries be involved. What Piaget discovered was that the same wrong answers were repeated over and over again by children of about the same age in different cities or even in different countries.

How are such uniform mistakes learned? They are not the sort of thing any adult would teach a child, so how do children all learn the same thing? Piaget's answer is that children do not learn in the sense that anyone teaches them, or in the sense of copying social models. Each child constructs the theory on its own. That is the core of the Piagetian revolution.

Freud had a somewhat similar idea. Virtually all children invent for themselves certain false beliefs about sex, childbirth, pregnancy, and castration as punishment, ideas that in most instances were not or could not have been taught the child. No doubt there are instances in which castration is threatened as a punishment for masturbation, but the number of boys who fear castration far exceeds the number who have actually been threatened. Freud thought of the false childhood beliefs as particularly related to topics involving sexuality and sex differences. Piaget picked up the broader implication that it is the child's whole belief system about all sorts of things that is constructed on a different model from the adult's.

A recent addition to the major points of view in the field of personality, growing out of the contributions of Piaget and not yet assimilated into most expositions, has been called *cognitive developmentalism*, structuralism, or constructivism. Probably all psychologists acknowledge the fact of cognitive development, just as all acknowledge the importance of behavior. What distinguishes cognitive developmentalism as a paradigm is taking that as keystone of the arch.

For many years American psychologists ignored the brilliant series of studies being published by Piaget, either from xenophobia or pique that he did not publish his results in standard journal format and style. In addressing the American Psychological Association, the physicist J. Robert Oppenheimer chided psychologists for neglecting Piaget's contributions (Oppenheimer, 1956). Once they became familiar with his work, the fruitfulness of his ideas was evident, and a flood of new research was loosed, mainly on aspects of intellectual development. Currently there is some reaction against the overenthusiastic and dogmatic application of Piagetian principles, but developmental psychology and indeed psychology in general have been forever transformed.

Piaget is above all a cognitive psychologist, and psychology in general has been becoming increasingly cognitive; it is difficult to say whether interest in

Piaget's work is either cause or result. Cognitive behaviorism (see Chapter 5) is not as similar to cognitive developmentalism as the names may suggest. Cognitive behaviorism, particularly as exemplified by social learning theory, is not primarily concerned with the developmental course of behavior; it puts greater emphasis on situational determinants of behaviors, and it is far less interested in the cognitive structures that the cognitive developmentalists discern in behavior. Other differences will become evident.

## PIAGET'S DEVELOPMENTAL PSYCHOLOGY

Piaget has contributed to developmental psychology in ways so rich and so varied that one cannot do justice to them in a brief account. He is one of psychology's few authentic geniuses. Therefore, some glimpse of his life may be justified. As a child he became interested in mollusks (snails) and studied them systematically. His first scientific publication, on a partly albino sparrow he had observed, appeared when he was ten; he published about twenty papers on mollusks, the first appearing when he was twelve years old (Flavell, 1963, p. 1). This background in a scientific approach to biology before becoming a psychologist is reminiscent of Freud's background in medicine and physiology. Piaget always continued to think of himself as a biologist, and biological concepts are fundamental to his theoretical system.

When Piaget turned to psychological problems, he worked for a time in the laboratory at the Sorbonne that Binet had founded and had headed until his death. Where Binet's primary interest was in turning heretofore qualitative differences in intelligence into quantitative ones, Piaget was fascinated by turning what had become primarily quantitative differences into qualitative ones. Piaget became preoccupied with just the things that Binet considered error. Why do children give the answers they do? They are not simply missing the adult's target, Piaget concluded; they are aiming at a different target. There is a structure or system to the child's thought, but one will miss it if all one asks is how close the child comes to achieving adult ways of thinking.

In his early work Piaget concentrated on the language and thought of the preschool and early school-age child. One book in the early series that has been particularly valuable for contemporary study of personality is the one on the development of moral judgment in the child; so it will be examined in some detail. That book stands out from the remainder of Piaget's work, which is mostly concerned with the development of perception, aspects of intelligence, and related theoretical topics. Piaget, along with his collaborator Bärbel Inhelder, was the first to articulate the idea of hierarchical stages (Tanner & Inhelder, 1956, 1960). Most of his later work on the development of intelligence, however, is not germane to the purpose of this book and will not be discussed.

## Early Studies

Piaget's first several books were built around the theme "that the child's cognitive structure, the kind of logic his thinking possesses, gets expressed in his use of language" (Flavell, 1963, pp. 270–271). In general, he began with careful observations of children, then devised interviews or experiments to bring out and clarify the salient features he observed in the child's thought.

First Piaget observed and recorded the speech of two six-year-old children (Piaget, 1926/1955). He found that almost half of their utterances was egocentric rather than socialized speech. In egocentric speech, the child was either talking to himself or was not attempting to communicate to the listener.

*Egocentricity* has been a key concept in Piaget's work. The child's language is egocentric "partly because the child speaks only about himself, but chiefly because he does not attempt to place himself at the point of view of his hearer" (Piaget, 1926/1955, p. 32). Typically, four-year-old children stimulate each other to speak but do not communicate with each other; thus they have collective monologues. Seeing only from his or her own point of view, the child assumes that everyone else sees the same way, and thus sees no real need to communicate on many matters. The child's premises are different from an adult's, but the child's are rarely made explicit. Part of Piaget's task was to make those premises explicit without distorting them.

Words such as *because* and *therefore* are rarely used spontaneously by young children, he found. When asked to complete sentences such as, "The door stuck because . . . ," they are unable to distinguish logical and physical causation from psychological or moral justification (Piaget, 1928/1959).

One subtest in the Binet-Simon scale asked the child to find the absurdity in the following statement: "I have three brothers, Paul, Ernest, and myself." (Girls' names were used if the examiner was a girl.) Rather than merely counting correct answers to such statements, as is done in the Binet test, Piaget analyzed the kinds of errors children make. The youngest children see "brother" as a class of persons rather than as a relation between people. Thus "I have three brothers" is not distinguished from "There are three brothers," and they see nothing absurd. Other children cannot take any vantage point other than their own. Therefore they do not see that "I" am a brother to "Paul," and they say there are only two brothers. Using a more detailed interview on the concepts of brother and sister, with inquiries concerning the child's own family as well as hypothetical families, three stages in the development of the concept of brother were shown. In the first, "brother" simply means boy. In the second, there must be at least two children in the family for one to be a brother. In the third, "brother" is understood correctly as a relation (Piaget, 1928/1959).

Similarly, Piaget distinguished three stages in the child's idea of dreaming. At about five or six years, the child believes that the dream originates outside himself and occurs in the room, so that he sees it. It may be punishment or retribution for a bad deed. At about age seven or eight, the child still believes the dream is in the room, but it originates in the head, or eyes, or voice. He or she understands, however, that the dream is not real. At about the age of nine or ten, the child understands that the dream is produced by thought and takes place in the mind or head or eyes (Piaget, 1929/1960).

In explaining physical causality, the small child has an equally egocentric view. The night is explained by people's need for sleep. The flow of the river is explained by men pushing with oars. The name of a mountain emanates from it and can be discerned by looking at the mountain carefully. The belief that the name of the mountain is a real thing subsisting in the mountain is an example of what Piaget called *realism*. Realism as he used the term is the opposite of objectivity. Realism makes no distinction between self and the world. The self is fused with reality. Thus the realistic subject is unaware of his own thought process (Piaget, 1929/1960). Egocentricity can be viewed as a corollary of realism.

*Artificialism* is Piaget's name for the child's belief that natural phenomena are made by people. For example, the Genevan child ordinarily believes that Lake Geneva originated when people dug it and filled it with water. Children may even believe that people made the sun.

That will not prevent the same children from declaring that the sun is alive because it moves. The latter belief is an example of *animism*. Small children are not bothered by such contradictions, a fact reminiscent of Freud's conception of primary process thinking, which also is unruffled by contradictions. The similarity between primary process and the thought of the child is no mere coincidence. What psychoanalysis shows is that characteristics of the thinking of the very young child live on in the adult in dreams and symptoms and other manifestations of the dynamic unconscious.

Thus Piaget has shown that the child has an *egocentric ontology* paralleling the child's egocentric logic.

### The Discovery

Take a series of frequent childish beliefs that Piaget has called to our attention (Piaget, 1929/1960):

"It gets dark so we can sleep."

"We think with our mouths."

"The sun is alive because it moves."

"Dreams come into the room from outside."

These are statements about ordinary events of everyday life. Every adult knows the statements are false; moreover, such matters are rarely discussed.

Piaget reasoned that these ideas are not random guesses or wild fantasies, because numerous children in different communities come up with the same ideas, often expressed in almost identical language. The kind of learning that various learning theorists study has nothing to do with the case, for no one teaches those ideas. Adults and older children take other explanations or versions for granted. No environmental contingencies or rewards or adult models account for learning such ideas. Where then do they come from?

Such ideas bear the mark of having been constructed by each child alone, independently of others. Children come up with the same wrong answers because they have basically the same intellectual equipment and the same facts to work with. To start with, they have the perceptual world. They cannot absorb complex explanations, no matter how they are taught them, until they have the appropriate mental structures to absorb the complexities, and that can only come one step at a time.

By far the most important part of what every person knows is not the kind of discrete facts that seemingly can be taught by association or by rewards (if anything can be taught be rewards) but rather the whole structure of knowledge, which no one teaches or could deliberately teach. That is why some psychologists call the Piagetian view *structuralism* (Piaget, 1970) (in a different meaning than the one attached to the experimental introspectionists discussed in Chapter 2).

Gestalt psychology (see Chapter 5) influenced Piaget's thought, as he recognized. But the Gestaltists neglected the child's development, putting their emphasis instead on the salience of "good" percepts, by which they signified, for example, symmetrical, regular, clearly outlined, and familiar figures. Like the experimental introspectionists, the Gestalt psychologists studied the perceptual process in normal adults, a population that did not interest Piaget. Where he most resembled the Gestaltists was in focusing on and showing the importance of the large context of thought rather than small, specific details.

Piaget's originality is not diminished by acknowledging that other psychologists, too, such as James Mark Baldwin and Heinz Werner, shared his vision of the child as constructing his own development. What uniquely distinguished Piaget's work is the wealth of experimental detail by means of which he brought the ideas to life.

## Method

In his early work Piaget perfected a new method of investigation, which he called the *méthode clinique*, or clinical interview. In the Binet-type test, the hallmark of the tester's interview with the child is strict adherence to a fixed set of rules. The questions that the child can be asked are all specified in advance, with very little leeway given for improvisation by the examiner or adaptation to the child's unique circumstances, abilities, or emotional problems. That innovation was a great advance over the days when physicians and teachers permitted their own biases and prejudices to affect the testing of a child.

Piaget chose to follow an opposite course. His method is a complex one, even harder to master than the difficult rules for giving individual intelligence tests, but it does have rules. The central idea is to probe the structure of the child's thought. An essential element is the *countersuggestion*: Whatever the child says, particularly if it seems illogical, the interviewer poses some objection that is more or less logically inescapable. If the child still clings to his or her original statement, it presumably represents a conviction, not just a fantasy or an accidental remark (Piaget, 1929/1960, ch. 1).

The great sin in doing Piagetian interviews is to suggest an answer to the child and assume when he or she then gives the answer that that is the way the child thinks. Children are learning all the time to adapt to the adult world and the adult's way of talking and thinking. That could be said to be their business. Therefore, under most circumstances their suggestibility to ideas coming from adults is for the best. It can defeat Piaget's purpose of probing the structure of the child's thought, however. Proper interview technique is said to take about a year to master.

The possible sources of children's answers are several, and the answers from the different sources must be treated differently. (1) The child may answer at random. If so, he will be inconsistent under questioning. (2) The child may answer purely in accord with its fantasy, possibly confusing fantasy with the real world. (3) The child may give an answer that has just been suggested to him or her by an adult. (4) The answer may be what Piaget called a "liberated conviction." That is an idea that first occurs to the child or is worked out in response to the interviewer's questions but is worked out on the child's own premises. (5) The child may answer out of spontaneous convictions. These answers are the most interesting. They are ready, are consistent, and cannot be shaken by countersuggestions. What the interviewer aims to bring out are the latter two types.

One mark of an answer based on conviction is that many children will have similar ideas. Another is that the ideas change gradually. For example, children who are moving toward an acceptance of a natural explanation of the origin of Lake Geneva will say that men dug the lake, then rain from the mountain filled it.

### Stages of Intellectual Development

Piaget discerned the origin of intelligence in the earliest behaviors of the infant. His studies of those behaviors began when he made extensive notes on observations of his own three children (Piaget, 1936/1963).

*Basic concepts.* Some reflexes, such as yawning and sneezing, occur in virtually the same way from infancy onward. Others, for example, sucking, though originating as reflex action, change with use, particularly at first. Sucking the breast or bottle, the way one usually observes it, is far more a learned than a reflex action. Piaget referred to sucking as a *scheme of action,* or *sensorimotor scheme.* ("Schema" is a more usual translation.) With each repetition, it becomes more skilled. Moreover, the baby soon learns to recognize the nipple of mother or bottle when it is hungry and reject it when not hungry. Appropriate objects, such as a pacifier or thumb, are sought when sucking is wanted for its own sake. Sucking is also a means of exploring new objects, such as a blanket or toy. These kinds of sucking are or become different from sucking a nipple (Piaget, 1936/1963).

*Scheme* is Piaget's term for a sensorimotor coordination, a pattern of stimuli and movements that is activated as a unity. It is not just an action, nor is it just a set of stimuli, nor is it a chance connection between a stimulus and a response, as implied in the idea of a conditioned response. It is the sensorimotor equivalent of a concept, and it is continuously broadened and refined with use. A scheme is the structure common to all those acts that from the subject's view are equivalent (Inhelder, 1969).

As the infant adapts its sucking to the occasion and the objects offered, it is displaying what Piaget calls assimilation and accommodation. *Assimilation* is displayed, for example, when every new object is first put into the mouth and sucked, that being what the small baby has learned to do, the scheme of action it has practiced. An example of *accommodation* is changing its pattern of sucking to adapt to whatever new material is at hand. In general, every action requires some balance of assimilation and accommodation. To the extent that old schemes are exercised on new materials, Piaget called the behavior assimilation. To the extent that the scheme changes in response to the stimulus, he described the activity as accommodation. The concepts of assimilation and accommodation Piaget saw as derived from biology; they show the biological roots of psychological activity. He meant assimilation to be understood as exactly analogous to the way the digestive system assimilates food.

*The sensorimotor period.* Piaget traced six stages of sensorimotor development, which constitute the precursors and first rudimentary stages of intelligence. He noted, of course, that these stages are not sharply defined and separate from one another.

In the first stage the infant practices impulsive and reflex actions independently of each other and for their own sake. Sucking is the most obvious, but the infant also looks, listens, grasps, and kicks.

In the second stage, self-sustaining circular reactions develop; some action, such as kicking or scratching or grasping a blanket, may be repeated many times. Gradually the infant begins to coordinate two or more schemes, for example, by looking at what is being grasped.

In the third stage, the infant begins to practice circular reactions for their consequences, for example, kicking in order to make the crib shake. These reactions become what Piaget called "procedures to make interesting sights last." Thus the baby is beginning to concentrate on the object of his actions, that is, the thing grasped or looked at.

In the fourth stage, the infant coordinates schemes and applies them to new situations. The beginning of intentionality is marked by the use of one scheme to activate another, for example, pulling a handkerchief away so that a toy underneath it can be reached. These accomplishments are elaborated by active experimentation. A new object or situation leads the baby to run through its repertory of schemes, giving the impression of experimentation. This stage, on average, rounds out the first year.

In the fifth stage, the active experimentation continues, but with greater novelty; each repetition involves some variation in the pattern. What is novel is pursued for its own sake.

In the sixth sensorimotor stage, the baby is able to invent new means by thinking rather than purely by groping. At the same time, the baby is learning about the permanence of objects. The concept of the permanent object refers to the baby's understanding that an object does not cease to exist when it can no longer be seen. At first infants lose interest in an object as soon as it is covered. By an ingenious series of experiments, Piaget traced the baby's developing sense of the continuing reality of the absent object. The mystery of how something can reappear in a different place from where it disappeared is solved when the baby understands that a thing can be moved around when the baby cannot see it.

*Development of operational thought.* Following the sensorimotor period, the child enters the *preoperational subperiod*, during which he or she learns to use signs and symbols to evoke and manipulate in thought absent objects and events. This period begins at about eighteen months or two years, when language, the most conspicious set of signs, begins. (For Piaget, *symbols* resemble what they signify, whereas *signs* do not. Signs are social, like words, whereas symbols are private.) Preoperational thinking extends to about age six or seven; the early stages of concepts such as brother and dreams (discussed previously) illustrate this stage. The preoperational child's thought is egocentric and fastens onto a single, concrete, external feature of an object or situation as the explanation for whatever is asked about.

In the stage Piaget labels *concrete operational,* the child reasons more or less correctly but only with respect to concrete and perceptible things and events. Both the preschool child, thinking at the preoperational level, and the school-age child, thinking at the level of concrete operations, use representations of objects and events; this fact distinguishes them from the infant in the sensorimotor period, whose thinking takes the form of direct action. What distinguishes the stage of concrete operations from the preoperational period is that the school-age child has "a coherent and integrated cognitive system with which he organizes and manipulates the world around him" (Flavell, 1963, p. 165). During this time the child masters concepts such as transitive relations (If A is older than B, and C is younger than B, then A is older than C) and, progressively, the various kinds of conservation (volume, weight, mass).

The problem of seriation can illustrate the difference between preoperational and concrete operational thought. Suppose a child is given a number of rods of varying length and told to arrange them in order of size. Typically, a three- or four-year-old will put together pairs of varying size but will be unable to carry through arranging all in a consistent order. Around the age of eight, children can easily arrange them so that each is larger than the one on the left, say, and smaller than the one on the right. Simple as the task may seem, it has significant implications. For example, it embodies the idea of transitivity, that if A exceeds B and B exceeds C, A must exceed C.

Probably the best known experiments are those on *conservation*, especially of volume. In one experiment, the child is shown two identical beakers with the same amount of liquid in each. The child agrees that the amount of liquid in the two is equal. Then, as the child watches, the liquid in one beaker is poured into another of different shape, say, a wide, squat one. Now the child is asked which has more. Some say the squat one has less, because they see that the level is lower; some say it has more, because they see that the diameter is greater. After a child has announced which has more, the liquid is poured back into the original beaker. The child now says the two are equal. Only older children understand that the amount is the same all along because nothing has been added or taken away. That understanding constitutes conservation of volume (Piaget & Inhelder, 1969).

Finally, in the stage of *formal operations*, the person reasons essentially correctly, even with respect to hypothetical possibilities. Piaget has also described this kind of reasoning as *reversible operations* and *operations on operations*. The chief interest in the account must remain, as was Piaget's, in the kinds of structure he found in the child's earlier mistakes.

One of Piaget's distinctive and most original contributions is the concept of *equilibration*. The child's thought is not a compendium of discrete bits of information. It is a system or a construction. When a child learns something new, it is not written on a blank slate, as Locke and the British empiricists seemed to assert. Rather, it is fitted into the structure of thought and understanding the child already has. This fact prevents too rapid shifts in the child's thought. A radically new idea is simply not understood; it does not register, because there are no categories for it. This fact introduces a strong force for stability in the child's way of thinking; that force is one way of understanding equilibration.

With respect to understanding the physical universe, when a child is equilibrated at a low level of thinking, discordant information can be counted on to be presented often enough and in enough different ways, simply by the wear and tear of everyday life, that ultimately the child will move up the intellectual scale. Only at the level of formal operations can equilibration finally succeed. Piaget has not been altogether clear on whether all normal adults do reach the stage of formal operations.

The topic of equilibration is potentially of even greater importance with respect to personality development than with respect to intellectual development, because the social environment cannot be counted on constantly to correct early-stage thinking. Some environments present only low-level models, carrying the danger of equilibration at such levels before the higher stages are attained.

### The Theory among Psychological Theories

Throughout his discussion of the origins of intelligence and the construction of reality, Piaget carried on a running battle with the proponents of alternative theories of intelligence, particularly classical behaviorism and Gestalt psychology.

The concept of the sensorimotor scheme defies alternative analysis in terms of stimulus and response. The stimulus as such does not exist prior to the response. The stimulus is partly constituted by the baby's ability to respond, that is, by the sensorimotor scheme that it brings into play and forms a part of. What the baby has no scheme for does not yet exist for it. A similar point had been made by John Dewey (1896), who influenced J. M. Baldwin, who was frequently cited by Piaget. No one before Piaget, however, had documented the details of the sensorimotor schemes.

The baby, Piaget argued, does not begin to apprehend the world by making a copy of it, by registering associations, or even by rewards and punishments. Each baby must construct the world anew, elaborating it bit by bit, beginning with a few reflexes and impulsive movements, exercising, altering, combining, and elaborating them through many experiences. Empiricists, including most behaviorists, see what is learned as an internal replica of experiences that come to the child already organized by the environment. But the environment can impose itself and be apprehended only in fragments; thus empiricism entails associationism to account for complex patterns of learned actions. This is a passive model of learning.

Piaget saw learning instead as an active process. Experience, he said, can be apprehended only to the extent that there is a structure to which it can be assimilated. The structure accommodates itself to each new experience by activity, and the outcome is a more differentiated scheme.

Thorndike's theory of learning by trial and error cannot explain the mechanism of intelligence, according to Piaget. Even seemingly random trial and error is always directed in part by a need, which organizes the experience. Thus even what appears to be pure groping for a solution never is.

The Gestalt theorists, by contrast with the behaviorists, see the structures of experience as given a priori, internally, without any prior history. The Gestalten, or structures, arise spontaneously in the nervous system through maturation, they believe. Piaget agreed with the Gestalt theorists that structures function as unities and are not imposed from outside by the environment. He disagreed that the structures arise by maturation and appear spontaneously without prior experience or are elaborated without deliberate intention. A scheme, he said, is a Gestalt with a history. It embodies past experience, it generalizes, it differentiates, and it can be applied in various ways.

Every sensorimotor scheme leaves in its wake a kind of vacuum that can only be filled by its repetition. This idea of Piaget's, never wholly explained, is similar to the repetition compulsion that Freud (1920/1955) discerned in children's play and in symptomatic behavior of adults. When a scheme is repeated, it inevitably changes just a little by the fact of repetition if by nothing else. By that means, it may generalize to slightly changed circumstances, or it may be made more discriminative with respect to appropriate circumstances. The child's need to exercise current schemes is the motor of the enterprise, at least at first, and serves the theory in place of all other motivations. That is different from accepted versions of psychoanalytic theory.

Piaget made the point that in the process of constructing reality or the world of objects, the child is also constructing self. Self and reality are differentiated out of a common matrix, the undifferentiated here and now of the newborn, what William James called "the big blooming buzzing Confusion" of the world for the newborn (James, 1892/1948). Piaget's point has also been made even more explicitly by psychoanalytic theorists (e.g., H. Loewald, 1951/1980).

A subtle intersection between the psychoanalytic paradigm and that of Piaget lies in the concept of scheme. How this concept enters psychoanalysis is most easily seen in Erik Erikson's discussion of the child's play as taking place in the *autocosmic sphere* of his own body, in the *microsphere* of toys, and in the *macrosphere* of play with other children (Erikson, 1950). In Erikson's discussion of cases, one sees a problem in one sphere being expressed in other spheres by the transposition of the scheme from one sphere to the other. That is the basis for play therapy. But play therapy is the counterpart to interpretation of dreams in adults, and there is a similar transposition of schemes in dream interpretation. Indeed, the essence of transference is transposition of schemes.

## The Concept of Hierarchical Stages

Disregarding the substance of the child's thought, one may look at the model Piaget has been using. His model of intellectual development differs from that of the psychometrician. Rather than seeing abilities as constantly increasing to a level of maturity, Piaget envisioned intellectual functioning as passing through qualitatively distinct stages. Each kind of thinking increases to a maximum as it displaces the previous kind, then declines as it is partially displaced by the subsequent kind. This model differs from the psychometric model of a nondecreasing function during the period of maturation. (This discussion will ignore the problem of the decline of abilities in middle and old age.) Piaget's model is more appropriate as a general model for personality development than the more usual psychometric model, which can be considered a special case of the Piagetian model. (See Figure 6.1.)

The stages in any single developmental sequence are arranged hierarchically. That is, each stage builds on the previous one, incorporates and transmutes it, and prepares for the next one. The order of the stages is not arbitrary, far from it. There is a definite sequence, and it is given by the logic of the stages. There is no way that a person could master formal operational thinking without

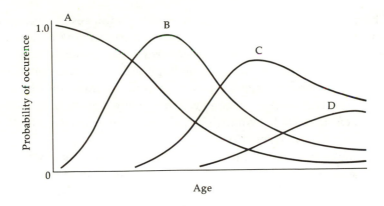

FIGURE 6.1 Kinds of growth patterns for personality. A, B, C, and D are signs of successive stages. (Adapted from Loevinger, 1976)

having first mastered concrete operational thinking. That is fairly obvious with respect to intellectual development, but Piaget's followers among personality theorists assert that it is equally true with respect to at least some aspects of personality development. The point is not beyond dispute, for some social learning theorists (e.g., W. Mischel & H. N. Mischel, 1976) argue that the order of the stages is given by environmental demands and other external contingencies. (See A. Blasi, 1976.)

The foremost difference between a true stage sequence and a developmental continuum that is not a stage sequence is that there are qualitative rather than purely quantitative differences along the continuum. However, Piaget and Inhelder recognized that underlying every qualitative sequence that proceeds by discrete jumps, quantitative processes must be going on, and also that qualitative changes underlie apparently quantitative ones (Tanner & Inhelder, 1956, 1960).

A Piagetian stage sequence has another essential characteristic, namely, that each stage has an internal structure. This structure is logically related to the concept of equilibration. The structure is defined by the connections between the various aspects of the stage; it is the framework within which the child thinks and acts in the environment (Blasi, 1976). The child understands and reacts to what he or she can put in personal terms in that framework. The process screens out markedly discrepant perceptions and ideas and preserves the stability of the stage. Persons in transition between stages cannot be characterized in such clear terms as those currently in a stage.

Piaget allowed for persons displaying responses or behaviors characteristic of more than one stage, a phenomenon termed *décalage*. That is a name, not an explanation. Décalage is not ruled out even for those in a stage, but it is specially characteristic of those in transition between stages.

The question of whether personality yields true stages or merely arbitrary though qualitative differences along an essentially continuous dimension is still at issue among those applying more or less Piagetian models to personality development. However, in view of the imperfections and unreliability of all present or foreseeable measures of personality development and of the vagaries of human behavior in testing situations, the question appears to be moot. (Stage models are discussed in Loevinger, 1976, chapters 7 & 8; J. R. Rest, 1979, chapter 3; K. W. Fischer & L. Silvern, 1985.)

To complicate the issue, Piaget specifically disclaimed that there are hierarchical stages of moral reasoning. Use of the term *stage* in presenting his study of moral judgment in the next section should therefore be understood as a looser meaning. Piaget used the term *period* as a superordinate category, covering a group of consecutive stages, as in "the sensorimotor period." As will be seen presently, Kohlberg uses the term *level* for that purpose, as in "the preconventional level," covering two stages. Loevinger, who, like Piaget, has a quasi-stage model, uses the term *level* for the transition between stages, as in "the Conscientious-conformist level," covering the transition between the Conformist and Conscientious stages. A further complication is that similar stage numbers are used by several authors, but there are no clear rules for matching stage number $X$ of one author with stage number $X$ of another.

### Moral Judgment

The foregoing studies affect the frame of reference within which the cognitive developmentalists view personality, but Piaget's study of moral judgment in the child contributes directly to the field (Piaget, 1932).

The research of Hugh Hartshorne and Mark May and their collaborators (see Chapter 5), meritorious as it was, epitomized the way Piaget did not want to study morality. For one thing, he noted that children do not generally consider cheating bad, particularly when it takes the form of cooperating with other children. Further, he was not interested in how well children conform to adults' ideas of what they should do. How can one bypass the child's natural tendency to conform to adult thinking and find out the child's real thoughts about morality? Piaget's approach was unique. He looked for an arena that would enlist the moral judgment of the child unhampered by adult judgment. This requirement led him to the game of marbles, precisely because no one much over the ages of thirteen or fourteen was interested in the game. His study of the game of marbles was done entirely with boys, probably because few girls were interested in it.

*The rules of the game.* Piaget's interview began by laying the marbles on the table, assuring the boy that the interviewer used to play as a child but had forgotten how, and then asking to be told how to play. With small children, who could not explain well, he would then have two of them demonstrate the game by playing together. Sometimes he would play with the children himself, purposely making conspicuous errors in the rules to see if the boy would catch the mistake. After ascertaining what the boy believed the rules were, the interviewer asked where the rules came from, whether they had always been the same, whether they could be changed, and so on. Finally the interviewer asked the boy to make up a new rule and to say whether it would be fair to play according to the new rule.

Piaget learned that children from the earliest age aspire to make correct use of the rules. They begin playing, however, by merely practicing arbitrary rituals or schemes of action with the marbles, such as rolling them down inclines. There are no real rules. That is the first stage, corresponding to the sensorimotor period of intellectual development.

As children become more aware of how others play, somewhere between the ages of two and five, they try to imitate. They may play by themselves or with their friends, following arbitrary rules, some made up on the spur of the moment to justify what they want to do. At first they do not understand the idea of competition or of winning but just take turns to keep the game going. They may believe that everyone can win. That is the second stage.

In the third stage, beginning around the age of seven or eight, there is incipient cooperation. Because each child now tries to win, the players must reach some agreement on the rules, but their ideas of the rules are still vague. Even two children who play together all the time may give contradictory accounts of the rules.

Between the ages of eleven and twelve, boys reach the fourth stage, characterized by codification of rules. The oldest players, Piaget found, had an enormously elaborate code of rules. Several different versions of the game were found, some local to a particular school or neighborhood. The rules covered such matters as the relative values of different kinds of marbles, how many marbles each boy put in the center as an original stake, how to decide who plays first, where to make the first shot, where subsequent shots are made, and so on. In addition to the ground rules, there was an elaborate set of exceptions to most of them, governed by special terms of consecration and interdiction. As an example, if one wants to play first when rules call for another to do so, one yells "Firsts." To prevent one's opponent from doing that, one must yell "No firsts" before the opponent says "Firsts." When members of the same class who played together were quizzed, they gave the same account of the rules. Girls' games, he found, were never so intricately codified, and girls displayed less interest in rules and their elaboration than boys did.

The consciousness of rules develops through similar stages though not exactly in tandem with the practice of rules. At first, rules are not understood to be obligatory. In the second stage of the consciousness of rules, they are believed to be sacred and untouchable; every alteration is seen as a transgression. Finally, in the third stage, rules are agreed on by mutual consent and can be altered by enlisting general agreement. The paradox is that rules are not obeyed reliably at the stage where they are considered sacred but only where they are understood to be democratically arrived at. The practice of rules, he found, is usually about a year ahead of the consciousness of rules.

*The method of choices.* The study of moral judgment is, like all of Piaget's work, too rich to be justly summarized here, but two more aspects must be mentioned, the problem of lies and the method of choices. The development of understanding of lies is intrinsically interesting and helps connect intellectual and personality development. The method of choices presages the method of dilemmas that is the chief instrument of Kohlberg and many of his colleagues.

The following pair of stories is a sample of the choices presented to the children:

> A. A little boy who is called John is in his room. He is called to dinner. He goes into the dining room. But behind the door there was a chair, and on the chair there was a tray with fifteen cups on it. John couldn't have known that there was all this behind the door. He goes in, the door knocks against the tray, bang go the fifteen cups and they all get broken!

> B. Once there was a little boy whose name was Henry. One day when his mother was out he tried to get some jam out of the cupboard. He climbed up on to a chair and stretched out his arm. But the jam was too high up and he couldn't reach it and have any. But while he was trying to get it he knocked over a cup. The cup fell down and broke. (Piaget, 1932, p.118)

After the two stories have been read to the child, the child is usually asked to repeat the stories to make sure he or she understands them. Then the child is asked if the two children in the stories are equally guilty ("la même chose vilain") and which of the two is naughtier and why. Younger children tend to see John as naughtier, older children, Henry.

Piaget called fixing blame in accord with the amount of material damage *objective responsibility*; it contrasts with fixing blame in accord with intentions, called *subjective responsibility*. Children of about seven years tend predominantly to objective responsibility, those of about nine or more to subjective responsibility, though there are many children who are inconsistent. No child over ten judged exclusively in terms of objective responsibility. The developmental trend argues against the different types of judgment being a matter of individual types or of family training.

Piaget believed that objective responsibility was the result of adult constraint and children's unilateral respect for adults and consequent willingness to accept their constraint unquestioningly. With respect to lies, however, he found a similar developmental sequence, which could not be laid to adults.

Children have, he said, a natural and universal tendency to lie. The injunction against lying, therefore, presents the child with a special problem. His subjects knew lies perfectly well when they heard them, even when they were only six years old, but when asked to say what a lie is, they identified them with "naughty words," such as oaths or indecent expressions. Both were simply moral faults committed with language. Neither their own fantasies nor the words they hear on the street seem bad to small children; they just accept that both are somehow forbidden.

A next step in learning about lies is to say that lies are statements that are not the truth. At first the difference between unintentional mistakes and conscious lies is not stressed as relevant. Thus this is an objective definition of lies, as Piaget used the term *objective*. Correct definition of a lie as an intentional falsehood comes at about age ten; however, many younger children, although they are unable to give a formal definition, do show in practical situations that they fully understand the meaning.

The interviewer presented pairs of stories, of which the following is an example:

> A. A little boy goes for a walk in the street and meets a big dog who frightens him very much. So then he goes home and tells his mother he has seen a dog that was as big as a cow.

> B. A child comes home from school and tells his mother that the teacher had given him good marks, but it was not true; the teacher had given him no marks at all, either good or bad. Then his mother was very pleased and rewarded him. (Piaget, 1932, pp. 144–145)

To test the child's understanding, the interviewer says something like, "Why did the boy say that?" Then the child is asked which of the children is naughtier and why.

The youngest children, about six years, believe that the bigger or more unlikely the falsehood, the worse the offense. Some even believe that the more incredible adults find it, the worse it is. Thus again it is a pure case of objective responsibility. Between seven and ten years objective responsibility disappears in favor of subjective responsibility. Correspondingly, the younger children believe it is worse to lie to an adult than to a child, whereas the older children believe either that it is the same or worse to lie to a child.

### Criticisms of Piaget's Work

Through Piaget's eyes it can be seen that however wrong a child's answer to a question may be, the answers at each stage represent a solid achievement as compared to the answers of the preceding stage, something intuitive parents and teachers have perhaps understood better than psychologists did. With

Piaget's help something of the structure of the child's thought at each stage can be discerned.

The behaviorist view that each child is infinitely malleable, given control of the contingencies of reinforcement, is opposite in thrust to the Piagetian cognitive developmental view, although possibly not directly contradictory. In the Piagetian view, the succession of stages is given by the inner logic of the developmental sequence, not by environment and not by heredity. A mistake frequently made attributes to Piaget an emphasis on environment, or, in some cases, on heredity. Neither is justified. Piaget acknowledged the importance of both heredity and environment, as everyone does, but he insisted that the logic of development is a kind of third force determining the direction development must inevitably follow.

Another frequent mistake, encouraged by the American emphasis on the psychometric approach, is to interpret Piaget's work as an attempt to determine norms of development by fixing an age for each achievement he describes. This enables some investigators to declare triumphantly that they have proved Piaget wrong, because they have found different ages for various stages among American children. Piaget, however, never claimed to be establishing exact age norms, nor was he the least interested in such a project. He frequently acknowledged that some experiments were done with lower-class children, who were probably somewhat slow in their development. He often interjected a sly comment to the effect that the reader's children are, no doubt, more precocious.

In addition to being uninterested in age norms, Piaget was not interested in speeding development along, hard as that is for an American reader to imagine. He was interested in developmental sequences for their own sake, for the insight they generated into the developmental process generally, not for the sake of altering anything. His indifference to the speed-up of growth is anathema to behaviorist and psychometrician alike.

As an experiment, attempts have been made to teach a child by reinforcement to see conservation of volume in a particular situation, say, one where water is poured from a tall, thin glass into a wide, squat one. What happens is that children will learn conservation or at least the correct answer in that particular setting but will not generalize to other settings. Moreover, the child is apt to forget the lesson after a time lapse. When, however, the child has developed a true grasp of conservation of volume, with the appropriate cognitive structures, conservation is immediately obvious in a new situation (Blasi, 1976).

Recently there has been increasing criticism of a strict interpretation of Piaget's concept of stages among developmental psychologists. The issue is often phrased as a failure of *synchrony*. The logic of a strict stage theory requires that the several aspects of a stage be manifest at approximately the same time, but that does not often appear to be the case. The failure of the various manifestations of a stage to develop synchronously is what Piaget has called décalage. But if décalage is extensive, the idea of each stage being characterized by a structure maintained by equilibration loses force.

Another issue that has generated recent research is whether or to what extent the structure of the child's thought changes, as distinct from an increase in breadth of knowledge and ability to articulate reasons. As an example, Merry Bullock has summarized studies of the child's conception of causality. She found that the youngest children who could be asked seemed to take for granted that a cause must be prior to or simultaneous with its effect; so that idea may even be inborn. The idea that there must be some mechanism connecting the cause with its effect children understand about the age of five. After that they improve in their understanding of and ability to explain particular mechanisms, such as the mechanism of the bicycle, but the structure of the idea of a cause apparently does not change (M. Bullock, 1985).

Kurt Fischer has addressed a number of the above criticisms of Piaget in his proposal for a skill theory. His theory combines structuralism and functionalism, that is, the capacity of the person to organize experience and the effects of specific environments in providing opportunities for practice. A skill in his usage is a modified version of Piaget's concept of scheme. By bringing in the practice effects specific to particular skills, he accounts for what Piaget does not, namely, horizontal décalage and lack of synchrony in the different skills of a given stage (Fischer, 1980; Fischer & D. Bullock, 1984). His version of the effects of practice is reminiscent of Thorndike's doctrine of specificity (Chapter 3): that the effect of practice is particular to the elements in just that performance. At the same time, he differs from Thorndike and resembles Piaget in his belief in the structural nature of child thought. The child, he says, although guided by others, must reinvent what is to be learned. For Fischer, structures of thought are narrow but strict; within a narrowly defined skill structure, the order of acquisition of developmental steps should be strictly predictable.

## COGNITIVE DEVELOPMENTAL RESEARCH IN PERSONALITY AND CHARACTER

### Kohlberg: The Moralization of Judgment

The best known contemporary cognitive developmentalist after Piaget is Kohlberg, whose research on the development of moral judgment is in part an outgrowth of Piaget's research on the topic. Many of the other researchers in the field either have been his students or have been influenced by his work.

*Method.* Kohlberg's method, the method of dilemmas, has evolved from Piaget's method of choices. The current version, the Moral Judgment Instrument (MJI), is most often presented as an interview with questions tailored to explore the individual subject's reasons (Colby, Kohlberg, Gibbs, & Lieberman, 1983). There is also a written form using standard questions.

The MJI presents the person with an ethical dilemma and asks what solution should be taken. An example of a moral dilemma is the following. Heinz's wife is dying of cancer, a druggist has a drug that would save her life, but Heinz cannot afford to buy it. Should he steal it? Whatever the person answers, the interviewer continues to press for reasons; only the reasons are scored. As in Piaget's clinical-interview method, Kohlberg's interviewers use countersuggestion to push the subject to justify, explain, and clarify the reasons. Several other dilemmas, along with the Heinz dilemma, probe different aspects of moral reasoning, such as the value of life, reasons for obeying the law, reasons for punishment, value of punishment, honoring contracts versus preserving personal relationships, and so on.

*Stages.* Piaget's study of moral judgment did not include children older than twelve or thirteen; Kohlberg began with the idea of extending the study through adolescence. Piaget discerned two stages (or forms) of moral judgment, *heteronomy* and *autonomy*, though one might include also a stage of *anomie* to describe the earliest sensorimotor schemes with which infants organize their play. When Kohlberg's study began, he expected to confirm those early stages and add further stages in adolescence. By a process not made explicit in his published writings, Kohlberg has extended his system to six stages.

Interviewing a large number of adolescent boys, Kohlberg found that moral judgment can be classed into three general levels — the preconventional, characterized by a concrete individual perspective; the conventional, characterized by a member-of-society perspective; and the postconventional, or principled, characterized by a prior-to-society perspective (Kohlberg, 1964). Each level is divided into two stages, as may be seen in Table 6.1, which is a recent version of the sequence (Kohlberg, 1976, 1981).

Stage 1 is characterized by a punishment-and-obedience orientation. That defines what the child thinks is good or right, and, by implication, punishment and obedience to externally imposed demands are major determinants of his behavior in problematic situations. Moral rightness is confused with power, importance, possessions, or other concrete or external characteristics.

At stage 2, the child's moral thinking is characterized by naive instrumental (or expedient) hedonism. The child is likely to have a firmer grasp of rules as such, compared to the child at the previous stage, for whom punishment may seem an entirely arbitrary exercise of power. However, the child adheres to rules primarily to serve his or her own short-term needs and desires or perhaps the desires of someone close. What the child understands of other people's motives is their own similar opportunism.

At stage 3, moral judgment is dominated by maintaining good relations and the approval of others; the child wants to be a "good boy" or "good girl." For the small child the people whose approval is sought will naturally be parents primarily, secondarily other family members, and later teachers. Older children and adults who remain at this stage may care chiefly about the approval of classmates or other friends. In contrast to previous stages, the moral rightness of an act is understood to depend on the actor's intentions.

At stage 4 the person is primarily oriented to conformity to social norms.

Instead of conceiving the norms in familial or peer group terms, however, as the third-stage person does, he or she sees them in terms of a larger social structure. Hence this is a law-and-order orientation. Respect for authority and the social order is less personal than at the previous stage and more a matter of principle. Even the authorities must obey the law, contrasting with the preconventional belief that authorities have the privilege of exercising arbitrary power.

At stage 5 the person has a sense of shared rights and duties as grounded in an implied social contract. At stage 6, which Kohlberg now acknowledges is hard to distinguish from stage 5, what is morally right is defined by self-chosen principles of conscience rather than by automatic adoption of society's rules. Kohlberg particularly emphasizes adherence to universal principles of justice.

The central question at every stage is Socrates's question, What is a virtuous person? What in school and society helps develop virtue? For Kohlberg, justice is the supreme virtue, and the core of each stage is a conception of justice. Higher stages are distinguished from lower stages in terms of having superior methods of solving problems related to justice. Every stage defines a kind of morality, but the moral systems of the higher stages are progressively more adequate and more equilibrated. For this reason, the preferred and precise description of the sequence is not moral development nor the development of moral judgment but rather the moralization of judgment.

Kohlberg insists that the order of stages is not only given empirically, though it is that too; primarily it is dictated by the logic of the stages. Because this logical justification is not particular to any society, it follows that the stages are culturally universal. A number of studies have at least partly supported this claim (Edwards, 1981). John Snarey has recently analyzed the assumptions underlying the claim and summarized relevant research, mostly confirmatory (Snarey, 1985). Because different societies obviously have different standards of virtue and justice, Kohlberg argues that it is the structure rather than the content of the moral reasoning that defines the stage. That again is a Piagetian type of argument, though not one that Piaget made clearly.

Kohlberg's claim for the logical necessity of the stage sequence is a mixture of logic, philosophy, analogy with intellectual development, and specific examples (Kohlberg, 1969, 1971), the latter illustrated in Tables 6.2 and 6.3. Each stage is shown to be more differentiated than the preceding one; it is also more integrated, as shown by the greater universality and self-consistency of higher than lower stages. The result is that higher stages are more equilibrated. They show increasing cognitive adequacy and take account of increasingly complex problems. At each stage morality is more internalized than at the previous one. The youngest children depend entirely on external constraint and punishment; next, on anticipation of rewards and punishments; then on approval and disapproval by those immediately present; then on social approval by the community; and finally, on self-chosen moral principles capable of universal application. Stated in (my) common sense terms, at each successive stage, the diameter of the circle of persons and situations considered in making a moral decision is wider.

TABLE 6.1. **Kohlberg's Six Moral Stages**

| Level and stage | Content of stage | | |
|---|---|---|---|
| | *What is right* | *Reasons for doing right* | *Social perspective of stage* |
| LEVEL I—PRECONVENTIONAL<br>Stage 1—Heteronomous morality | To avoid breaking rules backed by punishment, obedience for its own sake, and avoiding physical damage to persons and property. | Avoidance of punishment, and the superior power of authorities. | *Egocentric point of view.* Doesn't consider the interests of others or recognize that they differ from the actor's; doesn't relate two points of view. Actions are considered physically rather than in terms of psychological interests of others. Confusion of authority's perspective with one's own. |
| Stage 2—Individualism, instrumental purpose, and exchange | Following rules only when it is to someone's immediate interest; acting to meet one's own interests and needs and letting others do the same. Right is also what's fair, what's an equal exchange, a deal, an agreement. | To serve one's own needs or interests in a world where you have to recognize that other people have their interests, too. | *Concrete individualistic perspective.* Aware that everybody has his own interest to pursue and these conflict, so that right is relative (in the concrete individualistic sense). |
| LEVEL II—CONVENTIONAL<br>Stage 3—Mutual interpersonal expectations, relationships, and interpersonal conformity | Living up to what is expected by people close to you or what people generally expect of people in your role as son, brother, friend, etc. "Being good" is important and means having good motives, showing concern about others. It also means keeping mutual relationships, such as trust, loyalty, respect and gratitude. | The need to be a good person in your own eyes and those of others. Your caring for others. Belief in the Golden Rule. Desire to maintain rules and authority which support stereotypical good behavior. | *Perspective of the individual in relationships with other individuals.* Aware of shared feelings, agreements, and expectations which take primacy over individual interests. Relates points of view through the concrete Golden Rule, putting yourself in the other guy's shoes. Does not yet consider generalized system perspective. |

| Stage | What is right | Reasons for doing right | Social perspective of stage |
|---|---|---|---|
| Stage 4—Social system and conscience | Fulfilling the actual duties to which you have agreed. Laws are to be upheld except in extreme cases where they conflict with other fixed social duties. Right is also contributing to society, the group, or institution. | To keep the institution going as a whole, to avoid the breakdown in the system "if everyone did it," or the imperative of conscience to meet one's defined obligations (Easily confused with stage 3 belief in rules and authority; see text.) | *Differentiates societal point of view from interpersonal agreement or motives.* Takes the point of view of the system that defines roles and rules. Considers individual relations in terms of place in the system. |
| **LEVEL III— POSTCONVENTIONAL, or PRINCIPLED** <br> Stage 5—Social contract or utility and individual rights | Being aware that people hold a variety of values and opinions, that most values and rules are relative to your group. These relative rules should usually be upheld, however, in the interest of impartiality and because they are the social contract. Some nonrelative values and rights like *life* and *liberty*, however, must be upheld in any society and regardless of majority opinion. | A sense of obligation to law because of one's social contract to make and abide by laws for the welfare of all and for the protection of all people's rights. A feeling of contractual commitment, freely entered upon, to family, friendship, trust, and work obligations. Concern that laws and duties be based on rational calculation of overall utility, "the greatest good for the greatest number." | *Prior-to-society perspective.* Perspective of a rational individual aware of values and rights prior to social attachments and contracts. Integrates perspectives by formal mechanisms of agreement, contract, objective impartiality, and due process. Considers moral and legal points of view; recognizes that they sometimes conflict and finds it difficult to integrate them. |
| Stage 6—Universal ethical principles | Following self-chosen ethical principles. Particular laws or social agreements are usually valid because they rest on such principles. When laws violate these principles, one acts in accordance with the principle. Principles are universal principles of justice: the equality of human rights and respect for the dignity of human beings as individual persons. | The belief as a rational person in the validity of universal moral principles, and a sense of personal commitment to them. | *Perspective of a moral point of view from which social arrangements derive.* Perspective is that of any rational individual recognizing the nature of morality or the fact that persons are ends in themselves and must be treated as such. |

From Kohlberg, 1981.

TABLE 6.2   **Stages of Intentions and Consequences in Response to a Moral Dilemma**

In Europe, a woman was near death from cancer. One drug might save her, a form of radium that a druggist in the same town had recently discovered. The druggist was charging $2,000, ten times what the drug cost him to make. The sick woman's husband, Heinz, went to everyone he knew to borrow the money, but he could only get together about half of what it cost. He told the druggist that his wife was dying and asked him to sell it cheaper or let him pay later. But the druggist said, "No." The husband got desperate and broke into the man's store to steal the drug for his wife. Should the husband have done that? Why?

Stage 1.  Motives and need-consequences of act are ignored in judging badness because of focus upon irrelevant physical form of the act (e.g., size of the lie), or of the consequences of the act (e.g., amount of physical damage).

    Pro—He should steal the drug. It isn't really bad to take it. It isn't like he didn't ask to pay for it first. The drug he'd take is only worth $200, he's not really taking a $2,000 drug.

    Con—He shouldn't steal the drug, it's a big crime. He didn't get permission, he used force and broke and entered. He did a lot of damage, stealing a very expensive drug and breaking up the store, too.

Stage 2.  Judgment ignores label or physical consequences of the act because of the instrumental value of the act in serving a need, or because the act doesn't do harm in terms of the need of another. (Differentiates the human need-value of the act from its physical form or consequences.)

    Pro—It's all right to steal the drug because she needs it and he wants her to live. It isn't that he wants to steal, but it's the way he has to use to get the drug to save her.

    Con—He shouldn't steal it. The druggist isn't wrong or bad, he just wants to make a profit. That's what you're in business for, to make money.

Stage 3.  Action evaluated according to the type of motive or person likely to perform the act. An act is not bad if it is an expression of a "nice" or altruistic motive or person and it is not good if it is the expression of a "mean" or selfish motive or person. Circumstances may excuse or justify deviant action. (Differentiates good motives to which an act is instrumental from human but selfish need to which it is instrumental.)

    Pro—He should steal the drug. He was only doing something that was natural for a good husband to do. You can't blame him for doing something out of love for his wife, you'd blame him if he didn't love his wife enough to save her.

    Con—He shouldn't steal. If his wife dies, he can't be blamed. It isn't because he's heartless or that he doesn't love her enough to do everything that he legally can. The druggist is the selfish or heartless one.

Stage 4.  An act is always or categorically wrong, regardless of motives or circumstances, if it violates a rule and does foreseeable harm to others. (Differentiates action out of a sense of obligation to rule from action for generally "nice" or natural motives.)

    Pro—You should steal it. If you did nothing you'd be letting your wife die, it's your responsibility if she dies. You have to take it with the idea of paying the druggist.

TABLE 6.2   *continued*

Con—It is a natural thing for Heinz to want to save his wife but it's still always wrong to steal. He still knows he's stealing and taking a valuable drug from the man who made it.

Stage 5. A formal statement that though circumstances or motive modify disapproval, as a general rule the means do not justify the ends. While circumstances justify deviant acts to some extent they do not make it right or lead to suspension of moral categories. (Differentiates moral blame because of the intent behind breaking the rule from the legal or principled necessity not to make exceptions to rules.)

Pro—The law wasn't set up for these circumstances. Taking the drug in this situation isn't really right, but it's justified to do it.

Con—You can't completely blame someone for stealing but extreme circumstances don't really justify taking the law in your own hands. You can't have everyone stealing whenever they get desperate. The end may be good, but the ends don't justify the means.

Stage 6. Good motives don't make an act right (or not wrong); but if an act follows from a decision to follow general self-chosen principles, it can't be wrong. It may be actually right to deviate from the rules, but only under circumstances forcing a choice between deviation from the rules and concrete violation of a moral principle. (Differentiates good motives of following a moral principle from natural motives as following a rule. Recognizes that moral principles don't allow exceptions any more than do legal rules.)

Pro—This is a situation which forces him to choose between stealing and letting his wife die. In a situation where the choice must be made, it is morally right to steal. He has to act in terms of the principle of preserving and respecting life.

Con—Heinz is faced with the decision of whether to consider the other people who need the drug just as badly as his wife. Heinz ought to act not according to his particular feelings toward his wife, but considering the value of all the lives involved.

From Rest, 1969.

At the lowest stage, one considers only self; at the highest stage, one seeks universal principles applicable to everyone.

An important element in Kohlberg's conception both of justice and of moral development is the idea of role taking. Our decisions become morally more mature as we learn increasingly to take the role of the others involved in the situation. The highest morality is defined by this principle: The just resolution of a moral situation is one that would be assented to by any rational person who did not know which part in the situation he might have to assume. The philosopher John Rawls refers to this as the *original position* (Rawls, 1971). In Abraham Lincoln's words: "As I would not be a slave, so I would not be a master."

Although Kohlberg acknowledges his debt to Piaget both as to method and format of stages, he differs with Piaget on many particulars. Piaget hung his explanation of heteronomous morality on age and status disparities leading the

TABLE 6.3 **Motives for Engaging in Moral Action**

Stage 1. Action is motivated by avoidance of punishment and "conscience" is irrational fear of punishment.

> Pro—If you let your wife die, you will get in trouble. You'll be blamed for not spending the money to save her and there'll be an investigation of you and the druggist for your wife's death.

> Con—You shouldn't steal the drug because you'll be caught and sent to jail if you do. If you do get away, your conscience would bother you thinking how the police would catch up with you at any minute.

Stage 2. Action motivated by desire for reward or benefit. Possible guilt reactions are ignored and punishment viewed in a pragmatic manner. (Differentiates own fear, pleasure, or pain from punishment-consequences.)

> Pro—If you do happen to get caught you could give the drug back and you wouldn't get much of a sentence. It wouldn't bother you much to serve a little jail term, if you have your wife when you get out.

> Con—He may not get much of a jail term if he steals the drug, but his wife will probably die before he gets out so it won't do him much good. If his wife dies, he shouldn't blame himself, it wasn't his fault she has cancer.

Stage 3. Action motivated by anticipation of disapproval of others, actual or imagined-hypothetical (e.g., guilt). (Differentiation of disapproval from punishment, fear, and pain.)

> Pro—No one will think you're bad if you steal the drug but your family will think you're an inhuman husband if you don't. If you let your wife die, you'll never be able to look anybody in the face again.

> Con—It isn't just the druggist who will think you're a criminal, everyone else will too. After you steal it, you'll feel bad thinking how you've brought dishonor on your family and yourself; you won't be able to face anyone again.

Stage 4. Action motivated by anticipation of dishonor, i.e., institutionalized blame for failure of duty, and by guilt over concrete harm done to others. (Differentiates formal dishonor from informal disapproval. Differentiates guilt for bad consequences from disapproval.)

> Pro—If you have any sense of honor, you won't let your wife die because you're afraid to do the only thing that will save her. You'll always feel guilty that you caused her death if you don't do your duty to her.

> Con—You're desperate and you may not know you're doing wrong when you steal the drug. But you'll know you did wrong after you're punished and sent to jail. You'll always feel guilty for your dishonesty and lawbreaking.

Stage 5. Concern about maintaining respect of equals and of the community (assuming their respect is based on reason rather than emotions). Concern about own self-respect, i.e., to avoid judging self as irrational, inconsistent, nonpurposive. (Discriminates between institutionalized blame and community disrespect or self-disrespect.)

> Pro—You'd lose other people's respect, not gain it, if you don't steal. If you let your wife die, it would be out of fear, not out of reasoning it out. So you'd just lose self-respect and probably the respect of others too.

TABLE 6.3  *continued*

Con — You would lose your standing and respect in the community and violate the law. You'd lose respect for yourself if you're carried away by emotion and forget the long-range point of view.

Stage 6.  Concern about self-condemnation for violating one's own principles. (Differentiates between community respect and self-respect. Differentiates between self-respect for general achieving rationality and self-respect for maintaining moral principles.)

Pro — If you don't steal the drug and let your wife die, you'd always condemn yourself for it afterward. You wouldn't be blamed and you would have lived up to the outside rule of the law, but you wouldn't have lived up to your own standards of conscience.

Con — If you stole the drug, you wouldn't be blamed by other people, but you'd condemn yourself because you wouldn't have lived up to your own conscience and standards of honesty.

From Rest, 1969.

child to unilateral respect for parents. Kohlberg finds relatively little of unilateral respect at his stage 1, which he otherwise equates with Piaget's heteronomous morality. His stage 2 Kohlberg equates roughly with what Piaget calls autonomous morality. His later stages he does not find represented among the children Piaget tested.

In partial contradiction of Kohlberg, I would argue that Piaget's children have advanced somewhat farther up Kohlberg's scale than Kohlberg acknowledges, but only in regard to very limited contexts that are entirely within their control and ken. Here I would call on W. G. Perry's model (discussed later), that whereas the child's overall view of the universe is still strongly dualistic, there is one small area, games, and perhaps some aspects of relations within the family and school, where the child has advanced to a more relativistic conception (in Perry's sense of the word *relativism*). Piaget acknowledges such unevenness of growth with his term *vertical décalage*. No one can be expected to advance on all fronts at once, and such unevenness is probably a necessary precondition for growth.

In the current revision (Table 6.1) Kohlberg places a greater emphasis on cognitive aspects of social and moral perspective than in earlier versions.

*Tests of sequentiality.* The construct validity of the MJI has been pinned chiefly to proofs of the hypothesis of sequentiality. Kohlberg has reasoned that in a true stage progression, no one does less well on any occasion than on previous occasions (at least during childhood, adolescence, and early adult life, and barring major regressive experiences), and no one skips a stage if tested, say, every couple of years. The hypothesis of sequentiality states that the stages of moral judgment occur in invariant order, that no one advances to a later stage without passing through all earlier stages, and that in successive periods, people either stay the same or advance. Any substantial evidence of regression would contradict this hypothesis. Absent evidence for sequentiality, Kohlberg's claims for his moral stage theory are weak. Several studies by Kohlberg and his colleagues, both experimental and observational, bolstered the assumption. Although they did not find the pattern to be as invariable as Kohlberg had originally hoped and claimed, on average the generalizations held.

Kohlberg's major research project has been a longitudinal (using repeated observations over a long period of time) study of the moral reasoning of a diverse group of boys, first tested in connection with his doctoral dissertation. He began with samples of boys of ages ten, thirteen, and sixteen, equally divided between upper-middle and lower-middle classes and within each containing an equal number of popular and isolated boys. There were six boys in each cell thus defined, for a total of seventy-two boys in the initial sample. This was the original sample used to arrive at his sequence of stages. Before discussing results of retesting this sample, some smaller-scale tests of sequentiality will be considered.

In one study, subjects were first given Kohlberg's test; then they were given arguments as to what choice should be made in a particular dilemma. These arguments were ones that would normally be given by persons who scored at various levels on the scale. When asked to restate the arguments in their own words, they tended to rephrase them at their own level rather than at the level given them (Rest, Turiel, & Kohlberg, 1969). The following is an example of a statement concerning the story of Heinz illustrating stage 3 reasoning:

> If you were so heartless as to let your own wife die, you would feel terrible and everybody would really think you were inhuman. It would be terrible to think of what you allowed to happen to your own wife and what they must have thought when she realized that you weren't going to save her. (Rest, 1979, pp. 28–29)

The following response illustrates a misinterpretation. It shows no awareness of the concern for approval, substituting evasion of responsibility, thus showing stage 2 reasoning:

> He's sort of bringing everybody else into it. . . . It sounds like he is trying to cover up for it by bringing everybody else in. (Rest, 1979, p. 29)

In another study, subjects were coached in arguments one stage above their spontaneous level, two stages above, or one stage below. The only subjects who showed significant gain were those coached with arguments one stage higher (Rest, Turiel, & Kohlberg, 1969).

In another type of study, students were given the test, then given a semester's course that included discussion of moral dilemmas. The instructor saw to it that solutions a little higher than the students' normal level were presented. Experimental subjects showed greater gains on retest than control subjects (Blatt & Kohlberg, 1975). That result accords with the theoretical expectation that social models are effective only when the child's own thought structure is very close to that of the model, a consideration that does not seem to have been mentioned by the social learning theorists.

Although such studies were encouraging, some studies showed that regression did occur, contrary to Kohlberg's original assertions. In particular, his own longitudinal subjects showed some anomalous results. The original sample, first tested in their teens, have been retested every three or four years for about twenty years. As a number of cases could not be traced or retested, some additional cases have been added to the sample. About 20 percent of middle-class students who had scored the highest in high school, being firmly at stage 4, seemed to regress during their first two years in college, often to stage 2.

There are various ways to interpret such results. One might conclude that the strict stage model is not an accurate representation of how people develop. Instead, Kohlberg chose to interpret them as showing the need for revising his mode of scoring the test, and that project has continued for some years (Colby, Kohlberg, Gibbs, & Lieberman, 1983).

Using the data from a few subjects of the longitudinal study, Anne Colby, Kohlberg, and their colleagues have been endeavoring to arrive at a scoring system that will eliminate all reversals, thus a scoring system that will verify the assumption of a rigorous stage structure to moral judgment. The data for the remaining subjects, when rescored according to the new system, appear to support his claim to a large extent (Colby et al., 1983). Because, however, the cases involved are the same subjects that Kohlberg's group has been studying for a number of years, most psychologists will probably await confirmation of the findings from other research workers in other laboratories.

Kohlberg's inclusion of isolated and socially popular boys as part of his original research design was intended to test the hypothesis that opportunities for social interaction and for taking the role of others are part of the process by which development on this continuum takes place. This hypothesis is integral to the theory of cognitive development as originally proposed. The sequence is not prewired into the nervous system nor imposed by the environment, according to this theory. Rather it develops in the interaction of the developing child with the environment. This theory is compatible with Piaget's reasoning on this topic. It has not proved as fruitful as expected and is less stressed in current work. The part of the original design that has proved to be predictive of later progress in the stages has been socioeconomic status, exactly as traditional psychometric research would predict.

*Applications and applied research.* Kohlberg and his students and colleagues have studied the use of moral dilemmas not only as a way to measure moral development but also as a way to advance it (Blatt & Kohlberg, 1975). Coming out of those efforts, the idea grew up of designing a *just community*, a miniature democratic society within some setting such as a school or prison, governed by its own constitution and by-laws and meeting frequently to discuss issues in enforcing discipline on its members. The theory is that in this natural setting, with some aid from group leaders in showing the moral implications of the issues that arise naturally, optimal conditions are created for moral advance. Joseph Hickey and Peter Scharf have recorded one such study, its rationale, and its moderately successful outcome (Hickey & Scharf, 1980).

Creation of a just community represents a major institutional commitment as well as a commitment of time on the part of all participants for a notoriously inefficient form of government, namely, radical democracy. On a more restricted scale, many schools have instituted one- or two-semester courses or activities that are applications of Kohlberg's theory. This has occurred at junior high, high school, and college level. An even more limited application involves discussions on moral dilemmas interpolated into other courses or programs. A comprehensive objective evaluation of all such studies has yet to be produced. In general, courses lasting eight or nine months have produced measurable change; shorter-term efforts have not. The evidence is still fragmentary, however, mostly found in unpublished dissertations.

Any teacher or principal who believes that starting a program of discussions of moral dilemmas will solve the problem of disorder in the hallways, or even stealing or cheating, will be disappointed. That point of view is the one that Kohlberg labels the "bag of virtues" approach to moral development, which he contrasts with his view.

*Philosophy of education.* Kohlberg and Rochelle Mayer have described three different philosophies of education and child development—the Romantic view, the cultural-transmission view, and the progressive view (Kohlberg & Mayer, 1972). The *Romantic* view, whose ancestor is Jean Jacques Rousseau, among others, is currently typified by psychoanalysis, they assert. The Romantic view sees the child as born with high potential that society sets out to crush. Each child is born with a maturational program that, left unhindered, will flower and reveal his or her best intellectual and moral self. There are many variations in each school, and among psychoanalysts, writers such as Anna Freud and Bruno Bettelheim have stressed ego controls as essential to optimizing the unfolding process, Kohlberg and Mayer acknowledge.

The *cultural-transmission* view, whose ancestors include Locke and J. B. Watson, is currently typified by B. F. Skinner. It states that the intellectual and moral patterns that the child must learn reside in the environment, and the child picks them up there.

The *progressive* view embodies the insights of John Dewey and Piaget as well as those of Kohlberg. In this view the educational system cannot entrust the moral or intellectual development of the child either to a natural unfolding or to the child copying the rules and structures of the environment. Rather, the environment must present a graded series of experiences to the child, cued to the child's current intellectual and personality structure. In coping with new challenges in terms of his or her current structure, the child evolves a slightly more complex structure. That process, not simply letting nature take its course, is the mechanism by which development takes place. Presentation of conflict or problem situations of an appropriate level of difficulty is essential for the progressive approach to be successful in stimulating growth. Thus Kohlberg has taken what started as a method of measuring moral development, the method of dilemmas, and turned it into a philosophy of development and a principal mode of education.

*Development of gender identity.* Kohlberg has demonstrated the power of his cognitive developmental approach by a foray into a domain that none of the others in this group of psychologists has tackled, the domain of gender identity (Kohlberg, 1966). How, he asks, do children develop a firm sense of being boys or girls at around the age of four? He discusses the topic by marshaling a large array of empirical studies as well as his own reasoning.

Beginning, as Freud does, by discussing boys first, Kohlberg summarizes the psychoanalytic theory as follows: The little boy develops a passionate love of and desire for his mother. However, he fears his father's retaliation for this desire for exclusive possession of mother. As a protection against the feared retaliation (psychoanalysis specifies castration), he identifies himself with his father. Having defensively identified himself with father, he then internalizes father's role, and his sex-typed identity follows. It is as if his slogan is, "If you can't beat him, join him."

The social learning version Kohlberg renders somewhat as follows: The father is a major source of rewards, punishments, and control. Particularly the receipt of rewards from the father leads to identification of the boy with his father and to taking his father as a model. Imitating his father rather than his mother is rewarded by everyone throughout the boy's life, further strengthening the preferential imitation of male models. Having his father as his model, he identifies himself as male, like his father. A corresponding paradigm holds for girls.

Kohlberg disagrees with both of those models of development. He shows that children of two and three years are not at all convinced of the fixity of species. The transformation of one kind of creature into a totally different kind is natural to their way of thinking, with its credulity for magic. Kohlberg shows, for example, that some children of that age believe that a cat can be changed into a dog by clipping its whiskers. Similarly, a boy can become a girl by wearing a dress. Gradually, around the age of three or four, children learn that animals do not change species or sex, though they still do not understand for another two or three years that the genitals are the essential factor differentiating the sexes. Under the influence of the feature of childish thought that Piaget called artificialism, children are prone to believe that the girl's lack of penis is something done to her by people, hence their readiness to believe in castration.

Owing to his egocentrism, the three- or four-year-old believes that what is "like me" is specially good. Hence little boys believe boys are better, whereas little girls believe girls are better, though girls as well as boys recognize the superior power and prestige accorded to males in Western society. The belief in male superiority is partly a result of the concreteness of the child's thought. The greater size of men in general and of most fathers is conflated with belief in men's greater strength, greater independence, and so on. Studies have shown that these childish conclusions are not necessarily contingent on the presence of a male in the household. Nor will a child, for several years yet, have the idea that cultural norms mandate being satisfied with one's own sex. At four years the mechanism is simple: "I like what is like me." This is the basis for the special kinship of the boy with his father and the girl with her mother, according to Kohlberg.

Children begin to believe that their gender is a permanent feature at about the same time they believe that cats cannot become dogs and vice versa. Girls will remain girls, they will not grow up to be boys, nor will boys under any circumstances become girls. Once a boy has firmly identified himself as a boy, he recognizes his special kinship with his father, who is also male. Thus sex-typed identity follows naturally from a belief in the fixity of species. Having identified himself as a boy like Daddy, the boy wishes to be like his father. Modeling derives from gender identity, rather than giving rise to it. The special attachment of the boy to his father Kohlberg then derives from taking the father as a model. Thus the sex-typed identity is the original term of the sequence, with the identification with father, taking him as a model, and attachment to him as consequences.

*Critical evaluation of Kohlberg's contributions.* Kohlberg has been the most influential of Piaget's followers in recent years; his theory of moral development has been particularly popular outside the field of psychology. That popularity has made him a target for criticism both among other Piagetians and among non-Piagetians. A collection of essays by scholars from many fields that his work has touched on has been published recently evaluating his contributions to their fields; it contains thirty chapters, covering fourteen different areas (Modgil & Modgil, 1986). No attempt will be made to summarize those evaluations.

One of the first and most persistent criticisms concerns his claim to the cultural universality of his conception and sequence of stages. His opponents point to the fact that in many countries where some version of his test has been given, there are no persons who clearly test at the highest, or principled, stages. How, then, can he claim that that is the goal or endpoint for their development, as the sequence implies? He defines morality, they say, in the terms a liberal, intellectual Western male does.

There is no guarantee, however, that all stages will be present in all cultures. To demand that is to prejudge an issue that ought to be decided empirically: Do primitive cultures provide a situation in which the highest stages can develop? At any rate, Kohlberg sees every stage as a moral stage. The differences are in the kind of morality. Every child, he believes, is a moral philosopher.

The difficulties in the way of arriving at a decisive answer to the issue are formidable. Not only must the test be translated into the native language of the people being tested, not only must answers usually be translated back into English for trained raters, there is the larger question whether the dilemmas themselves are appropriate ones for a culture with different ways of living and a different value system. In fact, the dilemmas have been replaced by more appropriate ones in some studies with other cultures, but then the question arises whether the results pertain to the same test. The arguments and the evidence for and against cultural universality are presented by Carolyn Pope Edwards (1986) and Ian Vine (1986). The evidence for sequence is strongest for the first three stages, weakest for the principled stages.

Another criticism is ethical and political. Kohlberg has been criticized on the grounds that his system pigeonholes individuals within a stage, thus labeling them unfairly. This criticism, which has also been directed against other stage theories, is unfair and illogical. Whereas the IQ is presumably more or less constant throughout childhood, the essence of developmental stages is that they are constantly changing, at least potentially and minimally; thus, in principle no one is permanently labeled. (Parenthetically, research findings should not be circulated with any participating subject identified by name, a rule that is virtually always observed by researchers.)

Other psychologists within the cognitive developmental group have studied the development of various aspects of personality and character, including the sense of justice, the sense of responsibility, the capacity for interpersonal relations, ideas of friendship, the sense of self, the epistemological framework, among other topics. Several, though not all, of this group received part of their training with Kohlberg. The following sections will take up three principle directions in which the Piagetian paradigm has been extended, to cover girls and women, to cover younger children, and to use an objective test rather than an interview.

### Gilligan: Moral Development of Girls and Women

Carol Gilligan introduces her theory of the moral development of girls and women with the following observations: Major voices in the psychology of moral development have been those of Freud, Erikson, Piaget, and Kohlberg. Freud, despite the fact that from the beginning his patients were mostly women, claimed to the end that women remained a mystery to him. In particular, with respect to moral development, his main concern was to trace the development of boys. Piaget, by concentrating on the game of marbles, a game almost exclusively for boys, also produced a scheme of moral development having greater application to boys. Kohlberg's major study has been devoted exclusively to boys and young men. Moreover, somewhat like Freud, he found that girls and women tend to stabilize at stage 3 far more than boys and men, who typically advance to stage 4; at one time he accounted for this discrepancy by the greater opportunities for role taking in the life course of men, as compared to women, who are more often confined to home and the family circle. Only Erikson has shown concern for the specifics of female development; however, even he finds place in his charts of epigenetic development chiefly for the male version (Erikson, 1950, and elsewhere). The contrast between male morality and female morality is at least as old as the Old Testament. Contrast Abraham's willingness to sacrifice the life of his son Isaac to the Lord, with the mother standing before Solomon, who preferred giving her child to another woman rather than having it cut in half (Gilligan, 1982).

The data on which Gilligan's own theory depends come chiefly from three studies — an abortion-decision study, a college student study, and a rights-and-responsibilities study. For the abortion-decision study, twenty-nine women were referred from abortion clinics and pregnancy counseling services throughout a metropolitan area; twenty four completed the initial interview, and twenty one were reinterviewed a year later. In the college student study, twenty-five students who had taken a course on moral and political choice as sophomores were reinterviewed as seniors and again five years later; sixteen women who had dropped the course were also interviewed as seniors. For the rights-and-responsibilities study, thirty-six males and females, matched for age and other variables and ranging from six to sixty years, were interviewed intensively.

Gilligan appears to have begun with Kohlberg's dilemmas and his theory of moral development. Soon, however, she began to find themes in the way her subjects, especially the women, were construing moral problems that did not correspond to points on Kohlberg's scale. Her exact methods are not easy to reconstruct, since the specifics of her studies are as yet unpublished, though the results have been widely influential in changing thinking on female moral development. Apparently early in the studies, or perhaps before these studies were initiated, she had decided that Kohlberg's scheme did not do justice to women's development.

Her studies were not restricted to ascertaining where the persons fell on the Kohlberg scale, based on the choices they made to artificial dilemmas presented to them by the interviewer. She asked how they defined moral problems, what kinds of experiences were seen as moral problems, and how they responded to such problems in the context of real life. In the abortion study, for example, apparently all the subjects were referred because the question of whether to continue the pregnancy was experienced as a problem.

What Gilligan presents, largely in terms of illustrative excerpts from interviews, is not, however, a straightforward comparison of the developmental course of moral judgment in males and females. Rather, she traces two different developmental courses, namely, one course that takes fairness and justice as its essential theme and another that takes care and responsibility for others as its central theme. The former course is essentially the one that Kohlberg has traced. She states that on average more women than men follow the course dealing with care and responsibility. That theme evolves through stages, just as fairness and justice do in Kohlberg's account. Probably the study of women considering abortion was the initial stimulus; necessarily, those subjects were women, they faced a dilemma, and other persons (or potential persons) were necessarily involved in the dilemma.

Gilligan is far from the feminist school of thought that there are few real gender differences. She accentuates the differences between male and female psychology and quotes many authorities who have also discerned the difference in somewhat similar terms. Male psychology is traced as a progression toward separation, autonomy, and individuality, whereas female psychology progresses toward greater connectedness and intimacy in the search for identity. Gilligan adds the proviso that there are some boys and men with a feeling for relationships and responsibilities similar to that of girls and women, and in principle there are some girls and women just as interested in rules, rights, and justice as the typical male. What she objects to is taking the latter course as a yardstick to measure progress for the former sequence, inevitably with the conclusion that the average girl is deficient or that women are in a class with children on moral thinking.

In relation to the conflict over whether to have an abortion, women in the first stage construe the issue as one of self-interest in order to insure survival. The fun of having a baby and never again being completely lonely may be balanced against giving up freedom, going on welfare, losing the respect of one's parents, losing one's boyfriend, and so on, but always in terms of one's own interests. In the transition to the next stage, that way of construing the problem is labeled selfish.

In the second stage, all of the issues are recast in terms of responsibilities to others — parents, boyfriend, sometimes his wife or children, the potential baby, and so on. At this stage, the only moral solution is seen as one in which the interests of others are considered to the exclusion of one's own interests.

Ultimately that stage is seen as too asymmetrical. The woman at the center of the dilemma is a person too. Her search for goodness must give way to accommodate the truth, that she deserves to be one of the parties whose interests are considered. That represents the third and highest stage in this sequence. It resembles the Piagetian ideal of equilibration.

In related research, S. Pollak and Gilligan studied the reactions of eighty-eight men and fifty women students from a Harvard course in human motivation to a series of TAT pictures (see Chapter 4) (Pollak and Gilligan, 1982). Two of the pictures depicted achievement situations; two depicted people in close relationships. Men tended to tell more violent stories in response to pictures showing relationships, women in response to pictures oriented toward achievement. Men used somewhat more violent themes overall. Pollak and Gilligan interpret their results as showing that young men tend to see danger in and to be afraid of situations of intimacy, whereas they feel more secure in the well defined relations of achievement situations. Women, on the contrary, are afraid of isolation in achievement situations and tend to feel more secure in intimate relationships. These results, although pertaining directly to the realm of imagination and fantasy, confirm the different attitudes toward social relations typical of men and women in a way consistent with Gilligan's theory of women's moral development.

## Social and Moral Development of Children

Kohlberg's method of testing moral reasoning, posing classical moral dilemmas for solution, is suitable for adolescents and adults but not for very young children; yet the foundations of morality have generally been understood to be laid before such sophisticated topics as Kohlberg uses can be discussed with a child. Several psychologists in the cognitive developmental school have worked out methods for studying the beginnings of moral development. In the process, they have also raised some new questions for investigation.

*Selman and interpersonal perspective taking.* Robert Selman reasons that the child's understanding of social relations proceeds on a course parallel with moral development and sets a limit on moral development; thus he concludes that studying the understanding of social relations is logically prior to studying moral development (Selman, 1980). He sees the core of social cognition as lying in what is usually called role taking, but he prefers the term *interpersonal perspective taking.* By that term he calls attention to the progression from the egocentrism of young children, who do not distinguish their own perspective from that of others, to taking the perspective of the other, to taking a third-person perspective.

In order to make the thinking of school-age children accessible, Selman has devised dilemmas involving children participating in the kinds of things children normally do. The dilemmas can be presented orally or as film strips, with the parts played by children of appropriate ages, each film lasting six to eight minutes. An open-ended interview follows, conducted along lines similar to those used by Piaget and Kohlberg.

The specific topics Selman has investigated include friendship, peer-group relations, parent-child relations, and individuality, the last including subjectivity, self-awareness, and personality. To investigate the topics of individuality, subjectivity, and personality, the test presents a story about a little boy, Mike, whose dog, Pepper, has just run away. Mike's birthday is coming up shortly. His friend passes a pet shop in which he sees a new puppy, the last one in the shop, and wonders whether to buy it for Mike. Mike has said that he never wants to have another dog. What should the friend do? The test questionnaire concerns whether Mike could say he never wants another dog and not mean it, whether one can deceive oneself, and so on.

Selman sees five stages of role taking. At stage 0 the child sees individuals only in physical terms. People are described typically in terms of individual physical characteristics or in terms of global evaluations, such as good or bad. Personality change is not distinguished from physical growth.

In stage 1, that of individuals as intentional subjects, there is the beginning of understanding of motives. Actions are not just the doings of a physical being but are expressions of intentions. Personality change may be equated with practicing new skills.

At stage 2, when individuals appear as introspective selves, the child has a more complicated idea of both self and others as having something like two layers, an inner self and an outer self. One can feel one thing (sadness at losing one's dog) and openly express another (gratitude for the gift of a new puppy) in order not to hurt someone else's feelings. Personality may be seen in terms of habits, though not yet in terms of traits. Personality can be changed by deliberately changing habits.

Stage 3, that of individuals as stable personalities, marks the beginning of understanding ambivalence; one can both love the new dog and hate him for taking the place of Pepper. One can fool oneself, but only more or less intentionally. This stage also displays the conception of traits, which are more general and harder to alter than habits.

At stage 4, that of individuals as complex self-systems, the person spontaneously comes to the idea that people can have traits and motives of which they are not themselves conscious and that personal traits are organized into a system that is something more than a collection of habits or traits. Correspondingly, change may involve behavior and habits only, or traits, or the core of the personality organization.

In American children, stage 0 typically occurs at about ages three to five, which is below the age at which Selman's test is appropriate to give. Most children of seven years, about the lowest age for the test, can express stage 1 thoughts in an interview. At eleven years they typically can express stage 2 ideas; at fifteen, stage 3. Stage 4, which not everyone reaches, may develop between the ages of twelve and adulthood.

A story concerning friendship is about as follows. Two girls who have been friends since they started school have a date for next Saturday. Just after they made the date, a new girl at school called up one of them to ask her to come to the circus on Saturday, which will be the last day for the circus. The invited girl has to decide between breaking a date with her old friend, and missing the circus. The questionnaire goes into such topics as what is an ideal friend, what happens when friends quarrel, how do they make up, what trust develops in long-term friendships, and so on.

This story helps to delineate the development of the concept of friend. At stage 0, that of egocentric perspective, a friend is someone who lives near me or has nice toys or that I am playing with right now. At stage 1, that of subjective perspective, a friend is someone who meets my needs or wants. For example, if he gives me a present, we will be friends again. At stage 2, that of simple subjective reciprocity, the child sees self and friend as each aware of the other's feelings and point of view. For example, I like him because he likes me. At stage 3, that of third-person perspective taking and mutuality, people understand that friendship is based on mutual understanding built up over time. At stage 4, and higher, the person makes qualitative differentiations among kinds of relations.

A similar story concerning peer groups is followed by questions on leadership and loyalty. A story on parent-child relations is followed by questions related to punishment and conflict resolution in the family.

In one study, twenty-one students in a school for disturbed children tended to rate about normal in intelligence but significantly below a matched control group in regard to interpersonal perspective taking (Jaquette, 1980). Average children in the normative sample used stage 2 reasoning consistently at about ten and a half years, whereas on average the clinic children were close to thirteen years before they did so. There was some indication of greater inconsistency in clinic subjects.

In a longitudinal study of eight students in one class of the clinic school Daniel S. Jaquette observed them in class meetings once a week for a school year (Jaquette, 1980). In the meetings, real-life interpersonal problems were discussed, and the students were rated for the level of perspective taking in that context. They also were given Selman's test at the beginning and end of the year. The level they displayed in class meetings was lower than they displayed in a test situation with hypothetical problems. The students rather consistently displayed growth during the first two thirds of the year and decline during the last third, an effect that shows the possibility of some regression.

*Damon and hypothetical and enacted social reasoning.* William Damon has been interested in many aspects of the child's social development but particularly the development of a sense of fairness or justice (Damon, 1977). Like Kohlberg, he has taken as his adversary the social learning theorists, who represent social development as largely a matter of accumulating social norms and knowledge, in whatever order parents and others in the child's environment may present them. A related idea sometimes espoused by social learning theorists is that there is no close relation between the child's moral judgment and his or her actual morality and conduct. Damon points out that such comments usually contrast judgment with conduct or contrast thought with action. It is inconceivable, however, that anyone engage in social conduct without some thought, nor could one assess moral judgment without recourse to actual behavior, albeit verbal behavior. Indeed, most of what is called conduct has a large verbal element (Damon, 1977, p. 17). Damon thus substitutes for judgment versus conduct a contrast between theoretical or hypothetical moral judgment and active moral judgment in a real-life situation. Much of his research consists of parallel studies of moral problems in those two types of situations.

In one series of experiments, four children who do not know one another are brought together in a room with some strings and many colored beads and asked to make bracelets out of them. The task is stopped when one of the children has clearly made more than the others. One of the children, who is much younger than the others and has generally made the fewest bracelets, is taken home. The experimenter then says that A has made the "most and prettiest" bracelets, B is singled out as the "biggest boy" or "biggest girl," and C's bracelets are said to be "nice." The children are then told that they will be given ten candy bars as a reward, and they are interviewed separately as to how they would distribute the ten bars among the four participants. Then the three children are brought together to resolve their differences and arrive at a group decision. That is the real-life situation. A similar situation is presented to each child in an interview in order to see how he or she would decide in a parallel hypothetical situation.

Results from this series of experiments can be analyzed in many ways. All children give some candy to each participant. The youngest children tend to give the most reward to the child whose bracelets were labeled as "nice" and to themselves. Most of the children favored themselves somewhat, but the extra reward for the "nice" position probably represents the fact that this is an intelligible word of approval for the youngest ones.

A second result is a series of stages or levels in ideas of fair distribution or sharing. At level 0-A, the child's choice simply reflects his or her own wishes, without justification other than simply wanting it that way. At level 0-B, the choice still reflects the child's wishes, but it is justified on the basis of concrete realities such as size, age, or sex, though in an irrational, self-serving, and inconsistent fashion.

At level 1-A, choices reflect strict equality; everyone receives the same. At level 1-B, the notion of reciprocity enters, that is, persons are paid back in kind for good or bad deeds.

At level 2-A, moral relativity enters; different persons are seen to have different but equally valid claims. Claims may be compromised or special allowance made for special needs. At the highest level that Damon studied, level 2-B, equality, reciprocity, and moral relativity are all coordinated.

These stages are evident both in hypothetical and real-life situations. Stage of reasoning is highly correlated with age in the school children studied, ages four through ten. With age held constant statistically, there is still a significant though low correlation between hypothetical and real-life reasoning. Damon asserts that stages develop in the same order in both realms, but he has not demonstrated longitudinally that the stages must be passed through in the order given. It is quite possible that some children never adopt the reasoning of one stage but pass directly to the next one. That is a question that must be studied further.

Whereas Piaget had found that in his cognitive problems real-life reasoning tends to be in advance of reasoning about hypothetical situations, Damon found that hypothetical reasoning tends to be more advanced. He accounts for that discrepancy by the fact that in his situations, unlike Piaget's, self-interest enters to hold back the child's reasoning about real-life candy bars.

Damon's studies show that many young children do differentiate pragmatic from moral considerations, contrary to Kohlberg's implicit assumption. Kohlberg's original labels for the first two stages, punishment-and-obedience orientation and naive instrumental hedonism, both refer to pragmatic rather than strictly moral aspects. In early childhood there is, to be sure, some confusion of the pragmatic and moral aspects, but it is by no means true that no young child distinguishes them. It is true, however, that with increasing age the distinction become increasingly clear to more and more children.

*Turiel's view of conventions and morals.* In taking the game of marbles as his paradigm of moral development, Piaget was in effect asserting that children up to the age of twelve or so do not distinguish rules of the game from moral issues. Similarly, Kohlberg appears to assume that neither at the preconventional nor at the conventional levels do children differentiate conventional from moral issues; that is virtually implied by the names of the stages.

Social learning theorists also implicitly assume that children do not distinguish the moral domain from other rule-governed domains. A characteristic way of studying moral development among social learning theorists is to study the conditions under which children can sustain resistance to temptation. The temptations dangled before them are pieces of candy to eat or attractive toys to play with, with instructions to wait until the experimenter gives the child permission (see Chapter 5). Those actions are not intrinsically wrong; they are not even unconventional, as wearing pajamas to school would be. They are simply forbidden by the experimenter. The significance of the studies for moral development depends on assuming that the children do not know the difference between arbitrary and morally justified rules.

Elliot Turiel differs from Piaget and Kohlberg and from the social learning theorists with respect to whether children differentiate moral rules from social-conventional and arbitrary rules (Turiel, 1983). Turiel and his colleagues have shown that children from an early age distinguish acts that are wrong per se from those that are wrong because they are forbidden. Children have a structure of thought pertinent to evaluation of social-conventional acts; their understanding of society as a system and hence of social-conventional acts evolves in its own way, at least partly separated from the evolution of moral judgment. Unlike the social learning theorists, Turiel does not believe that rewards and punishments or social models are the chief determinants of children's evaluation of social-conventional acts. He is committed to the idea of intellectual structure and hence remains within the cognitive developmental school of thought. In a typical study by Turiel and his colleagues, children are asked to evaluate several acts, such as stealing, taking off one's clothing on the school playground, and calling teachers by their first names. A Piagetian-type interview explores the reasons behind the children's evaluations.

Donna Weston and Turiel studied a varied group of school children between ages of five and eleven (Weston & Turiel, 1980). (Their study will be reported here as if the same children were involved in all the parts, although that is not entirely true.) The children were given hypothetical stories concerning four acts — hitting another child, leaving toys on the school floor, taking all their clothes off on the playground, and refusing to share a snack. Most children in that age range distinguished hitting from the other three offenses as being bad per se. When asked to evaluate the acts without any statement about what the school policy might be, 95 percent evaluated hitting negatively, as compared with 45 percent and 60 percent evaluating the other acts negatively. No one evaluated hitting positively, though many did so for the other acts. Thus the evaluations of hitting were significantly different from evaluations of other acts, but the others were not significantly differentiated from one another. The five-year-olds were evenly divided on whether leaving toys and undressing were positively or negatively evaluated, but the eleven-year-olds were predominantly negative in their evaluation.

Then the children were asked to evaluate a school policy permitting each of the acts. Most of the children, 88 percent, evaluated negatively a policy permitting hitting, whereas on the other three acts, the majority, between 53 percent and 68 percent were positive. When asked to evaluate the acts, given a school policy permitting each act, a majority, 55 percent were negative only for hitting; 63 percent to 80 percent were positive for the others. Younger children, ages four to seven, tended to say that hitting was all right so long as school policy did not prohibit it, even though they rejected such a policy, as the previous results showed. This finding could be taken as supportive of Kohlberg's and Piaget's assumption of some confusion of conventional and moral, but only among children much younger than they assumed.

Given that there is no school policy, will the teacher respond to the situation if she observes such behavior? Half the children say yes with respect to hitting, but the majority, 60 percent to 65 percent, say no for the other acts. All ages say that it is all right for her not to reprimand or correct the child if there is no school policy.

Judith Smetana found that children of about three or four understood that specific moral transgressions were wrong even if there was no rule against it (Smetana, 1981). The four-year-olds understood that the acts would still be wrong in another context, but the three-year-olds did not understand the question about generalizability. These results again imply that very young children can distinguish moral from conventional domains.

The domain of social conventions is one that has its own stage sequence, according to Turiel (1983). The first level is simply an affirmation of concrete, observed uniformities of conduct. A six-year-old girl says that a man cannot become a nurse because "I have seen a lot of lady doctors, and you wouldn't really see a man a nurse" (Turiel, 1983, p. 107).

At level 2 that thinking is seen to be arbitrary and is no longer accepted uncritically. An eight-year-old girl says that a "boy could become a nurse because it doesn't matter. There are men nurses in hospitals. . . . His father might be old-fashioned and he would think that men could not take care of babies (ibid., pp. 107–108)."

At level 3, rules are seen in the context of a concrete conception of the social system. Thus a child should not call a teacher by her first name because "it was one of the rules of the school," said a boy of eleven years, five months. Without the rule, it wouldn't matter.

A boy a year and a half older, however, says that "If I were a teacher, I don't think it should bother a teacher that he be called by his first name. . . . but the way it is now, you really can't. . . . He could get himself in trouble" (ibid., p. 109). The latter response illustrates level 4, criticism of convention as related to rule and the authority system.

At level 5, conventions are seen in the context of a hierarchically organized social system that regulates social interaction. Thus a seventeen-year-old says, "You have to realize that you should have respect for your elders and that respect is shown by addressing them by their last names. . . . You have to go along with the ways of other people in your society" (ibid., p. 110).

Another seventeen-year-old, at level 6, is critical of level 5 thinking: "Just the fact that teachers in school have to be called Mr. or Mrs. is no valid reason for that. . . . The reason is to give the teacher in the classroom respect and give him a feeling of power and authority over the kids in class" (ibid., p. 111).

At the highest level, level 7, conventions coordinate social interactions and serve to integrate diverse elements of the social system. However, the illustration that Turiel gives involves a much more complex kind of reasoning than the foregoing quotations illustrate.

Turiel belittles the idea of conventionality as a stage in moral development. He sees everyone fitting in to some stage of the foregoing sequence, just as Kohlberg sees each of his stages as a moral stage. Levels 1, 3, 5, and 7 affirm the value of conventions, levels 2, 4, and 6 question, criticize, or negate the value of conventions, but everyone is equally concerned with conventions. After the very earliest years, say, three years at the latest, conventionality and morality are different domains.

Looking back at Piaget and Kohlberg, how much has been underminded by Turiel's criticism? With regard to Piaget's use of the game of marbles, Turiel has taken the adult view that it is just a game. Piaget has documented (as some oldsters may still remember) that in children's society the game was played with passionate seriousness. Marbles were the child's hoard, the prize possessions of that preplastic era when few had mechanical toys. The study of the game of marbles deserves to be reassessed in the light of Turiel's considerations, but it is not rendered completely irrelevant to moral judgment.

Concerning Kohlberg's stages, his data remain, of course, but perhaps he gave inappropriate names to the stages. A somewhat similar system of stages of ego development (see later) has used the term *conformist* instead of *conventional*, partly because some strongly anticonventional people appear to be rigidly locked into their own anticonventional code and hence have the structure or style of conformity at the same time that they abjure the content of conventionality. Again, further thought needs to be given to how far astray that misnaming of a stage may have led Kohlberg and his colleagues.

*Blasi and responsibility.* All of the foregoing topics — moral judgment, justice, conventionality, and social cognition — interrelated as they are, have a common thread in the theme of responsibility, a theme anticipated in Gilligan's studies of young women. Responsibility has many aspects, beginning before a choice of action has been made and continuing with accountability for the action and its consequences. These topics have been studied for many years by Augusto Blasi (1982, 1984). In his version of the moral-dilemma paradigm, children are presented with dilemmas pitting altruistic or helping actions against obedience to parental orders, institutional rules, or laws. The questionnaire that follows the story asks both what the hero should do and what he must do, for Blasi found early in his work that children differentiate free moral choices from strict obligations. Further, supposing the hero is punished, whether for disobedient altruism or for being obedient but not altruistic, then is the punishment fair? Who is to blame for the consequences? Thus responsibility is studied both in terms of choice and of accountability after the fact.

In one study, similar dilemmas regarding responsibility were presented to children of different ages. Although the actual content of the stories differed in age-appropriate ways, the structure of the dilemmas was the same for all ages. There were forty-six children in first grade, thirty in sixth grade, and thirty two in tenth and eleventh grades, approximately equally divided between boys and girls in each grade. The youngest were six or seven years old, the middle group eleven or twelve, and the oldest sixteen or seventeen. The youngest group was middle class, the two older groups divided between middle and upper-middle class.

The story for the youngest tells of a child left home alone with orders not to go outside. But he sees a little child falling in the yard and does not know whether to go out to help. He does go outside and is punished by his mother for doing so. Children in the first grade were more likely to choose helping (73 percent) than obeying. Whichever they chose, their reason was that that was what they wanted to do, or it referred to the specific circumstances of the story, such as the fact that the little child was small or helpless. When told that the hero was punished for helping and asked whether he should help next time, only 23 percent thought he should do it again. Punishment was then given as the reason for obeying. They could not give a justification either for the norm of obedience or the norm of altruism. They rejected the idea that there was any obligation to help. However, when asked whether the mother was fair to punish the child, the reasoning was more mature. Whether they said yes or no, they were more likely to give real reasons, less likely to regard their answer as self-evidently justified than in relation to the original choice.

The story for the sixth graders tells of a boy at camp who wants to bring food to another boy who is being punished, but this is against the rules of the director. He decides to obey the rules but is blamed by his father for not helping his friend. Sixth graders were more likely to choose to obey than to help, in contrast to first graders, but they always gave reasons for choosing obedience as a norm; they almost never gave impulse or their own needs as justification. Thus they understood the difference between their wishes and moral norms in a way that younger children do not. Norms were not tied to specific circumstances but to general principles, referring to order, duty, authority, and so on, considerations almost totally absent from the answers of the first graders. Obedience was not justified by the threat of punishment but by authority's greater knowledge, by maintaining order, or the like. By implication, if those contingencies are not met, obedience is not mandated. Further, there was much greater concordance between what they thought was right to do and what they thought there was a strict obligation to do. In general, there was a greater rejection of a sense of obligation in regard to the norm of helping than the norm of obedience. Almost one third mentioned the hero's knowledge of rules, circumstances, or consequences, or feelings of guilt; hence there was the basis for a sense of personal responsibility. Although almost all sixth graders gave reasons for their moral choice, only a small minority used a subjective perspective, such as conscience, to justify their choice. The majority relied on objective rules, especially the rule of obedience to authority and law. Sanctions against the hero were recognized as fair if they referred to sticking to the law, not if they referred to consistency with his own moral judgment. No sixth grader, even among those who accepted subjective responsibility for their moral choice, believed he should be blamed for not acting consistently with his own moral views.

The corresponding dilemma for the oldest children tells of a nurse who thinks about telling the family of a dying patient about the patient's true condition; however, this is against hospital rules. Afterward the patient's family blames her. The high school group was more heterogeneous than the younger children. More of them chose the norm of altruism than that of obedience; however, as the stories for different ages were not identical, this result needs to be checked further. Among the high schoolers, many who chose the norm of altruism saw it not only as the correct choice but also as a strict obligation. Some kinds of justification that are used by the eleventh graders did not appear at all among younger children, for example, a reference to a societal perspective or to universal human characteristics. In that sense, the oldest group is more objective, but they also rely more on their own subjective evaluation in their decisions, including references to the hero's personality, background, or interests. More than half of them use their own subjective evaluations in relation to one of the dilemmas. Another new element in the responses of some eleventh graders was deep feelings of the importance of being true to one's own values or self. Usually, however, they did not feel that others should blame them if they were not consistent with self-chosen values. Only four of the thirty two believed that it is fair to blame a person for not being true to his or her own values.

*Summary.* Piaget characterized the moral judgment of young children in terms of heteronomous morality and unilateral respect for their elders, and he advocated a more equalitarian upbringing as a partial antidote. The prescription was somewhat inconsistent with his own description of the intellectual capabilities of the small child, who is hardly equipped to understand how persons so unequal in size and ability as parent and child can be in some sense equal and merit equal treatment. Kohlberg, dealing with older children but again seeking the lowest stage, did not find evidence of unilateral respect but rather a punishment-and-obedience orientation at first, followed by a stage of naive instrumental hedonism.

Recent work has modified Kohlberg's description, at least as applied to young children. Between altruism and obedience, Blasi finds more first graders choosing altruism, a mode that hardly fits either of Kohlberg's first two stages, he has pointed out. Nor is what is conventionally or arbitrarily forbidden always confused with what is inherently bad, even by young children, contrary to apparent assumptions of Kohlberg and Piaget, as Turiel has shown.

What shows up repeatedly in studies of young children is that they do not understand abstract moral principles as mediators of moral choices. They tend instead to give concrete specifics as reasons for their choices. At the youngest ages, even these concrete aspects are arbitrary, irrelevant, and often self-serving: "He should get more because he is the oldest," or "I should get more because I am the littlest." The resort to specifics to answer a question asking for reasons is evident in the studies by Kohlberg, Selman, Damon, and Blasi.

This common thread in their findings should have been anticipated, because it shows the preoperational and concrete operational thinking of children ages four to seven. The illustrations of moral thinking in early childhood are nonetheless valuable for persons dealing with youngsters, enabling them to deal with children on a realistic basis. And the theme gives specific content to the idea of preoperational and concrete operational thought. After all, most of the time even adults are more comfortable operating in a concrete operational mode rather than an abstract, formal operational mode.

In early childhood, then, intellectual development places a cap on how far moral development can proceed. That appears to be less true in later childhood and adolescence, where the limitations in children's thinking demonstrate something other than intellectual constraints. Two examples that appeared in the foregoing accounts are the sharp distinction between what one ought to do and what one is strictly obliged to do, particularly in middle childhood. This was clear in Blasi's work and also in Weston and Turiel's data. In the latter instance, the children thought the teacher would condemn hitting even if there were no school policy against it but thought that it was all right for her not to do so. Thus public morality and private morality are distinguished, the former being what is strictly required, the latter what is required by a freely chosen morality (Blasi). Whether such distinctions are also made as often by adults does not seem to be known.

Contrary to what Piaget found for intellectual development, moral judgment in hypothetical situations appears to be more mature than in practical, real-life situations, as Jaquette (1980) (using Selman's test) and Damon (1977) found. The explanation appears to be intrusion of self-interest in real-life situations, which is less of a factor in intellectual performance.

Finally, Blasi found in his high school students a theme that did not appear at all in the younger students, valuing fidelity to one's own moral principles. The concept of personal moral integrity occurs rarely even at the eleventh grade. It is of course characteristic of the highest stage in Kohlberg's system. Again, the constraint on its appearance does not appear to be intellectual, for Blasi reports that a number of students explicitly considered the possibility of self-condemnation for not living up to one's own moral standards and rejected that possibility. The conception is understood, but it is not accepted.

In the foregoing studies, information about early moral stages is sought by studying younger children. They are a valuable source of information, but when they are the only source, there is a danger that other characteristics of the younger subjects will be mistakenly attributed to moral immaturity. This is true with preoperational and concrete operational modes of thought in the earliest stages. Thus other approaches are needed to discover the essential characteristics of the early stages, independent of the intellectual immaturity of early childhood.

### Rest: Objective Measurement of Moral Development

With all its richness, Kohlberg's test offers formidable difficulties to anyone learning to administer and score it. His senior collaborators say that one needs a full year's apprenticeship before reliable results can be anticipated. Many psychologists fascinated by the field of moral development are put off by the difficulties. In consequence, several research groups have been working out methods for overcoming the difficulties (Gibbs, Widaman, & Colby, 1982).

The best known and most objective of these tests is James Rest's Defining Issues Test, whose content is based on Kohlberg's conception of moral judgment development (Rest, 1979). The test presents on a printed form a series of moral dilemmas, some the same as and others similar to those Kohlberg presents. After one has chosen a solution to each dilemma (e.g., Heinz should steal the drug to save his wife), one turns the page and finds twelve statements of issues that might have affected the choice, such as whether Heinz and his wife have children. The issues have been selected so as to represent the kinds of concerns characteristic of the several stages. The subject rates each issue according to how important it was in determining the choice. At the bottom of the page, the subject lists the four most important issues in order of their importance for him or her.

There are different ways to score this test. The most used method is to count the number of principled issues, that is, issues representing Kohlberg's stage 5 or 6 reasoning, among the four issues chosen as most important, and to weight them in order of their importance. In line with his psychometric approach, Rest sees moral development in quantitative terms, rather than as a sequence of discrete stages, as Kohlberg does.

Rest acknowledges that the task presented to the person by his test is different from that presented by Kohlberg's test. Kohlberg's subjects must produce their own reasons, whereas Rest's subjects rate reasons presented to them. Learning theorists call this the difference between production and recognition; recognition is easier. Moral judgment is different from a strict learning task, at least as viewed by both Kohlberg and Rest; nonetheless, recognizing principled moral reasons is easier than producing them. Thus people tend to receive higher scores on the Defining Issues Test than on Kohlberg's moral judgment test. In other words, the views for which people express a preference are rated higher on the scale than the views they present spontaneously. There is, however, a substantial correlation between scores on the two tests.

What distinguishes Rest's approach, and Loevinger's, to be described next, is not so much their aspiration to be more objective in their measurement than others in this field nor even perhaps outstanding success in that endeavor. Their distinctive characteristic is that they make a somewhat different assumption about the variable they aim to measure. The strict Piagetians, including Kohlberg, Selman, and several others (Snarey, Kohlberg, & Noam, 1983), think of what they are assessing as being a logically coherent structure. A person is in one stage or another or at worst in transition from one stage to the next. Rest and Loevinger, on the contrary, conceive of what they are measuring as inherently quantitative and probabilistic.

Observable behavior, no matter what measuring instrument one is using, displays variability. No author claims that his subjects display behavior at only one level. The problem is how to think about that variability. For Kohlberg, it is error of measurement or error by the rater and of no theoretical interest. Rest sees each person in terms of a profile of stages; that is, he takes the percentage of responses that the person gives at each stage as representing appropriately the percentage of his thinking, or mental structure, that is at that stage. The weak point in Rest's position is that there has never been any evidence that the profile of scores on one cognitive developmental test matches the profile of the same person on another test. Thus the profile is probably a function of the measuring instrument rather than of the mental structure of the person. Whether the profile provides a truer picture of the cognitive apparatus than the idea of a unitary structure plus error of measurement is not known. Because all the measuring instruments have an unknown amount of error of measurement, there is no way to find out.

## Loevinger: Ego Development and Its Measurement

Beginning from a different point of view, my own research has gradually shaped a conception of ego development that resembles the conception of moral development, though it is a broader concept and the methods of study have been different.

*Objective measurement of mothers' attitudes.* The starting point was a project constructing an objective test of mothers' attitudes toward problems of family life, the Family Problems Scale (Loevinger & Sweet, 1961; Loevinger, Sweet, Ossorio, & LaPerriere, 1962). The women's groups that originally took the test came from widely different parts of the social spectrum, ranging from graduates of an Eastern liberal arts college to women marines. That fact influenced the course of the research.

Items were included to test different theories of how attitudes toward family problems are organized, such as the psychoanalytic theory of psychosexual stages and some everyday or quasi-psychiatric concepts such as punitiveness-permissiveness and acceptance of the feminine role. The psychometric problem that people tend to present socially acceptable self-portraits was met by making each item a forced choice between two alternatives and by writing the items in third person, so that they were pseudoobjective. Both alternative answers were, so far as possible, written so that they sounded socially acceptable. An example is, "No child should be permitted to strike his mother." The subject chooses between that statement and the following: "A mother should not be harsh with a small child who hits her."

Despite the care given in test construction, the results did not conform to expectations. None of the theories that we started with were confirmed by the data. Many women seemed to be responding in a stereotyped or socially acceptable rather than a candid way, even though we phrased the items to minimize that possibility. We were tempted to abandon the enterprise as a failure. One puzzling result encouraged us to go on: Some groups almost unanimously answered one way; other groups almost unanimously answered the same question an opposite way. Here was a challenging anomaly (see Chapter 1). Although we had not succeeded in measuring the traits or factors that we wanted to, apparently we were measuring something that bore a family resemblance to something that many other personality tests measured, or that obtruded into the measurement of other personality traits regardless of the test constructor's intent.

In the test protocols of the groups already tested, there were 202 from subjects who had answered every test question. This group of cases was used in a new study to investigate the structure of attitudes. Two thirds of the sample were mothers or pregnant, mostly the former, the remainder were students, most of them in college. The statistical analysis began by correlating every item with every other item; the items that formed natural statistical groupings were determined without reference to the content of the items. After the statistical grouping was completed we examined the content of the items.

No statistical groupings corresponded to the psychoanalytic concept of psychosexual stages and the (theoretically) corresponding character structures. Items related to toilet training were as closely related to eating items as to each other. The supposed personality manifestations of the oral character type were not confirmed; there was modest support for an orderly character type. Items that were supposed to test acceptance of the feminine role fell into two groups. One group measured acceptance of the biological aspects of the role, the other, acceptance of woman's traditional social role. Surprisingly, these two groups of items were related negatively; the higher a woman was in one respect, the lower in the other. Although the negative relation was small, it was enough to prove that acceptance of woman's role could not reasonably be seen as all one thing.

The most pervasive factor in the test came out of a group of items that was intended to measure punitiveness and permissiveness. But some questions that referred directly to punishing ("Hitting a child is one thing a mother should never do") had no relation to this cluster of items, whereas other questions that seemed to have no connection with punishment or permissiveness were excellent representatives of it. An example of the latter is "A mother should be her daughter's best friend," versus "A mother should not try to be her daughter's best friend." Another surprise was that it was the more punitive mothers who believed that they should be their daughter's best friend. By inspecting all the items included in the cluster and all that were excluded, we concluded that the most appropriate description of this set of items, or of the attitudes that they measured, was Authoritarian Family Ideology (Loevinger & Sweet, 1961; Loevinger, Sweet, Ossorio, & LaPerriere, 1962).

There was a striking similarity between Authoritarian Family Ideology as defined by the Family Problems Scale and the concept of authoritarianism that came out of the Berkeley studies of the authoritarian personality (Adorno, Frenkel-Brunswik, Levinson, & Sanford, 1950). The Berkeley studies began with a primarily political focus; their original intention was to study the origins of fascism and totalitarianism, and they expected to find some relation between such attitudes and psychosexual stages. They used more male subjects than females, including many prison inmates, and of course they asked different kinds of questions than we did. Their data, like ours, proved to be surprising. They found little or no evidence for the importance of psychosexual stages in determining political attitudes. Perhaps they originally hoped to find some pathological character type that was prone to a fascist or totalitarian attitude. If so, they were disappointed, for their results overall were more in line with the hypothesis that authoritarianism is a tendency that is latent in everyone. In subsequent research with children, Else Frenkel-Brunswik came to believe that authoritarianism is an aspect of immature persons (Frenkel-Brunswik, 1951).

The focus of our study was entirely small-scale domestic concerns, and all our subjects were women or adolescent girls, presumably normal. The communality in the Berkeley group's conception of authoritarianism and our conception of authoritarian family attitudes, despite differences in methods and in samples, lent additional weight to the conception. No matter what personality trait or factor one set out to measure, this aspect of personality tends to dominate responses, at least on such paper-and-pencil tests; the political implications of the concept of authoritarianism are gratuitous (Loevinger, 1958/1966).

Another insight helped to reshape this work. The variable Authoritarian Family Ideology, whose mature extreme is a liberal, nonauthoritarian attitude, does not have extreme authoritarianism as its other pole. Rather, authoritarianism is a midpoint on a scale whose lower extreme is more chaotic, anomie in Emile Durkheim's term. Some aspects of authoritarianism increase with increasing maturity at first and only later decline. This was another anomaly, because psychometric methods cannot handle such curvilinear relationships.

With these insights, we no longer sought merely factors affecting mothers' attitudes, nor could we be entirely satisfied with dependence on usual psychometric techniques. Because of the broad scope of the major variable, and because it bore a family resemblance to many variables that had appeared in varied contexts and that had been given various names, the new variable was called *ego development*. That term has drawbacks, for many psychoanalysts restrict the term to the first couple of years of life or to serious psychological disorders presumably originating in the first years. But no less inclusive term suffices.

That the variable was developmental was confirmed by a study of women tested postpartum (LaPerriere, 1962; Loevinger, Sweet, Ossorio, & LaPerriere, 1962). Women with previous experience in child rearing were significantly more mature on this test than women having first babies; women who had finished high school or attended some college were more mature than women with less education. These findings were confirmed in a later, more extensive study (Ernhart & Loevinger, 1969).

An article by C. Sullivan, M. Q. Grant (later Warren), and J. D. Grant, outlining a continuum that they called interpersonal maturity or the capacity for interpersonal integration, helped to flesh out the skeletal conception of ego development (Sullivan, Grant, & Grant, 1957). A new sample of women was given both the Family Problems Scale and a newly devised sentence completion test (hereafter, SCT). The correlation between them was to be a measure of the validity of the ego-developmental interpretation of Authoritarian Family Ideology. This project could not be completed without a way to score the SCT.

*Constructing a scoring manual for a projective test.* The SCT is a projective test, but we aimed to construct a scoring procedure that would be as objective as possible. The test consists of thirty-six sentence stems, which the person is to complete; informal studies showed that number to be about optimal, giving enough answers to obtain a reliable picture of the subject's personality without being so long as to be tiring or boring. A response to one sentence stem, whether an exclamation point, a word, a phrase, a sentence, or a paragraph, is counted as one response. Thus one problem of projective tests, how to interpret protocols with many or few responses, is obviated, at the expense of requiring the rater to score some incomplete or fragmentary or ambiguous responses.

The rule of scoring every response means that ego development in this method cannot encompass a single, logically coherent domain, such as Damon's fair distribution of rewards, or Selman's interpersonal perspective taking, or Kohlberg's moral judgment. Whatever the subject writes has to be judged with respect to whatever it may reveal about ego development. Indeed, this is why the term *ego development* was chosen to denote the domain; no other term seemed inclusive enough. Averaging responses over a wide domain, like fixing the number of responses at thirty six, reflects the psychometric and probabilistic orientation of this approach.

The SCT proved to be a more sensitive measure of ego development than the Family Problems Scale for several reasons. The main one is that, being a free response, or projective, test, it gives a more rounded and complete portrait of the subject's personality than an objective test could. Major efforts, therefore, were devoted to creating an objective scoring manual for the SCT rather than to further work with objective tests.

Although the details of the method of constructing the scoring manual are beyond the scope of this account, the essence is simple. We began with four stages similar to what Table 6.4 calls the Impulsive, Conformist, Conscientious, and Autonomous stages, though drawn more sketchily. The response to each stem was given a rating on that scale, without reference to other responses or other facts about the person. Then, reading a person's responses to all thirty-six sentence stems, we intuitively imagined what kind of person would give such responses and assigned a total protocol rating at that stage. Total protocol ratings were used to validate and improve on ratings of individual items. This process was repeated several times, with new and larger samples of subjects and repeated improvement in the test and the scoring technique. After the first cycle, item ratings helped in arriving at a total protocol rating. Thousands of cases have been used in this process, which after the first few years included boys and men as well as girls and women (Loevinger, 1985; Loevinger & Wessler, 1970).

The radical difference between our paradigm and Kohlberg's is illustrated by the following contrast: In constructing and using the manual for Kohlberg's Moral Judgment Instrument, the paramount rule is that every response must be logically consistent with the stage description whose rating is given. In constructing and using the manual for the SCT, the rule is that every response must be given some stage rating. To those using the manual for Kohlberg's test, the collection of answers at a given stage in the SCT looks illogical and incoherent, as Kohlberg has argued (Kohlberg, 1981b), whereas to those using the SCT paradigm, the moral judgment manual seems sterile and tautological, at least as a method for generating new insights. However, generating new insights, which is the rationale for the SCT manual, is not the purpose of manual construction for Kohlberg.

TABLE 6.4 **Stages of Ego Development Measured by the Sentence Completion Test**

| | Typical manifestations | | |
|---|---|---|---|
| *Stage* | *Impulse control* | *Interpersonal mode* | *Conscious preoccupations* |
| Impulsive | Impulsive | Egocentric, dependent | Bodily feelings |
| Self-protective | Opportunistic | Manipulative, wary | "Trouble," control |
| Conformist | Respect for rules | Cooperative, loyal | Appearances, behavior |
| Conscientious-Conformist | Exceptions allowable | Helpful, self-aware | Feelings, problems, adjustment |
| Conscientious | Self-evaluated standards, self-critical | Intense, responsible | Motives, traits, achievements |
| Individualistic | Tolerant | Mutual | Individuality, development, roles |
| Autonomous | Coping with conflict | Interdependent | Self-fulfillment, psychological causation |
| Integrated | | Cherishing individuality | Identity |

Adapted from Loevinger, 1976.

Because every response must be rated, there must be a wastebasket category, the Conformist rating, for fragmentary responses and ones that give no decipherable clue as to ego level. For the same reason, the rater is constantly stretched to find new and previously unsuspected manifestations of ego level. In that mission the project has been successful. The method has resulted in displaying unexpected facets of every stage and in refining the scale (Loevinger, 1979b, 1984). The skeletal conception that we began with has become a set of full-bodied character sketches of typical persons at each stage.

Raters periodically found it necessary to interpolate intermediate stages between ones that were being used. By this process, the original four-point scale has expanded gradually to become a nine- or ten-point scale (including transitional ratings not displayed in Table 6.4). Additional intermediate levels may become evident with further experience; so the levels should be described by names rather than numbers. Numbers inevitably lock the conception into whatever set of stages are current when numbering takes place. That ossification has taken place with every other system of stages. None of the other systems of stages has a procedure such as ours for empirical correction and expansion, though Kohlberg has changed his description at times, sometimes adding a seventh stage, sometimes stopping with stage 5 (Colby & Kohlberg, 1986).

Table 6.4 represents an abbreviated summary of our current conception.

*Stages.* The lowest stage that can be measured by the SCT is the Impulsive Stage. (Capitals will be used to denote stage names, whereas lower case will denote the corresponding everyday use of the term. No human characteristic arises all at once in one stage and disappears without a trace on passage to the next.) The Impulsive child is a creature of physical needs and is dependent on others for controls. The deep and dependent attachment to his or her caretakers is colored by those physical needs. Other people are understood in terms of the simplest dichotomies, such as good and bad, clean and dirty. For a preschool child, those limitations are primarily intellectual, but a few older children remain at this stage of ego development despite normal intellectual development. Lacking ability to conceptualize inner life, the child does not distinguish physical from emotional malaise. An older child at this stage will evaluate people entirely according to what they give or withhold. By the senior year in high school, persons at this stage are rare, and one almost never finds such a person in college.

At the Self-protective Stage (previously called Opportunistic) people have an appreciation of the world's rules, however wide their world may be, and know that it is to their advantage to play by the rules most of the time. Calculated opportunism characterizes only a few of the persons who remain at this level beyond early childhood. More characteristic is short-term hedonism and lack of long-term goals and purposes. People want immediate gratification and often exploit others to that end. Because they see interpersonal relations as exploitive, they are wary and self-protective. They are concerned with not "getting into trouble," which is often blamed on being with the "wrong people." Young children going through this stage in normal time cling to rituals and traditions. Perhaps the loss of those constraints in individualistic, adult Western society is what leads some older children and adults who remain at this stage to hostile humor. Some adults at this stage deserve to be classed as psychopathic personalities, but most Self-protective persons find a place in normal society and may even be successful, given good luck, good looks, intellectual brilliance, or inherited wealth.

Normal development to maturity depends on the child coming to the conclusion (not always warranted!) that people can be trusted, thus negotiating the transition from the egocentric Self-protective Stage to the group-centered Conformist Stage. The Conformist accepts the rules because the group does, a group that may progress from family to peer group to town to nation. The Conformist distinguishes feeling bad mentally from feeling bad physically, which less mature persons cannot always do, but the vocabulary for describing inner life is limited to banal terms like happy, sad, mad, glad, and fun. Although the received opinion is that clichés offer no information on ego development, we found that they are more characteristic of Conformists than of others. The same holds for most stereotypes, especially those having to do with gender roles. Interpersonal interactions are described primarily in terms of actions rather than feelings, except for the most cliché-like feelings, such as "love and understanding." Rules of conduct tend to be expressed in terms of always and never, no exceptions allowed. People of this stage tend to describe what people ought to be like and what they are like in terms of the same stereotypes; that is the phenomenon the psychometricians have called *social desirability*.

Originally the next, Conscientious-conformist level was conceived as a transitional level, but as it appears to be the modal stage for the population of the United States (Holt, 1980), it must be presumed to be a stable level. There is no clear criterion for deciding whether it should be called a stage or a transitional level, nor is it clear that there is a difference.

The group pressures that help people advance from the Self-protective to the Conformist Stage are less clear as a means of advancing beyond Conformity. One route beyond conformity may be the feeling that I am not quite the perfect, conventional person that the Conformist stereotype requires of me. Previously we called this level Self-conscious or Self-aware, but people thought those labels implied that persons at this level are not well-adjusted; there is no warrant for such an inference. If anything, as the modal group in American society, they have the best chance for a good adjustment.

Untying what-I-am from what-I-ought-to-be opens the way for beginning to differentiate one's real and ideal self. Interpersonal relations are seen not only as actions but also in terms of feelings. Rules of conduct are more likely than before to be somewhat qualified or contingent: "if you are old enough" or "if you are not married." Where the Self-protective person wishes to avoid trouble and getting caught, the Conscientious-conformist sees "problems," implying that there are reasons, an idea more clearly delineated at later stages. Inner life is described in more varied terms, but still with emphasis on self-consciousness, loneliness, and similar feelings of being apart from the group. Despite growth toward a richer inner life and greater conceptual complexity, the person at this level is still basically a Conformist.

Growth to the Conscientious Stage is another major and mysterious shift, for, as Freud pointed out, so long as sanctions for misdeeds come from outside oneself, they can be escaped, but a bad conscience is an ineluctable punishment (Freud, 1930/1961). How are people induced to make that shift? The psychoanalytic answer is identification; the social learning answer is that in the long run a person without conscience is punished or socially disapproved. Intuitively, however, conscience seems to be a less calculating thing than social learning theory implies. Research has no clear answer.

The distinctive mark of the Conscientious Stage is having self-evaluated standards: I approve or disapprove of a given course of conduct not just because my family or my schoolmate or my country does, but because that is what I personally feel. To take that stand, one must separate oneself from the group even more than at the preceding transition. In Blasi's work one glimpses how rarely adolescents hold themselves responsible for upholding their own standards. At the same time, the conscientious person is aware of individual differences in many traits and has a richly differentiated vocabulary for traits and for inner feelings. Blanket approval and disapproval of people declines; people are seen as complex, with good and bad characteristics. Work is no longer something to be avoided or got through but rather is often seen as an interesting opportunity. Achievement is valued not just for its competitive advantage, as a Self-protective person might do, nor just for social recognition, as a Conformist might do; finally they judge their achievements by their own standards. They have long-term purposes, goals, and ideals. They think in broad terms and see everyday events in their social context rather than solely in terms of personal impact. A negative aspect of this character type is that the person may feel excessive responsibility for others.

The transition from the Conscientious to the Autonomous Stage is called the Individualistic level. Beyond being able to describe individual differences, the person at this level has a sense of individuality, of the personality as a whole, of style of life; he or she has broad toleration for differences with respect to all of them. The inner self and the outer self are differentiated, but the outer or physical self is in some ways bound up with or expressive of the inner self. With regard to interpersonal relations, the sense of mutuality deepens. The problem of dependence that every adolescent faces is understood as more an emotional problem than just a physical or financial one. New elements at the Individualistic level, elaborated at higher levels, are a sense of paradox, a conception of persons as being different in their different roles (wife, mother, housekeeper, lover, working woman, daughter), the idea of psychological causation, and an interest in psychological development. An example of psychological causation and also of development is, "If my mother . . . had not been raised as she was, I feel I probably would have been quite different."

The Individualistic themes are elaborated at the Autonomous Stage. Beyond the recognition of emotional dependence as a problem, the person at this stage understands the inevitable interdependence of human beings. Another frequent theme is the quest for self-fulfillment, which partially displaces or modifies the need for achievement. Another change from the Individualistic level occurs with respect to the recognition of the inevitability of inner conflict. At the Individualistic level, situations are often seen as a conflict between my needs, say, for a career, and the unyielding environment — "If only I had a little more help with the housework!" Characteristic of the Autonomous Stage is a recognition of the intrinsic conflict between my own wishes and needs — "If only I had the time to pursue a full-time career and still be home with my children!" The defining characteristic of the stage is an appreciation of people's need for autonomy. Of course, even a two-year-old will demand to "Do it by self!" The demand for one's own freedom cannot, therefore, be the crucial sign; the touchstone is recognition of other people's need for autonomy, as, for example, when a mother recognizes her child's need to learn from his or her own mistakes.

Some typical responses for various stages are given in Tables 6.5 and 6.6.

TABLE 6.5A    **SCT Responses Illustrating Common Themes, by Ego Level**

Stem: If my mother . . .

| Stage | Response | Theme |
|---|---|---|
| Self-protective | had loved me more. | Dependent complaining |
| Conformist | were living, I would spend many hours doing things with her. | Actions, not feelings |
| Conscientious-Conformist | had a problem, I would try to help her solve it. | Helpfulness, "problems" |
| Conscientious | broadened her outlook, she would be a happier person. | Decentered from self, "broad outlook" |
| Individualistic | were less dependent upon her children, it would be easier for them to break away. | Dependence as emotional not just physical or financial problem |
| Autonomous | would allow me to live my own life, we would both be much happier. | Autonomy |

TABLE 6.5B

Stem: When they avoided me . . .

| Stage | Response | Theme |
|---|---|---|
| Self-protective | I laughed because my intentions were to avoid them. | Hostile humor |
| Conformist | I felt as if I wasn't wanted. | Fear of ostracism |
| Conscientious-Conformist | I felt very self-conscious. | Self-consciousness |
| Conscientious | I took stock of myself to find possible reasons. | Self-evaluation |
| Individualistic | I found I had been rather snobish to them, although unintentional. | Responsibility for unintentional actions |
| Autonomous | I wondered why they did—was it me? or was it them? or something else? | Conceptual complexity, three alternatives contrasted |

TABLE 6.5C

Stem: Most men think that women . . .

| Stage | Response | Theme |
|---|---|---|
| Impulsive | are bad but some are good. | Good-bad dichotomy |
| Self-protective | are good for just one thing. | Exploitive relationships |
| Conformist | are not their equals. | Stereotype |
| Conscientious-Conformist | are not quite qualified for most things. | Modification of stereotype |
| Conscientious | are as equal as them but just don't want to admit it. | Outside vs. inside layers of personality |
| Individualistic | are delightful and maddening creatures. | Paradox |
| Autonomous | are worth while to be with, but depending on the type of man and type of woman thinkings differ. | Relativistic thinking, individual differences |

The highest stage, like the lowest stages, will be left out of the account. Research shows that the great majority, probably 99 per cent of adults and even of children able to talk, are covered by the stages described. The modal stage is the Conscientious-conformist level. Most adults without a college education are at that stage or a lower one; most adults with a college education are at that stage or a higher one (Holt, 1980; Loevinger, Cohn, Redmore, Bonneville, Streich, & Sargent, 1985). The higher scores of the college educated may be an artifact of their greater verbal facility, but probably the qualities that enable a person to endure the frustrations and profit from the opportunities of college are both contributory to and evidence of further ego development.

*Applications.* The field of delinquency is one where ideas from the cognitive developmental school have found some of their most fruitful applications. Marguerite (Grant) Warren is one of the leaders of a group that includes Ted Palmer, J. Douglas Grant, and others, who have developed a differential treatment model for delinquents, based on a conception of the development of the capacity for interpersonal relations (Warren, 1977). The basic conception is similar to the conception of ego development, which was derived originally from their interpersonal integration model. In the work of the Warren group, delinquents are divided into subgroups, based first on the stage of interpersonal integration, then on some other considerations, such as passive versus aggressive and neurotic versus adapted behavior. Each subgroup is assigned to a treatment method theoretically and empirically appropriate to it.

TABLE 6.6   **SCT Responses Showing Similar Themes at Different Ego Levels**

|  | Stem | |
| --- | --- | --- |
| *Stage* | *A pregnant woman . . .* | *A woman's body . . .* |
| Impulsive | is fat. | is clean. |
| Self-protective | looks clumsy. | should always be kept clean.[1] |
| Conformist | is out of shape. | is beautiful and should be kept clean. |
| Conscientious-Conformist | often feels unattractive. | should be kept clean & sweet-smelling & modestly covered. |
| Conscientious | is physically ugly but spiritually beautiful. | should be kept healthy and strong in order to be beautiful. |
| Individualistic |  | is one thing she should take care of not only for health reasons but because it gives her self-confidence. |
| Autonomous | is a contradiction of unattractive bulk and vast femininity and womanliness. |  |

[1] Popular response occurring more often below the Conformist Stage and rated transition from Self-Protective to Conformist as a compromise.

Other fields where the SCT has been applied include clinical studies, educational intervention studies, and cross-cultural studies. The kinds of questions to which the method is pertinent include: Are some ego levels prone to particular kinds of pathology? Are some ego levels particularly appropriate for certain kinds of psychotherapy? Do chronic childhood diseases retard normal ego growth? What kinds of high school or college courses or curricula promote ego growth? What is the normal course of development for men and for women? Do some cultures promote or retard ego growth for some elements of the population?

All of those topics have, in fact, been investigated. Many of the studies are reported only in unpublished dissertations, or they involve small numbers of cases, or they are as yet incomplete. Definitive summaries of the topics have not been published.

Although no claims have been made for the universal applicability of the conception of ego development, the SCT has been used in many cultural settings, including a village in India, Curaçao, and Japanese cities. This area also awaits a definitive summary.

The chief value of the work with the SCT test, however, has been clarifying and sharpening some old insights into personality development, resulting in a modern conception firmly tied to at least one measuring instrument. The interplay of theory and data that construction of the manual has become is not ancillary to some other project. It is product as well as method.

### Perry: Development of Relativistic Thinking in College

William G. Perry, Jr., as the head of the Bureau of Study Counsel of Harvard College, became interested in studying changes in students' attitudes toward their studies in the course of their college careers (Perry, 1970). At first he and the other counselors attempted to study the problem by means of a true-false test, the Check List of Educational Values. They found, on interviewing some students, that students' reasons for giving some of the answers were opposite to what the apparent content of their answers seemed to imply. Therefore, they decided that only an interview would permit correct inferences concerning what the students were really thinking.

*The interview method.* As an example of the problem with a true-false or degree-of-agreement item, Perry cites the student whose answers at the beginning of his freshman year indicated a strong belief in absolutism and rejection of all pluralism or ambiguity. One answer seemed to be out of line. He had checked "Disagree" to the item, "There's nothing more annoying than a question that may have more than one answer." At the end of the year, when his interviewer asked why he had given that answer, he replied, "Well, when I came here I didn't think any question could have more than one answer—so why be annoyed?" (Perry, 1970, p. 64). This finding illustrates the difficulties in measuring personality by objective tests (see Chapter 4). (But those difficulties have not prevented Perry's admirers from trying repeatedly to create objective tests to ascertain the qualities that the Harvard study approached through interviews.)

Perry's main study was based on interviews done at the end of each of the four academic years for three samples of Harvard and Radcliffe undergraduates, seventeen students of the class of 1957 and sixty-seven members of the classes of 1962 and 1963. There were 484 interviews and 84 complete four-year sequences; one fourth of the subjects were women, but the major analyses were based on the men.

In order to make the interview as open and unstructured as possible, the interviewers led off with the question, "Why don't you start with whatever stands out for you about the year?" That way the student selected his own topic to begin with. Further prompts from the interviewer were equally noncommittal and served chiefly to clarify the student's train of thought. They included statements such as, "As you mentioned that, were you thinking of some specific incidents, or do any examples come to mind?" and "Well, now, do any other things stand out for you?" (Perry, 1970, pp. 19-20).

The interviews for the class of 1957 were scanned to see what categories fit the materials. The majority of the interviews seemed to delineate a developmental sequence. By marking out and describing distinctive points on that sequence, a scoring scheme was devised. The scoring scheme was used by the raters to rate separately each interview of the classes of 1962 and 1963. Comparison of ratings given independently by different raters showed exceptionally high interrater reliabilities even when all references to year in school were deleted and when excerpts rather than total interviews were rated.

*Developmental sequence.* The scoring scheme describing the developmental sequence has proved to be more important in its implications than the specific empirical results of the research have. It provides a way of looking at the potential development of every college student, not just those at Harvard. In order to avoid possibly gratuitous connotations of the stage construct, Perry refers to the steps on his scale as "positions" rather than stages. He recognizes, however, that his classification, like all classifications, is an injustice to many students. Nonetheless, it captures something of the process that most students go through to some degree during their college career.

Perry introduces the sequence with a hypothetical scenario:

> Let us suppose that a lecturer announces that today he will consider three theories explanatory of_____ (whatever his topic may be). Student A has always taken it for granted that knowledge consists of correct answers, that there is one right answer per problem, and that teachers explain these answers for students to learn. He therefore listens for the lecturer to state which theory he is to learn.
>
> Student B makes the same general assumptions but with an elaboration to the effect that teachers sometimes present problems and procedures, rather than answers, "so that we can learn to find the right answer on our own." He therefore perceives the lecture as a kind of guessing game in which he is to "figure out" which theory is correct, a game that is fair enough if the lecturer does not carry it so far as to hide things too obscurely.
>
> Student C assumes that an answer can be called "right" only in the light of its context, and that contexts or "frames of reference" differ. He assumes that several interpretations of a poem, explanations of a historical development, or even theories of a class of events in physics may be legitimate "depending on how you look at it." Though he feels a little uneasy in such a kaleidoscopic world, he nonetheless supposes that the lecturer may be about to present three legitimate theories which can be examined for their internal coherence, their scope, their fit with various data, their predictive power, etc.

Whatever the lecturer then proceeds to do (in terms of his own assumptions and intent) these three students will make meaning of the experience in different ways which will involve different assessments of their own choices and responsibilities. . . .

B's assumptions are of a form which includes the form of A's; and C's assumptions include, in a different and broader form, the forms of both A's and B's. This is evident in the different predicament of each student in the event that what the lecturer proceeds to do conforms to the expectations of one of the other students. For instance, Student C, faced with the lecture expected by either A or B, would have little difficulty in interpreting the experience accurately without revising his basic assumptions about the nature of knowledge. His assumptions logically extend to the possibility that a given lecturer might "have the point of view that" there was but one correct answer. Student A, however, faced with the kind of lecture expected by B or by C, must either revise his basic assumptions or interpret the experience in some such way as, "The lecturer is talking all over the place" or "This just doesn't have anything to do with the course."(Perry, 1970, pp. 1–2)

The ordering of the positions is not arbitrary nor is it chosen just to accord with Perry's personal values; it is dictated by the logic of the situation. Moreover, individual students tend to move from the position of A to that of B to that of C. Another and subtler confirmation of the ordering of positions appeared later in connection with deviations from the order.

*Positions in the sequence.* The first position, Basic Duality, is an extrapolation, as no instances were found by the end of the freshman year. In this position the student casts the universe into dualistic form, we versus they, right versus wrong, good versus bad. There are absolute Right Answers, known to Authority, whose job is to teach them. (Perry uses capitalization to indicate the absolutist nature of the conceptions of right and authority in the early positions.) Knowledge and goodness are accumulated bit by bit, through obedience and hard work. Independence consists of self-controlled obedience. Multiple opinions or possibilities, which Perry refers to as Multiplicity, are not perceived. At a sophisticated, cosmopolitan college, such as Harvard or Radcliffe, one can scarcely survive the year with such a narrow outlook. The students themselves come with conflicting certainties, which are discussed endlessly in the dorms. Even if each professor seems to be advocating a single point of view, different professors differ enough in their points of view to raise doubts about their collective infallibility.

The second position Perry terms Multiplicity Prelegitimate. In it the student perceives diversity but not as a sign of legitimate uncertainty; Multiplicity is perceived within the initial dualistic framework. The student may perceive multiple opinions as an exercise given by Authority "so we can learn how to find the Answer," or the diversity may be interpreted as a sign of confusion or error in the others, who are wrong. Those of conformist bent identify themselves with Authority, seen as right and possessed of absolute truth; others are confused or wrong. Those of oppositional bent may see Authority as wrong, muddle-headed, not knowing their subject, or needlessly confused; "we," who are right, are opposed to Authority.

In the third position, Multiplicity Subordinate, the student perceives diversity of opinion and uncertainty as legitimate in some areas; perhaps Authority "hasn't found The Answer yet." Even a benign and well-informed Authority cannot reduce uncertainty in such cases. Thus pluralism and uncertainty are recognized but assimilated to a basically dualistic framework. But then how can tests and essays be evaluated? The teachers clearly do not grade on how hard one tries or how many hours of work one has put in, as many high school teachers do. If there is no one right answer, they must be judging on the style of presentation, perhaps glibness or superficial cleverness, or on their own biases.

The fourth position is subdivided into two possibilities, Multiplicity Correlate and Relativism Subordinate. In Multiplicity Correlate the student perceives two realms, one in which there is an absolute correct Authority and another realm where diversity of opinion is legitimate and uncertainty prevails: "Anyone has a right to his own opinion." There are fields, such as, perhaps, literary criticism, where one cannot ever expect to find right answers. The area of multiplicity is relevant to the self, being experienced as confusing, liberating, or intriguing, rather than totally alien or confined to "them." An oppositional student may strive to expand the area of multiplicity, because in that area "They" have no right to make us feel guilty.

In the alternative version of position four, Relativism Subordinate, there is a beginning understanding of relativistic thinking, but it is seen as "how They want us to think," rather than as the nature of knowledge. The various possible opinions on a topic can be substantiated by facts and reasons. The value of a given opinion is not a matter of caprice but of how well the data are congruent with the proposition, or the propositions are coherent with each other or with a theoretical position. Some students may be introduced to this kind of thinking by their own challenge to the professors' opinions.

In the fifth position, Relativism becomes the predominant way of thinking. Where previously the world was perceived dualistically, with small pockets reserved for relativistic thinking, now the world is seen as essentially relativistic, with small areas reserved for absolute, right and wrong decision. That opinions should be supported and evaluated in terms of facts and reasons is no longer merely a task set by professors but a statement about the nature of knowledge in an uncertain universe. The professors too are engaged in a search for knowledge, struggling with facts and reasons the same way students are. Thus the professor-student relation is potentially more collegial and less hierarchical than in earlier positions. The major transition from a dualistic framework with an area of relativism to a relativistic framework with an area of dualism takes place gradually without the student being aware of it.

Perry proceeds to carry his account further through the anchoring of the student's now-examined beliefs into serious commitments. Most college students I have encountered, however, appear to be negotiating the transaction from multiplicity to relativism, and the foregoing part of his account seems most relevant to their concerns.

*Alternatives to growth.* Development along this sequence is not inexorable. Perry describes three alternatives to growth — temporizing, retreat, and escape. *Temporizing* means pausing for more than a year in one position, typically with awareness of the step ahead. *Retreat* occurs after some glimpse of multiplicity and involves an active denial of the legitimacy of the opinions of others. Typically it takes one back to extreme dualism. It may be seen in a dedicated reactionary, a dogmatic rebel, or in passive resistance to authority without espousing a cause. *Escape* typically entrenches the student in a middle position, using multiplicity or relativism in the service of alienation or cynicism or even of Authority.

These possibilities seem to undermine the developmental hypothesis, but a closer look reveals confirmation:

> Those students whom we saw as "progressing" made their own awareness of maturation clear, explicitly or implicitly, and conveyed a sense of satisfaction in it. Those whom we perceived as standing still, or stepping to one side, or reaching back, acknowledged that they were avoiding something or denying something or fighting something, and they regularly remarked on an uneasiness or dissatisfaction akin to shame. Some others referred to periods in which they felt they had "moved too fast" and had become alarmingly confused. In short, the students experienced quite consciously an urge toward maturation, congruent with that progression of forms we were learning to see in their reports. (Perry, 1970, p. 50)

Harvard and all liberal arts colleges with a similar atmosphere pose a paradox for the adolescent student. The normal urge to rebel against authority encourages progress along the sequence. But the college lends its authority to a relativistic, antiauthoritarian outlook, partly as a consequence of the commitment of individual professors and of the institution itself, partly as a consequence of the diversity of views among the professors. This atmosphere makes overcoming authoritarian tendencies easier for those inclined to conformity, because toleration for diversity is "what They want us to do." For some oppositional students, rebellion takes the anomalous course of return to a dualistic, authoritarian outlook, just because that is clearly not what the college is trying to encourage.

The dynamics, indeed the drama, of this developmental course Perry describes as follows:

> The impetus [to growth] seemed compounded of many "motives": sheer curiosity; a striving for the competence that can emerge only from an understanding of one's relation to the environment; an urge to make order out of incongruities, dissonances, and anomalies of experience; a wish for a community with men looked upon as mature; a wish for authenticity in personal relationships; a wish to develop and affirm an identity, and so on. It was the convergence of all such motives into an urge toward maturation that brought them under that encompassing inner standard to which each man held himself accountable.
>
> If the motives making up this urge to progress were the only forces operative in the students' development, there would of course have been no problematic balance, no drama calling for courage, and no meaning in a standard. Maturation did indeed have its joys of discovery and expansion, but its moral significances derived from its challenge by countervailing forces. At every step, the movement required the students to "face up" to limits, uncertainties, and the dissolution of established beliefs, while simultaneously it demanded new decisions and the undertaking of new forms of responsibility.
>
> This constellation of countervailing forces appeared to consist of such tendencies as the wish to retain earlier satisfactions or securities, the wish to maintain community in family or hometown values and ways of thinking, the reluctance to admit one has been in error, the doubt of one's competence to take on new uncertainties and responsibilities, and most importantly, the wish to maintain a self one has felt oneself to be (Angyal, 1965). Pervading all such motives of conservation lay the apprehension that one change might lead to another in a rapidity which might result in catastrophic disorganization. (Perry, 1970, pp. 51–52)

*An ameboid model for growth.* Perry's model for growth may be called ameboid. The individual moves forward with respect to some topic of special interest or personal relevance. Only gradually does the style of thinking about other topics catch up with the most advanced contingent. That appears to be what happened with the Swiss children Piaget studied. They had sophisticated conceptions of a democratic social compact with respect to the game of marbles. Piaget did not seem to notice that the same boys spent the rest of their lives in a society that did not allow women to vote, apparently seeing no violation of democracy or equality there.

The alternative model for growth, espoused by Kohlberg and his colleagues, divides cognitive and moral development into strictly logically defined subdomains (Snarey, Kohlberg, & Noam, 1983). Development in one subdomain is seen as necessary but not sufficient for development in certain other ones. For example, the appropriate level of cognitive development is necessary but not sufficient for a corresponding level of moral judgment development. The major difference between Perry's model and Kohlberg's lies in the fact that Kohlberg's group believes that everyone advances from one stage to the next in the same way, whereas Perry sees each person as finding a unique path. No measuring instruments are sufficiently refined to decide between these hypotheses. There is too much measurement error in every current test. To date, in fact, there has not been a strict definition of which stage in one sequence, say, cognitive development, would correspond to which stage in another domain. On balance, the evidence, such as it is, appears to favor Perry's model.

## COGNITIVE DEVELOPMENTALISM AMONG THEORIES

All the investigators classed in the cognitive developmental school are concerned with some broad aspect of personality or character, and their purviews overlap. All are committed to a view of an invariable developmental sequence, but how strictly that sequence describes the trajectory of individual persons varies with the investigator. There are a number of different measuring instruments being worked on, including several not mentioned in this summary.

First, the common elements tying together the systems of Piaget, Perry, Kohlberg, and others discussed here will be summarized. For all of them, thought is fundamentally structured rather than being a formless succession of ideas. Those structures are permanent or at least slow to change. Each person constructs his or her own framework (another way of describing structure) from babyhood on. The frame or structure is more important than the specific elements; the elements are assimilated to the framework. The structure changes slowly just because it is the framework. What cannot be accommodated within the present framework may be ignored or distorted to fit it.

Some familiar examples may clarify this view. You can teach a child who can talk to say that two times three is six. But the child who has no idea of the structure of the multiplication table will not retain it or generalize it. The child who has learned to think of multiplication as repeated addition can figure out missing elements of the multiplication table and retain more effectively what is learned. Both modes of learning are practiced in relation to reading: flash cards to teach single words and sounding out syllables to learn reading more analytically. Similarly, teaching a child to say that a particular experiment conserves volume does little good until the child has reached the age to understand conservation, after which it is no longer necessary to do so.

As with other paradigms that have been studied here, many of the major ideas were current in late nineteenth-century philosophical psychology. What is different about the twentieth-century version is the use of experimental or research paradigms to embody and to develop the detailed facts. Nothing less will be widely accepted today as a part of contemporary scientific psychology.

In contrast with other personality psychologists, the cognitive developmentalists say that the child's way of construing the world goes through stages that differ qualitatively, not just quantitatively; indeed, the qualitative difference is so great that adults can hardly understand the child's way of looking at things. The sequence of stages is determined not by environmental contingencies, as the behaviorists would have it, nor by hereditary physiological propensities, as psychosexual stages are, at least in part, but by the inner logic of the developmental sequence itself. The sequence is hierarchical; in this way, too, it is different from the sequence of psychosexual stages that psychoanalysis postulates (Loevinger, 1976, ch. 7). In the cognitive developmental view of true stages, each stage incorporates and transmutes the insights and accomplishments of the previous stage and prepares for the next stage.

As compared to the social learning theorists, the cognitive developmentalists lay less stress on the environmental contingencies in determining the behavioral course, more on the inner logic of development. They see behavior as related to mental structure (or structures) rather than seeing each item of behavior as independently determined by the situation. Different approaches to teaching and to psychotherapy are undoubtedly implied in these paradigms, but direct comparisons do not seem to have been made often.

Noam Chomsky, Skinner's antagonist in the field of linguistics, denies that children learn language by the reinforcement of specific word sequences (Chomsky, 1968/1972). The key to understanding language development, according to Chomsky, is the child's developing understanding of the "deep structure," or syntax, of spoken thoughts. The deep structure of a given utterance can be expressed in many alternative word sequences, which the child does not master as separate achievements but simultaneously by mastering the rules for generating sentences. Similarly, the cognitive developmentalists look beyond the structure of behaviors they study to the deep structure, that is, to the structure of thought being expressed in the given behavior. Unlike the Skinnerian behaviorists, they believe that the most important aspects of behavior are not established by reinforcement or reward but are expressions of the child's way of construing the universe. Specific behaviors obviously are influenced by rewards and punishments, but the way of construing the universe is not. Performance is partly governed by rewards and punishments, but basic competence is not.

Cognitive developmentalists, in viewing behavior as progressing through qualitatively distinct stages, differ from trait theorists, who view personality through lenses that render it in quantitative terms, as more or less of traits that vary from the least amount at one pole to the greatest amount at the other pole. The implied motto of the trait theorist is the saying of E. L. Thorndike that everything that exists in human nature exists in some amount, and that amount can be measured. The implied motto of the cognitive developmentalist is that everything in adult personality must have developed, and the developmental course can be traced.

## OPPOSITION TO STAGE THEORIES

Fischer and Silvern have summarized the arguments and evidence for and against stage theories. The opponents of stage theories begin from a different framework of assumptions than Piaget and the neo-Piagetians do. Piagetian stage theories can be looked at as beginning with an ideal, defined end point. In Piaget's study of intellectual development, that ideal end point is formal, reversible operations. The stages are then seen as hierarchically arranged steps toward that goal. The system is based on the metaphor of organic growth. Most of the evidence for stage theories, however, consists of little more than demonstration of qualitative change in performance with age. Such changes can always be accounted for in other ways, chiefly by physical growth patterns resulting in changes in demands from the social environment (Fischer & Silvern, 1985).

Even if one accepts the assumption (and as Fischer and Silvern pointed out, it is an assumption, hardly subject to empirical test) that psychological growth proceeds in terms of structural stages, one can still maintain that different people, or different groups of people, grow according to different patterns. That is the position of Gilligan with respect to gender differences in moral judgment, and it is implied by many critics who attack Kohlberg's claim to cultural universality.

Fischer and Silvern reconcile the stage theories with the evidence for individual differences by advocating a transactional or collaborational conception, that individual differences result from the interaction of the person's stage of growth with his or her current social circumstances.

But the major opponents of stage theories are not proponents of individual differences. Rather, the major opponents are those who claim that what seem like stages are the results of incidental growth and social expectations and sanctions, as programmed by the culture, the community, and the family. Mischel, for example, hardly champions the field of individual differences.

My conception of stages does not fit neatly into the foregoing categories. I believe that the variable I call ego development represents both a major dimension of individual differences within any age cohort (after early childhood) and the trace of a developmental or stage sequence. Thus the presence of the lowest stages in late adolescence and adult life indicates either arrest at or regression to early but normal stages. This hypothesis, if true, provides a parsimonious explanation of such syndromes as that of the impulse-ridden adolescent. Other proposed stage theories could also be looked at in those terms, but most theorists have pursued only minimally if at all the implied research strategy, that is, studying the range of individual differences within each age cohort.

As I read my data, consisting now of thousands of cases drawn from a wide spectrum of the American population (and others who have looked at similar data from other countries and other cultures have not disputed the point), there is neither warrant for discarding the idea of stages nor for construing development as a strict progression along a narrow, logically defined path. Fischer and Silvern are undoubtedly right that one's methodology determines the range of admissable results.

My methods are psychometric and thus are geared to accentuate individual differences. At the same time, I assume a basic stage structure. In consequence, my stages turn out to be "fuzzy sets," that is, patterns of more or less probable characteristics rather than a set of necessary and sufficient characteristics, as Kohlberg seeks (Loevinger, 1983). My conception fits with the pattern of growth depicted by Perry, where each person progresses from one stage to the next as a result of his or her own pattern of interests and social circumstances.

One of the troublesome things about current stage theories is their proliferation (Loevinger & Knoll, 1983). Structural stages have been sketched for moral judgment, sense of justice, interpersonal perspective taking, social conventionality, responsibility, ego development, and intellectual-ethical development, to mention just the sample chosen for the present review. If the stages really reflect a common "deep structure," the stages of those variables should all proceed in tandem. Such bits of evidence as there are indicate only a moderate relation among the various measures (Loevinger, 1979a). If they are not all evidence of the same structure, how many structures are there, and what should be the relations among them? Those are among the questions remaining to be answered in this field of research.

---

## REFERENCES

Adorno, T. W., Frenkel-Brunswik, E., Levinson, D. J., & Sanford, R. N. (1950). *The authoritarian personality*. New York: Harper & Row.

Angyal, A. (1965). *Neurosis and treatment*. New York: Wiley.

Baldwin, J. M. (1902). *Social and ethical interpretations in mental development*. New York: Macmillan. (Original work published 1897.)

Blasi, A. (1976). Concept of development in personality theory. In J. Loevinger, *Ego development: Conceptions and theories* (pp. 29–53). San Francisco: Jossey-Bass.

Blasi, A. (1982). Kognition, Erkenntnis und das Selbst [Cognition, knowledge, and the self]. In W. Edelstein & M. Keller, *Perspectivität und Interpretation: Beitrage zur Entwicklung des Socialen Verstehens* (pp. 289–319). Frankfurt am Main: Suhrkamp.

Blasi, A. (1984). Autonomie im Gehorsam: Die Entwicklung des Distanzierungsvermö-
gens im socialisierten Handeln [Autonomy in obedience: The development of dis-
tancing in socialized action.] In W. Edelstein & J. Habermas (Eds.), *Soziale Interaktion
und sociales Verstehen* (pp. 300–347). Frankfurt am Main: Suhrkamp.

Blatt, M., & Kohlberg, L. (1975). The effects of classroom moral discussion upon children's level of moral judgment. *Journal of Moral Education, 4,* 129–161.

Bullock, M. (1985). Causal reasoning and developmental change over the preschool
years. *Human Development, 28,* 169–191.

Chomsky, N. (1972). *Language and mind* (rev. ed.). New York: Harcourt Brace Jovanovich. (Original work published 1968.)

Colby, A., & Kohlberg, L. (1986). *The measurement of moral judgment.* New York: Cambridge University Press.

Colby, A., Kohlberg, L., Gibbs, J., & Lieberman, M. (1983). A longitudinal study of the
development of moral judgment. *Society for Research in Child Development Monographs, 48,* (1–2, Whole no. 200).

Damon, W. (1977). *The social world of the child.* San Francisco: Jossey-Bass.

Dewey, J. (1896). The reflex arc concept in psychology. *Psychological Review, 3,* 357–370.

Edwards, C. P. (1981). The comparative study of the development of moral judgment
and reasoning. In R. H. Munroe, R. L. Munroe, & B. B. Whiting (Eds.), *Handbook of
cross-cultural human development* (pp. 501–528). New York: Garland.

Edwards, C. P. (1986). Cross-cultural research on Kohlberg's stages: The basis for consensus. In S. Modgil & C. Modgil (Eds.), *Lawrence Kohlberg: Consensus and controversy* (pp. 419–430). Philadelphia: Falmer Press.

Erikson, E. (1950). *Childhood and society.* New York: Norton

Ernhart, C. B., & Loevinger, J. (1969). Authoritarian Family Ideology: A measure, its
correlates, and its robustness. *Multivariate Behavioral Research Monographs, 69–*1.

Fischer, K. W. (1980). A theory of cognitive development: The control and construction
of hierarchies of skills. *Psychological Review, 87,* 477–531.

Fischer, K. W., & Bullock, D. Cognitive development in school-age children: Conclusions
and new directions. In W. A. Collins (Ed.), *Development during middle childhood: The
years from six to twelve* (pp. 70–146). Washington, DC: National Academy of
Sciences Press.

Fischer, K. W., & Silvern, L. (1985). Stages and individual differences in cognitive development. *Annual Review of Psychology, 36,* 613–648.

Flavell, J. H. (1963). *The developmental psychology of Jean Piaget.* Princeton, NJ: Van
Nostrand.

Frenkel-Brunswik, E. (1951). Personality theory and perception. In R. R. Blake & G. V.
Ramsey (Eds.), *Perception: An approach to personality* (pp. 356–419). New York:
Ronald Press.

Freud, S. (1955). Beyond the pleasure principle. *Standard edition* (Vol. 18, pp. 3–64).
London: Hogarth Press. (Original work published 1920.)

Freud, S. (1961). Civilization and its discontents. *Standard edition* (Vol. 21, pp. 59–145).
London: Hogarth Press. (Original work published 1930.)

Gibbs, J. C., Widaman, K., & Colby, A. (1982). *Social intelligence: Measuring the development of sociomoral reflection.* Englewood Cliffs, NJ: Prentice-Hall.

Gilligan, C. (1982). *In a different voice.* Cambridge, MA: Harvard University Press.

Hickey, J., & Scharf, P. (1980). *Toward a just correctional system.* San Francisco: Jossey-Bass.

Holt, R. R. (1980). Loevinger's measure of ego development: Reliability and national norms for male and female short forms. *Journal of Personality and Social Psychology, 39,* 909–920.

Inhelder, B. (1969). Some aspects of Piaget's genetic approach to cognition. In H. Furth, *Piaget and knowledge* (pp. 22–40). Englewood-Cliffs, NJ: Prentice-Hall.

James, W. (1948). *Psychology: Briefer Course.* New York: World Publishing. (Original work published 1892.)

Jaquette, D. S. (1980). A case study of social-cognitive development in a naturalistic setting. In R. L. Selman, *The growth of interpersonal understanding* (pp. 215–241). New York: Academic Press.

Kohlberg, L. (1964). Development of moral character and moral ideology. In M. L. Hoffman & L. W. Hoffman (Eds.), *Review of child development research* (Vol. 1, pp. 383–431). New York: Russell Sage.

Kohlberg, L. (1966). A cognitive-developmental analysis of children's sex-role concepts and attitudes. In E. E. Maccoby (Ed.), *The development of sex differences* (pp. 82–173). Stanford, CA: Stanford University Press.

Kohlberg, L. (1969). Stage and sequence: The cognitive-developmental approach to socialization. In D. A. Goslin (Ed.), *Handbook of socialization theory and research* (pp. 347–480). Chicago: Rand McNally.

Kohlberg, L. (1971). From *Is* to *Ought*: How to commit the naturalistic fallacy and get away with it in the study of moral development. In T. Mischel (Ed.), *Cognitive development and epistemology* (pp. 154–235). New York: Academic Press.

Kohlberg, L. (1976). Moral stages and moralization: The cognitive-developmental approach. In T. Lickona (Ed.), *Moral development and behavior* (pp. 31–53). New York: Holt, Rinehart & Winston.

Kohlberg, L. (1981). *Essays on moral development.* Vol. 1. *The philosophy of moral development.* San Francisco: Harper & Row. (a)

Kohlberg, L. (1981). *The meaning and measurement of moral development.* Worcester, MA: Clark University Press. (b)

Kohlberg, L., & Mayer, R. (1972). Development as the aim of education: The Dewey view. *Harvard Educational Review, 42,* 449–496.

LaPerriere, K. (1962). Maternal attitudes in subcultural groups. Unpublished doctoral dissertation, Washington University.

Loevinger, J. (1966). A theory of test response. In A. Anastasi (Ed.), *Testing problems in perspective* (pp. 545–556). Washington, D. C.: American Council on Education. (Original work published 1958.)

Loevinger, J. (1976). *Ego development: Conceptions and theories.* San Francisco: Jossey-Bass.

Loevinger, J. (1979). Construct validity of the sentence completion test of ego development. *Applied Psychological Measurement, 3,* 281–311. (a)

Loevinger, J. (1979). Theory and data in the measurement of ego development. In J. Loevinger, *Scientific ways in the study of ego development* (pp. 1–24). Worcester, MA: Clark University Press. (b).

Loevinger, J. (1983). On ego development and the structure of personality. *Developmental Review, 3,* 339–350.

Loevinger, J. (1984). On the self and predicting behavior. In R. A. Zucker, J. Aronoff, & A. I. Rabin (Eds.), *Personality and the prediction of behavior* (pp. 43–68). Orlando, FL: Academic Press.

Loevinger, J. (1985). Revision of the sentence completion test for ego development. *Journal of Personality and Social Psychology, 48,* 420–427.

Loevinger, J., Cohn, L., Redmore, C. D., Bonneville, L., Streich, D., & Sargent, M. (1985). Ego development in college. *Journal of Personality and Social Psychology, 48,* 947–962.

Loevinger, J., & Knoll, E. (1983). Personality: Stages, traits, and the self. *Annual Review of Psychology, 34,* 195–222.

Loevinger, J., & Sweet, B. (1961). Construction of a test of mothers' attitudes. In J. C. Glidewell (Ed.), *Parental attitudes and child behavior* (pp. 110–123). Springfield, IL: C. C. Thomas.

Loevinger, J., Sweet, B., Ossorio, A., & LaPerriere, K. (1962). Measuring personality patterns of women. *Genetic Psychology Monographs, 65,* 53–136.

Loevinger, J., & Wessler, R. (1970). *Measuring ego development 1. Construction and use of a sentence completion test.* San Francisco: Jossey-Bass.

Loewald, H. (1980). Ego and reality. In *Papers on psychoanalysis* (pp. 221–256). New Haven, CT: Yale University Press. (Original work published 1960.)

Mischel, W., & Mischel, H. N. (1976). A cognitive social-learning approach to morality and self-regulation. In T. Lickona (Ed.), *Moral development and behavior* (pp. 84–107). New York: Holt, Rinehart & Winston.

Modgil, S., & Modgil, C. (Eds.) (1986). *Lawrence Kohlberg: Consensus and controversy.* Philadelphia: Falmer Press.

Oppenheimer, J. R. (1956). Analogy in science. *American Psychologist, 11,* 127–135.

Perry, W. G., Jr. (1970). *Forms of intellectual and ethical development in the college years.* New York: Holt, Rinehart & Winston.

Piaget, J. (1955). *The language and thought of the child.* Cleveland: World Publishing. (Original work published 1926.)

Piaget, J. (1959). *Judgment and reasoning in the child.* Paterson, NJ: Littlefield, Adams. (Original work published 1928.)

Piaget, J. (1960). *The child's conception of the world.* Paterson, NJ: Littlefield, Adams. (Original work published 1929.)

Piaget, J. (1932). *The moral judgment of the child.* New York: Free Press.

Piaget, J. (1963). *The origins of intelligence in children.* New York: Norton. (Original work published 1936.)

Piaget, J. (1970). *Structuralism.* New York: Basic Books.

Piaget, J., & Inhelder, B. (1969). *The psychology of the child.* New York: Basic Books.

Pollak, S., & Gilligan, C. (1982). Images of violence in thematic apperception stories. *Journal of Personality and Social Psychology, 42,* 159–167.

Rawls, J. (1971). *A theory of justice.* Cambridge, MA: Belknap Press.

Rest, J. R. (1969). Hierarchies of comprehension and preference in a developmental stage model of moral thinking. Unpublished doctoral dissertation, University of Chicago.

Rest, J. R. (1979). *Development in judging moral issues.* Minneapolis, MN: University of Minnesota Press.

Rest, J. R., Turiel, E., & Kohlberg, L. (1969). Level of moral judgment as a determinant of preference and comprehension of moral judgments made by others. *Journal of Personality, 37,* 225–252.

Selman, R. L. (1980). *The growth of interpersonal understanding.* New York: Academic Press.

Smetana, J. (1981). Preschool children's conceptions of moral and social rules. *Child Development, 52,* 1333–1336.

Snarey, J. (1985). Cross-cultural universality of socio-moral development: A critical review of Kohlbergian research. *Psychological Bulletin, 97,* 202–232.

Snarey, J., Kohlberg, L., & Noam, G. (1983). Ego development in perspective: Structural stage, functional phase, and cultural age-period models. *Developmental Review, 3,* 303–338.

Sullivan, C., Grant, M. Q., & Grant, J. D. (1957). The development of interpersonal maturity: Applications to delinquency. *Psychiatry, 20,* 373–385.

Tanner, J. M., & Inhelder, B. (Eds.) (1956). *Discussions on child development.* Vol. 1. New York: International Universities Press.

Tanner, J. M., & Inhelder, B. (Eds.) (1960). *Discussions on child development.* Vol. 4. New York: International Universities Press.

Turiel, E. (1983). *The development of social knowledge: Morality and convention.* Cambridge, Eng.: Cambridge University Press.

Vine, I. (1986). Moral maturity in socio-cultural perspective: Are Kohlberg's stages universal? In S. Modgil & C. Modgil (Eds.), *Lawrence Kohlberg: Consensus and controversy* (pp. 431–450). Philadelphia: Falmer Press.

Warren, M. Q. (1977). Correctional treatment and coercion: The differential effectiveness perspective. *Criminal Justice and Behavior, 4,* 355–376.

Werner, H. (1940). *Comparative psychology of mental development.* New York: International Universities Press. (Original work published 1926.)

Weston, D. R., & Turiel, E. (1980). Act-rule relations: Children's concepts of social rules. *Developmental Psychology, 16,* 417–424.

# CHAPTER 7

# Conclusion

A few themes have run through this book despite its wide range of topics. The three most prominent themes are: that different personality theories give access to different aspects of personality; that science always involves an intricate and intimate interweaving of theory, method, and data; and that theories are never wholly new but always draw on and reflect previous work as well as the spirit of the time and place.

Personality has many facets: the dynamic unconscious, behavior, traits, thoughts—including patterns, maps, and social models—and character. Each of those topics is central to a major school of psychology: psychoanalysis, behaviorism, psychometric trait theory, cognitive behaviorism, or cognitive developmentalism. That is the first theme, and those are the substantive chapters of this book. There are other schools of thought that many psychologists consider important, possibly more important than those selected for discussion in this book. On several occasions there has been mention of the school that seeks causes of behavior in physiology and temperament. Another theory or school of psychology is the existentialist school. That theory, if it is a theory, is left out here partly because one cannot be complete in short compass without becoming too superficial, partly because it does not accord with the second theme.

The second theme is that the interplay of theory, method, and data create something akin to what Kuhn calls a scientific paradigm. For each of the five major schools of thought I have sought the crucial empirical discovery that led, if not to a major scientific revolution, at least to founding a new school. Typically, the discovery is in a field outside that of personality: for psychoanalysis in psychopathology; for behaviorism and social learning theory in animal behavior; for trait theory and cognitive developmentalism in intelligence.

The very fact that there are five such disparate schools or systems of thought in contemporary psychology rules out the full meaning of Kuhn's idea of a paradigm, for he believes that in a mature science, one paradigm is accepted by all competent scientists. I believe there is no chance that that situation will come about in psychology, however long it ages. Character structure determines a person's frame of reference, the frame within which the person views the world, and a personality theory is part of the world that each person constructs according to his or her own system, or ego, or character, one could even say according to his or her own paradigm (Loevinger, 1976, ch. 11).

Using Kuhn's idea of paradigm as the model or at least the metaphor to organize this survey has had several purposes. The foremost one is to emphasize the empirical discovery at the foundation of each major school, in contradiction to a frequent view, particularly of newcomers to the field, that significant theoretical contributions are likely to come from pure thought. A second purpose is to show how each school characteristically invents or finds new methods of study and even new definitions of what are appropriate data for study. A third purpose is to show how those elements—the discovery, the theory, the methods, the data—are interrelated. Finally, I want to explore the possibility of substituting the logical structure of the system for previous authors' search for an explanatory principle in the founder's personal history or depth of commitment to a particular idea.

The third theme, which requires giving each school of thought its place in intellectual and social history, has been only sketchily carried out. That calls for a different scholarly discipline, and one beyond my competence. At the same time, an important dimension is missing if no mention is made of this topic.

I have tried to take seriously every theory presented. If it is not worth that, it should be omitted, for the field has a plethora of insights from different authors, too many for any one book. At the same time, every theory has its limitations, as indeed Kuhn's presentation predicts. To be true to Kuhn's model, the anomalies and recalcitrant puzzles must be indicated along with the insights and triumphs.

Psychoanalysis fits the paradigm most neatly, surprisingly, because much of its literature, both historical and contemporary, would not satisfy the loosest criteria of science. (In fairness, there are many current efforts to change that situation.) The great discovery in psychoanalysis, and it was a scientific discovery in the fullest meaning of the term, was that ideas can cause physical symptoms, or, for short, psychic determinism. Dreams, slips, and forgetting are excellent examples of new kinds of data.

Another element of Kuhn's idea of a paradigm is strikingly exemplified in psychoanalysis: Psychoanalysis has altered our view of the nature of the world in a way from which there is no turning back. Jung's analytic psychology and existentialism, whatever their merits, are more like reinterpretations of the world that Freud discovered than discovery of new worlds.

To say that many historically important schools of psychology did not begin with anything like a scientific revolution in Kuhn's sense is not to belittle the value of their insights. My purpose is not to pass judgment on the rightness or truth of any theory. For example, the history of psychoanalysis itself, with its latter-day return to ego psychology, shows that Adler was justified in saying in 1911 that Freud was neglecting ego psychology. That does not change my judgment that Freud and not Adler was the true revolutionary.

What I have eschewed is the analysis of Freud's own psyche or the explanation of his ideas in terms of his personal history. Such enterprises have their place, but I do not think an elementary exposition is that place. Too often they have eclipsed an examination of the logical structure of the system.

The close fit of psychoanalysis to Kuhn's model is what induced me to try the same exercise with other theories, where it is not always so successful; for each theory, however, the model brings out some interesting features.

Behaviorism's strong suit has always been prediction. One could say that the original discovery was how much behavior can be predicted without reference to anything in the organism, conscious or unconscious. Both Thorndike's learning curves and Pavlov's conditioned responses were functions of the experimental situation, not the psyches of their subjects. Food and other rewards used to shape response were obvious explanations of the strength of the response. Skinner's display of the dependence of the response curve on the schedule of reinforcement, almost independent of the species, is a fine example of a scientific discovery.

On the other hand, latent learning, the demonstration that learning is not or need not be contingent on reward, is an anomaly that some behaviorist systems must strain to account for. Skinner avoids the problems by not trying to account for behavior in that sense; for him, the mind of the individual is a black box, marked *DO NOT OPEN*. Perhaps the most devastating criticism of all reward and reinforcement theories is the demonstration of circumstances under which reward undermines intrinsic motivation. The extent of that phenomenon is an important field for further research.

The fact that some psychological variables, particularly intelligence, can be measured was a major discovery, because many respected philosophers and psychologists had long maintained that psychology is inaccessible to measurement, and, by implication, to a scientific approach. That idea still has its supporters. The measurement of intelligence seems doomed to political controversy. One cannot measure hereditary ability by any presently known method, most of us will grant. How then can one fairly make allowances for the handicapping effect of particular environments in judging the potentiality of a person?

A different kind of ambiguity dogs the measurement of personality. The richest, most revealing measures of personality are the projective tests, but they are just the ones hardest to quantify in any rational, statistically defensible way. The more precise objective tests of personality are the most likely to leave out crucial aspects.

A curious thing happens, however. Any test, projective or objective, that is used over a long period of time begins to yield remarkable insights in the hands of a wise clinician. The task of the psychometrician becomes to capture and codify the basis of those insights. However far that is possible will be the limits of personality measurement.

The most prevalent theory among contemporary personality theorists appears to be social learning theory, whether because of or in spite of the fact that its status as a coherent theory is most doubtful. Social learning theory is a subspecies of a broader class, the class of cognitive behaviorism. But is that a contradiction in terms? Can one be a consistent behaviorist and still acknowledge and deal with the cognitive dimension of behavior? Whatever the logicians and philosophers may answer, there is a large group of psychologists who hold to such a position. Indeed, a behaviorist must be exceptionally obtuse to deny the cognitive element in behavior.

Tolman and his colleagues and students deserve credit for establishing, via latent learning and the demonstration of maps and hypotheses in rats, for example, that the cognitive element is inescapable but can be described behavioristically. The animal-psychological origins, however, are almost never acknowledged by contemporary social learning theorists, who generally take a less historical orientation than is done in the present book.

In presenting the case for social learning, I included some of the major work of each of three well known theorists-- Rotter, Bandura, and Mischel. Then I was struck by how much more persuasive of the social learning position some bold social-psychological experiments are than the small laboratory studies of the social learning theorists themselves, hence the digression to the studies of Zimbardo and Milgram. These social-psychological experiments were not entirely diversionary, because they led back to issues in personality theory.

That people learn from other people as models, that goals and aspirations and expectation of success matter as determinants of behavior, that there is a weighing of small, immediate rewards against larger, long-range rewards — all of these facts are strikingly true, all were neglected by most previous psychologies, but none is truly revolutionary, and none alters our world view. Nonetheless, many rich details have been added to our understanding of the related phenomena by recent work.

Piaget, like Freud, was a truly revolutionary figure. In fact, some of Piaget's revolutionary ideas were anticipated by psychoanalysis. Piaget's great discovery was that many mistakes of children are not random but rather display a system, discernable by the widespread appearance of ideas that no adult believes or teaches to children. Freud made the same discovery, but in the limited area of children's beliefs about sexual functions and childbirth.

The concept of *scheme* can be seen as another link between psychoanalysis and the cognitive developmental school. Much of what is called symbolism in psychoanalysis is the use of a pattern in one medium to stand for the same pattern in another; a pattern in dreams or in children's play may represent the same or a similar pattern in the child's body or in interpersonal relations. Thus, for a very young child, bowel movements may come to mean the loss of part of its body or of a beloved person (Erikson, 1950), and a similar equation may occur unconsciously in the adult. The transposition of schemes is used to explain pathology, therapy, and normal psychic functioning in psychoanalysis. Transference is a prime example of the transposition of schemes. In Piaget's work, the elaboration of schemes is part of cognitive functioning and intellectual growth.

Even if one theory were true, whatever that means, and all the others false, a book like this should have been written. For, as Mill said, he who knows only his own side of the case knows little of that. Perry's description of the intellectual-ethical progress of college students deepens our understanding of Mill's discussion of liberty.

Presenting each of the five major theories in its own sphere with its own purview and its own methods has permitted me to play the more or less faithful advocate of each in turn, without being trapped into inconsistency. A minor theme pervading the book has been to emphasize the points on which the various theories confront one another, but to a considerable extent they are incommensurable.

In one respect I have not been a faithful expositor of the theories presented. Psychoanalysis is not the only theory with a metapsychology judged by its proponents to be the heart of their system. Two of the social learning theorists, Bandura and Rotter, also have theories that can be called metapsychological, and the methodological programs of some trait theorists serve somewhat similar functions. I plead guilty to some intolerance and some lack of understanding of all such metapsychologies. In psychoanalysis, the translation of clinical findings into the language of cathexis theory has always baffled me; currently it is passing out of style even among many prominent psychoanalysts (Gill & Holzman, 1976). Rotter and Bandura each has his own abstruse figural or quasi-mathematical representation of what are basically clinical or common sense observations. I find no substantive gain in those formulations, no outcome not otherwise obtainable. Therefore, I have spared the reader those difficult exercises.

It is a curious fact that efforts at making psychology formally rigorous often reduce it to a level of banality at which contradictory theories become indistinguishable, as I tried to show with respect to Rapaport's (1960) formalization of psychoanalysis (Loevinger, 1966). Justin Aronfreed has made a similar point with respect to Bandura's system, particularly Bandura's detailed empirical proofs of the importance of attention, retention, and rehearsal. The results are obvious and do not differentiate social learning theory from other theories (Aronfreed, 1972). Jan Smedslund, in a closely reasoned argument, maintains that when Bandura's theory of self-efficacy is translated into ordinary language, it can be seen to consist of tautological or logically necessary statements rather than empirically testable ones (Smedslund, 1978). Smedslund's argument, although beyond the scope of this book, has implications for other psychological theories as well. All such formalizations have been avoided in this book. There are other ways to approach the aim of rigorous thinking.

Perry's theme of contextual thinking has been built into the argument of the book: The theories, facts, and methods that make behaviorism salient in the context of behavior per se, make the findings of social learning theory of help in the context of immediate goals and social models for behavior and make cognitive developmentalism salient in the context of long-term goals and aspirations.

In my own research, detailed in Chapter 6, I have been concerned with the interplay of theory and data in a somewhat different sense. In the research that began with the Family Problems Scale and its measure of Authoritarian Family Ideology and progressed to the Sentence Completion Test as a measure of ego development, what has happened is that the very concepts being measured were being explored and shaped by the process of constructing a measurement. That idea is an old one in science, but the process rarely is pursued deliberately in psychology. Perhaps something like that happened with Piaget's demonstration of the stages of cognitive development. In personality, however, it is not usual. But the case of theory and data as mutual corrections implies a somewhat different view of science from Kuhn's, evolutionary rather than revolutionary.

These, then, are some of the themes that have been interwoven as I have traced a few major theories of personality: that different theories point to different aspects of personality; that theories always depend on previous work; that the core of science is the interweaving of theory, method, and data. It would belie the complexity of the topic to wrap it all up in one final conclusion. I hope I have shown, however, that one can work with personality as a whole while remaining faithful to the rigorous thinking that makes personality psychologists proud to think of their discipline as a science.

## REFERENCES

Aronfreed, J. (1972). A developmental memoir of "social learning theory." In R. D. Parke (Ed.), *Recent trends in social learning theory* (pp. 93–108). New York: Academic Press.

Erikson, E. H. (1950). *Childhood and society.* New York: Norton.

Gill, M. M., & Holzman, P. S. (Eds.). (1976). Psychology versus metapsychology. *Psychological Issues, 9,* (4, Whole no. 36).

Loevinger, J. (1966). Three principles for a psychoanalytic psychology. *Journal of Abnormal Psychology, 71,* 432–443.

Loevinger, J. (1976). *Ego development: Conceptions and theories.* San Francisco: Jossey-Bass.

Rapaport, D. (1960). The structure of psychoanalytic theory. *Psychological Issues, 2,* (2, Whole no. 6).

Smedslund, J. (1978). Bandura's theory of self-efficacy: A set of common sense theorems. *Scandinavian Journal of Psychology, 19,* 1–14.